Penguin Business Library

INTRODUCING MANAGEMENT

Peter Lawrence is a senior lecturer in operations management in the Department of Management Studies at Loughborough University. He studied history and sociology at London and Essex universities, and did educational research at Cambridge. He was formerly senior research fellow at the University of Southampton and lecturer in administration at the University of Strathclyde, as well as sometime research guest at LEST (Laboratoire d'Economie et de Sociologie du Travail) in Aix-en-Provence, visiting professor and Nuffield Social Science Research Fellow at the University of Konstanz, visiting fellow at the International Institute of Management in West Berlin, and research fellow at the Royal Technical University in Stockholm.

His books include *Georg Simmel: Sociologist and European* (1976); *Managers and Management in West Germany* (1980); *Technische Intelligenz und Soziale Theorie* (1981); *German Engineers: Anatomy of a Profession* (with Stanley Hutton, 1981); *Insight into Management* (with Bob Lee, 1984); *Management in Action* (1984); *Organizational Behaviour: A New Approach* (with Bob Lee, 1985) and *Small Business Breakthrough*, written with colleagues from the Small Business Unit at Loughborough University (1985).

Ken Elliott is Professor of Human Resource Management in the Department of Management Studies at Loughborough University. After obtaining a First in psychology from the University of Hull he was research officer at the University of Liverpool, then lecturer and later senior lecturer in psychology at the University of Bradford Management Centre, where he was also chairman of the doctoral programme. He is director of MCB (Ventures) Ltd, a member of the editorial advisory board of the journal *Management Decision*, and visiting professor at the Leicester Polytechnic School of Management.

He is the author of *The Documentation of Psychology* (1971) and of *Research Methods in Marketing* (1973). He was editor of *Management Bibliographies and Reviews 1979* and is a former managing editor of *European Training*. His teaching and research interests include managerial personality and performance, situational influences on interpersonal behaviour, behavioural aspects of organizational diagnosis, and various aspects of occupational psychology.

INTRODUCING

MANAGEMENT

Peter Lawrence and Ken Elliott

Penguin Books

PENGUIN BOOKS

Published by the Penguin Group
27 Wrights Lane, London w8 5TZ, England
Viking Penguin Inc., 40 West 23rd Street, New York, New York 10010, USA
Penguin Books Australia Ltd, Ringwood, Victoria, Australia
Penguin Books Canada Ltd, 2801 John Street, Markham Ontario, Canada L3R 1B4
Penguin Books (NZ) Ltd, 182–190 Wairau Road, Auckland 10, New Zealand

Penguin Books Ltd, Registered Offices: Harmondsworth, Middlesex, England

First published 1985
Reprinted 1988

Made and printed in Great Britain by
Richard Clay Ltd, Bungay, Suffolk
Filmset in Monophoto Baskerville

Contents

Preface

It may be helpful to say how we see this book, what it is and is not meant to be. In fact to start one square back it would be fair to say that there are two models for editing a book of this kind with a lot of different authors writing on subjects that are both separate and related. These are the control model and the facilitation model, and we have opted for the second.

The essence of the control model is the attainment of minimum standards, a high level of uniformity and the same sort of coverage per chapter throughout the book by means of very detailed specifications to authors, whose subsequent conformity to them is closely monitored. The facilitation model, on the other hand, proclaims a more open-ended, qualitative objective and tries to help contributors to realize it, in part through the absence of detailed controls.

The book as it appears is a testimony to the facilitation model. There are differences of style and stance among the contributors which we hope readers will find refreshing, not bemusing. Each chapter stands alone, and may be read and enjoyed on its own. At the same time, there are some overlaps, and a few gaps. But this could only be avoided by having more control, and arguably less originality, than we sought to exercise.

In both planning the book and 'making it happen' we have not shied away from the complicatedness of management. There has been no genteel promenade down the road to belief in a one-best way, no best structure, or unique formula for success. Management has its conflicts and imponderables, and these impinge on those who write about it as well.

At the same time the collection serves to advance our understanding of management, not just to reformulate received wisdom, and this comes out in several ways. Some contributors have drawn on their own research experience and findings, rather than on a secondary literature. Others have pursued unconventional lines of thought or argument, or organized data about a subject in terms of some piece of theorizing or intellectual perspective of their own making. Or again, some themes explored here are novel. For example, several chapters are concerned with national-cultural differences in management style or corporate structure, a topic that has only recently come to attract interest. And we have been more concerned that contributors should do these things than that they should struggle not to leave out anything, an exercise that can all too easily degenerate into a pallid attempt to say something about everything.

Finally, this is not a book about how to do it, or how to get it right first time, or to be MD at 35. Introducing means understanding, and putting in context, and sometimes seeking to understand the context as well.

Acknowledgements

We would like to thank our contributors for their scholarship, labours and indulgence. Their discipline made it possible to submit the manuscript to the publishers months ahead of schedule – no mean feat for a book with thirty-one contributing authors.

We would also like to thank our secretaries for their work in typing and word-processing: Chris Derbyshire, Maxine Badcock and Marion Aitkenhead.

Peter Lawrence and Ken Elliott

SECTION A

PERSPECTIVES

Introduction

There is a conviction that management can be depicted as a cycle consisting of planning, implementation and control. That the essence of management is the setting of objectives and elaboration of plans to realize them, the putting of these into operation, and controlling the extent to which objectives are thereby achieved. In some way the present book goes along with the idea of this cycle and implicitly or explicitly discusses the components of the cycle.

But this is not the whole story. Several of the authors in Section A, including Fores, Lawrence and Burgoyne, take issue with the rationality and overt intentionality of this cycle idea, arguing, in effect, that management is not really like this in practice. Perhaps the strongest implicit critique of the planning, implementation and control paradigm is that of Burgoyne, who turns the whole issue on its head by arguing that what managers do is more a reflection of what they are like as human beings and of how they manage themselves than it is a working-out of some higher administrative dynamic. There is a sub-plot, strong among the contributors to Section A but not exclusively confined to it, whereby present writers enter into a critical dialogue with the classical origins of the subject. These classical writers tended to emphasize the planned, intentional, rationally motivated and bureaucratic, and this provokes a reaction in a later generation.

We have drawn attention here to these differing views not so much to arbitrate but to illuminate the existence of different levels of understanding. One can answer the question, 'What is management all about?', in several ways – in terms of purposes attributable to founders of business organizations; in terms of an analytic appreciation of what must precede desired outcomes, or, with regard to the things managers observably do, the balance of this activity between the planned and the reactive; or even in terms of individual motives and aspirations. The contrary views that find expression in this book reflect some of the differences in the levels of under-standing.

This disjunction between the objectively rational and the subjectively real is important in another way. This is that the latter must not lose sight of the former, that the consciousness of managers must include cognizance of planned processes and outcomes. Education has on occasion been defined as communication between a culture and individuals. Education in a corporate context is in part about the communication of these rational and impersonally defined objectives, and the processes and determinants of this communication matter. Similarly, the, if you like, anarchic context of much management activity underlines the need for leadership, because it is the essence of the leader that such a person has objectives, has an idea of desired states of affairs that may be both planned and striven for. Again the processes of leadership are important.

CHAPTER I

Management: Science or Activity?

MICHAEL FORES

Virtually all the major works on management are from the present century. Yet it is clear that many complex operations were planned and performed, in a manner which might be called 'managerial' today, well before there was any formalized body of management knowledge and techniques.

The idea of management has come to be associated, in the literature and in the general English speech of the twentieth century, with the notion of 'organization'. We are often told that the first employing units, or 'organizations', which were large enough to warrant the need for separate arrangements in this special 'managerial' mode were the American railroads of the latter half of the nineteenth century (e.g. Chandler, 1978, p. 92). Yet Napoleon took an army of some 500,000 men to Moscow successfully, though it is true that he did not 'manage' to get them back with equal success. Why is it claimed that the need for the 'management of resources' became universal only in the twentieth century? After all, it is certain that this idea is much weaker in advanced countries like West Germany than it is in the USA or Britain (Sorge, 1978; Lawrence, 1980, Chapter 4). Is there perhaps something important that has to be explained in the arena of pre-suppositions? In this connection, it is worth considering five particular issues, which call into question the claim that management is a recent and universal innovation.

MANAGING AND ACHIEVING: A CONTRAST?

First, there is the perhaps unsuspected similarity between the effective deployment and use of resources, of materials, men and machinery, and those matters which English speakers have chosen to classify as 'managerial' in this century. It is inconceivable that the slave labour and the devices used for obtaining and moving huge masses of rock in the construction of the pyramids were not 'controlled' in some way that is akin to the way that that topic is covered in current management textbooks. Similarly, there must have been elements of executive effort akin to the 'planning' and 'coordination' of the textbooks. So this raises the question, can any hard line be drawn between 'management' and achievement in cooperation with others?

Second, there is an issue which follows from the fact that people at work are tool-users, who divide their labour in ways such that each will tend to concentrate on what they do best. Tools are machines of a type, being artifacts designed to operate in ways that can be described, analysed and predicted before working activity takes place. What we call 'organizations' today are similarly machines of a type, being devices which operate in predictable modes. Accordingly, as people at work divide their efforts with those of a range of machine-devices, it is clear that the human actors involved will have to specialize in those unprogrammable functions which do not suit machine behaviour. Machines will tend to deal with what can be analysed and described before work takes place, and with those parts of the total effort which are best thought of as the application of any rules, theories and other general propositions which may have a use. People at work, in contrast, must become specialists in the relatively unruly, and in what cannot be foreseen (Fores, 1982). So hopes expressed for a type of 'rational activity' by managers (e.g. Drucker, 1955), and for human activity as a form of 'rational decision-making' (e.g. Pollard, 1965, Chapter 6), must be compared with the harsh realities of working life, as business leaders normally lack the time and information to be able to act in this way (Carlson, 1951, 1978; Mintzberg et al., 1975; Jenkins, 1983).

Third, there is the question of discriminating what is expressly managerial activity from other activity which occurs within employing units. Drucker calls for a 'management science' to provide a 'general methodology, a synthesizing and integrating logic' for the human actor, to give a means of investigating 'all the alternative solutions' before arriving at a choice of action (1955). But many whose duties are not labelled 'managerial', such as machine operators and technical specialists, have to act in a similar manner by dealing effectively with resources within employing units and coordinating with others. Managerial activity cannot be considered to be any type of 'science' because of the nature of its main output, which is rarely if ever testable knowledge. The scientist observes aspects of the world and produces a testable record of these observations. Business executives cannot make a supportable claim that their work is scientific, because they measure, analyse and plan ahead; cooks and carpenters do this as well.

Fourth, there is the paradox of the efficient rat-catcher. Textbooks on management stress the prime importance of 'planning' for those who would act properly and effectively. For instance: 'The basic management function is planning, which begins with setting objectives and includes specifying the steps needed to reach them' (Dale and Michelon, 1966, p. 12). The accomplished rat-catcher catches rats so effectively for those who have hired him that he is always in danger of working himself out of a job. If the total 'management' of the employing unit is to be planned effectively in the way suggested by Frederick Taylor for instance (see below), the bosses will have little or nothing to do.

Fifth is a consideration which flows from the separate existence of business schools that have been set up on the American pattern. Many of the pioneers of formalized management were engineers (Smiddy and Naum, 1954). Yet, when the new management identity emerged, through a close link with courses of education and training designed for the needs of corporate bosses, it came to be involved mainly with organizing and running people-in-organizations. Business schools have been much more concerned with what the 'social scientists' have had to say than with inanimate things.

Thus, it is possible to perceive two contrasting depictions of how best to achieve results in employing units. There is what might be called the strong view: by the use of an organized corpus of the ideas and techniques that are associated with the 'management' idea. Then there is a weaker version which can be seen to be more pragmatic in type, according to which the boss-on-the-spot uses whatever parts of the body of management knowledge and dictates which appear suitable at the time.

THE NINETEENTH CENTURY AND BEFORE

One justification for starting a historical treatment of a separate management of employing units in the nineteenth century is that this period saw the first occasions when large groups of people were assembled together for work under conditions which were neither slave, nor feudal, nor military (Pollard, 1965, pp. 17–18). Slaves built the pyramids, and so there was not the special need for their bosses and supervisors to worry about the problems associated with keeping in employment people who might choose to leave. Those who fought under the great commanders such as Alexander, the Roman generals and Wellington would likewise not be free to take their labour elsewhere when they wished. Before recent times therefore there was not much experience of running large groups of employed people in conditions such as exist today; those of a free 'labour market' in which individuals could decide 'rationally' where to engage their own abilities to work (Weber, 1927/1981, Chapter 29).

With the emerging need for a separate managerial mode to be used in the controlling of resources, attention has to be turned to what might be a contrast between the function that economists call 'entrepreneurship' and the more humdrum concerns of simply running the show. Up to the eighteenth century, according to Pollard, the running of employing units was not such a separate matter, since it was 'a function of direct involvement by ownership, and if it had to be delegated either because of the absence of the principals [owners] or because of the size of the concern, then the business was courting trouble' (Pollard, 1965, p. 35). If someone called a manager had to be called in to aid the owner when the latter found he could not cope, this implied that the manager was not concerned with strategic choices associated with entrepreneurship. Books on management, of the strong type referred to above, however, depict the manager as the kind of boss who deals with strategy, as a type of entrepreneurial figure. Indeed one of the criticisms most often voiced of this depiction is that it is too much involved with the strategy, rather than the tactics, of running work (e.g. Jenkins, 1983).

The first factories which had to be run in the new way, with the owners not being able to keep all aspects of their business under their personal control, were those of late-eighteenth-century Britain. In contrast, the first formalizations about a separable managerial mode of behaviour were made in the USA in the latter half of the following century. The ideas and doctrines that have been built up in business schools subsequently have been most obviously American in origin and type (Mant, 1977). In this tradition, the 'manager of organization' is not simply the hired hand of the factory work place, brought in when the real boss needs some help on tactical matters of business. Accordingly, we have to consider the type which Boorstin has called 'the new species Businessman Americanus' (1966, p. 121).

The main function perceived for this new, mid-nineteenth-century American controller-type was as a 'booster' and builder of the urban settlements of mid-America, now idealized as Smalltown, USA; the sort of places that all true US citizens feel they ought to have come from. Thus, Businessman Americanus was someone who would be expected to throw over the old craft and occupational allegiances of the American East and of the Old World, to take a full and commanding part in the life of a fast-changing community. Here was the do-anything, go-anywhere individual of the Yankee ideal, transformed into the one who was helping to found the new cities of the mid-West, forged outside the influence of history (Noble, 1981). 'The very existence of an Upstart city depended on the ability to attract free and vagrant people. The strength of ancient metropolises came from the inability, the unwillingness or the reluctance of people to leave, but New World cities depended on new-formed loyalties and enthusiasms, shallow-rooted, easily transplanted' (Boorstin, 1966, p. 113).

To match the geographical mobility of those who helped to build up the new American cities, and were always prepared to move on quickly if things were not going well, is the idea of occupational mobility which warrants calling management a form of generalism. So Boorstin's type, Businessman Americanus, was someone whose personal versatility allowed him to be the storekeeper as well as the mayor, the dealer in real estate as well as the doctor, the lawyer as well as the promoter of railroads. He 'was not an American version of the enterprising European city banker or merchant or manufacturer. Not an American Fugger ... or Arkwright, he was something quite different ... a peculiarly American type of community maker and community leader' (Boorstin, 1966, pp. 115–16). The community was not only new itself, but also cast in a new philosophy of how to build up communities.

Here was 'the emerging businessman of the upstart cities', of whom it was said 'versatility was his hallmark', and whose personal wealth and reputation rose with the wealth and reputation of the place in which he had decided to pitch his tent. 'Rewards went to the organizer, the persuader, the discoverer of opportunities, the projector, the risk-taker, and the man able to attach himself quickly and profitably to some group until its promise was tested' (Boorstin, 1966, p. 123).

TWENTIETH-CENTURY DOCTRINES

Whereas the origins of modern management are to be found on the moving frontiers of nineteenth-century America, several twentieth-century writers have developed 'management' as a separate identity, idea and body of doctrines. Three people are often quoted as being influential; these are Henri Fayol, a French mining engineer; Frederick Taylor, the American who helped to found what is now 'work study'; and Max Weber, a German scholar, who is the only one of the three not to have worked as a 'manager of organization' in the business setting.

Weber was one of the founding fathers of sociology as well as of the management approach. His work bears on the second of the issues raised above (can man-at-work, as a tool-user, be a distinctively rational actor?). Weber is best known in the context of management for his ideas about 'authority structures'. Weber and his followers discerned three types of authority domination in employing units, and three modes of human working activity. The 'traditional' mode of authority is associated with rites and uses that are handed down through the generations, remaining relatively unquestioned. In 'charismatic' or 'affective' authority, the leader of the group engages his personal qualities to make things work properly: James Watt, Richard Arkwright and other founders of the 'industrial' order are generally thought to have operated their businesses in this way. In 'rational-legal' authority there are relatively well-specified arrangements of reporting to superiors, the clear and formal specification of goals, and limitation of the power of individuals. Many of the ideas about 'management of organizations' are related to this type of authority.

Weber attempted, like Marx, to explain the rise of capitalism. Weber contrasted 'capitalist' forms with those that were 'pre-capitalist', in a way different from that of Marx. Marx thought that the 'industrial workers' of a new era had a completely different lot from their forebears because they no longer owned their tools, the means of production; also, these new operatives had become slaves to the mechanical contrivances which they used. 'In handicrafts and manufacture, the worker makes use of a tool; in the factory the machine makes use of him' (Marx, 1867/1887). But for Weber, 'Capitalism is present wherever the industrial provision for the needs of a human group is carried out by the method of enterprise, irrespective of what is involved. More specifically, a rational capitalistic establishment is one with capital accounting, by calculation according to the methods of modern bookkeeping and the striking of a balance' (Weber, 1927/1981). Crucial parts of the type of era that followed the shifts from traditional times are held to be: 'the rational permanent enterprise, rational accounting, rational technology and rational law, but again not these alone. Necessary complementary factors were the rational spirit, the rationalization of the conduct of life in general, and a rationalistic economic ethic' (Weber, 1927/1981). This description seems to fit well with Drucker's blueprint of a developed 'management science' being something concerned centrally with 'a general methodology' that is to be used in support of a 'rational activity'. Those who are deemed to be proper managers should isolate clearly and explicitly the problems they face, they should discern 'all the alternative solutions' and cost out each alternative before coming to a choice about what to do (Drucker, 1955).

A major objection that can be levelled at this attempt to link together rational types of behaviour with rational types of working arrangements is associated with the first three of the potential difficulties to the management standpoint raised in the second section. For those who are simply keen to achieve results in terms of producing goods and offering services competitively, 'the organization' is something which is designed to operate in the manner of a machine. Effective performance in running such a construction depends much less on 'the rules of logic and research', than on gaining a good grasp of particulars (Sorge, 1982).

Given that machines of all types are designed to operate in a predictable fashion, it should be clear that human actors ought to be ready to step into those places whose features are so unpredictable that machines cannot be used successfully. By the 'rules of logic' of the workplace division of labour between men and machines of all types, rather than by the rules of something more arcane, such as those attributed to being 'scientific', a new era (in terms of arrangements of working procedures) leads to a period in which man-at-work is *less* likely, rather than more so, to have to operate in the manner of 'rational decision-making'.

In general, 'to a very great extent people do not know what they are doing until they have done it, if then. The extent to which people act with a clear idea of their ends, knowing what effects they are aiming at, is easily exaggerated. Most human action is tentative, experimental, directed not by a knowledge of what it will lead to but rather a desire to know what will come of it' (Collingwood, 1946, p. 42). In particular, although the notion of expressly rational action by human beings has been linked with both managerial and 'scientific' practice, the events of the new capitalistic era dealt with by Weber have given would-be achievers the chance to succeed in collaboration with a host of machine-like devices, which are the real specialists in work of the predictable type. It is often the case that, in Weber's words: 'Precision, speed, unambiguity, knowledge of files, continuity, discretion, unity, strict subordination, reduction of friction and of material and personal costs ... are raised to the optimum point in the strictly bureaucratic administration but the main purpose for setting up such an arrangement is so that its human participants can act in those non-rational modes in which they specialize when operating with predictable machines.'

While Weber is best known as an academic, Fayol is remembered as someone who qualified as an engineer in his native France, became the chief executive of a mining company and published in 1916 a book which has been translated into English as *General and Industrial Management*. His idea of a separable set of five elements implies a universal approach to management.

First is the element of 'organization', concerned with the building-up of 'structures' within the unit. The bosses of such units must plan, design, and put into operation certain parts, forms and procedures: how job-holders should report to their superiors; how information should flow generally within the unit; the levels of responsibility for taking decisions; how new employees are hired; and so on. Machines, materials, money and men all have to be put to use in the employing unit, so that they can be employed effectively to generate things in demand outside the unit.

The second element, 'command', invokes a military parallel. A good civilian commander has to be able to keep his subordinates well primed to be able to undertake their specified duties. There is no point in having the best articulated rules and procedures of the type considered under 'organization', if people working in such units do not apply their interest and initiative to their work. So the corporate boss, even the man at the very top, will normally have to lead by example, as well as by instruction and formalized control.

The third element, 'coordination', is only barely separable from 'organization' owing to the division of specialized human effort. The organization chart of any large employing unit will show many functions and departments, whose separate names seem to imply a separate existence. Yet, the disparate efforts of corporate specialists and others have to be bound together effectively to give the customer what is wanted at a suitable price.

The fourth element of 'control' includes the exact and detailed monitoring of operations of employing units to discover whether 'everything occurs in conformity with established rule and expressed command'. If the bosses of employing units are to try to 'reduce uncertainty and adapt to changing internal and external conditions by planning ahead' (Atchison and Hill, 1978, p. 511), it is obvious that they will have to be able to assess quickly what has really happened. Did carefully laid down predictions work out as expected? Information has to be available quickly and errant behaviour has to be brought back to the required norms. A separate staff function may be built up to do this, although, of course, this function will still have to be 'coordinated' within the unit like any other.

The fifth element, 'planning', includes an ability to forecast in order to provide material used in 'controlling' the employing unit. So this involves: 'examining the future and drawing up the plan of action'. It feeds into 'control' by helping to point to appropriate corrective action when there are discernible deviations between the plan and the real outcome. This process has to recognize that the future is always risky.

Fayol's scheme, as outlined briefly here, has been used as the pattern for schemes of analysis adopted by other writers. It has been criticized as being distinctively the view from the very top of employing units (e.g. Atchison and Hill, 1978). It is certainly the case that such an elaborate way of looking at things suits the managing director better than the factory foreman. The same criticisms can be used of Fayol's approach as can be used of Weber's; that there is an element of Fayol's five elements in *all* human activity and not only in separable management *administration*.

It may seem appropriate on paper to break up executive concern into the five elements discussed. But a key weakness is that managers are not hired to act out the working role of machines; they must tend (like everyone else) to be specialists in the unruly and apparent dysfunction, rather than in planning and its adjuncts. 'The conventional theory is that he [the manager] should strive to reduce uncertainty. It would be more realistic to say that he must tolerate uncertainty. Better still, he can elect to welcome uncertainty, not as its victim, but confronting it, purposefully. Management is improvisation, not application of tried and tested methods' (Jameson, 1979).

Further, the specific human skill of Everyman includes an ability to be able to deal with *all* the 'resources' that are within reach. The human contribution in work involves each individual's ability to use intelligence and intuition in the particular case, and so full executive control is impossible. The bosses may well want to discover all that is discernible about the units they aim to run; but even machinists are managers of a sort, and very often they are the only ones who know enough of what is going on to be able to act appropriately. Top people's information is very distorted (Carlson, 1978).

The work of Taylor, Philadelphia blue-blood turned self-made engineer, established a fully separable management identity in the USA, where it has prospered most visibly. But Taylor and 'his successors [who] showed how rational approaches to the design of work could increase efficiency through the implementation of specialization and division of labour' (Atchison and Hill, 1978, p. 28), were not primarily concerned to generate a comprehensive 'science of managing'; this is despite the title given to Taylor's best-known book, *The Principles of Scientific Management* (1911). Instead Taylor was more the efficiency expert, concerned with operative work to be designed and organized by others, rather than with the design and functioning of executive work. Taylor is remembered most widely for his contention that there is 'one best way' of doing jobs on the shop floor. This 'best way' for conducting operative work was to be derived from exact study and analysis of what has to be done. Taylor suggested that specialists could observe and change working practices more effectively than the person doing the job. Component elements of manual work could be examined and improved, with regard to the sequence of effort, and the design and use of tools. A major duty of the manager was to 'develop a science for each element of man's work, which replaces the old rule-of-thumb method'. Further, he must take responsibility for hiring the right man for the job, training him adequately, preparing him for what has to be done, and rewarding him in such a way that the 'principal object of management should be to secure the maximum prosperity for the employer, coupled with the maximum prosperity for each employee'.

It may have suited the spirit of the age for would-be pioneers of new schemes such as this to suggest that they were helping to produce a sort of 'harmony through technological order': this, 'through presenting technology as a [specifically American] frontier force capable of liberating mankind from the irrational complexity of civilization and fulfilling the progressive prophecy that a harmonious natural simplicity was the final earthly paradise' (Noble, 1981, p. 37). But a down-to-earth criticism of Taylor's system concerns two facts: that the 'one best way' to do a job is rarely discernible; and requirements for running his allegedly scientific arrangements play havoc with optimum organizational arrangements.

In that part of Taylorism which relates to the arrangements made in employing units, in order to produce his type of rational behaviour, the author claimed that: 'The shop (indeed, the whole works) should be managed, not by the manager, superintendent, or foreman, but by the planning department. The daily routine of running the entire works should be carried on by the various functional elements of this department, so that the works could run smoothly even if the manager, superintendent, and their assistants outside the planning room were all to be away for a month at a time.' So the fourth issue in the list at the start of this chapter is relevant in this context. A major effect of Taylorism has been the strengthening of the 'staff' functions at the expense of the 'line', and so to make the specifically managerial view of such units characteristically that of the non-line specialist.

FURTHER DEVELOPMENTS

In time, a reaction to the 'classical' view of management in general, and to Taylorism in particular, led to the 'human relations' approach. This attempted to compensate for the fact that earlier writers had over-simplified the record about how human actors operate and react when working communally. If the habits and activities of particular work-groups are examined closely, it becomes apparent that monetary reward is not normally the only benefit which is sought from going to work. Indeed the individual at work seems to have such a sophisticated attitude towards his immediate colleagues, and how they all act, that ideas of 'economic man' and of human self-interest turn out to be wide of the mark. So those who favour the Human Relations approach have come to stress the importance of the work of social scientists. A typical example was the famous Hawthorne Experiment of 1927–32 at the Western Electric factories in Chicago. The experimental circumstances themselves seemed to have encouraged the working group whose behaviour was being examined; and schemes of individual wage-incentives which had formed a major part of Taylorism were questioned. One important general finding from the study is that the so-called worker is as keen to do a good day's work, according to his own estimation of what that is, as is the so-called manager.

The main findings of the Hawthorne studies indicated: 'The point of view which gradually emerged ... is one from which an industrial organization is regarded as a social system.' The working behaviour of groups of operatives will not be understood well 'without considering the informal organization of the group and the relation of this informal organization to the total social organization of the company' (Roethlisberger and Dickson, 1939). What is held to be the specifically 'human' aspect of employing units is given by the way that they may be split up for purposes of analysis and understanding by outsiders, into two main, interlinked elements: 'the technical organization' which is concerned with products, processes and the physical items of the enterprise; and 'the human organization' which is concerned with matters such as 'social needs' and includes both the 'formal organization' generated by the employer and the 'informal organization' which his employees design and run for themselves.

This approach to the study of employing units, which is closely linked with observation of what really happens in them, has 'contributed much that can be of value to the manager who wants to understand why his apparently sensible and logical plans are often frustrated. If he looks at a job only from the classical point of view he will think of the tasks that have to be done, but not of what it is like for the person who has to do them. An understanding of the latter is one guide to why a person in that job may behave in a particular way' (Stewart, 1970, p. 20).

Drucker has argued that the 'manager works with a specific resource: people'; whereas 'the days of the "intuitive" manager are numbered', owing to the rise of formalized management with its articulable 'fundamentals' (Drucker, 1979). But Dale and Michelon have denied this absolutely, by claiming that: 'Management is not an exact science like physics or chemistry. Although many things have been discovered about it, it is essential that the manager use judgement, based on good sense and experience' (1966, p. 11).

It has been argued earlier that the scientist proper aims to produce a testable record of what has been observed; or else he aims to test knowledge and ideas about the observable world – always with the intention to produce what will be generally accepted as the best knowledge available at the time. The most characteristic feature is a concern to match observation with abstraction, as given by the definition of science as tested knowledge. In these conditions, the scientist should only seek to set down theories or generalizations or laws, when these are supportable by observation

(Fores, 1983). Many commentators have claimed or have implied that properly 'scientific' activity since the time of Newton should be concerned centrally with the production of generalization. So the three famous 'laws of motion' conceived in the seventeenth century have blinded others with an ambition to achieve a similar type of breakthrough in knowledge and understanding of our complex world. And there have been various conceptions of the 'management of organizations', put together with support from a kind of science pursued in the social setting, the authors of these notions having assumed that management is overwhelmingly a human sort of affair. Some are influenced by Weber's ideas about rational activity by humans at work, some by Taylor, some by the Hawthorne studies, and some by a string of mostly American social commentators on motivation to work.

In this tradition of social science the most important finding of the Hawthorne work is the isolation of the informal organization, or perhaps an 'informal system'. Yet, exactly because this is a *general* finding, in the tradition of generalizing social analysis, it lacks vital utility in the *particular* workplace. There, all generalizations turn out to have only slight relevance in the course of establishing working success.

Writers using the systems approach to the 'management of organizations' (such as March and Simon, 1958) have stressed how employing units should be considered as single entities, and so have tried to avoid some of the pitfalls of analysis that have been discussed. 'Social systems' are arrangements with boundaries, including that which separates the unit from its environment, which operate in ways similar to biological systems. If you examine what is going on at particular boundaries, it is claimed, you begin to understand interactions and interrelationships that may have been lost to view in the more 'classical' approach which stresses separation; of function from function, organism from organism.

Another approach is known as information systems, stemming from the wartime use of operational research. 'An organization can be looked at as a mechanism for processing information', with 'management information systems' designed to help make the boss 'a decision centre', and executive work being seen as 'decision making' once more (Stewart, 1970). This is the view of the employing unit as 'an "adaptively rational" system, adapting and responding to a variety of internal and external constraints in arriving at decisions' discussed by Cyert and March (1963).

But, even if these treatments of the subject are an improvement, troubles still exist which are inherent to what Bacon called 'the idols of the theatre' and 'the idols of the market'. People tend to think in a 'theatrical' manner, because the phrases that they use to communicate, and the ideas and words with which they express themselves, influence the ways in which they frame questions that they expect to be answerable. 'The idols of the market are the most troublesome of all. For men imagine that their reason governs words, whilst in fact words react on the understanding.' So, an approach to a particular subject, such as the analytical approach to management through the use of social inquiry, becomes heavily stamped by its own early assumptions: 'The human understanding, when any proposition has once been laid down ... forces everything else to add fresh support and confirmation', even though evidence may be there to deny the proposition; for it does not want to 'sacrifice the authority of its first conclusion' (Bacon, 1620, *Aphorisms* 59, 46).

CONCLUSION

From the foregoing, it should be apparent that the writer believes, after a consideration of some English speakers' idea of 'management', that the weaker pragmatic version is preferable to the stronger one of an organized system of ideas and techniques. It is not clear that any discriminate set of functions performed by people at work is well enough identified to justify the setting up of a special range of practices, techniques and theories.

Management may have been thought of as something like 'getting things done through people'; and faith may have been placed in the analytical approaches of 'scientific' types of inquiry to provide insights for the manager; but this has often provided a false trail of exhortation, not closely enough linked with what really goes on in employing units. We are still close to the conditions which Smiddy and Naum have seen as the 'era ... of management as an art; that is the application of knowledge without systematization, and ordinarily on a definitely personalized basis' (1954, p. 4).

. This is not to argue that particular elements of what has been discussed here should be neglected because the whole is suspect. Rather it is the systemization itself which is at fault, together with the influence of the disaggregating, analytical tradition of apparently scientific inquiry on what is essentially a holistic activity. It may appear from the record that 'control' is separate from 'coordination', 'social systems' from 'technical systems', and so on, because separate words have been used to deal with them; but on the ground they are often the same thing. So the act of analysis itself can add an unwanted degree of complexity for those who heed it.

This can be linked with earlier comments about the specifically American origins and development of the idea of management. As sketched out above, those living in the USA have for some time been familiar with a depiction of their own world, and of their own lot, as being one that should be especially simple and free from cultural blandishments. So science in general, and social science in particular, have been thought to hold out a particular and special hope for them, although these are part of man-made culture themselves. Science is expected to serve a major function in banishing the complexity that Americans are taught to hate; it may offer citizens of the USA hope of achievement of a special American 'harmony' – such as that sought between theory and practice – in their search for a worldly Eden in the New World.

Science, however, has often been offered to Everyman as a miracle. We see two entirely separate things, the book of knowledge and the activity engaged in by human beings to derive it, called by the same name, 'science'; and this entity has been made into a mystic, powerful and totemic force (Fores, 1983). Much the same thing has happened over 'management', which also appears as a mystery of modern times. For Drucker, for instance, active businessmen are encouraged to be very precise about matters such as: 'What is our business and what should it be?'; 'Who is the customer?'; 'What is value to the customer?' (1979). He also stresses the importance to the businessman of instituting a regime that is linked to 'method rather than opinions' – 'the knowledge organization demands clear decision authority'. But there is none of this required clarity about 'management', the expressed concern of a book in which others are exhorted to think very clearly. It waves about in the wind as 'a body of knowledge', as a 'discipline', as 'people', as 'tasks', and as other things besides, in what is clearly a celebration of the topic discussed (1979, pp. 7, 14). So it is that we have been encouraged from the USA to praise 'rational' human behaviour, to stand in awe of the power of 'science', and to accept the stronger version of 'management' as a mystic force in a world where human actors have been rendered machine-like.

CHAPTER 2

The Real Work of Managers

JOANNA BUCKINGHAM and PETER LAWRENCE

The main thrust of this chapter is descriptive, not exhortatory. It is about the way managers spend their time, the activities they engage in, as revealed by several studies. It is not about the way managers ought to manage their time, or the strategic objectives they should embrace.

Michael Fores has cast some doubt on the classical idea of management in the last chapter. In particular he has questioned the view that management as an activity must be based on a body of knowledge called management science. This in turn implies that we cannot equate management with rational decision-making, even though such decision-making may be one dimension in the work of managers. Neither can management as an activity be equated with the contemplation of the corporate future.

It should be said straight away that studies of the work that managers do give much support to the Michael Fores notion of management as an intuitive and extemporizing activity, dealing commonsensically in the here-and-now. Not that the research literature on the real work of managers is very extensive. An American writer (Mintzberg, 1973) lists a mere fourteen such studies, three of which in fact deal with the work of foremen rather than managers. Mintzberg himself in the book containing this enumeration presents an important study of management work, of which more later, and there are also a couple of subsequent British studies. Our purpose, however, is not a systematic exegesis of this research literature, whatever its extent, but rather a selective use of it to explore the main themes.

In our view three general, albeit contradictory, propositions emerge from this literature. Put very simply they are:

1. What managers do is different from what people think.
2. Management work is all the same.

3. Management work is all different.

THE WORK OF MANAGERS: EXPECTATIONS AND REALITY

There are three ways to discover 'what managers do all day'. They may be asked to fill in diaries in which they record their activity over an agreed period, they may be observed at work by a third person, or be made the object of activity sampling, where the researcher checks what they are doing at fixed intervals and attempts to build up a comprehensive activity profile from these samplings. Most such studies have in fact used the diary method, including ten of the fourteen listed by Mintzberg.

The first and probably most famous of these studies, pioneering the diary method, is neither British nor American, but the work of a Swedish economist and business adviser, Sune Carlson. It is a study of nine Swedish managing directors, and it represents a dramatic working-out of our first proposition, that management work in reality differs in many respects from the popular conception. And for that matter the study showed very clearly that the managers who were its subjects also harboured many illusions about the nature of their work.

The managers in Carlson's sample worked long hours, between eight and a half and eleven and a half a day. This conforms to the popular image, but perhaps more interesting is the fact that the managers concerned did not realize how hard they were working and, when told, tended to represent the period of the study as atypically hectic. This was not the only element of self-deception. These managers put a lot of importance on making regular tours of the works, showing one's face and so on, but close inquiry again showed they did this only rather infrequently.

It has become a commonplace that top managers have an important function as representatives of their companies in the wider society, yet Carlson's study is probably the first occasion on which this fact is actually documented. Some 44 per cent of the managers' recorded working time was spent away from the companies which employed them: 8 per cent working at home, 3 per cent travelling, and a massive 36 per cent at meetings and visits at other places. Once again there was an element of self-deception: the managers underestimated the time spent on these representational activities, tended to depict this state of affairs as only temporary (quite wrongly) and were inclined not to make preparations and arrangements for periods of absence.

The idea that the top manager is an Olympian figure, remote from the hurly-burly of the company and oriented instead to the general, strategic and long term, is heavily undermined by Carlson's study. His managing directors spent some 80 per cent of their time in meetings and discussions with others and only 10 per cent working alone. Much of this 10 per cent was made up of very short periods too brief for the accomplishment of any task requiring sustained attention.

An analysis of the content of meetings and discussions again showed a preoccupation with current operations rather than future developments, an emphasis on matters of application rather than policy. What these top managers saw themselves as doing was continually 'getting information', a heading used twice as frequently as any other in the diaries.

Even in matters of communication these managers ran counter to the stereotype of the august senior executive. They showed little enthusiasm for formal communication, and wrote on average only two to three letters a week. Their preference was for telephone contact and face-to-face communication and they tolerated a regime of often brief interactions and frequent interruptions. So much for Olympian detachment.

It is only fair to add that Carlson detected some awareness among these managers that their pattern of work activity left something to be desired. In particular, they were conscious of the neglect of policy matters and regretted the extent to which their time was determined by the needs of others. It is also clear that there is something of a vicious circle in operation, where too little emphasis on policies to guide action leads to too many specific requests for rulings – and even less time for policy formulation. Carlson coined the phrase 'administrative pathology' to denote this phenomenon where the manager is conscious of deficiencies yet is apparently unable to break out of the vicious circle.

This notion of administrative pathology receives further support from a much later study of production managers in British companies made by one of the present writers (Hutton and Lawrence,

1982). This study showed all sorts of things which were amiss in terms of both the content and the context of the work of these production managers, which for the most part they were aware of without being able to change. Like Carlson's managing directors these production managers spent only 10 per cent of their time alone, had an even more fragmented work pattern and an almost exclusive orientation to what Carlson calls 'current operating' but what in this context could be more aptly dubbed as 'fire-fighting'. Now to some extent this is as it should be: production management is not meant to be an ivory tower. At the same time the pressure and fragmentation does imply some neglect of the planning and system aspects of the job.

A new element to emerge in this production management study is the fact that relations between the various departments or functions – production on the one hand, and inspection, maintenance, engineering, purchasing, sales and finance on the other – are often quite bad, so that the production manager may spend a lot of time trying to 'stage manage' these interdepartmental relationships, getting things by 'special pleading' rather than in terms of normal interdepartmental cooperation, and on occasion engaging in internal warfare.

Delivery punctuality, getting orders to customers on time, is another example of this phenomenon from the world of the British production manager. All the evidence is to the effect that the overall performance of British industry on delivery punctuality is quite dreadful, and observational studies of the work of production managers illustrate many of the reasons. These range from the late arrival of parts and materials the company has bought elsewhere, through inadequate maintenance crossed with junky equipment, to restrictive working practices and other industrial relations problems. Again the interesting thing is that the production managers involved are all too poignantly aware of such causes yet seem powerless to 'change the course of history'.

Industrial relations is yet another instance. Well below the level of headline-making strikes there are a myriad of industrial relations issues – about working conditions, overtime, demarcation, work allocation, discipline and so on – all of which impinge on the production manager's time and attention (Lawrence, 1984). Not only is the production manager typically unable to remove such issues 'at source' but the system of recruitment to production posts in Britain tends to advance individuals who are skilful in dealing with industrial relations problems, and who even enjoy it. This in turn is a part of a larger phenomenon, the fact that the demands of production management put a premium on resourcefulness so that occupants of production management posts come to embody this virtue to a high degree. It may be helpful to elaborate this point.

Production management is a complicated and demanding job in any circumstances. In comparison with the way that production managers in West Germany structure their working day (Hutton and Lawrence, 1979), one can see that certain features in Britain – industrial relations, under-investment, an often poor interface between corporate functions – add to the difficulties. So the challenge is enormous, but there has been a response. The challenge has thrown up a corps of production managers with the right skills and aptitudes who can face the difficulties, even thrive on them. So the work gets done and morale is high.

At the same time it is the *immediate* challenge these managers are responding to, in the form of the interlocking inefficiencies of British industrial life. So the emphasis is on fire-fighting, endurance, resourcefulness and winning through. These managers are keeping a creaking system going but they are not on the whole a force for regeneration. Or to put it another way, questions of planning, system and policy are neglected while those who understand how to sort the immediate problems get on and sort them. But this will not stop the same problems arising tomorrow.

We have pursued the moral of this study of production managers in Britain not only because the findings are largely consistent with those of Carlson and provide dynamic manifestations of his concept of administrative pathology, but for other reasons as well. Studying what managers do is a legitimate academic exercise, but it is more than this. The findings clearly have implications for training and performance improvement, as well as for selection and job design. But it is also possible that such studies may serve the ends of cultural critique or illuminate areas of malaise and malperformance (Lawrence, 1983).

THE PRESUMPTIVE HOMOGENEITY OF MANAGEMENT WORK

We turn next to the second general proposition about the real work of managers, namely the idea that management work is homogeneous, that a certain pattern of activities holds good for most managers most of the time. In a certain way this idea also began with the work of Sune Carlson, since for many years his was the only study of managers at work. There was a tendency to assume that the pattern he exposed, of long hours and high pressure, of a highly interactive work role concerned with 'hot information' handling rather than strategic planning, was the dominant character of management activity over a wide front.

Yet it is the American researcher Henry Mintzberg, writing some twenty years later, who has done most to sustain the idea of the homogeneity of management work (Mintzberg, 1973). Generalizing both from earlier research and on the basis of his own study of the work of a sample of business leaders and municipal administrators, Mintzberg offers a brilliantly perceptive account of the distinctive commonalities of managerial activity. Indeed he claims that managers' jobs are 'remarkably alike' (Mintzberg, 1973) meaning that the same frame of reference may be used to characterize the work of managers at different levels, from foreman to chief executive, and for managers in civil as well as business organizations.

The essence of management work, Mintzberg argues, is that it is challenging and non-programmed, even if, like all jobs known to man, it contains some ordinary or routine elements. Mintzberg has made this point with beguiling simplicity; yet it is very basic. Management work is unprogrammed (and therefore fun) in the sense that the content of activities cannot be predicted in any detail. One can only advance general predictions: that a manager will face problems, take decisions, have meetings, receive information, and so on. Yet even the most 'predictable' meeting, say one that is scheduled and recurrent, may produce any number of challenges or creative opportunities.

Mintzberg extends his characterization of management work by arguing that the manager's power is based on his information. This information enables him to make decisions, at least more effectively than his subordinates could make them. Yet much of this information is in the form of oral gleanings rather than in that of a formal data base; as such, the information is difficult to handle in a systematic way, and so the decision-making is difficult to delegate.

There is little science in management work according to Mintzberg, in the sense that the manager works with verbal information and intuitive processes. At the same time this lack of formal structuring makes the job open-ended and the range of issues to be dealt with gives managerial responsibility an unrelenting nature.

Management work is highly interactive, not contemplative. Its essence is meetings, talks and discussions, and for the managers and administrators in Mintzberg's study scheduled meetings are the most time-consuming single activity. The manager's predominant contacts are with his subordinates, these accounting for somewhere between a third and a half of his contact time.

The demands and pressures mean that management work, in Mintzberg's famous phrase, is characterized by brevity, variety and fragmentation; that it is in the form of many brief and varied segments of action and that even the manager's engagement in larger issues tends to be fragmented, or dispersed in time and context. What is more, managers appear to like this variety and interruption, and gravitate to the more active elements in their work. The accompanying danger, of course, is superficiality.

Neither Mintzberg nor those whose findings have fuelled his generalizations have said 'the last word'. But Mintzberg has produced a very insightful characterization; and the weight of research findings is such that one can speak of 'the nature of managerial work' as an entity at least stretching from chief executives through general managers to several levels of production manager. Or to put it another way, these main-line management jobs from managing director to first-line supervisor appear to have much in common. But this main-line formula is in turn a clue to patterned differences.

PATTERNED HETEROGENEITY IN MANAGEMENT WORK

It is only fair to say that Henry Mintzberg has also paradoxically contributed to the idea of some patterned diversity in management work, even if he is best known for his general characterization. He does this by positing three general roles for managers – the interpersonal, informational and decisional – then subdividing them further, and finally illustrating all of them from his own study (Mintzberg, 1973). This role typologizing, however, is in terms of relative emphasis, and is in any case an analysis in terms of function rather than activity.

The idea that there may be quite observable and tangible differences in the work which managers do is associated above all with Rosemary Stewart. In her first book specifically on this issue she presents the findings of a diary-based study of 160 British managers (Stewart, 1967). This sample, it should be said, is a complete *mélange* in terms of type of company and hierarchical level. What is more they were distributed over several functions and specialisms, with a variety of job titles – works manager, production manager, chief engineer, maintenance engineer, general manager, chief executive, cost accountant, sales manager, marketing director, and so on. This last point, the range of particular jobs represented, is critical for the development of Rosemary Stewart's theory.

The most general finding from this study is that there are all sorts of tangible differences in the way these managers spent their time. To start with a basic fact the actual hours of work differ markedly, with the mean figure for the sample being forty-two hours per week, but at the two extremes eleven managers in the sample worked less than thirty-five hours and three worked more than sixty. The places where the managers 'did their time' also varied; to take one example, the mean figure for the sample for time spent in their own establishment (as opposed to head office, other plants in the group, or simply somewhere else) is 75 per cent of the recorded working time, compared with 66 per cent for Carlson's chief executives. And again there is much difference at the extremes, with sixteen managers spending under half their time there, while another forty-two spent more than 90 per cent of their working time at their own establishment. There are similar variations for time spent in own office, with the mean being 51 per cent, as opposed to 35 per cent for Carlson's chief executives; yet ten of the managers in Rosemary Stewart's sample spent less than 30 per cent of their working time there, while seventeen spent more than 80 per cent of their time in their own offices. Or again the mean figure for time spent travelling was 8 per cent (a general speeding-up since Carlson's chief executives logged a trifling 3 per cent!), yet for twenty-eight managers in the sample no time at all was spent in travelling, while another nineteen spent over 20 per cent of their working time in this way.

If we turn to the content of activity rather than its location or duration, these variations, the leitmotiv of Rosemary Stewart's study, persist. The mean figure for time spent on paperwork is 36 per cent compared with a mere 10 per cent for Lawrence's British and German production managers, and less than 10 per cent for Carlson's chief executives. Again twenty-eight managers in the sample spent less than 20 per cent of their time on paperwork, while 10 per cent spent over 60 per cent of their time on it. The figures/ proportions for time spent telephoning, in informal discussion and in committee meetings show a similar variation.

The same holds for the interactive elements of the manager's work. The mean figure for time spent working alone is 33 per cent for Rosemary Stewart's sample, compared with only 10 per cent for the Carlson and Lawrence samples, but with four managers spending less than 10 per cent of their time working alone at one extreme, and another four spending more than 70 per cent alone at the other. Or again the mean figure for time spent with immediate subordinates is 26 per cent but with two managers in the sample spending no time in this way and five spending more than half their complete working time in discussions with such subordinates. And by way of comparison the mean figure for time spent with one's boss is 8 per cent, with eight managers spending over a fifth of their total working time with their boss, and another fifteen spending no time at all in this way.

There are two further particular points to be made with regard to this first Stewart study. In one phrase, she questions the classic elements of variety and fragmentation. Take fragmentation: the mean figure for fragmenting/fleeting contacts is 12 per day, yet three managers recorded less than 3 per day while another ten recorded more than 23. Or to regard the continuity – fragmentation phenomenon from the other direction, the mean figure for periods of half an hour or more alone, without interruption, is 9 in four working weeks, but five of the managers had no such uninterrupted half hour in the whole month of the study, while another five had more than 25 blissfully undisturbed half hours.

On the question of variety Rosemary Stewart sought to illuminate the experience of her sample of managers by contrasting in percentage terms the difference between their minimum and maximum weeks. For instance, with regard to time spent reading and writing, seventy-five of the managers, nearly half the total sample, had a 10–20 per cent variation between their minimum and maximum weeks. Reading and writing work, that is, varied as a proportion of all work by up to 20 per cent in the four weeks of the study. For time spent in their own office, fifty-one of the managers, nearly a third of the sample, showed a variation of 20–30 per cent between the minimum and maximum weeks. Or again for time spent with subordinates 101 managers, or getting on for two thirds of the sample, showed differences of 10–30 per cent between their minimum and maximum weeks. There is much more of this kind in Stewart's study supporting the theme of the variety, rather than the homogeneity, of, management work.

We have spent some time presenting selected findings from this study precisely because it is in sharp contrast to its most famous predecessors in putting the emphasis on structured variation rather than on quintessence. What is more, in treating variety and fragmentation as *variables* rather than as *fundamentals* Stewart is striking at the core of Mintzbergian orthodoxy. The main thrust of Stewart's study is simply to note, document would be a better word, the extent and dimensions of variation. On the subject of its determinants there are simply references to such factors as the size and type of organization, its market situation, whether or not the individual manager is involved in *general* management, and his particular job. But it is the last of these, the particular job, which becomes pivotal in her second study.

This second study is more empirically ambitious and theoretically sophisticated (Stewart, 1976). Its pilot stage comprises interviews with 180 managers, again in many different jobs; a main stage consists of a questionnaire-based interview with 274 managers; and an intensive stage studies representatives of sixteen managerial job types using interviews, work monitoring and diary recording. This is the most comprehensive study of management work we have, and we have clearly come a long way from Sune Carlson's pioneering study of nine top managers.

The findings are organized in terms of two analytic schemas. The first is an analysis of the job-holders' contact pattern. It answers the question, what is the range and balance of his contacts with peers, subordinates, other juniors, his boss and people outside the organi-

zation. By crossing the internal and external (or both) distinction
with the nature and direction of contacts distinction (in the sense
of upwards, downwards or sideways contacts), and by variations on
this scheme, Stewart identifies twelve types of management jobs.
These twelve types are meaningful in terms of data concerning the
managers' contacts, though to some extent they cut across conventional job titles.

The second analytical schema is in terms of other characteristics
of the work pattern including the duration of activities, the time-
span of decisions, the presence or absence of recurrent elements in
the work, the balance between expected and unexpected work
assignments, the incidence of crises, the prevalence of deadlines and
whether these are self-imposed or externally imposed, and whether
the manager's work is largely proactive or reactive. Analysing the
findings in terms of these variables suggests four basic work
patterns: systems maintenance, for example most production
management jobs and branch manager posts; systems administration, for example the work of accountants and office managers;
project work, for example jobs in design and product development;
and mixed jobs, usually more senior positions or general management posts.

REFLECTIONS

Rosemary Stewart has put the emphasis on the variation between
management jobs, and the second study described above is written
up in a book provocatively entitled *Contrasts in Management* (Stewart,
1976). But it is important to add that she is not arguing that this
variation is determined in any unilateral way by the conventional
labels, for example sales manager, management accountant, chief
engineer, which attach to jobs. Industry does not have standardized
job titles, after the manner of military ranks, and even similar labels
may conceal differences of responsibility and activity. Stewart has
simply noted that many, for instance, production managers have
this particular contact pattern or that particular work pattern.

Two of the themes we have sought to illustrate, the likeness and
unalikeness of management jobs, are in stark contrast. It is only fair
to add that there is a way to reconcile these differences. As has been

suggested, there is a high degree of agreement between the findings of Carlson, Mintzberg and other studies discussed by him, and Lawrence. These studies all emphasize the hectic and trouble-shooting aspect of management, the manager as hot-information handler, and the idea of brevity, variety and fragmentation. And what these studies have in common is that all deal with managers variously having direct responsibility for men and money, plant and products. In other words there appears to be a line running from top management through general management and various levels of production management down to the production supervisor, and jobs anywhere on this line seem to have classic Carlson–Mintzberg features. But when a researcher takes a sample of managers, embracing accountants, engineers, marketing specialists, research managers, and so on, then high levels of variation in terms of work and contact pattern emerge.

We quoted Mintzberg at an earlier stage to the effect that management work is complex. It is worth adding that all the studies tend to confirm this. While one may say with some justice that management work is 'about going to meetings' or 'talking to people' or 'taking problem-solving decisions', such formulas leave unanswered the range of questions about how, with whom, for how long, where, to which deadlines, in how fragmented a way? The studies considered in this chapter address precisely these questions.

Lastly, there is a tendency for studies of management work to be rather deterministic, to suggest that how managers spend their time is determined by the overall dynamics of management or the exigencies of particular jobs or organizational locations. This is not untrue, but tends to play down the element of individual choice, the subject in fact of Rosemary Stewart's most recent work (Stewart, 1982), or, to put it another way, the idea of management style, popular with journalists and consultants, is under-researched in general and poorly related to studies of management activity.

Managers may choose between alternative activity means to accomplish their general objectives, and the choice is a dimension of personal style (Hutton and Lawrence, 1979). And of course another approach is to argue that the personal style of a manager will in no small measure reflect the way he manages himself – but this is a theme of the next chapter.

CHAPTER 3

Self-Management

JOHN BURGOYNE

Our normal view of a manager is perhaps of someone who has a desk in an office, receives letters, goes to meetings, issues instructions, writes reports, studies figures, and so on. Like the person whose activity can be described as placing one brick on another, building a wall, building a cathedral or glorifying God, so the manager's activity can be described at many 'levels'.

Some of the available 'theories' and forms of 'practical advice' to managers focus on the bricks of managerial work: the management of time; the organization of resources in the form of money, materials, plant and equipment, and people; and the division of managerial work into general tasks like planning, organizing, directing, controlling, staffing, motivating, and budgeting (Mintzberg, 1973). Another traditional approach is to speculate, theorize about and attempt to research the psychological traits or characteristics underlying or causing effective managerial behaviour (Campbell et al., 1970).

We have therefore two approaches to understanding management. On the one hand, managers organize resources external to themselves to get things done; whilst on the other hand the question of how, and how well they do it, is answered in terms of 'inner' psychological characteristics: knowledge, skills, attitudes, personality characteristics, etc.

Combining these two ideas leads to the question whether it makes sense to think of managers, and indeed all of us, as managing our 'inner' resources as a basis for managing the 'outer' world and our relationship to it. The self-management approach to thinking about management is the positive answer to this question. This is the world of manager as self and self-management. The remainder of this chapter is devoted to the explanation of this area, and how it relates to the external world of management action, work organization, the management of people and resources to produce goods and services in society.

This involves a consideration of:

1. Ways of thinking about what is within us as people and as managers.
2. The idea of managing outer resources through managing inner resources.
3. Self-understanding and awareness, and self-initiation of learning as fundamental to self-management and improving effectiveness.
4. The implications of this way of thinking for a number of traditional areas of 'practice':
   a training and education;
   b careers;
   c managing people;
   d the nature of good management.

WHAT IS SELF?

If we look at the terrain of 'ourselves', what are the features and landmarks that we report, what are our inner resources, tools, assets? We are likely to identify: ideas, concepts, skills, values, attitudes, feelings, emotions, sensitivities, knowledge, self-esteem, self-concept. Also, if we think about ourselves trying to answer this question we may be tempted to add something like 'self-awareness' or 'self-consciousness' to cover the fact that this is what we seem to be using even to think about the question. And in pursuing this line of thought we may come to the question 'Who is doing the thinking?' Shotter (1975) refers to this as the 'essential I'.

The manager, and the person, were depicted earlier as at the centre of their own world surrounded by their immediate environment of office, pen, telephone, secretaries, etc., working through these to influence or manage an area of activity, which in turn is part of a work organization in society. The effects of a person's 'work' can be seen as radiating out through these zones, rather like the ripples from a stone thrown into a pond (and as in that situation, there are many other ripples, and the influence of any one action is more difficult to discern and isolate the further away it gets).

It seems reasonable, also, to think of 'inner resources' as varying in terms of their nearness to the core of the 'essential I', or to the 'surface'. Thus a technical skill, such as ability to type, is near the surface and intimately tied up with a piece of equipment in the immediate environment. Deeply held values (what we might fight and die for), or self-concept (what we set a lot of store by being), are closer to the 'essential I'. Roles that we perform, such as manager, student, mother, father, wife, husband, are likely to be

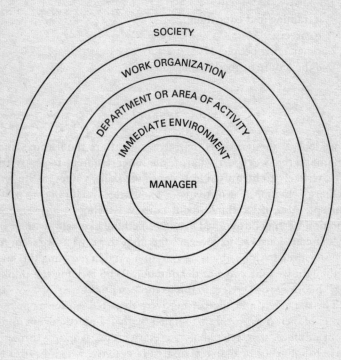

1 The manager's outer world

in the middle ground; as are attitudes to particular areas of activity (race, sex, competitiveness, etc.), which may in a sense 'translate' our fundamental values into the stance we take to particular issues. General 'areas of knowledge' that we develop, like engineering, accountancy, psychology, etc., are also in the middle ground, having some relation to what we want to be and providing a background to the particular practical competences that we wish to apply. This way of thinking about ourselves and other people can be loosely called the 'onion skin' model of personality.

The different layers are not independent of each other. The inner layers need the outer layers in the appropriate form to 'apply' them;

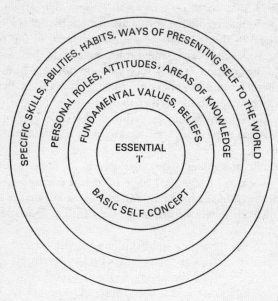

2 The 'onion skin' model of personality

thus the surgeon deeply personally committed to saving life and relieving suffering needs manual dexterity and physical skills to 'express' this in the performance of a delicate operation.

Looked at this way, the surface skills and immediate performance are the essential bridge or channel between inner values and beliefs, and influence in the world.

WHAT IS SELF-MANAGEMENT?

The argument being developed here implies that *everybody* is, to an important extent, a 'manager', by virtue of managing themselves and the resources immediately around them, in whatever role or roles they occupy in society. However only some roles in society are formally defined as 'managerial', and it is these, and the people that occupy them, that are of primary concern here. The argument is that the performance of formal management activities is likely to have its roots in the processes of self-management of the people occupying the formal management roles. Because of this, management as an occupation or profession may be different from most other professions and occupations, having its basis in the role occupant's approach to life, rather than in a set of professional or occupational techniques and procedures. This may explain why managing seems to be more idiosyncratic than most other occupational activities.

One way of attempting to describe some of the 'inner resources' brought to bear on the performance of formal managerial roles, without denying the intrinsic individuality of the activity, has been to attempt to delineate broad categories of inner 'qualities and skills' used in the activity.

A study of the 'qualities and skills' regarded as important by people in managerial work, by people who have attempted to do research on this subject, and people facing the practical problems of selecting and training managers has produced eleven broad categories of managerial skills and qualities (Burgoyne and Stuart, 1976). This categorization of managerial skills and qualities takes up the idea of Bateson (1973) that there are different levels of learning, and that learning can itself be an important managerial skill and process.

First Level

At the first level, learning is simply the taking on board of simple factual information, like someone's telephone number or the price of a ton of coal. At this level there are two general categories that seem relevant for managing:

1. *Command of basic facts.* For any particular job or situation there are a host of bits of information that need to be known: names, procedures, locations, facts and figures, descriptions of plans, what is going on. Note that many basic facts are temporary or 'transient' bits of information, like the amount of money in the bank, or the level of stocks of certain products, and as such they have to be 'relearnt' continuously.

2. *Relevant professional knowledge.* Many people become involved in management after doing the professional or technical job which they manage – a nurse may become a manager of nurses, an engineer may become a manager of engineers, and so on. 'Professional knowledge' is the understanding of the process being managed which is, in these cases, regarded as necessary to being able to manage them. Professional knowledge is a necessary input to managerial decisions in such cases. There are other areas of professional knowledge relevant to some managerial roles which do not have their origins in the technology of the process being managed, for example labour relations law for the personnel manager, and corporate tax regulations for the financial manager.

Second Level

At this level, learning is the acquisition of skills, abilities and other 'qualities', which when combined with the relevant *basic facts* and *professional knowledge* enable a person to 'manage' a specific situation. Skills, etc., in this category are at a different 'level' from those above because they *create* and *use* the factual information.

3. *Continuing sensitivity to events* is that set of skills and abilities that enables people to know what is going on, to pick up information. They can be thought of as the skills of perception. It is through the use of their skills that people acquire and keep up to date their *basic facts* and *professional knowledge*. These skills can be thought of as a spectrum from 'hard' information – interpreting figures, reading

balance sheets – to 'soft' – sensing the attitude of someone else, or the mood of a group of people.

4. *Analytical, problem-solving, decision-making/judgement-making skills* include all the skills and techniques of logical problem-solving and decision-making, weighing pros and cons, setting costs against benefits, planning and optimizing. It also includes the more intuitive processes of judgement involved in making decisions without 'perfect' information, where there are uncertainties involved, where effects of actions have to be estimated, and where plans for an unknown future have to be drawn up.

5. *Social skills and abilities* are all those skills concerned with working with and through people: leadership, communication, influencing, etc. They include both cooperative skills, as in team work, and competitive skills, as in negotiating and bargaining.

6. *Emotional resilience* refers to all the qualities and skills that help people cope with the emotional stress and strains which arise as a natural consequence of managing, where uncertainty has to be faced, different interests have to be reconciled, failures and setbacks occur. There are a whole variety of ways in which individuals may 'cope' with such stress, but the concept of 'resilience' is that the person can both 'absorb' stress and not be deformed by it.

7. *Proactivity* is the inclination to respond purposefully to events. This set of 'qualities' may be thought of as attitudes and personal goals. Proactivity means having some notion of direction and purpose, and the tendency to try to exploit situations as opportunities to move in these directions. It can be thought of as the opposite of *reactivity*: the passive attitudes of waiting for a problem/crisis to arise and trying to solve it.

Third Level

This level of learning relates to the second level in the same way that the second relates to the first, that is, it is those skills and qualities that enable us to develop and change the skills and qualities at the second level. They are the qualities that we acquire by 'learning to learn'. Level two skills are likely to be specific to particular roles or functions, whereas level three skills are those that enable people to adapt very quickly to a change from one job to another that is very different in terms of the tasks that make it up.

8. *Creativity* includes all the skills and features of the person that enable them to accept or develop something new, and to find a new application for existing ideas. As used here, it involves not only having new ideas oneself, but also the ability to recognize, understand and accept a new idea from someone else. Mental and emotional openness and flexibility might be another good label for this characteristic.

9. *Mental agility* is a kind of applied high-level general intelligence, the general ability to deal with complex ideas quickly and accurately, and to switch from one situation to another.

10. *Balanced learning habits* covers the whole range of learning skills and attitudes of mind that facilitate learning. These involve skills of taking ideas from experts and others, skills in learning by discovery and experiment, relating theory to practice, analysing experience, avoiding getting 'trapped' into fixed ways of seeing or interpreting events.

11. *Self-knowledge* is expressed through all the other skills. It involves the abilities to have, be aware of and change one's concept of oneself, as it relates to the 'essential I'.

Self-management can therefore be seen as the way in which we manage our inner resources, and through this manage ourselves in relation to our environments. A very important aspect of this process is the way we ourselves form and re-form our inner resources, in the light of our experiences of managing ourselves in our environments. This is the process of learning which will be discussed further in the next section, 'What Is Self-Development?'.

The focus of this discussion, and the central argument of this chapter, does however concern the everyday, public process of managing as carried out in factories and hospitals, shops and schools, and all work organizations. The conclusion is that this public 'managing' is likely to be the outer manifestation of the self-management of the people involved in the process. The approaches, styles, techniques that people bring to formal managerial roles are likely to be based on those that people take to managing themselves and their personal environments. Just as the formal activity of research can be seen as the explicit systematization of how researchers introspectively interpret themselves as learning, so management, as a formal activity, can be seen as the externalization, systematization and making explicit of a process of self-management.

The aim of this chapter is not to develop a theory and prove it right, but to articulate a perspective on management that may add to our understanding of it. The usefulness of such a view may be judged, in part at least, by its ability to give us a way of thinking about problems that puzzle us. Two such problems are worth exploring. The first is the seemingly obstinate refusal of managing as an activity to become formally professionalized in the way that law, medicine and accountancy have become, and the second is the continuing uncertainty and diversity of views about what is appropriate education and training for management. If managing is very much an extension of self-management, then this may be the reason why it is difficult to draw a neat boundary around it, and its body of method and technique, as a professional activity. Because managing is something everyone does, it is not possible for management to be the exclusive property of a learned profession. Similarly if managing is very much part of living, then learning to manage must be very much tied up with the general process of learning to live. In addition 'natural learning', the kind that happens without direct help from teachers, education and trainers, must play a large part in the development of managerial competence. If this is the case it is going to be difficult or impossible to agree on a generally valid formal system of education and training for managing. Education and training may have an important part to play, but they must be complementary to these natural processes and to education and training for life, and as such are likely to vary much from situation to situation.

WHAT IS SELF-DEVELOPMENT?

The discussion of self-management has shown how much learning and development, and the self-initiation of these processes, are a part of managing. The ability to change, learn and develop is very much a human characteristic. The notion of self-development is therefore by this argument an intrinsic part of managing. There seem to be two important dimensions of self-development (Burgoyne, Boydell and Pedler, 1978): development of self and development by self.

Development of self can best be described in terms of the 'onion skin' model of personality used earlier. Changes in features of people nearer the outer surface, such as technical skills, are likely to be less to do with 'self' than ones near the 'core', such as self-identity and personal values. Development of self therefore means changes in those aspects of people near to the 'core'. Development of self as an important aspect of learning to manage follows from the central argument of this chapter, that management is based on self-management. Put another way, learning to manage cannot be just the learning of a number of procedures and techniques (which is not to deny that these are important).

Development by self refers to processes of learning in which the person in some way takes the initiative and manages the process, rather than the process by which a person learns as a result of something that is 'done' to them. Again, it is a central part of self-management and management. It follows from this that learning to learn can make a very useful contribution to learning to manage. A variety of ideas and approaches have been developed which offer some help with this (Kolb et al., 1971; Juch, 1983; Pedler, Burgoyne and Boydell, 1978).

The idea of development by self should not however be taken as an argument against formal education, training, study, serious research and literature on management problems, and seeking help from experts, and as an argument in favour of learning everything from scratch through personal discovery. On the contrary all these things are major resources for the self-managing learner and represent the accumulated wisdom of civilization and the experience of previous generations. What is important is the person's attitude to such accumulations of formal knowledge. The self-managing learner is likely to see these as a rich source of hypotheses and ideas to apply to their experience and problems, rather than as a set of absolute truths to be passively taken on board.

IMPLICATIONS AND CONCLUSIONS

It should by now be clear that the argument of this chapter is that self-management is not just one aspect or part of management, however important, but a different way of looking at management as a whole. The argument is that 'management' occurs initially or primarily in the process by which all people understand, use, develop and organize their personal resources, and from this base influence their immediate environment and the broader world. However formal, explicit, objective and systematic some processes of management in formal organizations may be, they are the externalization of, have their origins in, and can be changed by, the process of self-management. By way of conclusion, the meaning of this different view will be elaborated in the context of a number of different issues likely to be of concern to anyone concerned with formal or informal management: training and education, career formation, 'managing' other people, and the ultimate criterion for good or effective management.

The great majority of discussions, writings and approaches to education and training are based on the assumption that education and training are something 'done to' people, rather than something 'done by' people for themselves. The self-management view is that people are at least capable of being 'agents' (capable of initiating things) rather than 'patients' responding passively to 'treatments' (Harre and Secord, 1972). The argument here is that if people are to be truly good managers then they must start by managing themselves, and they must start this by managing their own development. However, people are capable of accepting 'patient' self-concepts; and as Mintzberg (1973) correctly points out, training, in this form of indoctrination, is one of the main forms of organizational control of people. This form of control is only gained at the cost of destroying, at its core, the individual's ability to manage. Education and training can be organized on the basis of giving people the opportunities and facilities to manage their own learning, both in terms of acquiring specific surface 'skills' which they may find relevant, but also in being as self-aware as possible about the ideas and concepts that they internalize into their own self-images from the cultural and organizational consciousness that surrounds them.

The word 'career' has many different meanings attached to it. Here it is intended in the broad sense of the biography of a person's work life, even if this would be thought of as 'just a series of jobs'. Most people wonder from time to time what 'shapes' their careers, and if they could have been different in the past or be different in the future. Some mixture of personal choice, luck, management, some undefined 'them', opportunities thrown up by economic, political and social processes, are usually seen by people as forming their careers. Where career planning or management is carried out by organizations or governments it tends, like training, to be thought of as a process of managing passive resources: moving people among jobs like pieces on a chess-board. The self-management view would obviously put considerable emphasis on personal choice, but without in any way denying that opportunities may be restricted and personal aspirations quite frequently thwarted by circumstance. Schein (1978) articulates a viable view of career formation: that careers are 'negotiated' over time between individuals and those who act as employers on behalf of work organizations. At a practical level he argues that someone has to plan the work and job to be done on behalf of work organizations. Thus individuals need to be clear with themselves what they want to give to and take from work, and there should be continuing dialogue between these two processes to exchange information and ultimately to 'negotiate' work roles. Such a procedure is the realistic context of career self-management.

Much of the 'theory' of management, particularly in the behavioural area, is concerned with the issue of managing people. Topics like leadership style and maturation arise in this context. Many of these models and theories make 'deterministic' assumptions about those managed if not about those doing the managing. That is to say, they are based on the belief that the ultimate theory of, say, motivation would render people's behaviour totally predictable, and therefore controllable by the pressing of the right motivational buttons. This involves making the 'patient' rather than the 'agent' assumptions about people discussed above.

In the 'self-management' view, it has to be acknowledged that the 'managed' as well as the 'managing' are capable of self-management. There seems to be a certain amount of evidence in support of this view. Firstly the conspicuous lack of success of the endeavour to find 'good' theories of motivation and leadership, despite vast amounts of research effort, increasingly supports the view that the underlying task is futile. Secondly, studies like those by Lupton (1963) show in fine detail how the traditionally 'managed' workers and operatives very successfully 'manage' their work, output and payment systems. If the self-management view is right, then all work arrangements must basically be seen as being negotiated between self-managing people. This is not of course to deny that power may be very unequally distributed in such negotiations, but it is to argue that people can be best understood if they are thought of as responding intelligently to attempts to manage, motivate and lead them in the light of their own rationality and in the context of their own plans for managing their work and their lives. It is ultimately fallacious to think of people as 'human resources' in the same sense as plant, machinery, goods and raw materials. They are better thought of as 'resourceful humans' (Morris and Burgoyne, 1973).

Perhaps the clearest indication of the differences of the self-management view, and its strange mixture of radicalness and traditionalism, comes from a consideration of what may be regarded as 'good', 'productive' and 'effective' management. It is fairly common amongst many managers, particularly those in the commercial sector and those in producing industries, to regard certain supposedly 'objective' indices, such as production, profit, output, as the ultimate criteria of good management. A considerable amount of research effort has also followed this view, and searched for such 'objective' indices (see Campbell et al., 1970, for summary). In much of contemporary society the production of goods is somehow seen as more worthy than the provision of services (presumably because the products seem more tangible and enduring). Also, some organizations, broadly those in the private sector, are described as 'wealth producing', and others, which are supported by taxes on that wealth, passed through the medium of the state to public sector organizations (education, the health service) are seen as 'wealth consuming'.

What is 'good' is ultimately a moral question rather than a technical question of measurement. The heart of the self-management view is that 'good' finally accrues in the well-being of people, and that, since people are self-defining and self-managing, what counts as well-being must be defined by individual people rather than deduced from a theory. Viewed in this light, and also as common sense tells us, the production of 'goods' in the sense of physical objects is not an end in itself, or is only a useful end if the objects are 'good' for someone. Arguably no one wants a washing machine for its own sake, but only as a means of providing a self-laundry service, which is itself only of value in as much as that service enhances the well-being of people. Thus 'services' are nearer to worth than physical goods since the latter are a means of achieving the former.

The traditional meaning of the word 'wealth' and the derivation of the word itself is something like 'collective well-being' rather than the contemporary corrupted meaning of individual, corporate or state 'cash in the bank' (Carter, 1968). Viewed in this way, public service organizations, such as those for health and education, contribute most directly to wealth in the traditional sense. Other forms of organization produce the resources that contribute more indirectly, but are necessary, to the generation of wealth. Against this background, work organizations can be seen as arrangements of people at work which involve transactions with people as employees, owners, suppliers, customers, clients, neighbours and sub-contractors. Managing can be defined as creating, by negotiation, these arrangements with these people, and maintaining these arrangements by continuous renegotiation. 'Good' may accrue to all the parties to this transaction, and the effects of good management are to create the arrangements that enable this to happen.

This is a way of looking at management effectiveness, rather than an argument for a different technology for measuring managerial performance. Indeed, within this view, objective efficiency of quality and quantity of production, economical management of money and resources, the avoidance of physical waste and destruction, are of crucial importance; since it is these objective and material arrangements that 'carry' the contribution to well-being which it is the purpose of work organizations to create. The paint and canvas of the artists, the pen, ink and paper of the poet, 'carry' their creations, but their essence is something else.

CHAPTER 4

Management of Organizations

IAN GLOVER

A management team has two major and overlapping tasks: to organize and supervise the work of others; and to supply ideas and information. The constraints of structure often seem impersonal and static, especially to observers, yet they change and vary considerably in practice. The technical demands of tasks to be done, the internal politics of employing units and the environment of units lead to variations in ways of organizing people and jobs. This chapter will describe some of the main ways in which thinking about the organization of work has developed in this century, and show that these ideas can have practical relevance in spite of their often theoretical and confusing nature.

SOME PRACTICAL EXAMPLES

We can all think of examples of work organization which results in wrong tasks being done, or in tasks being done badly or not at all. The mechanization of coalmining in Britain after the Second World War involved the sweeping reorganization of patterns of work, the destruction of established teams of miners and degradation of their skills: all this using principles previously applied to mass production in manufacturing industry. This led to poor levels of output and to considerable dissatisfaction amongst employees. Reorganization had ignored several of the unique physical problems of mining, and the special skills and working traditions of miners. The benefits of mechanization were only secured after the needs of the task and its relationship with the habits and skills of miners were fully understood (Trist and Bamforth, 1951; Trist et al., 1963).

The reorganization of the National Health Service in 1974 also illustrates the problems which can result when units are organized without proper respect to the needs of their main tasks. A complicated administrative hierarchy was superimposed on a system in which the sub-units had traditionally enjoyed a good deal of local and professional autonomy. This seems to have been to the detriment of patient care and participation by laymen; and to have generated many unanticipated administrative costs. These costs were not merely financial; there were also practical costs in the form of bureaucratic complexity and inflexibility (Child, 1977, pp. 219–21).

Other examples of poor organization affecting efficiency in the author's recent experience include heavy-handed financial control in an old-fashioned family-owned department store, which irritated and antagonized customers because transactions took several minutes longer than necessary. In a very efficient food-processing factory all outside telephone calls to the loading bay had to go through the central switchboard. Most of the calls to the switchboard were for the loading bay, and so lack of a direct inside line to it delayed many other important calls. A new and rapidly expanding private long-distance bus company had failed to organize an effective booking system. Most of its bookings were made by telephone, either direct from customers or from travel agencies and some overbookings simply resulted from the inadequate design of the form used to record the number of seats booked for each journey. More resulted from travel agents issuing tickets and failing to ring the company to see if seats were available and from the office mislaying and damaging booking forms using a filing system in which different bills and forms overlapped. Taken together these examples illustrate the rich but often frighteningly complex variety of ways of organizing tasks.

THE IDEA OF BUREAUCRACY

The first major statement of the systematic study of work organization, the idea of bureaucracy by Max Weber, was introduced by Michael Fores in the first chapter of this volume. The word bureaucracy, literally rule by officials, has been used in several partly incompatible ways to mean both administrative efficiency and inefficiency. When used by social scientists it refers to large-scale 'formal' organization, with tasks planned and executed 'rationally' in relation to clearly defined goals. In popular usage, approval is focused on efficient and impartial instances of administration; disapproval on inefficiency, over-adherence to rules and the human problems associated with impersonal large-scale organization.

Bureaucracy in the technical sense existed in China from around the second century A.D. However the modern feeling that bureaucracy had two faces was originally expressed most forcefully by French novelists and polemicists in the eighteenth century. Until this century the term was generally used in a political sense, to describe state administration. Mosca (1884, 1939) argued that there were two major forms of government: feudal and bureaucratic. Under the former the ruling class was organized simply, so that any member of it could exercise direct personal authority over others in the economic, military, judicial or administrative spheres. In bureaucratic states these spheres had become sharply differentiated and exclusive to particular sections of the ruling class, with salaried officials employed to perform them. Unlike many nineteenth-century thinkers, Mosca felt that minority (rather than democratic) rule was inevitable. He felt that public officials defined the character of the modern kind of ruling class, and that they formed a very important part of it, and were not merely useful servants of constitutional government.

Thinking about bureaucracy was broadened further by Michels (1915/1967). He also saw the inevitability of large-scale formal organization in modern states and showed how all forms of organization, not just state ones, might increasingly become 'bureaucratic'.

In spite of the importance of Mosca's and Michels's ideas, it took Weber (1947, 1948), writing in the early twentieth century, to produce something approaching a rigorous definition and theory of bureaucracy. He clarified the concept and fitted it into a theory of domination. He regarded domination as a form of power relationship in which the ruled saw it as their duty to obey the orders of their rulers (see Fores). He identified three major kinds of domination: charismatic, traditional and legal-rational.

Weber felt that more than one type of domination could coexist within any unit. He explicitly warned against the view that there was any kind of historically inevitable transition from charismatic or traditional to legal-rational domination. His idea of bureaucratization coincided with ideas of rationalization. He saw the latter as producing 'progressive disenchantment', a decline of magic, spontaneity and mystery, which was a central feature of modern experience. The main defining features of rational bureaucracies are explicit goals, a hierarchical authority structure and substitutability of personnel. These emphasize clear specifications of tasks and of positions in the hierarchy, unified control and disciplinary procedures, as well as systems of employment which emphasize the possession of formal qualifications, formal career and salary structures, promotion on the basis of merit or seniority, and checks against attempts by staff to appropriate their posts or the resources which went with them.

His attitude towards the bureaucratization of work was resigned and pessimistic, although he tended to neglect its ritualistic and possibly inefficient features, which imply changes in 'bureaucratic' practice. Weber's ideas have underpinned the near-exponential growth of studies of work organization since the 1950s. Today such studies influence and are influenced by work in most of the social sciences. Knowledge of economic and political decision-making, employee motivation, industrial conflict, management styles, the design of jobs, and the growth, choices and status of occupations has been informed by the understanding of work organization which grew out of the 'debate with Weber's ghost'.

BUREAUCRACY: RESPONSES TO WEBER

Weber's theory of bureaucracy has been criticized on three main grounds: he played down the inefficiency which it might help to produce; he was too pessimistic about the progressive rationalization and disenchantment of the world; and his notions about rationality were misleading. Less significantly, some have suggested that he confused the issue by adopting the term bureaucracy as a tool for scientific analysis in spite of its often emotive everyday usage.

Although Weber never stated that bureaucracy was the most efficient way, he did argue that the desire for technical efficiency was built into it. Social scientists have been concerned with bureaucratic inefficiency for the best part of fifty years. Merton (1940) wrote about relationships between bureaucracies and the personality of the bureaucrat and was led to modify the idea that bureaucratic administration is specially rational. For Merton, the training and the expert knowledge and skills of bureaucrats spelt 'trained incapacity' whenever situations changed, since they were over-disciplined and devoted to means rather than ends. Interaction between bureaucrats led to the development of attachments and loyalties which interfered with their supposedly objective treatment of clients and cases.

Selznick (1943), who studied the work of the Tennessee Valley Authority in the USA in the 1930s, showed how sub-units could develop goals of their own which could conflict with those of their parent organization. A common remedy for this was to set up new sub-units to monitor and counteract these tendencies but unfortunately this 'remedy' often generated more sub-unit goals (see also Burns and Stalker, 1961). Gouldner (1955*a*, *b*) criticized the fatalistic pessimism of Weberian and other theorizing about bureaucracy. He felt that the size and complexity of many units was unavoidable, and argued that some members of 'representative' bureaucracies regarded rules as being necessary on technical grounds and as being in their own interest. Such bureaucracies were different from 'punishment-centred' ones, in which compliance was reluctant, with job holders feeling that rules had been imposed on them by an alien group. In a similar way Crozier (1964) and Krohn (1971) felt that bureaucracies could shelter and even nurture talent as well as stifle it. Blau (1956) argued that bureaucratic efficiency could not be guaranteed by tethering job holders to rigid sets of rules unless these rules identified the aims of the organization and were consistent with it.

Parsons (Weber, 1947) queried the internal consistency of Weber's model, noting how Weber had apparently assumed that administrative staff had professional expertise as well as the right to issue orders. From Parsons's viewpoint, administrative staff gave orders, whereas professional staff were employed to provide them with expertise. Weber had assumed that the functions would be performed by the same individuals, whereas conflict between line 'doers' and staff 'advisers' was prevalent in modern organizations. Differences between Anglo-American and German systems of education and training suggest that Parsons may have misunderstood Weber's use of the term *Beruf*, which is often taken to mean profession but which refers to any skilled occupation or vocation. Comparisons of Anglo-American and West German occupation formation show professionalism to be far weaker in Germany, where line and staff tasks are often performed by the same individuals (Child, Fores, Glover and Lawrence, 1983). Therefore Parsons's criticism of Weber may have been based on weak assumptions. On the other hand a good deal of well-regarded research into British and American settings (see for example Burns and Stalker, 1961, and Lawrence and Lorsch, 1967) has shown how units staffed and organized bureaucratically can be run in ways which allow them to cope successfully with complex and threatening external forces. Also Simon (1954; see also March and Simon, 1958) was probably right to suggest that Weber's ideal type projected an unjustified aura of timelessness.

We have already noted how Weber did not equate formal rationality with efficiency. Rationality in this context only meant 'correct calculation' which Weber felt could be pernicious in certain circumstances. He did not feel that it was either necessary or desirable for societies to base their social arrangements on monetary calculation and legal codification alone. His theory was intended for broad historical comparative analysis, but many students of work organization and management have forgotten this and have assumed that alternative organizational forms were somehow irrational or deviant. Empirical study has generally shown that organizations which approximate to the bureaucratic ideal often adapt poorly in rapidly changing commercial, technical and political environments, and that they probably only form a significant minority of all organizations. But the general value of the idea has been stressed by writers like Eisenstadt (1958) who discuss processes of 'bureaucratization' in a sociologically rigorous way and at a high (societal) level of abstraction which specifies conditions under which bureaucracies rise and fall. This kind of thinking has increasingly been applied in cross-cultural comparisons of work organization (see for example Lammers and Hickson, 1979, and Sorge and Warner, 1980). Blau and Scott (1963) agreed that it would be useful to test whether particular elements of the bureaucratic ideal type taken singly or in combination might produce administrative efficiency. By suggesting that Weber had offered a merely intuitive account of possible influences on efficiency they stimulated many recent micro-level investigations of bureaucratic structure and operations.

Weber's statements on bureaucracy can be expected to continue to exert a powerful influence. Most employing units seem to manifest at least some feature of bureaucracy because their leaders seek economies of scale, technical efficiency and legitimacy; and most large enterprises employ specialists in managerial-level jobs in ways which reflect the practices of the early-twentieth-century civil service in Britain or Germany. Much current research into work organization is still inspired by a concern with bureaucratic complexity and rigidity, with the displacement and subversion of bureaucratic goals, and with the routinized disenchantment apparently characteristic of the experiences of many employees. Since the 1930s research has increasingly shown how units with similar goals can be organized and run in very different ways. Three partly complementary and overlapping ways of explaining such differences which have evolved out of this research can be labelled constraint, choice and culture.

Constraint

Constraints are the various practical and technical factors which limit the ways in which units should or may be organized. Any unit's internal structure is affected by its size, by the nature of the products or services which make up its outputs, by the physical and intellectual nature of its operations, by its relationship with its 'markets', and by the nature of its dependence on other units. This approach is known as contingency theory. Its main practical implications are that as a unit becomes larger, it enjoys more opportunities for decentralizing many advisory and managerial tasks to specialists. Its top job-holders need to rely, in turn, on formal documentation and standard procedures, rather than personal supervision, in order to coordinate activities and to maintain control. When tasks and technologies for processing materials or information have a relatively routine and stable character, jobs should be specialized and defined quite firmly, with relatively little discretion, with supervision largely separate from advisory and technical tasks, and with everything coordinated according to established plans and procedures. When the unit's tasks, methods or situation are less stable, when innovation becomes more important compared with control, then less 'bureaucratic' and more loose and flexible methods of organization and supervision are called for. These broad conclusions have been summarized by Lupton (1971), Child (1972, 1973, 1977) and Watson (1980).

The studies and evidence which helped to produce contingency theory emphasized the variety of situations in which different units find themselves, and the necessary variety of appropriate responses. Classic studies by Burns and Stalker (1961) and Woodward (1965, 1970) showed how relationships between function and form could vary in different units. Pugh et al. (1968, 1969) showed that the constraints of task and technology generally operated most forcefully in smaller units and around the 'operating cores' of all types of unit. In larger units and away from the operating core the influence of size and of dependence on other organizations was more important. Thus general bureaucratic-administrative principles and the impact of the external environment became more relevant away from the core, and especially in larger units. Lawrence and Lorsch (1967) took thinking about the effects of the environment on organization further by focusing on the methods of differentiation and integration used to cope in different situations. Companies in the plastics industry in uncertain situations characterized by rapid technical and market change found that the time horizons of their research and development, marketing and production departments needed to be different. Research and development people had to think and plan a long way ahead, while being adaptive to current developments. Marketing people needed to focus more on short-term issues while they still faced a good deal of uncertainty. Production's time horizons were the shortest, and its managers' lives were more predictable than those of managers in research and development or marketing. The task of integrating the work of the three types of department, each with managers with very different outlooks and patterns of behaviour, was much harder than in more stable industries such as food manufacturing. Top job-holders in plastics needed to devote a great deal of effort to integrating the activities of the three functions, which they did by emphasizing direct contact and open confrontation, and by setting up interdepartmental teams and coordinating units.

The overtly practical emphasis of contingency theory has not been without critics, who have attacked it as a new 'conventional wisdom' which suggests, just as earlier 'universal' approaches did, that organization and management are largely or purely technical matters (Child, 1972, 1973). Such an idea obviously neglects a considerable body of evidence on the political character of managerial and organizational decisions, often by exemplifying and drawing on biological and sociological 'systems thinking'.

This approach to organization defines each unit as part of the wider social system, that is, society or its environment, as being made up of a set of interdependent parts or sub-systems which exchange resources and problems between themselves and the environment. 'Thus, a manufacturing company imports raw materials, converts them into products, and acquires a profit from selling the product' (Lawrence and Lorsch, 1969). Other inputs and outputs include people and their skills, supplies, power, information and decisions.

The usefulness of this kind of thinking to contingency theory and the great practical value of its emphasis on the interdependence of (and cooperation between) sub-units should be obvious. However, its critics, such as Silverman (1970), argue that it tends to invent and to exaggerate the importance of organizational goals at the expense of those of individuals. Systems theorists respond that organizations and their goals do have a reality over and above their members and their goals, simply because the Ford Motor Company or the United Nations (for example) form part of the world we define as real and deal with.

Choice

The term 'choice' refers to the fact that top job-holders or 'strategic decision-makers' normally have some freedom of action in organizing their units within the limits apparently set by practical constraints. They may also decide to be less than efficient and, indeed, to ignore the constraints facing them or to opt for different ones, for example by moving into new markets, using different production processes, diversifying, scaling operations down, and so on. Decisions to be less than efficient are made possible by the fact that no unit operates under conditions of perfect competition, and they occur for many reasons, including the moral ones which persuade some managers to spend money on employee welfare, to harmonize jobs, or to support charities. Such choices are often seen to be political, ideological and personal and influenced by the values and interests of the individual. This is known as the social-action perspective, which emphasizes individuals' thought and actions; their conflicts of interest, the diverse aims and backgrounds and the private character of their decisions to comply with or to deviate from organizational norms. Whereas contingency theory emphasizes the practical requirements of tasks, the notion of 'strategic choice' emphasizes political influences (Child, 1972, 1973).

Culture

The notion of culture has been used recently to develop a more comprehensive and perhaps all-inclusive perspective. The basic idea is that organizational variety does not develop in a social, historical or political vacuum. It recognizes the ways in which attitudes and habits change and develop in new circumstances, in ways which are 'arational' in the sense that they lose touch with the original reasons for their existence. As different countries have different economic and political priorities which affect their systems of education and training, so jobs are staffed with people having different types and levels of skills who relate to each other in different ways.

Broad differences of this type and the reasons for them were discussed by Weber, and more recently Mintzberg (1979, pp. 294, 295) attributed some variations between and within cultures to fashion as well as to more fundamental forces. Dalton (1959) and Crozier (1964) discussed the strength of 'traditional' bureaucratic approaches to work organization in European settings, compared with more flexible North American approaches, and their studies of aspects of American and French management support the idea that work organization is first and foremost a product of cultured human action. This idea only began to be explored and tested systematically by organization theorists in the 1960s. Until then research seemed to be preoccupied with issues of rationality and efficiency, usually within particular units and cultures. Most research was, and still is, conducted in North America and Britain, countries which once seemed to exemplify industrial success. Cross-cultural comparison has become more fashionable in Britain and North America after assumptions about Anglo-American superiority began to fade. For example, Lawrence (1980) suggested that German manufacturing firms are significantly more production-dominated than their British counterparts. The interdependence of national economies and the importance of the multinational corporation are also factors which stimulate a 'culturalist' approach to work organization.

The culturalist approach suggests that attempts to structure the execution of tasks rationally on the basis of theory are unlikely to work. It accepts the existence and the importance of constraints and it regards them, as it does 'political' choices, as integral to human institution-building.

This kind of argument was used by Fores and Sorge (1978) in a discussion of the 'rational fallacy' and it has been applied to the study of work organization by Sorge (1977, 1980). Sorge defined culture as consisting of all human artefacts, physical and mental, and 'social entities distinctive for having common ... elements' (language, tools, social habits, etc.). Organizational life should not be 'divided into a "strategic" part at the top, where "dominant coalitions" exercise choice, and a more reactive part lower down, where contingencies are given aid and exercise constraint'. This implied a unidirectional kind of causation, from the environment/ context through the boundaries of organizations, into their structures, their roles, and ultimately behaviour. In fact the ideas of constraint and choice had too often been employed as spurious opposites. So too had 'cultural norms' and 'recognized contingencies', the needs of 'tasks' and 'institutional factors' or 'power relationships', stability and change, rational and non-rational action, and, most important of all perhaps, practice and theory.

All of these supposed opposites were spurious because each item was, in every case, entirely dependent on and complementary to the other. A culturalist perspective highlighted this by emphasizing the interdependent nature of all aspects of life and the folly of producing simple models of causation.

Contrasts between the worlds of theory and practice were especially dangerous whenever practice was thought of as the 'application' of theory. Scientific work inevitably tended to contrast and differentiate things which, in reality, were interdependent and mutually interactive rather than opposed. Accounts of the 'perceived world can [never] consciously articulate its own transcendence when this is an emergent phenomenon'. This was because 'mute practice always moves ahead of verbose theory'. Theories concerned with human action could never produce watertight statements about causes. Nor should they be expected to produce anything other than highly tentative, limited and temporary predictions. Practice meant much more than the application of theory and ignorance of this fact inevitably led to 'a suppression of cultured activity, through scholastic theory and petrified practice'.

The work of Sahal (1978, 1980) has shown how the production of human artefacts, including organizations, can never be culture-free. Only *natural* phenomena could be that. People very often acted before they thought, so that the practical relevance of systematically ordered scientific knowledge was limited by definition, as were 'rationalistic' concepts of human action.

SOME RELATED THEMES AND CONCERNS

A generation or more of studying and theorizing about work organization has witnessed many other concerns.

Goals

The idea that the activities engaged in by members of organizations is not simply random, that units 'have continuity and do accomplish things', is clearly a reasonable and useful one. These goals are however dynamic things, abstractions which evolve through interaction between members of units and their environments. Official or stated goals are rarely quite the same as 'operative' or 'real' ones (Etzioni, 1961; Perrow, 1970, 1972). Their determination is a political process involving competition, the formation of alliances, bargaining, and so on. They are often very difficult to establish or be sure of, especially in large units – when outputs are intangible and hard to quantify, and when the environment is unstable. Excessive control stifles innovation and the performance of routine tasks. Official goals are easily displaced either for internal political reasons or because of over-conformity. Individuals usually have several goals, and any organization has at least as many goals as it has members. Official goals and the rules to help achieve them are often simply invoked by individuals coping with the conflicting demands of their jobs (Zimmerman, 1973; Manning, 1977).

Typologies Study & interpretation of types.

There have been many attempts to develop typologies of organizations, but unfortunately the attempt to produce an 'adequate' typology is rather like trying to produce lists of the occupations performed by the citizens of a town by using burial records. Even so, attempts to develop typologies to help understand the variety of organizations have produced several useful insights. Thus while units cannot be usefully or meaningfully abstracted from their environments, typologies can be useful aids to comparative study. Most seize on particular aspects of organization, such as the technical complexity of production processes, authority structures, the functions that units perform, or more simply on their size or type of ownership. For example, Woodward (1965) distinguished between unit or small batch, large batch and mass, or process systems of production, showing how different structural configurations were appropriate to different technologies. Etzioni (1961) distinguished between forms of power (coercive, remunerative and normative) and forms of member involvement (alienative, calculative and moral) as respectively experienced in prisons, business firms and churches. Blau and Scott (1963) produced a typology designed to answer the question 'who benefits?', and distinguished between four main kinds of organization and their 'prime beneficiaries': mutual benefit (members are the prime beneficiaries), business (owners), service (clients) and commonweal (the general public).

A practical typology distinguishes functional, product, area-based, project and matrix structures. Functional structures are designed around specialist departments and often suit smaller types of unit. Product structures are used when an organization's outputs are of two or more discrete kinds: specialization is first by product, then by functional and/or occupational specialism. Area-based structures are specialized first by geographical location, then by functional specialisms and/or products. Project structures are specialized by particular tasks, which usually have a temporary nature: for example they are often used by medium-sized and larger house-building firms. Matrix structures are composite, mixed ones which are subdivided according to the diverse and varying demands of functional expertise, products, geographical location and time: they appear to suit many multinational corporations and they represent, in part, much more permanent forms of project structure.

Mintzberg (1979) also described five types, the first consisting of the simple structure, centralized, with specialization usually of a functional kind and with power very much at the top, often found in small, young and growing units such as new government departments or medium-sized retail stores. The machine bureaucracy is a much more complex functional structure, doing routine, standardized work. It is akin to a rigid Weberian bureaucracy with line and staff functions very distinct, little horizontal decentralization, many formal procedures, and usually operating in a simple, stable environment; it was typical of many airlines, prisons, and steel-manufacturing or car-manufacturing companies.

The professional bureaucracy also employs standardized skills but tasks are more complex, so that experts have to be given power and autonomy. Specialization of tasks has a strong horizontal flavour and professionals work closely with clients but independently of most colleagues. The environments of such units tend to be complex but stable. Examples include hospitals, accountancy practices, craft production firms and universities. Standards often come from outside, rather than from inside as with the machine bureaucracy. Tasks and authority are very decentralized, both vertically and horizontally, with parallel hierarchies and a democratic atmosphere.

The divisionalized form is typical of many large industrial corporations. Each division has its own structure, which relates to a particular product, service or market and which resembles a machine bureaucracy. Outputs tend to be standardized, and the partly autonomous departments and divisions are coupled together by a strong administrative structure. The span of control at the top is often very wide, and decision-making often very centralized. Performance depends heavily on the efforts of line management.

Head offices usually handle strategy, allocate overall financial resources, appoint divisional managers, monitor divisional behaviour, and provide support services common to all divisions. Environments (or markets) are diverse and could be stable or dynamic, simple or complex. Older organizations such as machine bureaucracies tend to diversify and divisionalize, in order to decrease risk.

Finally, the adhocracy, typical of innovative and often young units like advertising agencies, some electronics firms and *avant-garde* film companies, is very complex but not highly structured. They manifest high levels of job specialization, usually based on formal training, considerable use of project teams and liaison devices, and a great deal of selective decentralization to the project teams. Line 'doers' and staff 'advisers' are hard to distinguish, there are few formal procedures, and there is little emphasis on planning and control. Strategy is very often implicit and structures change continually. Environments/markets are usually very diverse, dynamic and complex. Techniques used are often very sophisticated, with decisions decentralized and made at all levels in a democratic atmosphere.

Conflict

As might be expected, conflict has preoccupied many students of work organization. It is integral to all areas of social life, given differences of interest, ability, knowledge and value; and within particular social units it acts as a kind of mechanism whereby such differences are balanced. Conflict can be 'healthy', although much of it is not. Differences in age, promotion prospects, rewards, and specialist or departmental background are very common sources. The selection of individuals for promotion is officially determined on objective and meritocratic grounds but in reality many peripheral and political characteristics are often crucial. From studies of American managers, Dalton (1951, 1959) listed membership of the Masonic Order, being Germanic or Anglo-Saxon in ethnic origin, not being a Catholic, and belonging to the local yacht club and to the Republican Party as being useful assets.

The power enjoyed by different sub-units usually provides much of the structure within which conflicts occur. Hickson et al. (1971)

suggested that the power of a sub-unit will be greater if it is not dependent on other sub-units, if other sub-units cannot be substituted for it, and if it is central to the aims of the dominant coalition. Sales departments often enjoy a good deal of power in manufacturing because of their 'strategic position with respect to the environment' (Perrow, 1970). Much less important sub-units of various types often enjoy surprising amounts of power because, like minority parties in 'hung' elections, their political support is valuable to top job-holders. Expert specialists are often able to bias important information to their own advantage (Pettigrew, 1973*a*).

The growth or decline of any unit is usually a rich source of conflict as it alters the internal balance of power, simultaneously presenting new threats and opportunities to 'yesterday's' and 'tomorrow's' men (cf. Burns, 1955; Dalton, 1959; Burns and Stalker, 1961). Conflict within management tends to take place informally between specialists, whereas conflict between managements and lower-level participants is often more structured and formal. Pfeffer (1981) attributed increasing politicization in American organizations to the effects of scarcity associated with the USA's relative economic decline, an increasingly heterogeneous workforce with different values, attitudes and beliefs, and an erosion of organizational authority.

Decision-Making and Control

The study of managerial decision-making and control also emphasizes political factors along with more 'objective' structural ones. Decisions can be understood as complex and lengthy processes, informed by values, interests, ignorance and inertia (Dubin, 1962; Mintzberg, Raisinghani and Théorêt, 1975; Glover, 1979). The data discussed by Mintzberg and by collaborators suggest that 'decisions' are very often rationalizations after events which have happened to lucky and/or politically competent managers. Cohen, March and Olsen (1972) described organizations as collections of decision-makers looking for opportunities to implement preferred outcomes, solutions looking for problems to which they might be the answer, and feelings looking for issues on which they can be aired. The assumptions upon which decisions are based are very often unspoken. When politically dangerous issues are not raised they are sometimes described as non-decisions (cf. Lukes, 1974). Control is not a simple concept either. Marglin (1976) attributed the growth of managerial hierarchies in manufacturing industry to a desire to purchase material and social advantage by reducing uncertainties associated with independent labour power, rather than to any technical necessity. Tannenbaum and Cooke (1979) suggested that hierarchy and oligarchy are nowadays the norm across a wide range of industrial and developing capitalist and socialist countries, irrespective of the existence of 'temporary', 'organic' or 'participative' systems of management.

HOMO FABER AND RATIONALITY

There is an important sense in which the use of the term 'organization' is ideological when used to describe the units in which people work, represent their interests, play and so on. The word obviously implies a rational ordering of people and events, but the preceding discussion suggests that units are not typically structured or run in very rational ways. Elsewhere, and after examining evidence on the nature of managerial activity, I concluded that the most sensible model of man for social science to adopt was that of *homo faber*, man the tool-maker and tool-user, the maker and doer (Glover, 1979, 1980; see also Dahrendorf, 1973). The evidence suggested that most other models of man sometimes adopted by students of human behaviour were inadequate.

Homo sapiens, with his large and powerful brain, was not as wise or rational as the possession of this distinguishing characteristic seemed to suggest. *Economic man*, a product of economic theory, too often lacked the knowledge and also the inclination to act in the thoroughly rational income-maximizing ways predicted. *Homo sociologicus*, the performer of socially prescribed roles, was a much more dependent and passive creature than experience suggested. The existence of a distinctive *psychological man* appeared doubtful given the diversity of psychology. If he did exist in lay minds he was probably a sub-Freudian character with unfathomable and sometimes dark motives. Such a model simultaneously explained everything and nothing. A more modern psychological model might be akin to an extremely complicated computer, processing environmental stimuli and responding with programmed bits of behaviour on a basis of past learning. While this model fully admits the possibility that behaviour is normally poorly informed and often far from the rational *homo sapiens* and *economic man*, it does little to explain the active, creative nature of human life.

In contrast to all of these models, *homo faber* was superior for explaining both the darker and less rational features of man's nature, as well as the brighter, more successful ones. It helped to explain how man's culture, his tools, habits, traditions, beliefs, skills and abilities have developed. It showed how man was the only really self-made animal, how his culturally transmitted characteristics and artefacts distinguished him from other animals, whose attributes were to a much greater degree inherited. It was broad enough to explain evolution and revolution, destructiveness and creativity, conflict and order, and to do so comprehensively.

Compared with other animals, *homo faber* was far less guided by instincts and was distinctive through the creation of artefacts in the form of tools, machines and institutions. Human behaviour contained a large element of 'playfulness': goals were often unknown and were normally under-specified, and relevant facts were often wilfully and cheerfully ignored (Gehlen, 1977). Human purposes and the means to achieve them were often defined simultaneously. Action and behaviour were normally arational, 'based on accumulated intuitive experience which can be rationalized ex post facto, but remains inarticulate ex ante'. Human instinct had always guided action but it was a cultural artefact itself, whereas it was natural in the case of other species. This had not changed since primitive times and education, civilization, science and planning could not help it to change. Large-scale planning which tried to anticipate goals and outcomes was either alien to the species (and literally inhuman) or 'a ritual celebration at a particular point in history, or a bit of both' (Sorge, 1980, p. 24).

CONCLUSION

Events in most employing and other units often suggest that they might more usefully be called 'disorganizations' than 'organizations', but despite this and the virtually infinite number of influences on work organization, certain regularities can usefully be discovered and compared. At least one well-known manufacturing company, which is (perhaps a little unusually) large, British and successful, has been influenced by the ideas discussed in this chapter (Jones and Marriott, 1970, Appendix 7).

CHAPTER 5

Communication in Organizations

TONY KEENAN

It is obvious to even the casual observer that communication is an all-pervasive aspect of organizational life. There have been relatively few real-life studies of communication in organizations, however, and many authors have been reduced to generalizing from studies carried out in other contexts, particularly investigations carried out under laboratory conditions.

DEFINITIONS OF COMMUNICATION

Communication, in common with many other terms from everyday language used in social and management science, suffers from the paradox that, while it is intuitively meaningful to most people, a generally agreed definition has eluded researchers. For example, Dance (1970) found no fewer than ninety-five definitions. No attempt will be made in this chapter to distinguish between the pros and cons of the various definitions, but a working definition to illustrate some of the salient features of the concept will be adopted. Communication refers to the process by which *senders* endeavour to transmit *information* to *recipients* along one or more *channels*. The key terms in this statement are left deliberately broad.

Senders can be individuals, groups or organizations, and *recipients* can be individuals, groups, organizations or society at large. Farace and MacDonald (1974) suggest that research has been carried out at four levels: individual, dyad, small group and the intact organization. Individual-level studies have covered a variety of issues, such as the frequency and duration of communication contacts, individual reactions to communications, and so on. Dyadic communication between pairs of individuals is generally considered to be the simplest form of interpersonal communication. Communication in small groups which allow face-to-face interaction between members is the third level. Finally, studies of intact organizations concern communication between groups, departments, divisions and other sub-units which comprise the organization.

Information is also interpreted broadly to include not only factual data, but also messages about the sender's attitudes. Face-to-face communication has a particularly rich information content, including expression of attitudes, emotions, intentions, motivations, etc., much of which is used by the recipient to interpret the true meaning of the message.

Amongst the variety of *channels* for information transmission, oral or written verbal communication are obviously important, but we also use non-verbal signals such as facial expressions, posture and gestures. These can complement verbal information, and often convey emotional and attitudinal information.

The use of the word 'endeavour' in the definition indicates that information is not always successfully transmitted. This can occur in a variety of ways: the recipient might misperceive the message, might not accept it as accurate, or refuse to behave in an appropriate manner. This can be illustrated by an example of a superior attempting to give a subordinate negative feedback in the course of a performance-appraisal interview. The subordinate may delude himself into believing that the message was not really very negative (misperception); he may decide the superior is wrong and reject the implied criticism (refusal to accept); or he may make no effort to change his behaviour in the desired direction. These issues are important in many 'communications problems'.

FUNCTIONS OF COMMUNICATION

If failure to communicate effectively is bad for organizations, it implies that communication serves important functions. Greenbaum (1974) distinguished four functional sub-systems of communication. First, *regulative communication* concerns managerial control and consists of orders and instructions designed to ensure conformity to plans in relation to tasks by the use of procedural statements, rules and regulations. *Innovative communication* attempts to facilitate the organization's ability to adapt and change in the interest of increased effectiveness, and might use suggestion schemes and problem-solving meetings. *Integrative communication* functions to maintain employee morale and it can operate in a variety of ways, such as praise by superiors or promotion. *Informative-instructive communication* enables individuals to execute job demands effectively and includes such items as bulletin board notices or training activities.

An important function of communication for managers is feedback. This refers to information about the appropriateness of an individual's past job behaviour which can perform two main functions for the recipient (Ilgen et al., 1979). First, the directional function tells the individual which job behaviours are most appropriate, by, for example, clarifying duties and responsibilities, or indicating parts of the job done well or badly. Second, the motivational function of feedback spells out what kinds of rewards or other outcomes are likely for particular job behaviours. Feedback can thus influence behaviour at work by providing information about what is required and by indicating the consequences of certain behaviours. Feedback can be used in all four functions given by Greenbaum.

Consideration of Greenbaum's dimensions and feedback should dispel the misconception that the main function of communication is to exert downward influence. Although Greenbaum's regulative communication deals largely with downward communication, the other functions indicate the importance of same-level and upward communication. Subordinates do provide feedback to their superiors on occasion, but this may be subject to considerable filtering and suppression.

CHANNELS OF COMMUNICATION

A number of studies have been concerned with the characteristics of different modes of communication. It is possible to distinguish between non-verbal and verbal modes, and, within the latter, written or oral forms.

Several aspects of non-verbal behaviour have been studied, including body motion, para-language and proxemics (Duncan, 1969). Non-verbal signals in conjunction with oral communications often convey information about the feelings or attitudes of the sender. For example, eye contact, head nodding and smiling can be used to indicate approval or disapproval and so function as feedback. This influences the feelings and behaviour of recipients in a variety of tasks. To take just one of many possible examples, Keenan (1976) demonstrated that non-verbal signals of disapproval sent from interviewers to candidates during selection interviews affected the candidates' feelings towards the interviewers and resulted in a deterioration in their performance. The candidates in this study were unaware that the interviewers were using non-verbal signs of disapproval, suggesting that this mode of communication can have its intended effects without conscious awareness by the recipient.

As far as verbal communication is concerned, the relative merits of oral and written communication have been of interest to a number of writers. Each mode has advantages and disadvantages. Oral information is more immediate and allows the sender to incorporate subtle non-verbal cues and to obtain clues as to how the message is being received; but it is subject to distortion, especially if several receivers relay a message to each other along a communication chain. As well as being more accurate in some cases, written information can be stored permanently. Which of the two modes is used most commonly by managers, and under what circumstances is one preferred over the other? We have only limited information on which to base our conclusions. Some studies have shown that senior managers prefer spoken rather than formal information, apparently because the former gives them more insight into organizational phenomena (Mintzberg, 1972). Diary studies of managerial activity also indicate that managers spend considerable time in oral communication, but this seems to depend on the nature of the data managers deal with. For example, Keegan (1974) found that those in highly structured jobs, such as finance, tended to use documentary sources of information whereas those in less structured jobs, such as general management, were more likely to use verbal information.

One study of the retention of information found that oral material was better retained than written, and that the most effective method combined oral and written. However, absorbing information and accepting the message (for example, by changing one's attitudes or behaviour) are not necessarily the same. Porter and Roberts (1976) concluded from a review of communication studies that comprehension may be better with written information and that opinion changing is greater with face-to-face communication.

Most organizations have formal or 'official' lines of communication. Typically, these operate on a hierarchical basis, with information being passed downward from the top. Of course there are also officially sanctioned lateral lines of communication, for example between departments or sections. In addition to these official communication linkages, many organizations also develop informal networks where information is transmitted on the so-called grapevine. Structural properties of organizations influence the development of formal and informal communication patterns.

Vertical Communication

Vertical messages are about twice as frequent as lateral ones (Porter and Roberts, 1976), and those higher up the hierarchy have more formal communications than those lower down (Zajonc, 1963). There is little evidence on the relative frequency of downward and upward communication, although there is an indication that downward communication increases while upward communication decreases as an organization grows in size (Donald, 1959).

A key element in superior–subordinate communications is the unequal distribution of power, so the reward power of superiors over subordinates inevitably affects communications between them. For example, Lawler et al. (1968) found that managers had more favourable attitudes towards interactions with superiors than with subordinates, presumably because of the former's greater propensity to reward them. The authors suggested that this could mean that communications from below are therefore given less value than they ought, thereby discouraging upward-influence attempts. Schilit and Locke (1982), pointing out that upward influence is an important component in organizational effectiveness, identified nine methods which subordinates used to try to influence superiors. These ranged from ingratiation and manipulation to the use of rational argument and appeals to higher levels of management. Shilit and Locke asked a group of subordinates about their past successful and unsuccessful influence attempts, and a separate group of superiors about subordinates' attempts to influence them. Both groups were in broad agreement that the most common method of influence was logical presentation of ideas and this was more often mentioned in successful than in unsuccessful situations. Both groups also agreed that repetition or persistence, trading job-related benefits, and going over the superior's head were frequently used for both successful and unsuccessful influence attempts. However, a disparity emerged when they were asked why influence attempts failed. Superiors usually mentioned the communication content whereas subordinates ascribed failure to the closed-mindedness of the supervisor. This illustrates an important source of distortion in the tendency to attribute failure to other people.

This raises the issue that managers and subordinates have quite different views about how much information is passed down the hierarchy (Webber, 1970). Superiors and subordinates also disagree about the usefulness of different types of feedback for subordinates. Greller (1980) found that supervisors consistently underestimated the importance subordinates give to task feedback, comparisons to the work of others and co-workers' comments, and overestimated the importance of formal rewards, informal assignments and comments from the boss.

Problems are also found with the information communicated upwards by subordinates. Porter and Roberts (1976) found 'that individuals in low power positions, when sending messages upward, do screen out certain types of information that would tend to bring unfavourable reactions from the individual who has potential control over them'. This is hardly surprising but it is a problem for the supervisor trying to obtain an accurate picture of what is happening within his area of responsibility.

Horizontal Communication

About one third of all communication within organizations is horizontal, including communication within and between workgroups, between departments and between line and staff positions.

Many interactions within workgroups take place in the context of problem-solving and decision-making, and so researchers have tried to analyse the dynamics of group problem-solving. Much of this has been under laboratory conditions. Several interpersonal factors inhibit effective communication and decision-making in groups, including: conformity pressures to reach uniform decisions; the influence of dominant personalities; unequal participation by group members; and concentration of power (Hoffman, 1965). Given these inherent problems, there is clearly a need to devise techniques for improving communication in groups, as outlined by Eils and John (1980).

In communication between groups there is potential for conflict and intergroup rivalry where differentiation of activities 'creates a sub-unit orientation rather than an organizational perspective' (Porter and Roberts, 1976). This preoccupation with the work unit rather than the total organization results in poor communication by encouraging distortion and suppression of information.

The Grapevine

Ever since the advent of human-relations theories of management, considerable emphasis has been placed on informal relationships and their influence on organizational life. Rumour has been defined as unofficial information of high interest value to the recipients, but, despite popular beliefs, the evidence indicates that rumours are relatively infrequent and not necessarily widely disseminated (Caplow, 1946; Festinger et al., 1963, and Back et al., 1950). Only a few individuals are actively involved in the transfer of grapevine information (Davis, 1953; Sutton and Porter, 1968). Guetzkow (1968) concluded that 'These studies seem to reveal no characteristics which distinguish rumours in any fundamental way from other communications.' The tendency to vilify grapevine communications as undesirable has also been challenged by suggesting that it may be of value if properly 'managed' as a means of upward communication (Davis, 1959).

Structural Influences on Communication

Structural properties of organizations and their sub-units can influence the flow of communication. Bacharach and Aitken (1977) studied verbal communication in forty-four administrative bureau-cracies and found that size, shape, decentralization and boundary spanning were related to the amount of communication between subordinates but had little relationship with the communication patterns of department heads. Schilit and Locke (1982) found that subordinates in small, private organizations were particularly likely to adopt informal methods of upward influence.

The dearth of organization-level studies of structural effects on communication contrasts with the large number of investigations into structural properties of small, face-to-face groups. Most of these studies have been carried out in the laboratory using experimental subjects and have typically been concerned with centralization or decentralization. In a decentralized network each individual can communicate directly with every other individual, whereas in centralized nets individuals can only communicate indirectly by routing information through a central person. Shaw (1964) in summarizing many of these studies concluded that for simple tasks centralized structures are more effective while for complex tasks decentralized structures lead to better problem-solving. Group members are more satisfied in decentralized structures, irrespective of problem complexity. It is difficult to know how far these results would apply to real life, given the complexity of organizations and the highly developed interpersonal relationships of workgroups. Cohen, Robinson and Edwards (1969) illustrated the problem of generalizing from laboratory to real life when they tried to simulate an aspect of real-life group functioning not ordinarily taken into account in the laboratory. Small groups do not exist in isolation in real life, but are embedded in larger groups, and their findings indicated that many of the earlier results need to be qualified, since subjects' behaviour and attitudes were clearly influenced by the larger network in which the small groups were embedded.

EFFECTIVENESS OF COMMUNICATION

The question of the effectiveness of communication is obviously critical, especially from the viewpoint of the practising manager. It is clearly important to try to determine how and why communi-cation processes are often less effective than they might be. This can be usefully considered at two levels: the organizational and the interpersonal.

Organizational-Level Communication

There has been concern about the nature of the information available to managers to aid them in decision-making. Is there too much or too little? How can the quality and quantity be improved? Do managers really use the information provided when making decisions? Organizations may be considered essentially as information-processing systems. They collect and absorb data from the internal and external environment and process them ostensibly for use in making decisions about alternative courses of action. Since organizations are composed of reasonably intelligent individuals, it might be expected that it would be used rationally in decision-making. Feldman and March (1981) argued that this is often far from true and suggest three basic reasons. First, in many organizations there is an incentive to collect more data than is really necessary, with the result that decision-makers are overloaded and cannot properly absorb them. This arises partly because those who gather information are not the people who use it, and this means that there is little incentive for gatherers to avoid overloading users. Decision-makers also have a tendency to feel that it is better to have surplus information than to lack something that is necessary, and so they demand more information than they need. Wildawsky (1983) suggested that to avoid overloading executives, information should be systematically reduced and summarized as it is passed up the hierarchy. Executives would then not have information as such but chains of inferences drawn by subordinates at successive levels in the hierarchy.

The second point of Feldman and March is that often the wrong kind of information is collected. Much of the information is irrelevant to decision-making but is collected in a kind of surveillance or monitoring role.

Third, they suggest that collecting and passing on information may be based on strategic considerations, rather than as an aid to decision-making. Information is a form of power used to serve personal interests: for example, keeping essential information in one's head, rather than committing it to paper, helps to make an individual's services more difficult to dispense with. Information thus becomes subject to 'strategic misrepresentation', making it unreliable and ambiguous for the user. A consequence of these three organizational phenomena is that decisions tend to become divorced from information. More information is collected than is needed, but less is actually used.

Interpersonal Communication

The focus here is the effectiveness of message transmission from one individual or group to another. To be effective a message must be accurately perceived and accepted by the recipient, and this involves sender encoding. Encoding is the process of the sender translating the information for transmission into an appropriate form such as written or spoken language.

There appear to be two major forms of inaccuracy in encoding messages: omission where the message is incomplete and distortion where the information sent is biased. Campbell (1958) has suggested a number of mechanisms by which these processes occur. When messages are passed along a chain of communication, condensation and accentuation can occur. In condensation, successive encoders shorten the message, perhaps by dropping what they judge to be minor details. Accentuation is the process of enhancing contrasts by exaggerating some differences and losing others. In assimilation, information is distorted, in order to make it fit better with the sender's previous knowledge or attitudes; or in line with the recipient's attitudes, knowledge or beliefs.

Decoding is the process whereby the message from the source is perceived or interpreted by the recipient. Obviously, the sender's intentions may or may not be perceived accurately, but even if a recipient succeeds in doing this, he may still refuse to accept it, or to act upon it, and so the communication must in a sense be deemed ineffective.

Roberts (1971) suggested that the effects of communications follow a principle of least effort, in that individuals try to maintain a relatively stable image of reality and are therefore more predisposed towards accepting messages which are consonant with their existing beliefs and attitudes. The corollary of this is that they will resist messages which challenge pre-existing beliefs. In relation to feedback messages Ilgen et al. (1979) concluded that people perceive positive feedback more accurately than negative, and feedback which is consistent with what has gone before is more readily accepted than that which is inconsistent.

The recipient's beliefs about the ability and motivation of the sender also influence his perception of messages. A key element here appears to be beliefs about the sender's credibility. Credibility has a number of components, and two of the most important are perceived expertise and perceived trustworthiness. Recipients are more likely to accept a communication where senders are believed to possess relevant expertise and are judged to be trustworthy (Ilgen et al., 1979).

IMPROVING COMMUNICATION IN ORGANIZATIONS

In considering possible ways of improving its effectiveness, it is useful to focus separately on the different levels of communication since the problems and their possible solutions are rather different at each level. The three levels considered are: the organizational level, workgroups and dyadic communications.

At the organizational level it is necessary to examine systems of gathering and using information. In particular, is there too much information in the system leading to overloaded managers who are consequently unable to use it rationally? Is the available information actually directly relevant to the process of deciding between alternative courses of action? Many organizations should give some thought to the relationship between their formal system of communication channels and the extent and nature of grapevine networks. Have the latter grown up because of inadequacies of the formal structure? Does the grapevine aid or hinder management?

At the workgroup level, various processes inherent in group functioning impair communication and decision-making and suggest that training programmes should be devised to develop more appropriate interaction styles and modes of decision-making. Eils and John (1980) describe a number of techniques which have been used to improve group communication and decision-making. These include restricting group interaction, mathematically combining individual judgements to reach group decisions, giving groups an explicit communication strategy by means of a set of verbal instructions, and providing more detailed systematic feedback about individual judgements to each group member prior to group decision-making.

Two particular problems stand out in considering the inaccuracy of dyadic communication. First, the superior–subordinate link has strong potential for misunderstanding and inaccuracy. On the one hand subordinates distort upward messages in trying to exert influence; and on the other, they often misperceive superiors' messages or refuse to accept them. These problems are to some extent inherent in the superior–subordinate relationship and are unlikely to be eliminated, but they can probably be minimized if steps are taken to develop an atmosphere of openness and trust. Some organizations find participative management techniques successful in creating such an atmosphere. Sensitivity training and related techniques can change an individual's attitudes and behaviour in the direction of greater openness and interpersonal trust (Smith, 1975).

The second problem with dyadic communication relates to feedback. There is no doubt that feedback is a powerful tool for improving effectiveness, yet as we have seen it often seems to function less well than it might. People need to know clearly what is expected of them and they need regular communications about where they are going wrong. Perhaps even more important, organizations should give individuals clear indications as to the kind of job behaviour that will be rewarded and in what ways. Of course this presupposes that organizational rewards are linked in a rational way to performance effectiveness, which is not the case in some organizations.

SUMMARY

Communication has a number of important functions in addition to transmitting factual information relating to work tasks. These include upward influence and feedback, both of which can have important motivating effects. Communication is not just about written information, as much of it is face-to-face, which is the preferred mode by managers: it is more effective in changing attitudes than the written form. Problems which are inherent in superior–subordinate communications seem to be due largely to the reward power of the superior. These include filtering of information by subordinates and inadequate feedback from superiors to subordinates. The effectiveness of communication within groups is reduced because of certain fundamental properties of groups, such as conformity pressures and the emergence of dominant personalities. Intergroup communication is often characterized by a conflict of interests. Informal communication exists in most organizations, but there seems to be no reason for making a sharp distinction between the formal and informal modes. Informal communication may have some useful functions for management. Organizations often fail to collect and use information in a rational way. Not only do they collect too much, leading to overloading, but they often collect the wrong kind of information for decision-making. At the level of dyadic communication encoders reduce the accuracy of messages by the processes of omission and distortion. For their part, receivers often misperceive messages. These problems arise in part because individuals interpret messages in the light of their previous knowledge, their attitudes and values, and their motivations.

CHAPTER 6

Leadership

ALAN BRYMAN

Leadership was once the lodestone of management research. In everyday life and speech we refer to A being a born leader or B having the right leadership qualities, and those recruiting future leaders usually believe, or perhaps entice us to believe, that they know what to look for in potential leaders. This appears to be a natural field for social scientists to examine systematically the attributes of leadership and determine whether any proposed qualities or styles had predictable outcomes. Yet there is a pervasive gloom among leadership researchers, at the time of writing. While some writers detect grounds for optimism, many point to the inadequacies or failures of leadership research. There have been moments of great hope and excitement as new theories or empirical approaches have provided what appeared to be important insights, but these have invariably foundered on the rocks of empirical examination.

A critical turning point in the study of leadership was in the late 1940s when Stogdill (1948) reviewed a vast amount of evidence on the personal qualities of leaders and found no clear evidence that leaders could be identified by a number of psychological traits. It seemed that the identification of psychological traits was a blind alley, and in the years that followed researchers concentrated upon what leaders did: their style(s) of leadership. The thrust of leadership research turned to mapping out the different styles people in leadership positions adopted and determining which promote performance. The leadership positions ranged from first-line supervisors to higher management, and their non-manufacturing counterparts in organizations ranging from military combat units to hospitals. This has often led to difficulties, in that one could readily anticipate that the style of leadership appropriate to a middle-manager of a plastics firm not necessarily be appropriate for the sergeant of a combat unit. This leads inevitably to the suggestion that relationships between style and outcome may be situationally specific, paralleling development in organization theory over the same period (e.g. Scott, 1981, Chapter 6). Increasingly most working definitions of leadership have seen it as a form of influence in which the leader seeks to have an impact upon subordinate attitudes and behaviour in line with a prior and often predetermined goal or constellation of goals.

OHIO: A TALE OF THREE QUESTIONNAIRES

The first exhibit is the research which emerged in the early 1950s out of Ohio State University in a highly ambitious attempt to describe the leadership styles of a range of leaders and their impact on various measures of outcome. The earliest of their questionnaires was the Leader Behaviour Descriptions Questionnaire (LBDQ) which asked subordinates about their leader's behaviour. A factorial analysis of the 100 items revealed that two dimensions were particularly prominent: consideration (C) and initiating structure (IS). *Consideration* reflects the extent to which an individual is likely to have job relationships characterized by mutual trust, respect for subordinates' ideas and consideration of their feelings. *Initiating structure* reflects the extent to which an individual is likely to define and structure his role and those of his subordinates towards goal attainment (Fleishman and Peters, 1962, pp. 43–4).

Two further questionnaires were developed from this analysis: the Supervisory Behaviour Description Questionnaire (SBDQ) and the Leadership Opinion Questionnaire (LOQ), both of which are specifically geared to the examination of C and IS. The former (like the LBDQ) asked subordinates, and the latter asked leaders, how they believed they ought to behave.

An important property of C and IS was that these two dimensions were independent, so that leaders could be described in terms of both variables simultaneously. Early research at Ohio, which proceeded in a climate of great optimism (Fleishman, 1973) tended to find C to be positively associated with subordinate satisfaction and negatively with grievance rates and absenteeism. Higher IS seemed to enhance effectiveness but result in more grievances. At a very early stage there was a clear recognition of the complexity of many of these relationships. A study at International Harvester showed a large number of relationships to be curvilinear, suggesting that, for example, the impact of C on grievance rates is greater at some sections of the scale than others (Fleishman and Peters, 1962). Further, this study found an interaction between C and IS in that, though IS is positively associated with grievances, among high-C foremen it was not. In other words, IS could be enhanced among such leaders without increasing grievances. Practically, such results are of interest since they would seem to suggest that the ideal leader will be high on both dimensions (cf. Fleishman, 1973, p. 37).

Unfortunately, the solid promise of the Ohio studies melted somewhat. When Korman (1966) reviewed studies employing the Ohio measures he found that the results were often highly inconsistent. Clear determinate patterns in the relationships could not always be observed. He chastised researchers for inferring that particular leadership styles result in particular outcomes (performance, job satisfaction, morale, etc.) when the relationship could easily be the other way round. This accusation, which has some empirical foundation (Lowin et al., 1969) could easily be applied to the bulk of leadership research.

Korman (1966) also argued that Ohio research did not sufficiently emphasize situational factors which might moderate the various relationships. As Kerr, Schriesheim, Murphy and Stogdill (1974, p. 63) point out, many of the Ohio researchers were aware of this point, and one of the main exponents of the approach, Fleishman (1973, p. 37), mentions factors like pressure for production and climate as candidates for situational exploration. Kerr et al. (1974) have systematically sought to instil a situational interpretation into the literature deriving from the Ohio tradition, and to derive some propositions therefrom. For example, while higher levels of IS typically result in lower job satisfaction, there is evidence that when a group is under pressure IS may even enhance satisfaction owing to the greater tolerance of subordinates. Similarly, they observe that when there is intrinsic task satisfaction the relationship between C and job satisfaction is reduced. They also suggest that greater intrinsic satisfaction is likely to produce a less negative relationship between IS and subordinate satisfaction and a less positive relationship with performance. The need for the introduction of situational variables into research is now widely accepted, but this makes for difficulty in applying the results to the task of training leaders, as the parsimony of the early research is lost in a maze of complex situational interactions.

Another attempt to account for some of the inconsistent results has been carried out by Schriesheim, House and Kerr (1976) in the context of the different Ohio questionnaires. They point out that the LOQ is particularly prone to producing inconsistent and weak empirical relationships. Their review of the evidence, as well as their own research, suggests that when the LBDQ is used there is a positive relationship between *IS* and subordinate satisfaction and a negative one when the SBDQ is employed. Moreover, the question of whether *IS* and *C* are genuinely independent appears to depend upon the questionnaire. A large part of the explanation appears to derive from the greater inclusion of 'punitive, autocratic and production-oriented leader behaviours' to measure *IS* in the SBDQ (Schriesheim et al., 1976, p. 302).

It is difficult to imagine what leadership research would look like without the Ohio studies, so pervasive has been the impact of their central ideas, or more particularly their measures. Further, in spite of Korman's (1966) influential review, it is possible to say that some consistent results have been obtained, particularly that *C* is nearly always associated with subordinate satisfaction and often with productivity. Even the much vaunted combination of high *C* and high *IS* scores has been questioned by Larson, Hunt and Osborn (1976) and by Nystrom (1978), though the basic tenets of the Hi-Hi combination and its benefits are by now well enshrined in managerial-grid training (Blake and Mouton, 1964), which proclaims the advantages of 'team management' with its simultaneous concern for production and people. Problems remain, though they are not exclusive to Ohio, in that the direction of causality is unclear. An experimental study (Lowin and Craig, 1968) and a panel study (Greene, 1975) attest to the possibility that performance and satisfaction cause particular leadership styles. The adequacy of the statistical properties of the scales has been severely criticized (e.g. Schriesheim and Kerr, 1974).

Virtually no approach to the study of leadership has provoked as much controversy as Fred E. Fiedler's (1967, 1971) contingency model which seeks to predict leadership effectiveness in group contexts. While the empirical basis for the approach has undergone some changes, its central article of faith is the 'Least Preferred Co-Worker' (LPC) Scale. A leader is asked to describe a person with whom he has worked least well, now or in the past, using twenty pairs of adjectives, for example pleasant–unpleasant, friendly–unfriendly. Each of the twenty scales comprises eight points, with higher scores reflecting a positive evaluation (e.g. pleasant) and lower scores indicating a negative description (e.g. unpleasant). At this juncture, the reader might legitimately ask how this measurement device is linked to the study of leadership. Fiedler's studies suggest that the leader who achieves a high LPC score, and who is therefore providing a favourable description of his LPC, 'tends to be permissive, human-relations-oriented, and considerate of the feelings of his men', whereas the low scorer 'tends to be managing, task-controlling, and less concerned with the human relations aspects of the job' (Fiedler, 1965, p. 116). The scale seems to distinguish person-oriented from task-oriented leaders.

The next question is how far this distinction can be related to leadership effectiveness. Fiedler's research was conducted in a variety of contexts (including basketball teams, civil engineering teams, open-hearth shops, consumer cooperatives). Apparently inconsistent empirical results in this diversity of contexts led him to conclude that the link between style and effectiveness depends on the favourableness of the situation for the leader. The notion of 'situational favourableness' was taken to include three dimensions: *leader–member relations* (often called group atmosphere) refers to the extent to which the leader is liked and trusted by his subordinates and their preparedness to be loyal to him; *task structure* indicates whether the task at hand is tightly defined from above; *position power* refers to the extent of the leader's authority to hire, promote, fire or demote. Fiedler classified his studies in terms of these criteria and found that the low-scoring LPC leaders perform most effectively in either favourable or highly unfavourable situations. By contrast, high LPC leaders (that is, more permissive and considerate) perform most effectively in the middle range of favourableness.

One of the most controversial aspects of Fiedler's approach derives from his view that his studies shed considerable doubt upon the value of training leaders in a particular style. He argued that it may be more realistic and productive to change contexts to suit styles, rather than vice versa, since a person's leadership style is an outcome of personality and may not be amenable to change through training. Fiedler's alternative is for managements to vary the situational context in order to achieve a better 'fit' with leadership style (Fiedler, 1965). Fiedler, Chemers and Mahar (1976) devised self-assessment instruments for leaders to determine how far their style matched their situation. They also suggest that such considerations should be taken into account by leaders in deciding whether to accept a job offer and in recruiting subordinates who will themselves be leaders.

One of the most difficult problems with Fiedler's contingency theory is the meaning of the LPC scale, particularly in view of its centrality to the overall approach. The link between scores on the scale and style is not obvious (Schriesheim and Kerr, 1977, pp. 22–4) and certainly debatable. Stinson and Tracy (1974) have shown that LPC scores correspond poorly with subordinate accounts of leader behaviour, as measured by the Ohio SBDQ. Shiflett (1973) asked how one might interpret the significance of leaders' scores which are in the middle of the range for achieving a fit between style, as measured by the LPC scale, and context. Since LPC is treated as a unidimensional scale which is correlated with performance, such inferences would not be obvious. The statistical properties of the LPC scale have also been shown to be questionable (Schriesheim and Kerr, 1977).

The 'situational favourableness' dimension has also been a source of controversy. One obvious difficulty is that there are many other situational contingencies which might logically be relevant to the LPC–performance link, and the absence of a definitive theoretical justification for Fiedler's most preferred dimensions has added to this difficulty. The impact of size, technological and bureaucratic variables might be usefully assessed and may be less theoretically contentious.

Most damaging of all to Fiedler's approach, and largely as a result of the problems mentioned above, other writers have often failed to replicate Fiedler's results (Hosking, 1981).

As with the Ohio studies, the static quality of most research within this tradition has meant that even if the correlations were consistently in the anticipated direction, it might be premature to infer that style causes performance (Hosking and Schriesheim, 1978, p. 500; Greene, 1975). Research cited by Schriesheim and Kerr (1977, pp. 25–6) strongly suggests that leaders' scores on the LPC scale may change over time, and that leaders may adjust their styles, as indicated by LPC scores, in response to group performance. A finding such as this also leads one to doubt that an individual necessarily has a 'natural leadership style' (Fiedler, 1965, p. 121).

THE PATH–GOAL THEORY OF LEADERSHIP: THEORY IN SEARCH OF FACTS

The work of Fiedler and the earlier Ohio researchers was based on the development of empirical measures of leadership and the derivation of subsequent empirical relationships. While a theoretical basis for the two programmes had been developed, much of the work was not guided by a clear theoretical rationale. In this respect, the path–goal theory developed by Robert J. House (House, 1973; House and Dessler, 1974; House and Mitchell, 1974) is quite different for it explicitly adapts a psychological 'expectancy theory' to the study of leadership. Simply put, this theory asserts that an individual will behave in a particular manner if he believes his behaviour will have desirable outcomes for him and that his effort will result in the attainment of these outcomes. In the leadership context, this perspective was translated into attention being focused on the leader's ability to facilitate subordinates' expectations that their efforts will enhance their ability to achieve their valued goals and how the successful provision of this expectation produces greater satisfaction and better performance among subordinates. At a very early stage it was recognized that virtually all of its central tenets were likely to be situationally contingent.

The theory has gone through a number of revisions, particularly in respect of the relevant dimensions of leadership style. House's

(1973) early research tended to emphasize the Ohio dimensions of *C* and *IS*. For example, *IS* tended to enhance job satisfaction of subordinates, but when controlled for role ambiguity the relationships were no longer present. The sample upon which this research was conducted was involved in largely ambiguous tasks, so, House reasoned, *IS* redressed this ambiguity so that leaders were able to 'increase the clarity of path–goal relationships and increase satisfaction' (House, 1973, p. 152). A later version of the theory (House and Mitchell, 1974) focused on four types of leadership behaviour: *directive* leadership (often called instrumental) entails a clear stipulation of what is expected of subordinates and a delineation of the paths for achieving that goal; *supportive* leadership denotes a friendly, approachable leader who is concerned for subordinates; *participative* leadership is characterized by consultation with, and a serious consideration of, subordinates' opinions; and finally, the *achievement-oriented* leader sets high expectations of subordinates' performance, sets them challenging goals, and makes clear his confidence in their ability to attain his expectations.

Two broad classes of situational factors were deemed likely to affect relationships between behaviours and outcome. The personal characteristics of subordinates moderate the impact of leadership through such aspects as their ability and how powerless they feel in relation to their environment. Environmental factors are important and include the nature of the task and the broader organization structure.

The research by House and Dessler (1974) and the review provided by House and Mitchell (1974) looked promising for the theory. For example, House and Dessler (1974) found that directive leaders were less likely to have satisfied subordinates when tasks were more structured; but when tasks were unstructured, they tended to have more satisfied subordinates. The task may serve as a substitute for the clarifying quality of directive leadership in structured contexts, so that too much directiveness in fact becomes counter-productive for subordinates; where the task is unstructured, direction is very functional for them. Subordinate personality variables may also mediate the effects of task ambiguity: highly authoritarian subordinates appeared to be more satisfied with directive leaders when carrying out structured tasks than with non-directive leaders. Supportive leaders tend to enhance subordinate satisfaction when the task is stressful or dissatisfying.

Early research within the path–goal framework seemed to have established successfully different types of leadership style and the circumstances in which each style could be related to subordinate satisfaction and performance. Unfortunately, the rocks of empirical examination again took their toll. Sheridan, Downey and Slocum (1976) could provide little empirical support for the theory and pointed out that the interaction between leader behaviour, task structure and satisfaction and performance was far more complex than the theory seemed to indicate. Other studies have had difficulty in replicating House's finding that task structure moderates the relationship between *IS* and satisfaction (Dessler and Valenzi, 1977). A very thorough study of managerial and clerical employees by Schriesheim and Schriesheim (1980) found instrumental leadership did not relate to satisfaction even when situational factors were taken into account, though it had an anticipated effect on subordinates' role clarity. More importantly, supportive leadership did have a strong effect upon job satisfaction and role clarity, but this did not vary, as path–goal theory would lead one to predict, by task structure, job type or organizational level. By contrast, two studies reported by Greene (1979) supported House's finding that instrumental leader behaviour results in greater subordinate satisfaction when the task is unstructured, but that dissatisfaction ensues when it is structured. Similarly, instrumental behaviour was found to enhance role clarity when task structure was not high. However, the relationship with subordinate performance was much less consistent with the theory, particularly since the findings suggested that increased instrumental leadership is a response to poor performance. Greene found that subordinate performance influenced the extent of leader supportiveness. Inferences of this kind, which are only possible when longitudinal studies are conducted, clearly throw into doubt generations of static studies in this field.

The picture is again a bleak one. The initial promise of the theory and early research findings has given way to doubt and uncertainty in much the same way as in the Ohio and Fiedler programmes. To be fair, the theory is much younger and there is a clear recognition that the measurement devices used to test the theory have often been inadequate (Schriesheim and Kerr, 1977; Schriesheim and von Glinow, 1977) and not sufficiently sensitive to the theory. In addition, a broader range of situational factors needs to be considered, though this would diminish the neatness of the theory.

The preceding discussion involved an assessment of three of the major approaches to leadership in the past thirty years. Through them it is possible to discern a preoccupation with leadership styles and their impacts on criteria such as job satisfaction and performance. The emphasis has become increasingly situational, and other approaches such as Vroom's decision-making perspective (Vroom and Yetton, 1973) have systematically introduced this orientation. It is also possible to detect the ebb and flow of promise and disappointment that the field as a whole has yielded. The introduction of a new situational variable into the testing of a particular approach may be a valid short-term expedient but in the context of the development of the leadership field it is little more than clutching at straws. Even the question of the direction of causality is in doubt. Similarly, there is doubt about the extent to which leaders have particular leadership styles, since there is evidence which suggests that leaders may adjust their behaviour in response to different tasks (Hill and Hughes, 1974) or in line with the job experience of their subordinates (Seeman, 1957).

More recent theoretical and empirical work has stimulated interest in the latitude within which leaders operate. To some extent this kind of question goes some way towards accounting for some of the discrepant findings which have been noted. Two areas of work are particularly relevant. First, a distinction has been drawn between discretionary and non-discretionary leadership in that sometimes leaders have substantial control over their behaviour, sometimes not (Hunt, Osborn and Schuler, 1978). Leaders are not always free to function in an entirely unfettered manner and the constraints of organizational structure may limit the latitude a leader has in adopting a particular style. Not only might this affect the extent to which a particular leadership style leads to enhanced performance, it also influences subordinates' perceptions since they may react differently to a particular style depending on whether they see the leader as acting voluntarily, or as constrained by wider circumstances. Non-discretionary rather than discretionary leadership has a greater impact upon subordinate satisfaction. By inference, ideas such as these point to the inadequacy of conceptualizing leadership style as a 'free-floating' variable, in which a leader is free to adopt a particular pattern almost at will.

The second suggestion in the literature which addresses leaders' spheres of latitude is one which is implicit in the various situational-contingency models. Kerr and Jermier (1978) have argued that there are many contexts which may work against the leader's ability to have an impact upon the satisfaction and performance of his subordinates, and that 'substitutes for leadership' neutralize leader behaviour. Characteristics of the subordinate (e.g. ability and experience, professionalism, need for independence), characteristics of the task (e.g. unambiguity, intrinsic satisfaction) and organizational characteristics (e.g. formalization, close-knit work groups, inflexibility, organizational rewards not within the leader's control) were argued to be potential substitutes. However, Howell and Dorfman (1981) found that of the potential substitutes they examined only organizational formalization (explicit goals, plans, responsibilities) was an unambiguous substitute. These approaches strongly point to the need to bring the study of leadership much closer to organization theory. The study of leadership has too often been plucked out of any clear context and studied in isolation, so that broader environmental factors have served merely as moderators of empirical relationships. Bennis (1976) goes even further and argues that leaders are increasingly having their authority and autonomy curtailed not only by internal but also by external constraints. Factors rarely addressed in leadership studies are likely to have a direct impact upon spheres of latitude, in addition to the internal factors to which Hunt et al. and Kerr and Jermier refer. These factors include governmental regulations, the interorganizational network in which a leader is embedded, and guardians of performance like boards of directors. Thus when Salancik and Pfeffer (1977) investigated the impact that US mayors could have on city budgets they found that their effect was generally minimal, and particularly weak in those cities where powerful interest groups severely limited their range of discretion. Similarly,

Lieberson and O'Connor (1972) found that major leadership changes in a range of manufacturing companies had a limited effect upon a range of performance criteria. Characteristics of the company or the industry generally appeared to have a more pervasive effect on performance. The basic point which can be drawn from these perspectives is that leaders' spheres of latitude may be'very narrow and that much leadership may have over-emphasized the importance of leadership styles.

WHAT IS TO BE STUDIED?

It may seem bizarre that after over eighty years of intensive research this question should be asked, but a number of writers are indeed concerned about the correct object of study. There is concern, for example, over the extent to which behaviour associated with leadership is properly separated, and separable, from those behaviours associated with executive or managerial functions (cf. Tosi, 1982). Presumably leadership is not synonymous with management, so one might legitimately ask how much of the management role involves leadership behaviour, as typically conceptualized by researchers. Considerations of this nature raise the possibility that an individual may be a good manager but a poor leader. Further, this problem would contaminate observed relationships between measures of style and outcome, and may at least in part account for some of the disappointing findings in this area. Similarly, the tendency to examine the leadership behaviour of formal leaders has meant that a possibly large arena of research has been closed off. As Pondy (1978, p. 152) has observed, we know far too little about informal leaders. This is surprising since studies of organizations in the 1940s and 1950s had repeatedly pointed to the emergence of the 'informal organization' (cf. Blau, 1956) within the context of a formal organizational blueprint. Research of this kind frequently pointed to the emergence of informal leaders who gained credibility in terms of a well-articulated structure of values and behaviour. In part, the neglect of informal leadership can be explained in methodological terms. Studies of informal organization were invariably based upon case studies, usually utilizing participant observation and unstructured interviewing. The leadership studies which have been examined here have invariably been static, cross-sectional studies involving the use of survey instruments. Such research designs are not well suited to the detection of informal leaders, so that researchers have typically examined the styles of formally designated leaders. More recently writers like Pfeffer (1977) and Calder (1976) have argued that leadership ought to be viewed as an attribution that is made of people who come to be so designated. While the examination of an approach such as this invites questions about the selection of formal leaders, in terms not simply of style or qualities but also of social characteristics, it raises additional questions about the interaction processes which result in the emergence of informal leaders.

The majority of the studies have concentrated upon formal leaders in relatively low positions within their institutional hierarchies. As a result, as Dubin (1979, p. 227) has observed, most leadership research has been about leadership *in* but not *of* organization. Similarly, McCall and Lombardo (1978, p. 152) point out that there is insufficient evidence about chief executives, company chairmen and top leaders generally. As a result, it can be argued that many broader, more fundamental issues about the function of leadership have been ignored. In particular, the notion that the leader has a vital role as the promoter of values in organization has been given short shrift in the analysis of leadership.

Selznick (1957) pointed out that institutional leaders define the role and mission of an enterprise. They move beyond the rational delineation of an administrative machinery in the cause of efficiency and in order to infuse an organization with a value system and create a social structure which embodies it. This process which Selznick referred to as the 'institutional embodiment of purpose' seeks to mobilize the commitments of its members to a broad normative consensus. As a result we find a

> ... unity that emerges when a particular orientation becomes so firmly a part of group life that it colours and directs a wide range of attitudes, decisions, and forms of organisation, and does so at many levels of experience (Selznick, 1957, p. 138).

Such a conception seems rather abstract and a far cry from the relationship between LPC scores and job satisfaction. But it is no further from, and possibly a lot nearer to, the realities of organizational life. Thomas Peters of McKinsey and Company has pointed out that 'the shaping of robust institutional values' (Peters, 1979, p. 170) is a vital aspect of top leadership in that they provide the vital premises which underlie the setting of goals and the selection of policy options. Indeed, when Peters's company examined the management practices of thirty-seven particularly well-run organizations, they found that one of the most prominent characteristics of such companies is that their chief executives promote clearly articulated values which 'are pursued with an almost religious zeal' (Peters, 1980, p. 205). Company employees are socialized into the cultures of these corporations, a process which seems almost as important as the development of appropriate technical skills. Nor is the development of organizational cultures isolated from organizational performance. The McKinsey workers have come to recognize that if organizational style is out of phase with aspects of its operations, performance may well be jeopardized (Waterman, Peters and Phillips, 1980, p. 22). Similarly, Peters (1979, p. 170) notes that leaders themselves are often more effective to the extent to which they systematically develop values and seek out a consensus.

In developing value premises and their structural implementation, leaders have to be sensitive to their product, market, the backgrounds of subordinates and a myriad of other factors. Evidence of these processes can often be discerned in accounts of prominent leaders. John F. Welch, the chairman of General Electric, aims to create 'an atmosphere where people dare to try new things – where people feel assured in knowing that only the limits of their creativity and drive will be the ceiling on how far and how fast they move' (Morrison, 1982, p. 53). In order to implement this culture, he removed the structural constraints on innovation by departing from a context of tight control and centralization and enhancing decentralization and risk-taking. He seeks to explain changes fully to his officers and to maintain close contact with a wide range of operations. A more extreme case of leadership through values is provided by Jim Treybig, founder-president of the enormously successful Tandem Computers. The company's philosophical principles, which can loosely be described as 'people oriented' (Magnet, 1982), are clearly articulated in company magazines, in a book entitled *Understanding Our Philosophy* and through courses.

Employees carry around a clear sense of the corporate culture which establishes the importance of the individual as an end in itself (e.g. 'You never have the right at Tandem to screw a person or to mistreat them'). The climate is reinforced through minimal controls, unstructured vertical and horizontal communication, minimal role specification and undefined hierarchies.

In each of these cases it is possible to detect leadership vision in which the leader seeks to create an atmosphere to generate motivational commitments on the part of subordinates. To refer to what they do as a particular style in the manner of most leadership research seems to miss the point. Like most major leaders, they seek to bring all elements into alignment by fusing them into an overall programme. They are in the business of the promotion of values, in Selznick's (1957) sense, once they seek to define their programme in this manner. Leadership research misses most of these points because of its comparative lack of interest in major institutional leaders and its tendency to collapse leadership categories into shorthand depictions of leader behaviour, when in fact, as Pondy (1978, p. 90) has observed, it is the variety of strategies which is of interest.

CHAPTER 7

Control

PAUL FINLAY

At its simplest, an organization can be viewed as a conversion process: inputs are converted to outputs via some process. The inputs are resources of people, materials, capital and energy and the conversion is to an output with a higher value than the inputs themselves. The conversion process may be depicted as in Figure 1 below.

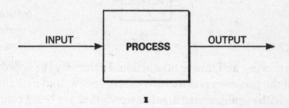

INPUT   **PROCESS**   OUTPUT

1

Inputs to the process would come, either directly or indirectly, from its environment. Even if this environment were completely unchanging (no changes in the price or quality of raw materials for example), it would not normally be appropriate to allow the process to continue without check: the process may become unable to produce the required output, as would happen, for example, if a machine gradually became worn, and began producing items that were outside acceptable tolerance limits. Thus the cycle of activities depicted in Figure 2, overleaf, needs to be carried out. First, the process needs to be monitored to see that all is well; if not, planning is required whereby the options open to correct the deficiency are explored. In the light of this exploration a decision is made to alter the process, and this is then followed by action to implement the decision. Further monitoring is carried out and so the cycle is repeated continuously throughout the life of the process.

Where the environment is changing, it is wise also to monitor the environment so as to anticipate the effects of environmental changes

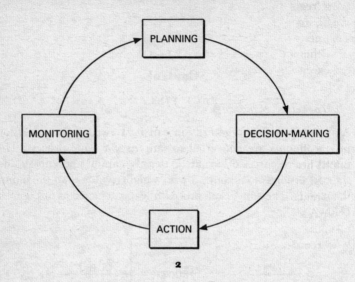

2

on the process, and thus to take action. In this way the appropriateness of the processes is constantly under review, and activities kept in line with requirements: in other words they are being controlled.

Control is an intimate and integral part of a manager's professional life. Managers spend a great deal of time creating and operating control procedures for the business processes for which they have responsibility. The control they exercise is often subtle, because in most businesses managers are concerned with human-activity systems, and humans are notoriously difficult to control. For this reason it is much more appropriate to begin a discussion of the principles of control by describing physical systems of the sort developed by engineers: systems in which human activity is either absent or plays only a minor part.

DESIGNED PHYSICAL SYSTEMS

Engineers have long understood the need for control which is central to the science of cybernetics. The term cybernetics comes from the Greek word meaning 'steersman', and this gives flavour of one aspect of control. Other dictionary definitions include the words 'regulate', indicating a clearly defined preferred state for the system, and 'guide', suggesting a much vaguer idea. Apart from machines with artificial intelligence, an appropriate and serviceable definition of control for designed physical systems will be taken as 'to keep something within prescribed limits'.

A Domestic Central-Heating System

Most of the basic principles of control in designed physical systems can be illustrated by considering the operation of a domestic central-heating system. One form of a conventional system is depicted in Figure 3a: here a gas-fired boiler is used to heat water that circulates through radiators, which in turn heat the air in the house. A sensor measures the air temperature at a suitable point in the house and a comparison is made in a thermostat between this measurement and a preset value. If the measured temperature is

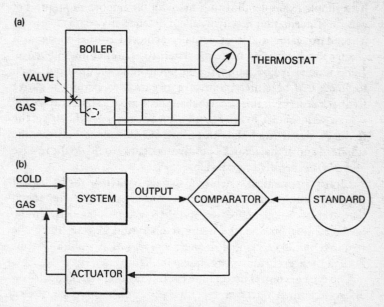

3 *a* a domestic central-heating system;
b conceptualization of a domestic heating system

below the preset temperature then a signal is sent to turn on the boiler. This causes the water to be heated, the radiators get hot and the air temperature rises. The heating continues until the sensor records a temperature equal to the preset value and then the boiler is turned off.

A generalization of the central-heating system is shown in Figure 3b. Here the system (house) is shown as having two inputs: an environmental input that cannot be controlled (cold or negative heat) and a controllable input (gas, whose rate of input to the boiler can be controlled). An output from the system (the air temperature in the house) is measured and compared in the comparator (the thermostat) with a standard (the preset temperature). If the measured output differs from the standard in what is considered to be an undesirable way, then a signal is sent to the actuator (the gas valve) to alter the controllable input to the system (the gas).

Retroactive Control

This simple example illustrates many of the important features of control. Information specifying the difference or variance between a standard value and that actually achieved is used to signal a change to one of the inputs to the system so as to alter this difference. Information is fed back from the output to influence the input. Such feedback can be either positive or negative. Generally negative feedback is desired: this occurs when the feedback signal causes the system performance to alter in such a way as to *reduce* the size of the feedback signal (and thus to reduce the difference between the standard and actual values – positive feedback would do the reverse and this is generally undesirable).

Clearly, in practical systems the signal to switch on the boiler will not be sent unless the difference between the standard and actual temperatures is a degree or so, and there will be a lag between the boiler coming on and the house temperature getting up to the required value. Overshoot or over-compensation will also occur. Both of these occurrences are shown in Figure 4.

The type of control used in the central-heating system described above is termed retroactive control: control is exercised after a variance between standard and actual has occurred. The house must cool below the required temperature before action is taken.

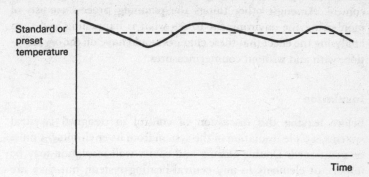

4 Overcompensation in a control system

Most financial control systems in business rely on retroactive control.

Proactive Control

Proactive control has more inherent subtlety than retroactive control. Changes in the values of the environmental variables for which compensation is desired are monitored, and compensation applied before the system is significantly affected. Some sophisticated central-heating systems have such a facility. A thermometer outside the house measures the rate of change of the outside temperature and, if the temperature is falling, a signal is sent (fed forward) to activate the boiler before the interior thermostat has registered any fall in temperature. This is desirable because the insulation in the house walls prevents an instantaneous change of the inside temperature as the outside temperature falls. Monitoring the change in the outside temperature allows compensation to be made for the otherwise inevitable lag between an internal temperature fall and the resultant injection of heat to restore the required temperature. The modulations shown in Figure 4 are reduced and smoothed out.

Thus proactive control provides the possibility of protecting the system from a severe buffeting caused by environmental change. To use a nautical analogy, the hatches are battened down and the sails trimmed before the main force of the storm reaches the ship. Financial and corporate planning in business is a form of proactive control. Amongst other things the planning process consists of monitoring the environment to see what is happening and then analysing the effect that these changes would have on the organization, with and without countermeasures.

Insulation

Before leaving this discussion of control in designed physical systems, simple insulation of the system from its environment must be mentioned. Double glazing and cavity-wall insulation may be important elements to any central-heating system, but they are only capable of slowing down the effect on the system of changes in the environment. Insulation alone is well suited to counter short-term random and cyclical environmental change, but is not appropriate for longer-term changes. Holding stocks of raw materials and finished goods in business is a form of insulation. A stock of items allows one process to be isolated (although only partly) from those taking place before it and after it.

In summary, reactive control is invoked only after an undesirable state of affairs has been reached; whereas proactive control is the way of so organizing the system that it is prepared for environmental change. Insulation is a means of reducing the link between cause and effect. A combination of all these methods of control will be used in most systems.

HUMAN CONTROL OF DESIGNED PHYSICAL SYSTEMS

Human activity was ignored in the discussion of the domestic heating system. People would have been involved in its design however and would be involved in its operation. The domestic central-heating system has been depicted as a system in which all the actions that the system should take have been preprogrammed, so that a wide range of variance can be coped with automatically. In such a system, the standards set and the rules of operation have been defined outside the system. Such a system is termed a cybernetic control system, and is obviously of the kind appropriate to designed physical systems. The tenant of the house may be included if we widen the extent of the control system. At its very simplest the tenant decides on the required temperature and thus the thermostat setting. In doing this he acts as a higher level of control.

A central-heating system that includes the tenant is an example of a homeostatic system – a system in which control is exercised by the system itself. Hofstede (1978) likens this to the actions of a biological cell, whereby, within wide limits, the cell controls itself and adapts to its environment. If the government decided to charge a higher price for fuel, then the homeostatic system could adapt to this, perhaps lowering the thermostat setting, while the cybernetic system could not adapt. Homeostatic systems tend to be more flexible and adaptable than are cybernetic ones, but they tend to be slow to implement (since the rules of self-control have to be learnt) (Hofstede, 1978).

Hierarchy of Controls

The discussion above highlights the concept of levels of control: the tenant controls the central-heating control system through setting the standard, and the government influences the way the tenant runs the system. This concept of levels of control is extremely important in business and it might be summed up by the aphorism 'even the boss has a boss'.

So far two methods of controlling the temperature of the house have been mentioned: either to alter the input (in this case the quantity and/or price of the gas used) or to alter the standard itself (alter the required temperature). These are termed first-order and second-order control. A third method of exercising control is to change the system itself by altering the process by which inputs are converted to outputs. In the central-heating case, for example, a violent rise in gas prices might call for a more efficient boiler to be installed.

What has yet to be considered is the design of the control system and the role of the designer. To proceed, it is convenient to introduce a little systems terminology.

Output, Control and Environmental Variables

Formally a system can be defined as a 'purposeful set of interrelated parts and processes'. In systems terms, output variables are used to evaluate the system; environmental variables may significantly affect the system but cannot be controlled; and control variables can be changed to effect control of the system. The link between these variables has to be known to design a control system. In the case of the central-heating system, it is necessary to know that an increase in the amount of gas to the boiler will ultimately enable the house temperature to reach the standard temperature in the face of a decrease in the environmental temperature. The relations specifying links such as these form a model of how the system will perform for various combinations of control and environmental variables. Without a knowledge of these relations, the designer would not be able to design and the controller would be controlling in the dark. Figure 5 shows this requirement for a model of the control system added to the system.

The designer would use this model to investigate the types of control system that might be installed, testing each possibility against a range of values of the environmental variables. For example, environmental temperatures higher than the required temperature could be tried on the central-heating control system. If this were done with a conventional central-heating system, the controls would not be adequate to cope: the system's only response

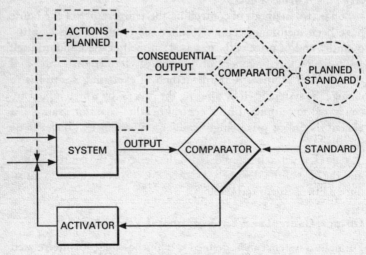

5 A control system and its 'model'

to such conditions would be not to make matters worse (that is, not to switch the boiler on). An air-conditioning system able to extract heat from the house would be needed to get the house temperature back under control. A model allows for this possibility to be examined before the system is installed.

CONTROL IN HUMAN-ACTIVITY SYSTEMS

While management is concerned with the effective use of all types of resources, the most difficult management problems often concern human resources. Control in human-activity systems is different from control in designed physical systems. As this is so, it is necessary to question whether the model of control depicted in Figure 5 is applicable to such systems. Four basic assumptions of cybernetic control are:

1. that standards can be devised and can be stated precisely;
2. that achievement can be measured;
3. that variance information can be fed back;
4. that this feedback information will be sufficient to maintain control.

These assumptions may be met where human activities are similar to those in designed physical systems or machines. Such human activities may be termed structured activities: 'Structured activities are in general stable, repetitive activities or procedures which can be economically analysed and systematized, such as clerical or assembly line tasks' (Dermer, 1977). At the other extreme are unstructured activities, which are novel activities requiring judgement. Many of the tasks undertaken by top management are unstructured activities.

For structured activities, cybernetic controls of the sort described for the simple central-heating system still have a major role to play, although the human element means that they are unlikely to be effective on their own. For systems comprising many unstructured activities – sometimes called managed or discretionary systems – the validity of cybernetic control systems is more questionable. Their characteristics must be investigated to see whether the assumptions underlying cybernetic control will be met.

Assumption 1: Standards Can Be Devised and Can Be Stated Precisely

Most organizations do not start off with ready-made standard values for their operations; they have broad, rather imprecisely stated goals summing up what is seen as the mission of the organization. For example, a business organization may see its primary goal as one of survival, with other goals likely to be to make an adequate profit, to obtain a certain market share for their product, to provide useful and interesting work for the employees, and so on. Such goals are often not specified precisely enough to act as cybernetic control standards, and so they must be hardened into precisely defined objectives. The setting of objectives can be straightforward; for example, a company manufacturing cars would have little difficulty in setting objectives in terms of cars produced per shift or cars produced per man hour. In other cases it can be very difficult. What objectives should be set for a personnel department? Some of its outputs can be precisely defined (such as the number of employees recruited, or the number of wrongful dismissal cases brought against the company), but other outputs, such as responsibility for employee development and training, are much more difficult to specify. This is also true for many other parts of an organization, such as the public-relations and legal departments. In this case, substitute or surrogate measures may be used as output measures: for example, absenteeism as an inverse indicator of morale; or the number of employees sent on courses as an indicator of employee development.

The problem with using surrogate measures is that they often put the emphasis on efficiency rather than on effectiveness. Efficiency is a measure of the performance of a process in converting inputs to outputs – usually defined as:

$$\text{efficiency} = \frac{\text{outputs}}{\text{inputs}}$$

This should be contrasted with effectiveness, which, although containing the notion of efficiency, has in view the wider concept of the value of the output of the process to the overall or higher good. For example, factory A may be much more efficient than factory B in producing shoes (that is, wasting fewer materials, using fewer man hours, etc., for the same output); but if factory A produces all size 13 shoes for which there is little demand, while factory B produces the most popular sizes, then factory B can be considered highly effective in that it meets the higher good of protecting people's feet. So it can be seen that efficiency is a measure only of the process itself as a converter and says nothing about the value of the outputs: in Drucker's phrase – efficiency is doing the thing right, effectiveness is doing the right thing.

So returning to the issue of surrogates, using them can lead to an emphasis on doing the thing right, when the organization should be doing the right thing, because surrogates are almost always simpler measures working at a lower level than is really required.

A further problem is that it is often not possible to devise a single standard for an organization, and in fact most organizations have multiple objectives encompassing such things as profits, employee morale and market share. This is not necessarily a problem in itself, but becomes one when these objectives are in conflict. Profit may seem to be the one and only objective of a commercial enterprise, but generally higher profits in one year have to be tempered by considerations of the need to pay for long-term growth and increased productivity which may reduce profits in the short term. What happens in fact is that organizations tend to set minimum values on each objective and then strike a balance (often very subjectively) between the values that will feature as the standards.

With human-activity systems, the problem of multiple objectives is compounded by the fact that individuals in an organization have objectives of their own which may not be the same as those of the organization. Indeed it is said that organizations don't have goals and objectives, only individuals do, and what passes for organizational goals are those of the dominant individual or coalition (Perrow, 1970).

Assumption 2: Achievement Can Be Measured

If an agreed standard cannot be set, then there is no point in measuring achievement as part of the control process. However, even with an agreed standard, the measurement of achievement can pose severe problems: such problems often occur as an adjunct to the use of surrogate measures as standards. For example, if one were interested in 'controlling' morale and used absenteeism as a surrogate measure for this, then one's measure may be invalidated if a flu epidemic occurred – crude use of the raw figures on absenteeism would lead to the view that morale had slumped. A further concern is that an organization will tend to use easily and precisely measurable objectives, whereas these may not be the important ones.

Assumption 3: Variance Information Can Be Fed Back

Unstructured activities involve a considerable element of judgement. One-off projects and much research and development work fit into this category, as does some of the work of legal and public-relations departments. In such cases direct feedback of information is not possible, as exactly the same activities are never repeated: indirect feedback takes place through the accumulation of knowledge of how similar activities might be performed in the future. Such a link between past and on-going activities is a far cry from the direct feedback implicit in cybernetic control. The variance information will be amalgamated with other experience to be used in a wider way. Hofstede (1978) also cites the communication difficulties that are likely owing to the controllers very often being of a different class or group to those who are controlled: this class difference being a difference in aspiration, ways of thought and, indeed, ways of speech.

Assumption 4: The Feedback Is Sufficient to Maintain Control

The inability of a conventional system to cope with environmental temperatures above the standard was mentioned in the discussion of a domestic central-heating system. The tenant is powerless to effect control with such a system. This illustrates a very important concept of control: a controller can only be expected to control a system if he has control variables at his disposal that are at least as effective in altering the system outputs as are the environmental variables that he wishes to counter. This, in slightly simplified form, is the law of requisite variety as expounded by Ross Ashby (1970).

Without sufficient control variables, the controller has been given responsibility without power and the two need to be balanced. For example, it is not sensible to hold a manager responsible for the labour costs in his department, if a company-wide wage agreement over which he has had no influence comes into force. He can only be held responsible for some of the factors making up these costs such as the number of people employed in the department or the amount of overtime worked.

In analysing the assumptions underlying cybernetic control, it can be seen that they are not a close fit to the realities of unstructured activities. Most of the formal control systems in operation in business today rely on cybernetic control, and thus are often not a totally appropriate mechanism. However, they are a firm requirement in most organizations, usually augmented by informal non-cybernetic controls.

CONTROL SYSTEMS IN BUSINESS

By far the most used business-control systems are systems organized by management accountants that revolve around the annual budget. An annual budget is a detailed financial forecast of the income and outgoings of the organization for a financial year. The forecasts act as the standards against which subsequent control is exercised. Often, however, the controls are not directly in terms of financial quantities but involve such 'physical' things as quantity of waste, machine loadings and overtime.

In setting up a control system based on an annual budget, four decisions need to be made:

1. What are the centres of responsibility in the organization?
2. Within each centre, what processes are to be controlled?
3. What is an appropriate reporting period?
4. How are variances to be reported?

Centres of Responsibility

Most business organizations are structured on a functional basis. It is natural that the centres of responsibility will follow this functional split and also the natural splits within functions. In short, each manager will head a part of the organization responsible for using resources or generating income and each manager should be in charge of a unique responsibility centre.

All responsibility centres are not of the same type, however, and a hierarchy of three types can be identified: cost, profit and investment centres.

At the lower levels in an organization, for example in a section concerned with processing customers' orders, a manager would only be responsible for the costs incurred. If the processes were stopped, no costs would be incurred. A responsibility centre such as this is termed a cost centre.

At a higher level, managers would become responsible also for revenue as well as costs. Being responsible for both revenue and costs means that the manager is responsible for the profit generated by his unit. Such a manager would be described as being in charge of a profit centre.

While the top managers in a company would be responsible for profits, they may not have responsibility for the use of them and of the other assets they use. Managers in an independent company would have such responsibility, but where the company is one of a group it may be only at group level that decisions about the use of profits and other forms of capital are taken. Thus there is a distinction between a profit centre and an investment centre: only the latter has the responsibility for investment decisions.

The Processes to Control

Since they consume resources or generate income, all processes need to be controlled. The question remains, however, of the level of detailed control. For example, should stationery be controlled as a general commodity or should it be divided into pens, paper, paperclips, etc.? The level of aggregation will depend on the monies associated with each subdivision and the effort required to control them. What is considered an important sum of money, and thus needing control, will be a reflection of the size of the organization.

What should be sought, therefore, is a match between the degree of control exercised and the importance of the resource controlled.

The Appropriate Reporting Period

In the cybernetic control model, the outcome from the process to be controlled is compared with its standard. While in the automatic control of machinery (process control) almost instant comparisons are made and control exercised accordingly, in most business systems the operation of a process is monitored for some time before the comparison is made. The time period over which data are gathered is governed partly by the administrative effort required to perform the aggregation and make the comparison, but mainly by the need to obtain sufficient data in order to reduce the effect of random factors. For example, if the use of a raw material in a production process were being monitored, it would probably be inappropriate to compare the actual usage with the standard usage over a period of one hour – in any one hour, a failing that has negligible cost implications might set the alarm bells ringing. Setting the reporting period involves a fine balancing act between a period long enough for random fluctuations to be smoothed out, yet short enough to pick up any systematic trends quickly. Typically a period of a shift or a day is used for operational control, of a week or a month for managerial control and of a month or a quarter of a year for board-level control.

The reader may be puzzled in trying to compare the sort of reporting period discussed here with that described for the central-heating system. There, as with any process control system, the conditions under which action should be taken are completely prescribed, and there is no fixed reporting period. Business-control systems based on this principle, called 'exception reporting', have been implemented but are not in common use. Basically no fixed time period is set. The outcome from the process is continually compared with an appropriately 'moving' standard: if the outcome remains within a prescribed tolerance, no report is produced; if the outcome goes outside the tolerance then management is informed.

One reason for the dearth of business-control systems based on exception reporting seems to be that management likes to have a periodic report if only to be sure that the control system is working correctly. More fundamentally, however, the prior determination of what constitutes cause for concern and what does not will not take account of the fact that, as the context of the process changes,

so will the relevance of different sizes of deviation from the standard.

Often a compromise between exception reporting and reporting
periodically is used, in which outcomes well below standard are
highlighted to indicate where action may be needed.

Variance Reporting

At the end of a reporting period, the costs actually incurred, and
the revenues actually received, are aggregated for each type of cost
and revenue within each responsibility centre. The actuals, the
standards and the differences between them (termed the variances)
make up the report to management.

It is not always the case that what is aggregated forms a directly
convenient measure for comparison with the standard. In controlling the usage of a raw material, for example, if the overall cost of
the material used to produce a given volume of finished goods were
higher than the standard, is this adverse variance due to higher
material prices or to a greater usage? To unearth the cause of the
variance, the gross variance needs to be analysed. The technique
for doing this, using as an example the calculation of a raw material
variance, is as follows.

Standards will be set for the unit price paid for the material and
for the quantity needed for the standard unit of production.

The following equations can be written:

standard material cost = standard unit price × standard
                                        quantity

actual material cost = actual unit price × actual quantity

The material cost variance is defined as:

material cost variance = standard material cost − actual
                                        material cost

                        = (standard unit price × standard
                          quantity) − (actual unit price × actual
                          quantity)

Rearranging this equation we have:

material cost variance = standard unit price × (standard
                       quantity − actual quantity) + actual
                       quantity × (standard unit
                       price − actual unit price)

The first term represents the material usage variance; the second term the material price variance.

In this way the overall variance is decomposed into its constituent parts. This is important as it isolates the real cause of the variance. It is particularly important to do this if different managers are responsible for different features of the total cost: in the case of raw materials, very often a purchasing manager would be responsible for the price paid for the raw material, while another manager would be responsible for its use.

If, for example, the standard quantity of a commodity were 10,000 with a standard unit price of £1, the standard material cost would be £10,000. With an actual quantity of 12,000 and an actual unit price of £0.90, the material usage variance is calculated as:

$$£1 × (10,000 − 12,000) = −£2000$$

while the material price variance is calculated as:

$$12,000 × (£1 − £0.90) = £1,200$$

Thus it can be seen that the adverse variance – the variance which has an adverse effect on the organization performance – lies only in the material usage, and not at all in the material price. Continuing in this way it is possible to pinpoint the areas of concern, and the managers responsible.

Problems with Conventional Budgeting Control Systems

Conventional budgetary-control mechanisms are invariably cybernetic in operation with the deficiencies already examined. The main problems centre around devising appropriate standards (especially difficult for unstructured activities) and with obtaining goal congruence. Management by objectives (MBO) is one technique designed to secure this congruence and is discussed below. Even where cybernetic controls may be appropriate, however, the conventional budgetary approach suffers by being devised on an incremental basis: the previous year's budgeted and actual figures form the basis from which the next budget is constructed. Almost every process that entered the previous budget is entered into the next; the only differences being changes in the associated costs and revenues due to different expectations of demand, inflation, and so on.

The problem with incremental budgeting is that no assessment is made of whether a process should be undertaken at all, and, if it should, whether there is a better way of doing it. This problem is particularly severe with fixed costs and with unstructured activities. An approach called zero-based budgeting (ZBB) aims to overcome this deficiency by forcing a review of the use of all resources.

Zero-Based Budgeting (ZBB)

As with incremental budgeting, the starting points for ZBB are the current processes for which a manager is responsible. From a breakdown of these processes, discrete activities are identified. Where a break is made from the conventional approach is that the manager is obliged to identify and evaluate alternatives to each activity, and to develop what are called 'decision packages' for each. A decision package is a document that describes an activity in such a way that management can rank it against other activities competing for resources, and accept or reject it. For example, a manager might be responsible for a system that pays employees: alternatives to the current method of, say, using an in-house mainframe computer system might be to use an outside firm or to purchase a microcomputer system to do the job. For each of these identified options, the manager would make out a case, giving both the pros and the cons. He would then nominate one option as the preferred option.

An option so chosen would indicate the general preferred approach – perhaps to purchase a microcomputer system for the payroll application above. Within this option the manager would now be required to identify the 'base-case solution' – the solution that would just achieve the objectives required for that activity. In the payroll case the minimum objective would be to pay the employees the correct amount of money. Together with this base-case he would be called upon to look at 'incremental options' – other possible solutions following the same general preferred approach and which necessitate an increment of spending on top of that called for by the base-case. Returning to the payroll example, incremental costs might be incurred by having an extra terminal to the microcomputer, or by buying more comprehensive microcomputer software that would allow personnel records to be held as well. A formal document stating the options considered, both broad and incremental, together with the pros and cons, constitute the decision package.

A decision package would be developed for each activity, although on occasion no feasible alternative to the current method would be identified. The next step is to rank the decision packages in order of decreasing benefit to the organization. The organization is then in a position to decide, for any given level of overall expenditure, those activities which should continue unchanged, those which should continue albeit in a modified form, and those that should be stopped.

Pyhrr (1977) discusses the problems of ranking. This needs to be done at a high level in the organization, as an overview of all activities is needed. Since the activities are being assessed at lower levels, a large number of decision packages would reach top management if no filtering were used. A simple solution is reached by establishing a cut-off expense line at each organizational level. Management at that level then review in detail and rank only the decision packages involving expenditures below that cut-off level. Packages above that level are reviewed by the next management level.

Proponents of ZBB claim that it has several advantages over conventional, incremental budgeting. It allows comparisons to be made across functions and allows resources to be allocated in a manner that is considered best for the organization as a whole: it forces alternatives to be actively sought and evaluated and indeed the rationale for all activities to be questioned. On the other hand it seems a time-consuming exercise. However, Pyhrr himself does not see ZBB being an annual procedure where the activities of the organization are reasonably stable and where management is satisfied that operations are effective and efficient.

Management by Objectives
Earlier in the chapter, the inapplicability of cybernetic control to unstructured activities was discussed. Two problem areas were the impossibility of determining standards (and subsequently compar-

ing actuals with them) and goal congruence – of ensuring that the goals of the individual were consistent with those of the organization. Management by objectives is a technique that, through personal commitment, attempts to overcome these two deficiencies.

In managing by objectives, a start is made by each subordinate developing his own set of objectives. Concurrently, his boss will have developed a set of objectives for the unit in which the subordinate works that are consistent with the organizational objectives. In the light of the objectives of the organization, the boss and the subordinate then review the subordinate's objectives until agreement is reached. For each objective in the agreed set, measures of performance are developed against which the subordinate will later be evaluated.

Proceeding in this way, it can be seen that a subordinate has much greater control over setting his own standards than in conventional control systems, and thus is more likely to be motivated to meet them. Also, given an agreed set of quantifiable standards, evaluation can be made against achievement, rather than on subjective assessments coloured by the way the subordinate goes about his job. On the other hand, the time taken to obtain agreement on a set of objectives with many subordinates can be too demanding for many managers. An organization needs perhaps three to five years to implement management by objectives successfully. More fundamental, however, is the assumption made in management by objectives that the separation of goals into separated objectives can actually be achieved.

SUMMARY

In order to thrive, every organization must control its activities. In businesses, the major formal control system is that created and maintained by accountants for financial control. Such systems revolve around setting a budget and comparing actual performance against a desired standard of performance. One deficiency of most budget control systems is that they tend to be incremental, in the sense that one year's activities and performances are expected to be similar to those of the previous year, only incremented to take account of small changes in data values. Zero-based budgeting is a technique for preventing the unthinking nature of incremental budgeting, by forcing management to seek alternative ways of doing their current activities (including not doing them at all). Financial control systems tend to be of the cybernetic type which, although reasonably appropriate for structured activities, are inapplicable to unstructured ones. Two major problem areas apparent in attempts to use cybernetic controls for unstructured activities are in setting standards and in ensuring a fair measure of goal congruence. Management by objectives is a technique designed to overcome this problem: it does so but only at the expense of much time and effort by the whole organization.

SECTION B

THE CONTEXT OF MANAGEMENT

Introduction

The fundamental and simple idea which pervades this section is that management does not take place in a vacuum but in a finely structured context. An appreciation of this is made more poignant by the fact of a certain tension between what we might rather crudely call high-level context and low-level context. On the one hand are environing culture and its effects, the structure of business ownership and controls, government economic policy and legislation, and the national system of industrial relations. On the other hand are the more immediate questions of the ethics of individual actions, the internal politics of the organization, the fact and effect of worker participation in decision-making processes, and so on.

The first set, the dimensions of high-level context, are about restraints, general emphasis, the patterning of options. The second set, the dimensions of low-level context, are more about action and choice and individual responsibility. The ability of individuals to effect – still less shape – the first is severely limited, yet at the lower level their freedom of action is considerable, and their responsibility inescapable. Section B seeks to chart these levels.

Again there is a sub-plot, which is to underline the notion of cultural relativity. There is little in the fact or context of business which is absolute, which is always and everywhere the same. The pattern of ownership and control, for instance, varies even among the western industrialized democratic states; the system of industrial relations varies markedly among even neighbouring western European countries; or again France and West Germany, Sweden and England, show significant differences in the degree and style of government involvement in economic life. This sub-plot becomes more explicit in the last chapters of the section which take up such questions as how does national culture affect the character of management, and are, say, American or Japanese companies operating outside their homelands noticeably different.

CHAPTER 8

Ownership, Management and Strategic Control

JOHN SCOTT

This chapter examines changes in the ownership of large business enterprises, and their implications for management.

The environment of these organizations influences the type of control used in them. An important aspect of the environment is the market situation of the firm: its position in product, capital and labour markets. No firm can survive for long in unfavourable market situations, and so control will always be constrained by the dictates of the market. Large enterprises may, and often do, dominate the markets within which they operate; but they still operate in and through markets.

The activities of the state are a second key element in the environment. Political action not only maintains the general framework of law and administration within which markets operate, but also influences direct intervention in business. Public enterprises, governmental agencies and planning policies provide additional constraints upon the enterprise.

The third element of the environment consists of other organizations with which the enterprise is involved: employers' associations, cartels, interlocking directorships, trade unions, and so on. The enterprise is not a monolithic social group but a federation of competing groups with divergent interests. Shopfloor workers respond to the labour market situation by joining trade unions to enhance their ability to further their interests within the enterprise. Similarly, top executives join bodies such as the Confederation of British Industry or the Engineering Employers Federation to strengthen the position of the enterprise in negotiations with government, trade unions and other organizations.

The business enterprise can be considered as an organized group of employees divided by economic interests and political outlook, but unified through their subjection to the control exercised by the 'dominant coalition' of directors and executives. This dominant coalition must draw on the resources available to it to exercise control within the constraints imposed by the environment of the firm. Before this can be analysed further, it is necessary to discuss the meaning of 'control'. In fact it has several different meanings, some of which are discussed in other chapters of this book. In this chapter 'control' refers to 'the power of determining the broad policies guiding the corporation' (Goldsmith and Parmelee, 1940, p. 99). This power is exercised at two levels: strategic and operational. Strategic control involves decisions over diversification, mergers and general objectives aimed at coping with environmental constraints (Ansoff, 1965). Strategic control must take account of these constraints but will also attempt to alter them to enhance the position of the enterprise within its environment. The operational sphere involves activities to implement corporate strategy, and so operational control concerns budgeting, wage determination, choice of suppliers, and hiring and firing. Strategic control sets the framework, while operational control involves the day-to-day administration of company affairs. Operational administration is carried out by a managerial hierarchy working within a framework of financial targets set by those who exercise strategic control. The remainder of this chapter will show how the dominant coalition is formed and how capital ownership is related to its ability to exercise strategic control *within and over* environmental constraints.

OWNERSHIP AND CONTROL

The Debate

The industrial enterprise of nineteenth-century Britain was essentially small. It was typically run by a family or a small group of partners, based on one plant, and involved little or no delegation of authority by the owners who had full control over both strategy and operations. The characteristic form of business enterprise was larger and differently organized in the non-manufacturing sector: railways, banking and insurance. In these sectors the joint-stock company, a firm in which the capital was subscribed by a large body of shareholders, had arisen as a way of meeting their greater capital requirements. From the 1870s the increasing scale of industrial production forced many manufacturing firms to convert themselves into joint-stock companies so that they could draw upon a wider pool of capital. Amalgamations and mergers among these companies meant that by the turn of the century a number of markets were dominated by large business enterprises.

In the USA a similar process occurred, but the transition from the entrepreneurial firm to the large enterprise occurred more rapidly. A handful of New York financiers, headed by J. P. Morgan, were active in the amalgamation and restructuring of capital which produced a number of industrial giants. Public concern over the concentration of wealth and the resulting power led to an official inquiry and to the Clayton anti-trust laws, which attempted to prevent the monopolization of particular markets. In the United States even a tradition of academic research into these problems developed, particularly about the separation of ownership from control in the large joint-stock company.

The classic statement of this idea is in the work of Berle and Means (1932). They argued that the joint-stock company involves a legal separation of two aspects of ownership: shareholders are the owners of the company, but not of its assets. The assets are owned by the company itself and are, therefore, subject to the control of whoever is able to dominate the company's affairs. In the old entrepreneurial firm the owner of industrial property had full rights over it, but in the joint-stock company there is a dissolution of these traditional property rights. The shareholders who supply the capital and own the company may not be identical with those who determine the uses to which this capital is put. In this situation the question of who is able to control corporate strategy becomes all important. Berle and Means claimed that shareholdings were becoming less important as bases for strategic control and that, in consequence, internal managers had enhanced opportunities for this control.

This theme of the 'managerial revolution' seemed to strike a popular chord. Berle and Means thought that the 1930s were a period of transition from owner control to management control, but their hypothesis about the future of managerial power was widely accepted as an established fact (Zeitlin, 1974). James Burnham made a particularly influential statement of this view in his book *The Managerial Revolution* (Burnham, 1941). He argued that the 'finance capitalists' who controlled the US economy in the inter-war period were destined to be displaced by managers who played an indispensable role in the technical direction and coordination of the production process. This rise to power of managers in industry would be paralleled by the rise of those who manage the state apparatus. He argued that the USA was experiencing a class revolution which would eventuate in a managerial society. Burnham's broader claims have not been widely accepted, and most writers follow the less extreme statement of Berle and Means. Galbraith (1967) typifies this traditional belief that the increasing size of the business enterprise has led to the growth of a vast managerial hierarchy filled with technical specialists. This 'techno-structure' becomes the locus of power within the enterprise, and hence the modern corporation is the managerial corporation.

Although the notion of the managerial revolution has been disputed (see Scott, 1979), much academic research has in fact documented its pace. Some of the difficulties of this view will be presented in the following two sections, but it is necessary here to discuss a little further the main concepts and methods which have been used in this research.

The starting point is that the opportunities for internal and external funding of investment of an industrial enterprise are determined by its position in the capital market, and its position in product and labour markets. Relationships in the capital market constitute the most important aspect of an enterprise's control situation. The dominant coalition is the outcome of the balance of power between the participants in these relationships: the executives, shareholders and financiers who attempt to dominate corporate strategy. Each participant can draw on different resources from the enterprise and its environment, and their differing interests create a potential for conflict and struggle. The distribution of the share and loan capital of an enterprise constrains the possibilities of action for shareholders, financiers and executives in the overt or latent struggle for control (Scott, 1982*a, b*).

Berle and Means constructed a widely employed typology of modes of control. They distinguished situations in which a group with a majority of the voting shares is able to use this position to dominate corporate strategy from those situations in which no such majority shareholding exists. In the latter situations, control depends not upon legal majority control but on some additional 'extra-legal' basis. The two types of such control which they defined are minority control and management control:

> ... control is more often factual, depending upon strategic positions secured through a measure of ownership, a share in management or an external circumstance important to the conduct of the enterprise (Berle and Means, 1932).

The voice of executives and financiers can become greater as that of shareholders is diluted by a dispersal in share ownership. Minority control is where 'working control' can be secured by a group with some 20 per cent of the shares facing an anonymous mass of small shareholders. When the bulk of the shares are widely dispersed it is only necessary to hold sufficient to constitute the nucleus of a majority of those actually voting to be able to influence corporate affairs. The crucial point is that numerous small shareholders tend to be apathetic and not to attend company meetings, so that only a fraction of the total share capital is actually voted. Debate has raged over the precise level of shareholding necessary to secure minority control, with the Berle and Means figure of 20 per cent being variously lowered to 10 and 5 per cent (Larner, 1970; Burch, 1972). However, Zeitlin (1974) has correctly argued that no such arbitrary cut-off point can be specified *a priori*. The level of shareholding required is variable from case to case depending on the actual patterns of shareholding and the relative power of other contenders for control.

According to Berle and Means, management control occurs where the shares are so widely dispersed that no group has sufficient to gain minority control. Under these circumstances there is no effective shareholder participation in control, and the way is open for the internal executives to form themselves into a self-perpetuating controlling group. Gordon (1945) developed the idea that such circumstances also create opportunities for financiers from banks and insurance companies which provide loan capital. Thus management control is a situation where control rests with a board of directors which perpetuates its position on a basis other than its shareholdings. This broad view of management as those who participate in the top levels of business decision-making has generally been ignored by later writers, who have equated 'management' with the internal, salaried executives. The Berle and Means thesis was that the transition from owner control to management control was a process in which the constraints inherent in shareholding were weakened. Many of those who have taken up this argument have altered the idea of the 'managerial revolution' to one which holds that there has been a long-term trend towards the dominance of career executives (Galbraith, 1967; Kerr et al., 1960).

The Evidence

Much of the available evidence does *seem* to support the idea that ownership has become progressively separated from control. Tables 1 and 2 present summaries of the results of the most widely cited studies in Britain and the USA.

TABLE I   *Control in the top 200 US non-financials (1929–63)*

	Percentage of corporations		
	1929	*1937*	*1963*
Majority control	11.0	21.0	3.0
Minority control, per cent			
(a) 30		18.5	
(b) 20	23.0		
(c) 10		23.5	9.0
No dominant ownership interest	44.0	37.0	83.5
Other	22.0*	—	4.5**

Sources: The data are taken from Scott (1979), Tables 2, 5 and 7.
Original sources are: 1929 (Berle and Means, 1932); 1937 (Goldsmith and Parmelee, 1940); 1963 (Larner, 1970).
* 1 per cent in receivership, the remainder being controlled through legal devices.
** All controlled through legal devices.

Berle and Means claim that the years following the First World War saw a progressive dispersal of shareholdings as majority control gave way to minority control, and that the period in which their own study was carried out was that in which management control became an important phenomenon. Table 1 shows that just under a half of the top 200 non-financial corporations had developed to a stage in which no single ownership interest was able to exercise effective control over corporate strategy. Twenty-one

TABLE 2   *Control in large U K non-financials (1936–75)*

	Percentage of corporations		
	*1936**	*1951**	*1975**
Majority control	25.5	13.3	10.6
Minority control, per cent			
(a) 20	27.7	27.6	14.9
(b) 10			15.4
No dominant ownership interest	46.8	59.2	59.1

Sources: 1936 and 1951: Florence (1961), Tables V A and V B.
1975: Nyman and Silberston (1978).
* Figures relate to English companies – ninety-four in 1936 and ninety-eight in 1951. The percentage figures, which are based on fewer than 100 cases, do not add up to 100 because of rounding.
** Figures relate to U K companies – the top 250 less 42 which were unknown or unquoted.

per cent were classified as controlled through a 'legal device' – that is, majority or minority voting control by another company or by means of a voting trust. If these corporations were reclassified according to their ultimate control type, the figures for majority and minority control would be considerably swelled. Goldsmith and Parmelee classified their own data in this way, and concluded that the 1930s saw an increase in the significance of both minority and management control. Whereas Berle and Means took 20 per cent as the cut-off for minority control, Goldsmith and Parmelee lowered this to 10 per cent. Although 18.5 per cent of non-financial corporations had a minority group holding in excess of 30 per cent, almost a quarter of corporations were controlled by groups with between 10 and 30 per cent. Although the proportion of companies with no dominant ownership interest appears to be lower in 1937 than in 1929, the differing cut-off points employed make it likely that the ten-year period saw an increase in the proportion of major companies with no group holding more than 10 per cent. The data for 1963 show a massive increase in this proportion: over four fifths of the top 200 non-financials had no dominant ownership interest. On the basis of his results, Larner claimed that:

> ... it would appear that Berle and Means in 1929 were obser-
> ving a 'managerial revolution' in process. Now, thirty years
> later, that revolution seems close to complete (Larner, 1966).

The evidence for Britain seems more ambiguous (see Table 2). In 1936 almost a half of the very largest companies had no dominant ownership interest; by 1951 this figure had risen to well over a half. Over the same period, the number of majority-controlled companies fell substantially and the number of those which were minority controlled remained constant. It seems that this period involved a trend towards greater dispersal of share-holdings. The figures for 1975 suggest that there has been little change since then, but this appearance is dispelled when it is realized that the figures relate to a much larger group of companies. The 1975 data relate to a wider spread of sizes, and if it is assumed that any trend towards greater dispersal would be more character-istic of the largest companies, then it can be argued that the post-war period as a whole has seen a continuous extension of the trend away from majority control. One caveat must be made, however, that many of the unquoted companies not analysed by Nyman and Silberston would be majority controlled by families or foriegn companies, and the post-war period has seen an influx of American and then European subsidiaries. Realistic British data might be expected to show this and also to show the increased importance of state enterprises. By comparison with the USA, where both the state and foreign capital are less important, it might be expected that the British economy should show an *increased* proportion of majority-controlled enterprises. The figures in Table 3 show that this is indeed the case.

TABLE 3   *Control in the top 200 UK non-financials (1976)*

	Percentage of companies
Majority control	38.5
*Minority control**	21.0
No dominant ownership interest	40.5

Source: Scott (1982b), Table 6.12.
* Cut-off point 10 per cent.

The figures for majority control in Table 3 include 6.5 per cent of companies in which the state held a majority of the shares or which were organized as public corporations. Foreign companies,

families and individual entrepreneurs were the majority shareholders in the remainder. The number of majority-controlled companies in the top 200 non-financials was very similar to the number
in which there was no dominant ownership interest, a situation
rather different from that found in the USA.

But what do these results in fact show? In both Britain and the
USA the growing significance of companies with no dominant
ownership interest seems to suggest a trend towards management
control. A number of commentators, however, have suggested some
problems in this interpretation. Chevalier (1970) has shown for the
USA that the category 'no dominant ownership interest' includes
a large number of companies in which a big shareholder had 5 per
cent or more of the shares, and Blumberg (1975) found that there
were often a number of such shareholders in each company. A
particularly important finding has been the changing nature of the
large shareholders. In Britain and the USA, the proportion of
shares held by individuals has fallen over the post-war period and
today the large shareholders tend to be financial intermediaries
rather than individuals. Pension funds, insurance companies and
other investment companies hold about two thirds of the shares in
British companies. This suggests that dispersal of shareholdings has
resulted not in a mass of anonymous individual shareholders but in
the emergence of groups of aggressive and well-informed financial
'institutions'.

This has been described as control through a constellation of
interests. This mode of control requires that a substantial block of
shares be concentrated in a small but diverse group of shareholders
and that the remaining shares be widely dispersed. This group of,
say, twenty large shareholders will collectively hold a majority or
substantial minority of the shares, but are too diverse to vote this
in a coordinated way. Such shareholders must nevertheless achieve
some kind of *modus vivendi* and the board of directors cannot disregard their interests. This situation differs from all the control
types defined by Berle and Means. The board will reflect the
constellation of interests and is unable to achieve the autonomy
from particular stockholder interests which is characteristic of
management control, yet the dominant shareholders do not constitute a cohesive controlling group. The research reported in Table
3 has shown that this is characteristic of many large British enter-

prises and no examples of management control were found amongst the top 200 British non-financials.

But control through a constellation of interests should not be equated with the simplistic view of the control of industry by financial companies. The financial intermediaries themselves are increasingly controlled through constellations of interests. There is a circularity in control relations: financial companies are the major shareholders in industrial companies, and the pension funds of many large industrials have become important shareholders in both financial and industrial companies. Property ownership and the associated relations of control have become increasingly depersonalized. Ownership is vested in interweaving shareholding and investment interests, and this transformation in ownership provides the context for the struggle for control between shareholders, financiers and executives. The dominant coalition which occupies the boardroom and the key executive positions will reflect the balance of power between the various participants in the controlling constellation. This results in the creation of a considerable number of interlocking directorships. Networks of intercorporate capital relations are associated with the existence of personnel links between the boards of companies. Interlocking directorships constitute alliances between organizations which effect capital-based relations of control, but which also have an independent significance. Business information can flow through the network of interlocking directorships, and this information becomes an important part of the environment of each enterprise (Stokman, Ziegler and Scott, 1984).

The Implications

Has there been a managerial revolution? There has been a transition from personal forms of possession to the more impersonal forms involved in 'institutional' shareholdings. Individual enterprises have become increasingly independent from particular ownership interests, becoming simply units in a structure of intercorporate relations. The various modes of conrol which have been discussed do not, however, directly indicate the dominance of particular leadership groups but point to the differing patterns of constraints within which shareholders, financiers and executives struggle for control. Although personal ownership has declined in significance, it remains important in many sectors and new entrepreneurial capitalists are constantly emerging. In many companies family holdings have been diluted from majority to minimal minority holdings, and the executives have become less and less the appointees of dominant shareholding interests. At the same time, the growth of institutional shareholdings and the increasing significance of credit has undermined the ability of executives to achieve effective autonomy from shareholders and financiers. In entrepreneurial firms, and in those controlled through a constellation of interests, the top career executives play an important part in strategic control, but they rarely exercise undisputed dominance.

Company boards, then, comprise varying combinations of executives, shareholders, financiers and their representatives. These dominant coalitions emerge from the struggle for control, and the various participants must work within the constraints of the ownership relations and other environmental constraints. In the struggle for control, executives are able to structure the information received by board members. They may, for example, seek generalized approval for a course of action by presenting the minimum of detail and limiting the options available to their fellow directors. Shareholder and financier representatives on the board may in fact be prepared to encourage such manoeuvring as a way of controlling the executives who have to work hard and efficiently to preempt board decisions. Increasingly, non-executive directors take a watching brief on behalf of controlling constellations, and so long as a company successfully meets its financial targets they will have no incentive to disrupt executive strategies.

These conclusions are only an intermediate step in the analysis of ownership and control and it is necessary to review some of the implications of the transformation in ownership patterns. Strategic control has been studied mainly at the level of the overall administrative structure. Chandler (1962) has argued that the move away from majority control was an important precondition for the emergence of centralized and later multidivisional structures. From the standpoint of the argument presented in this chapter, that argument must be recast: although the weakening of majority control may have been an important precondition, the consequent transformations in administrative structure were due to the active role played by investment bankers and to the emergence of control through a constellation of interests. The 'Chandler thesis' has been considerably amplified by European writers, who have shown that the longer survival of family majority ownership in Britain, France and West Germany is an important factor in explaining the belated adoption of multidivisional organization (Channon, 1973; Dyas and Thanheiser, 1976). National variations in patterns of ownership and control are related to national differences in the pace and direction of administrative reform.

Chandler's argument has been very influential in studies of management, but in recent years it has been extended and elaborated by writers who have been critical of some of its main tenets. They have argued that it tends to depict a universal trend from the entrepreneurial to the multidivisional firm, and that it neglects certain important features of the exercise of control in large enterprises. Drawing on the influential work of Braverman (1974), it has been claimed that large enterprises have shown a diversity of organizational forms and modes of control over their employees. Strategic control relates not only to forms of control over managerial subordinates, the topic of greatest concern to Chandler, but also to the control exercised over office and shopfloor workers. The day-to-day exercise of operational control requires that the managerial hierarchy should possess the capacity to produce the necessary levels of effort from workers in the enterprise (Wood, 1982; Friedman, 1977; Storey, 1983; Baldamus, 1961).

These arguments connect the study of ownership and control with the key issue of industrial relations. Chandler's notion of administrative structure has been extended to cover 'the various organizational forms and personnel which entrepreneurs have used to recruit and maintain a labour force; to monitor, discipline, and reward workers; and to deal with trade unions' (Gospel, 1983). Central to this is the issue of whether industrial relations are ceasing to be defined in purely operational terms and increasingly to become a strategic question. In its turn, this raises once again the whole notion of 'control'. If control is to be seen as a consequence of the totality of social relations which constitute the environment of the enterprise, then the increasing salience of the labour market and labour relations means that organized labour has the potential for a much greater influence over the determination of corporate strategy. The dominant coalition must increasingly respond to, and perhaps coopt, the representatives of organized labour. But it has been emphasized that the enterprise is a federation of competing groups with divergent interests, and so it cannot be assumed that the trade unions will acquiesce in this. The divergence of interests, the struggle over what Baldamus (1961) has termed the 'effort bargain', may mean that strategic control will become the major focus of the conflict between capital and labour.

CHAPTER 9

Government Policy and the Economic System

JULIAN LOWE and ELEANOR J. MORGAN

Even in free-market economies, legal, political and economic factors have an important influence on the management of private enterprise. Many Western countries now have mixed economies in which the impact of government on business has increased in importance over a long period. In some, a number of major industries are directly owned by the state and these have often been used as instruments of national economic policy. In addition, government policies have a major effect on the private sector and so they are part of the coalition of interests, alongside the workforce and shareholders, who have to be considered in framing business policy.

As well as the interdependency of interests between business and government, the firm must also operate within the context of the economic and legal systems. These different considerations may have a major impact in formulating policies or they may merely represent a minor constraint. Some firms and industries are more affected than others. The pharmaceutical industry, for instance, must be fully aware of and responsive to changes in government policy since its research, production and marketing are heavily regulated, and its major customer in the UK is the government-funded National Health Service. Other industries may be influenced less directly by the political and legal system, although most will be subject to some controls in both the labour and product markets and all will be affected by changes in the overall economic environment and taxation by central and local government.

Factors such as company size and dominance in markets also affect the extent of government regulation of the firm. Large firms have most potential power and are more visible than their smaller counterparts; they are more likely to be targets of government control. At the same time, by virtue of their size and resources they can also exert more influence on the nature and form of government intervention. Large multinational companies operating in several countries are particularly privileged in this respect. Although they may act in close cooperation with their own domestic government, they are outside control by any one state, especially if their home base is not confined to one country (e.g. Anglo-Dutch Shell). Their ability to locate production facilities in different countries may increase their power to obtain concessions from governments. In the past, large firms have found government support more forthcoming for research, employment maintenance and protection from foreign imports, but they also had to bear the brunt of government policies towards prices, incomes and monopolies. There are now clear signs in many Western economies that the small-sized and medium-sized firm is rapidly becoming a focus of government interest, and government-backed programmes give specific help to this sector and promote entrepreneurship in general. Management has to try to understand the changing external environment and its likely impact, so that it can predict and react to changes and also so that it can try through various channels to influence government intervention.

The Nature and Rationale of Government Intervention

To predict and influence the nature and form of government intervention, industry needs to understand the political philosophy and economic basis underlying government policy towards the business sector. Many of the economic grounds for government intervention have been neatly summarized by a recent Nobel Prize winner in economics (Meade, 1975). These reasons relate essentially to a market-based economic system characterized by free competition between producers but with additions necessary to protect basic social and legal objectives. This is based on the assumption that the welfare of society both as producer and consumer is maximized when there is free and fair competition between firms, although government intervention may be required to achieve this when the market fails to operate efficiently. According to Meade, government intervention may be justified on the following grounds:

1. It helps to control and stabilize fluctuations in capital, labour and product markets.

2. It submits to appropriate control the use of monopoly power by large firms and labour unions.
3. Where economies of large scale are important, government either encourages or through state ownership facilitates various enterprises joining together to reap these potential cost reductions.
4. Government provides certain goods and services which by their nature could not be bought separately by individuals but which could be purchased and enjoyed in common by all members of the community.
5. Intervention provides equality of opportunity and rewards effort and current worth.
6. In some areas individuals cannot take a long enough view of the future, and so government has to make some long-term decisions which industry would not take on its own, for example in control of natural-resource depletion.
7. Certain interventions are needed where the free operation of the market might neglect to take account of social as opposed to economic costs and benefits, for example social costs of pollution.

These reasons for intervention do not, of course, command unanimous support but they form the basis of much policy towards business in Western economies since the Second World War. Alternative grounds for government intervention advocate a socialist planning approach (Holland, 1976) and a free and unregulated market system as proposed by the 'Austrian School' (Littlechild, 1978). This latter philosophy has particularly influenced recent conservative governments in the US, UK and West Germany.

It is unlikely, however, that actions by government can necessarily be predicted from a detailed understanding of their philosophy. More often than not, government decisions about industry and the economy are the result of conflict resolution between competing goals and constraints. This can be seen for example in the 1970–74 Conservative government's decision to renationalize Rolls Royce, rescue several large ailing firms through massive subsidies and introduce a statutory incomes policy. More recently, extensive subsidies in the labour market and continuing investment aid to large firms strained the Conservatives' traditional dislike of intervention in the interests of protecting employment. Policy may sometimes be a result of *ad hoc* pressures and have little to do with a careful evaluation of various policy alternatives. This 'government by reaction' is exemplified in an item of environmental legislation, the Deposit of Poisonous Wastes Act 1972, which passed through Parliament in twenty-two days after a few examples of poisonous waste disposal had caught the public imagination. Government had a policy before this, but there was intense political pressure for government to be seen to be doing something immediately (Kniber, Richardson and Brookes, 1974).

This highlights the external pressures upon government, but despite the importance of such *ad hoc* pressures, public policy towards industry generally does have some predictable and common thread based on the government philosophy and the administrative background. There have been definite swings towards and then away from emphasis on central planning of production and markets with changes in government, but these policy changes are not always as sharp as one might expect. In the UK the permanent civil service has alleviated the severity of change because this body of policy-makers is not subject to the same major ideological and political changes as Parliament itself. The civil service with its long time horizons and different perspective may well be a major force for either stability or reaction, depending on one's point of view. Politicians themselves do not always plan ahead in the same way, as a recent investigation noted:

> We found widespread recognition and concern about the divergence between political and industrial timescale which led us to conclude that there was a mismatch between political and administrative time scales. We were not considering ideological aims or plans of political parties which are by definition long term but the practical interrelationship between industry and government. With the exception of one senior member who believes government takes a long term view whilst firms are only concerned with their cash flow on an annual basis, all other interviewees said it was government which took a short term view and industry which had to look and plan in the longer term (Hansard Society, 1979).

This is an important point because intervention in industry is often justified on the grounds that government takes a longer view in the interests of both current and future generations, whereas this evidence suggests it is unlikely to be true of politicians, as opposed to civil servants.

THE MEANS OF GOVERNMENT INTERVENTION AND CONTROLS

The Economy

Even in the most market-oriented economies, government seeks to influence the economy as a whole in pursuit of its major policy goals of price stability, high and stable employment levels, economic growth and a satisfactory balance of payments. The chief instruments are monetary policy, affecting the cost and availability of credit; and fiscal policy, acting through taxation and public spending programmes. Direct controls such as prices and incomes policy, hire-purchase restrictions and foreign-exchange regulations may also be used to achieve particular objectives. These policies have an important influence on the business environment and so the health of the economy and national economic policy influence the performance of individual firms.

Fluctuations in economic activity and changes in economic policy associated with altered circumstances lead to difficulties for managers predicting developments accurately enough to plan their company's future. Government and large businesses prepare detailed forecasts of the economy as an aid to public and private decision-making. Although these forecasts have sometimes been accurate, events such as the unexpected rise in oil prices in 1973-4 and 1979-80 highlight the difficulties of predicting economic trends in the present turbulent environment. It can be argued that international events have become a greater source of instability facing the business sector than variations in domestic macroeconomic policy have ever been.

Whatever their political hue, most Western governments now go far beyond control of basic fiscal and monetary factors. Attention is paid to promoting specific aspects of economic performance in industry by attempting to alter demand and cost conditions of individual industries and sometimes specific firms. This attempts to encourage either the more efficient operation of market forces, for example, through competition and monopoly policy; or the re-direction of market forces by selective intervention.

Competition and Anti-Trust Policy

The purpose of government competition policy is to promote indus-trial efficiency and consumer welfare by controlling monopolies, restrictive practices and other potential abuses of monopoly power. Such policy developed early in the Unites States but most Western countries now have competition laws. Firms operating in the EEC are also subject to EEC competition policy which is designed to secure free and fair competition between member states. Legislation varies considerably both in scope and strength. The United States probably takes the strongest anti-trust stance but recently some aspects of its policy have been modified, while other countries, including Britain, have strengthened their competition laws and the agencies responsible for enforcing them.

In the United States the Sherman Act prohibits the creation of a monopoly position but in practice a distinction is increasingly made between monopolization by superior efficiency, which might be expected to operate in the public interest, and other means. In Britain, as in West Germany and the EEC, market dominance itself is not prohibited and policy is based on preventing the abuse of monopoly power. Structural remedies, such as ordering firms to sell off part of their activities, are uncommon outside the United States; instead the firm's behaviour is regulated where necessary.

Similarly, in the United States there are very strong prohibitions against firms in the same activity merging if this might sub-stantially reduce competition. In Britain, mergers can be investi-gated with a view to banning any found detrimental to the public interest, but a fairly permissive attitude has been taken. Evidence of the generally poor performance of merged firms has, however, led several countries to contemplate introducing or strengthening their merger controls, and since 1979 large mergers in Britain have come under more scrutiny.

Competition policy controls restrictive practices which limit competition between apparently independent firms. In some countries, including the United States, particular practices are declared illegal *per se* whereas in others any behaviour which is anti-competitive in effect is outlawed, with the interpretation being left to enforcement agencies and courts. UK policy is mainly directed towards defining the types of restrictive practices which can be taken to court and banned if not shown to be in the public interest, but the 1980 Competition Act has given additional powers to the Office of Fair Trading to investigate any practice which is anti-competitive in its effects. The Office of Fair Trading deals with other aspects of the conduct of industry which may be either anti-competitive or directly against the public interest, such as excessive or misleading advertising, low product standards, and so on.

Selective Intervention

The aim of competition policy is to make markets work more efficiently, but governments have long recognized that for various reasons it is necessary to redirect or alter market forces through selective intervention policies. This might be for political or social objectives, such as the redistribution of the ownership of production leading to nationalization; or for economic reasons, often because the market does not work fast enough and the time taken to adjust to changing circumstances can be both economically and socially expensive. Subsidies for declining industries and training programmes are examples of economic reasons.

Major structural domestic readjustments have required increased intervention in particular firms and industries in many Western countries in response to other factors, such as the reductions in tariffs following the General Agreement on Tariffs and Trade; the growing economic importance of Far Eastern countries; changes in technology; and world recession. There have also been ebbs and flows in policy. In Britain, the Labour government of the 1970s emphasized public ownership through the National Enterprise Board whereas the Conservative government of the 1980s is trying to reduce state involvement and is returning some state-run companies to private ownership. The overall importance of public participation and government influence has hardly declined, however, despite this apparent turnaround.

The growth of industrial subsidies in many advanced Western economies is an important aspect of intervention (Burton, 1979). Table 1 indicates the extent of public expenditure on trade,

TABLE 1 *Public expenditure on industry, trade, employment and energy (£ million)*

	1982–3	
	£ million	%
General support for industry		
Selective assistance	146	
Support services	21	
Finance for British Leyland	360	
Assistance to steel industry	108	
Shipbuilding loans and assistance	134	
Aviation investment and services	40	
Promotion of tourism	33	
Total	842	14.4
Regional support		
Regional development grants	600	
Selective assistance in assisted areas	13	
Provision of land and buildings	49	
Other regional support	1	
Total	663	11.3
Support for nationalized industries (excluding transport)	791	13.5
Industrial innovation		
General industrial R & D	200	
Aircraft and aero-engine R & D	30	
Space	64	
Concorde development and production	18	
Rolls Royce and other aircraft projects	105	
British Technology Group	23	
Nuclear	221	
Total	661	11.3
Promotion of international trade	174	1.0
Functions of the labour market		
General services	258	
Redundancy and maternity fund	457	
Special employment measures	352	
Manpower Services Commission	1,233	
Other	140	
Total	2,440	41.6
Health and safety	79	1.3
Regulation of domestic trade and industry and consumer protection	79	1.3
Central and miscellaneous services	127	2.2
Programme total	5,854	100.0

Source: The Government's Expenditure Plans, Volume II, Table 4.1, HMSO, London, 1983.

industry, energy and employment in Britain. In addition to general programmes of aid, individual industries receive support including microelectronics, shipbuilding, steel and the aircraft industry. Particular firms receive substantial aid – a prime example is British Leyland. Various activities also receive assistance at certain times and the current subsidies for firms introducing microprocessors are a typical case. Regional subsidies feature prominently and in the decade to 1980–81 regional aid in Britain totalled nearly £5 billion. Governments have tended to concentrate on subsidizing capital but, faced with rising unemployment, labour subsidies have increased and about 42 per cent of the expenditure shown in Table 1 goes to the labour market.

The United States has relied less on subsidies, but it is increasingly resorting to other measures to protect its domestic industry. A variety of other means of selective intervention are available including specific regulations and controls as well as protective measures in areas of employment, investment, production and marketing. These policies may be interlinked, and procurement is used to enforce proper attention to equal opportunity and to health and safety laws such that only firms which exceed minimum requirements are even allowed on government tendering lists (Weidenbaum, 1981). The UK government has favoured particular suppliers and this has a major effect on policy in the computer and pharmaceutical industries.

MANAGING THE GOVERNMENT/BUSINESS INTERFACE

Forecasting Change

The overall scope of government intervention is very substantial. An important question for the individual firm concerns the extent to which it can forecast and influence the framing of this policy.

Predicting changes in the economic and political environment is an important aspect of top management's information system. Unfortunately an ability to predict does not guarantee that the firm will be able to deal effectively with all the changes in the business environment. As noted earlier, many changes in domestic economic activity are reflections of major shifts in trading patterns through-

means

to changes ...

US. During the perio... ~~and the Economic System~~ of world money markets

1980s, firms were often stuck wit... ~~e~~ particularly sensitive

structure which made them highly vulner... ~~to~~ changes in the

demand for goods and services and in exchange and inte... ~~1970s and~~ ~~a debt~~ in

A classic example of a firm overstretching itself and being unable to retrieve its position was Laker Airways which was caught by a recession in the airline industry as well as fluctuating exchange rates affecting the cost of servicing its foreign debt.

Similarly, even when given adequate notice of various legal and structural changes in the system, firms may still fail to adjust their marketing and production sufficiently. In the area of environmental control, for instance, many firms have had to merge or shut down altogether following the onset of more stringent pollution control regulations. The textile and iron-founding industries have been particularly badly hit in the UK (Low and Lewis, 1981). In the US, firms across a whole spectrum of industries have been forced out of business even though the new regulations they faced were publicized many years prior to their implementation. Similar impacts have been noted in equal pay and equal opportunity, health and safety at work, prices and incomes, and various other aspects of customer protection. A good example of the effects of control in this latter category is the stricter legal liability for manufacturers of faulty products. This has caused bankruptcies and reduced research effort in many industries and its results have been particularly noted in the pharmaceutical industry (Grabowski and Vernon, 1977). The tobacco companies diversified substantially during the 1960s when faced with mounting evidence on the health effects of cigarettes. Firms involved in the asbestos and lead industries have made similar strategic moves following predictions of greater government regulation and control in those areas. Generally the ability of firms to predict the economic and political environment adequately is a necessary but not a sufficient condition for survival. In addition firms try to influence the nature of government policy.

...become involved in the process of Managem...ince ...ishes to adopt a purely passive or at best influe... on government–business relations. Various an..... influence involve firms either acting on their own or as a group. The channels of influence are both formal and informal, and are aimed at politicians, civil servants or the voting public in general. Many firms/industry groups try to allay the need for regulation backed by legislation through self-regulation. One of the best-documented examples of self-regulation is in the area of advertising. Through voluntary codes of conduct established by the Advertising Standards Authority and the Independent Broadcasting Association, advertisers regulate the nature of advertisements across a wide spectrum: advertising to children, cigarette and alcohol advertising, as well as the acceptable content of advertisements and the claims of advertisers are all controlled. This approach is adopted in other countries too, notably West Germany, and appears to be a successful means whereby industry takes much of the potential impetus out of possible public regulation (Chiplin and Sturgess, 1981).

Despite voluntary codes of conduct, many firms and industries still have the spectre of public control to deal with; pressure groups and lobbying activity come into their own in this context. Through the operation of pressure groups firms may:

1. affect the implementation of existing policies and legislation;
2. affect innovation within existing legislation; and
3. help in the policy formulation of new legislation.

Thomas (1982) provides a useful distinction between the various forms of pressure groups which may have both conflicting and complementary aims: those involved with particular sectors, for example trade associations and employer associations; vocational or professional groups representing professional institutes and associations; groups on a geographic basis; and 'peak' groups which are the national bodies of those groups mentioned above, for example the CBI and the Institute of Directors.

The first stage in securing successful representation is to establish the right to be heard or consulted. This can occur at various stages through a direct audience, in writing or via media coverage. The right to be listened to does not come easily and successful pressure group activity suggests that a long process of negotiation and interaction may be involved (Moran, 1981). Since much pressure group activity will be aimed simultaneously at executive action and policy evolution, MPs, ministers and civil servants must all be influenced. Given the growing power of the EEC in developing community-wide legislation and in providing various types of subsidies, the importance of establishing a voice in Brussels is increasingly being recognized by firms in member countries. It is necessary to coordinate pressure at several levels and through more than one channel, including public channels such as the media. Many other factors are involved in successful pressure group activity. In particular, the representativeness of the group and the ability to respond quickly to alternatives put forward by government are crucial. Most pressure group activity is concerned with the drafting stage of legislation and so usually the civil service and certain key members of government will be the ones who have to be influenced and lobbied. However, where parliamentary amendment is required, MPs in the house become the natural target of this representational effort.

Generally British industry has not been successful in pressure group activity (Grant and Marsh, 1977; Hansard Society, 1979). This failure cannot be attributed to the intransigence of government since other groups like the agricultural lobby have had considerable success. Until recently industries have been poorly represented and their efforts fractionalized. Contacts with policy-makers have not been regular enough, and tended only to focus at times of crisis.

Besides operating through the relevant trade associations and business pressure groups, many of the larger firms make their own efforts to influence government policy. Consequently firms need to give senior managerial responsibility to those concerned with government relations. In the US the Consumer Product Safety Commission requires that the chief executive of a company sign and certify information sent to the commission. Again in the US, the Occupational Safety and Health Administration insists that chief executives of firms must be willing to accept the responsibility for occupational health and safety as an integral part of the job (Weidenbaum, 1981).

The government relations function has also become more central in the UK as well. Recent research suggests that, currently, over twenty of the top companies in the UK have a specialized government relations department, of which thirteen are in the top twenty-five by size, but none outside the top 150 have yet set up a government affairs department (Grant, 1982). Each of the firms with a government relations function had established it during the 1970s and four explanations were advanced by the companies themselves for this development: the increase in government intervention during the 1970s; particular events such as the failure of the 1970–74 Conservative government; long-run changes in the political system including long-run economic decline, the decreasing role of the traditional establishment as a mediating mechanism and the growing importance of other pressure groups; a degree of imitation of similar activities in closely connected US companies.

The extent and nature of this government relations function varies from one of keeping information and briefing top executives in meetings to proactively maintaining regular and frequent contacts with politicians and civil servants at various levels. While the government relations function receives a varied response in other departments of the companies, in several it makes an important input into the corporate-planning function and in a small number of firms it provides valuable information for use in overall forecasting and strategic management. It seems likely that this important aspect of activity will increase in large companies, with smaller firms continuing to operate mainly on a cooperative basis through industry associations.

CONCLUSION

Management has to make decisions in an environment constrained by economic and political forces sometimes totally outside its control. While the ability to understand and predict change cannot be considered complete protection against change, it certainly helps, and the amount of effort expended on business forecasting as well as the growing importance of government relations departments in large firms emphasizes this need. Management can and should attempt both to anticipate and to influence policy. To do this, it needs to be listened to by the key decision-makers in government, which requires an effort on industry's part to understand the political philosophy and economic rationale of intervention and to secure effective representation.

CHAPTER 10

Industrial Relations

JON CLARK

Industrial relations are about trade unions and strikes – or so runs the conventional wisdom. While this is undoubtedly true, ultimately it misses the point. Trade unions and strikes are important elements of something more fundamental and certainly less newsworthy – the day-to-day working life of the employed population, their relationships at work, the decisions about what work they do, how they do it and when they do it.

Industrial relations, then, are about the rules which govern relations at work, and the processes and institutions through which these relations are controlled. These rules, processes and institutions are like all social phenomena: they are both created by human beings and independent of them. Human beings establish and administer the rules that govern their employment, but these rules also take on a life of their own, exerting a powerful influence over the behaviour and thinking of those who created them.

What is the significance of industrial relations for management? Clearly they are an important social context of managerial behaviour, both a constraint limiting managerial discretion and a resource enabling management to achieve its objectives more effectively. But industrial relations are also about the quality of life of the population as a whole. For not only do working people spend a significant proportion of their lives at work, but wages, hours and other conditions of employment also have a crucial influence on their (and their families') standard of living and way of life. It is this that makes industrial relations such a complex, wide-ranging, sensitive and also exciting subject.

INDUSTRIALIZATION AND INDUSTRIAL RELATIONS

In 1490 B.C. Hebrew brickmakers in Egypt rebelled against being ordered to make bricks without straw; nearly 3,000 years later, in A.D. 1387, the serving-men of the London cordwainers revolted against the 'overseers of their trade'. These are just two of the many recorded examples of 'labour problems' in pre-industrial societies. However, industrial relations as we understand them today are a more recent phenomenon, closely bound up with the advent of the 'industrial revolution' in the second half of the eighteenth century and the appearance of paid employment as the cornerstone of work relations.

Prior to this, people were obliged to work in the main as a result of wider social and political bonds (e.g. slavery, serfdom, membership of a tribe or community) under terms and conditions determined by these bonds. In industrial-capitalist societies, however, work is an exchange relationship based on a contractual agreement – a contract of employment – between an employer and an employee. In exchange for a wage or salary, the employee is obliged to carry out certain work under the direction of the employer and under 'freely' agreed terms and conditions. Industrial relations, then, are not all work relations, but only those between employers and employees. The concern of industrial-relations study is to analyse the individual and collective, the social, economic, political, legal and psychological forces which shape these relations.

Industrialization has shaped the social and economic environment within which industrial relations are conducted in a number of ways. In the first instance it has led to a massive increase both in the size of the working population – seven million in Britain in 1841, over twenty-six million in 1981 – and in the proportion engaged in paid employment as opposed to other forms of work relations (e.g. the self-employed, employers). By 1981 around 93 per cent of the working population in Britain were classified as 'employees', and were thus involved in industrial relations to determine the basic terms and conditions of their work.

The development of industrial-capitalist society has also seen major changes in the industrial structure of British society. While the percentage of employees engaged in 'production' industries (manufacturing, mining, construction, electricity, gas and water) has remained remarkably stable over the past 150 years at just under 50 per cent, the proportion of people involved in the 'primary' extractive industries such as agriculture and fishing has declined substantially. On the other hand, the percentage involved in service industries like education, health, commerce, finance, leisure and entertainment (the 'tertiary' sector) has increased greatly. Thus, while in 1801 35 per cent of the working population were engaged in agriculture, the number had declined to under 2 per cent in 1981. In contrast, while only 32 per cent were involved in service industries in 1841 (largely in private domestic service), the number had increased to over 50 per cent in 1981.

This change in the industrial structure has been accompanied by a massive increase in the division of labour. This has led to a growth in the complexity of the occupational structure (300 occupations listed in 1830, over 30,000 in 1981) and, more recently, to a relative decline in manual compared with white-collar jobs. As late as the 1911 Census, for example, 75 per cent of the working population were held to be in manual occupations as opposed to 19 per cent in white-collar jobs (with 7 per cent classified as employers and proprietors). By 1981 the numbers were virtually equal.

Three other changing features of the employment structure affecting the nature of work and employment also deserve mention here. These are the growth in public-sector employment (almost negligible before 1900, now approaching one third of the working population); the growth in female participation in the labour force (around 25 per cent of the labour force in 1841, over 40 per cent by 1981); and the increasing size of the organizations in which people work (one important aspect of what sociologists call 'bureaucracy' or the bureaucratization of work and employment).

How could we best summarize the general meaning of these statistics? In short, a cross-section of 'typical' employees in Britain 150 years ago (in 1831) would have been dominated by male manual workers in relatively small establishments under private ownership working on a material product (food or other 'production' goods). A minority of employees would have worked in white-collar occupations and in service industries (the latter mainly women in private domestic service). A cross-section of 'typical' employees in the 1980s still work predominantly in the private sector, but in much larger, multiplant establishments, and now split equally between manual and non-manual occupations and between production and service industries. A substantial proportion of employees are now female, and nearly a third are directly or indirectly employed by the state. Quite clearly the revolutionary nature of industrial capitalism, both in altering the foundation of people's working life and in continually modifying the structure of employment, is a crucial element of the environment within which industrial relations are conducted.

THE STUDY OF INDUSTRIAL RELATIONS: SOME BASIC CONCEPTS AND FRAMES OF REFERENCE

Academic interest in the subject grew very much out of the public identification of industrial relations as a 'social problem', and to this day it has generally failed to establish itself as an independent discipline in its own right. There is, though, a degree of consensus about some concepts and focal points of the subject. The core unit of industrial relations is the individual employment relationship, the relationship between individual employer and the individual employee. The rules which govern this relationship are rarely determined by these two parties alone, however, and one of the main tasks of industrial-relations study is to examine the ways in which different elements of this relationship are determined and the reasons why they are determined in the way they are.

Generally, we distinguish between five methods of 'job regulation': unilateral, customary, joint, statutory and tripartite.

Unilateral regulation means that one party alone determines the rules governing a specific issue. On the whole, managements reserve the right to decide on the overall size of the workforce, and who to employ, to promote and to dismiss. Unilateral trade union or employee regulation is less common, but a prime example is probably the 'pre-entry' closed shop where a trade union requires the employer to employ only people who are already members of a particular union.

Customary regulation (custom and practice) means that a rule has come to be accepted through tradition and convention rather than because it has been formally laid down by one party or another. Informal rules governing rest breaks and manning levels, for example, are often the result of custom rather than explicit agreement or regulation.

Joint regulation means that two parties, usually representatives of employers and employees 'collectively', participate jointly in determining the rules. This extends from weak joint regulation, such as consultation with employee representatives and employees, to stronger forms of joint decision-making such as negotiation or collective bargaining. Collective bargaining is in fact the prime method of determining basic terms and conditions of employment in most major industrial-capitalist countries.

Statutory regulation means the establishment of rules or norms by the state. This ranges from the establishment of the legal framework of industrial relations to governmental measures such as incomes policies. In Britain and some other countries it also includes regulation by specialist semi-state agencies in areas such as health and safety, arbitration, and sex and race discrimination.

Where these latter agencies operate with the consent and participation of employers and trade unions we usually speak of *tripartite regulation*. The third party can either be, as in the case of the labour courts in West Germany or the industrial tribunals in Britain, a state official, such as a judge or civil servant, or, as in the case of the governing body of the Advisory, Conciliation and Arbitration Service (ACAS), an independent expert.

It should be stressed that, when we talk of these different methods of job regulation, we are referring not just to the process of deciding on the rules governing employment, but also to the enforcement or administration of these rules. Much of day-to-day industrial relations is concerned less with the more glamorous or newsworthy task of making the rules (for example, annual wage negotiations) than with interpreting and applying them to the complex realities of working life.

These five methods of rule-making are important concepts in the toolbag of the industrial-relations specialist. However, they are not just descriptive concepts, but can also be used prescriptively, implying preferences and prejudices for and against particular methods. A useful way to explore and understand this conflict between different methods of conducting industrial relations is to analyse them in terms of competing 'frames of reference'. What we mean by this is that, as a result of their position in the work organization and the particular values and beliefs they have, people tend to adopt a particular 'frame of reference' towards industrial relations. Our view of industrial relations, and our preference for one method of job regulation over another, will depend to a great extent on whether we adopt a 'unitary', pluralist' or 'radical' view of the work organization and the wider society.

A *unitary frame of reference* sees work organizations as unified by a common purpose and with one focus of allegiance. Employees are held to have an obligation of loyalty towards the organization and its leaders, but in return the leaders and the organization are obliged to care for the employees in a way which inspires such continued loyalty and trust. The vision underlying this frame of reference is closely akin to that of the football team or the 'ideal' family, and is generally hostile to trade unionism. It is typically prevalent in large, high-technology, North American multinational companies and small family businesses, and is clearly more common amongst company directors and senior managers than amongst clerical workers and operatives (for further discussion see Bain, 1983, Chapter 4).

A *pluralist frame of reference*, in contrast, sees the work organization as a coalition of different groups with divergent interests, with no one dominant source of leadership or allegiance. Common purpose can exist, but tends to be fragile and conditional. The work organization operates through the recognition and reconciliation of divergent interests, particularly through compromise and accommodation between the major interest groups. This frame of reference tends to predominate amongst managers and trade unionists involved in the day-to-day conduct of industrial relations, especially in their bargaining roles.

A *radical frame of reference* sees industrial relations as part of a wider structure of inequality in wealth, influence and power in industrial-capitalist societies, ultimately dominated by the interests of employers. The rules governing employment may therefore be modified in certain respects by employees and their trade unions, but negotiations and agreements are temporary truces in a broader, more fundamental and ultimately irreconcilable conflict between the forces of capital and labour. This frame of reference has wide support within the socialist labour movement and provides the basis of much Marxist analysis of industrial relations.

It is rare to find one of these frames of reference in its 'pure' form, nor shall we always find that the main actors in industrial relations adopt a consistent view on all questions. In fact, employers, managers, trade unionists and employees often favour different methods of job regulation and different frames of reference according to the particular issue and the particular group of employees. For example, many managers support a pluralist view on the regulation of wages, accepting the need for joint regulation with trade unions, but reject the involvement of unions in decisions concerning investment policy. Similarly, many managers believe that trade unions are legitimate for manual workers but unnecessary and unacceptable for middle and senior managers. However, by using the concepts and frameworks outlined above we will not only be able to clarify our own views on the controversies surrounding industrial relations, but also to begin to understand the relation between social structure, beliefs and human behaviour which lies at the heart of all social science.

THE MAIN ACTORS IN INDUSTRIAL RELATIONS

Employers' Organizations

The function and significance of employers' organizations in industrial relations varies from country to country, and from industry to industry. In general they have four main functions: the negotiation of terms and conditions of employment; the establishment of disputes procedures; the provision of advice and counselling services; and representation (see Bain, 1983, Chapter 5). In Britain, employers as a whole are represented nationally by the main confederation, the CBI, which is largely a pressure group on government. However, the other main functions are largely fulfilled by industrial federations such as the Engineering Employers' Federation (EEF).

In many advanced capitalist societies the most important function of employers' organizations remains industry-wide bargaining, that is, bargaining which determines the basic wages, hours and holidays of employees for a whole industry (for example, chemicals, engineering, construction, textiles). The major exception to this rule is the USA, where basic terms and conditions of employment have usually been decided at company or plant level. In recent years, however, there has been a move in a number of countries away from industry-wide bargaining, both upwards to a national-political level and downwards to a company, plant and workplace level. This has tended to undermine the traditional role of employers' organizations in some industries and placed increased weight and attention on the role of management in industrial relations.

Management

Personnel management is considered elsewhere in this book, so it will be dealt with only cursorily here. Management in industrial relations, however, is concerned with more than just the personnel function. Personnel departments may well develop company and plant-wide strategies on industrial relations, recruitment, training and career development, but the success of such strategies depends much on how far senior management and line management understand and identify with them in the day-to-day operation of the organization. Good management is concerned not only with ensuring the most efficient achievement of organizational objectives, but also with providing reasonable terms and conditions of employment and meaningful work and career opportunities for its employees (see Bain, 1983, Chapter 4).

Trade Unions

Around 100 years ago, under 10 per cent of the employed labour force in Britain were members of trade unions. By the early 1980s the figure had reached over 50 per cent. Indeed, in most industrialized countries, trades unions are involved in national-political life as well as in the day-to-day conduct of industrial relations.

What is a trade union? One of the most widely quoted definitions is that of Sidney and Beatrice Webb, who wrote on page one of their *History of Trade Unionism* (1894): 'A Trade Union ... is a continuous association of wage-earners for the purpose of maintaining or improving the conditions of their employment.' The first important phrase in the definition is 'continuous association of wage-earners'.

People become members of trade unions because they are employees working for employers in exchange for a wage. This is their common 'objective' economic position; at a general level this gives trade unionists across organizations, industries and even across nations their common feeling and purpose. Unlike employers, who have at their disposal a mass of social and economic power (money, buildings, machinery, human resources), employees or wage-earners generally have little or no social power as individuals. At the heart of trade unionism since its inception, therefore, has been the recognition of the need for employees to combine together independently of the employers. The term 'continuous association' not only stresses the importance of collective organization ('association'), but also the need for permanent, 'continuous' organization (unlike many of the organizations of employees from the fourteenth century onwards, which were formed as a result of particular grievances and then disbanded soon afterwards).

Next, we come to the 'purpose' or objectives of trade unions. In different organizations, industries and regions, in different countries and at different times, trade unions have had different types of objectives. These range from the so-called '3 Ts' (teas, towels and toilets) to demands for political revolution. But common to all trade union movements, however different the significance they may attach to it, has been the objective of 'maintaining and improving' the terms and conditions of employment of the employed labour force. This has been, and remains today, their basic social purpose.

As far as 'maintaining' the conditions of employment is concerned, trade unions have striven, from the beginning of the industrial revolution in England, to defend existing conditions against changes which threatened the livelihood and the work of their members. This has meant that trade unions have often been regarded as ultra-conservative, resisting attempts by managements to increase efficiency and remain competitive. Seen from a different point of view, though, such defensive union stances could be regarded as legitimate protests against employers who introduce changes without due regard for their effects on employees. This particular aspect of the trade-union role can thus be interpreted in different ways, according to the frame of reference adopted.

As to 'improving' conditions of employment, there is little doubt that trade unions have pioneered and fought for a number of social and economic objectives, including shorter working hours, a more equitable distribution of income, longer holidays and an end to discrimination in employment.

The general objectives of trade unions have been less the subject of criticism in recent years, however, than the methods used to achieve them, particularly the use of the strike. The complexity of this issue prohibits a detailed analysis here of the use and meaning of strikes in industrial relations (for a detailed discussion see Hyman, 1977; Smith, 1978; Bain, 1983, Chapter 9). It should be pointed out, though, that the strikes which do take place tend to be concentrated in those industries and areas of employment (that is, production areas) where the content, conditions and pace of work are most soul-destroying. It should also be remembered that in 1970, when the number of days lost through strikes in Britain reached a new post-war peak, just over ten million working days were lost, compared with 20 million through industrial accidents, 300 million through sickness, and well over 200 million through unemployment, which then stood at one million (see Hyman, 1977, p. 34).

In most industrialized countries, trade unions have striven to achieve their objectives predominantly by attempting to subject an ever-increasing range of issues to joint negotiation. In addition, they have also advocated statutory regulation on issues such as health and safety standards. This has usually come about through legislation, since the judges and the courts have traditionally been seen, not without justification, as 'anti-union'.

As far as trade-union structure is concerned, there are a number of different types of organization in different countries. 'Structure is a function of purpose', wrote the former General Secretary of the TUC, Walter Citrine, and most trade-union organizations reflect both the objectives they set themselves and the social and political history of their respective countries. In Britain the gradual development of industrialization and the lack of radical political upheavals (through revolution or war) have led to a piecemeal development of trade-union structure. The foundation of craft unions, set up to defend the interests of highly skilled workers threatened by the introduction of machinery, was followed at the end of the nine-teenth century by the establishment of general unions for the semi-skilled and unskilled, and 'industrial' unions in the railways and the mines. In more recent times occupational (e.g. white-collar) and sectoral (e.g. public sector) unions have been founded to cater for new groups of employees.

Today, trade unions everywhere are facing new challenges: from management, governments, new technology, changes in the employment structure and from their own members. Some of these challenges and possible trade-union responses will be discussed below (see also Bain, 1983, Chapters 1–3). What is beyond doubt is that trade unions are in many respects inadequate to meet the rapidly changing economic and political environment. But that is also true for managements, political parties and nations. One of the most important areas in which the future role of the trade unions will be decided is at the grass roots, in other words at workplace and establishment level.

Employee Representation at the Workplace

While industry-wide bargaining remains the backbone of many industrial-relations systems, a second 'system' of industrial relations, at the level of the organization (company, establishment, workplace), has come to assume ever-increasing importance since the end of the Second World War. It is here that the corporate policy objectives of organizations are implemented and where the form and content of individual employment relationships are finally determined. In some countries, such as West Germany, employees in large private companies are given the statutory right to representation on the boards of their organizations. Indeed, the Commission of the European Economic Community has been advocating for some time the extension of the West German system to the rest of the community countries. The foundation of any system of employee representation in work organizations, however, is to be found in the system of representation at the workplace.

In most industrialized countries there is a statutorily regulated system which defines in law the form, rights and obligations of employee representatives. The West German system, for example, is based on the works council, a body elected by all employees with rights of joint decision (co-determination) on issues such as wage-payment systems, working time and individual dismissals, and rights to consultation and information on issues such as manpower planning, training and investment programmes. With these rights, however, go certain powerful obligations, including the duty to cooperate with the employer 'in a spirit of mutual trust' and not to strike or advocate strike action.

A different system operates in most areas of British industrial relations, based on shop stewards or departmental representatives. They are elected by trade-union members and accountable both to the 'shop' or department (usually composed of around forty employees) and to the trade union. It has been calculated that by the late 1970s there were around 300,000 shop stewards in British industry representing their members individually and collectively on issues ranging from the '3 T's' to wages, dismissals and redundancies.

The shop-steward system has all the advantages and disadvantages of the 'voluntary' system of British industrial relations. They are generally in daily contact with their 'constituents', flexible and relatively non-bureaucratic, and 'more of a lubricant than an irritant' (Donovan Report, 1968, p. 29). On the other hand, they are subject to few obligations, are not elected by all employees, and their rights to co-decision and consultation are uneven and generally poorly formulated.

In some companies, particularly American-owned ones, senior managements have a policy of discouraging trade unions and encouraging company-based systems of employee representation such as staff associations and consultative committees. It remains to be seen which of these models of employee representation becomes more dominant in the future: the voluntary, trade-union based, British shop-steward system; the legally regulated, employee-based, West German works-council system; or the voluntary, non-union, company-based system. What is clear is that the choice by managements and employees of a particular system will have vital implications for the operation of their organizations and the conduct of industrial relations.

The State

Chapter 4 examined many of the ways in which work organizations are influenced by the political, legal and economic climate. Indeed, much of the recent public debate about the 'politicization' of industrial relations has revolved around the way in which state economic and social policy (anti-inflation policy, employment policy, welfare and taxation policy) affects the general climate of industrial relations (see Bain, 1983, Chapters 14 and 17).

Apart from this wider function of economic and social policy-maker, however, the state has a number of distinct functions in industrial relations which need to be distinguished. Firstly, the state as legislator establishes the broad legal framework for the conduct of industrial relations (see Bain, 1983, Chapter 15). It can provide a strong legal framework, establishing in detail the rights and obligations of the parties, as in West Germany; or it can leave most major issues (particularly collective ones) to the parties themselves, as it has traditionally done in Britain. It can encourage joint regulation and trade-union organization, as did the Labour government of 1974–9; or it can weaken them and encourage an increase in unilateral management control, as did the Conservative post-1979 government (see Clark and Wedderburn, 1983).

Secondly, the state can establish agencies to deal with specific issues by tripartite regulation. In most countries there are now tripartite agencies dealing with manpower policy, conciliation and arbitration, health and safety, individual employment disputes (industrial tribunals), and equal opportunities (including race and sex discrimination), as well as with wider economic policy developments.

Thirdly, the state is now a major employer. In Britain around 30 per cent of the employed labour force work in the 'public sector', and in this capacity the state establishes a general climate for the conduct of industrial relations (see Bain, 1983, Chapter 7).

Fourthly, the state (here meaning not just the government, but the political system in general) reflects to a greater or lesser extent the degree of wider consensus in society. In other words, it reflects the values and ideas which form the basis of some kind of national integration. Industrial relations are not sealed off from the wider society; indeed, they may be an important factor in determining the degree of national integration. In this and other ways, the last two decades of the twentieth century are likely to see the state continuing to play a prominent role in industrial relations and more generally in our social and economic life.

THE CONTRACT OF EMPLOYMENT

If the individual employment relationship is the core unit of industrial relations, then the contract of employment is its formal legal expression. In most industrialized capitalist countries, employers have a legal obligation to present new employees with written contracts of employment including details of certain basic terms and conditions of their employment. In Britain these comprise: the parties to the contract; date of commencement; scale and rate of remuneration; payment intervals; hours of work; holidays and holiday pay; sickness and sick pay; pension schemes; notice on both sides; job title; notification of disciplinary rules and procedures; and the person to be contacted in case of grievance or disciplinary action. This apparently exhaustive list seems at first sight to be a prime example of statutory regulation, but it should be stressed that the employer's statutory obligation towards the employee is mostly procedural and formal rather than substantive. In other words the law lays down the procedure to be followed and which issues should be in the contract, but does not generally determine the substance of the terms and conditions of employment such as wage levels, hours of work and holidays.

In fact, much of the substance of the individual contract of employment is not determined directly by the contracting parties, but is incorporated into the contract from other sources, such as collective agreements (scale and rate of remuneration, hours of work, holidays, grievance procedure) and unilateral employer regulation (disciplinary rules and procedures). In most countries there are also some areas in the contract, such as public holidays, notice and sick pay, where employers are under a legal obligation to conform to statutory minimum standards. Because of the force of these joint, statutory and other rules, and despite the legal fiction of the 'equality' of the parties to a contract, the individual employee rarely has the power to influence the major terms and conditions of the contract of employment offered by the employer.

The contract of employment is often remarkably silent in one area, the actual duties to be carried out by the employee when at work and the way these duties shall be organized (that is, the area of job content and work organization). The employer is required to give the employee a job title, but this is usually very general and leaves open a wide area for managerial discretion. More recently, particularly in the public sector, employers have produced more detailed 'job descriptions' outlining the duties of employees, but the whole area of job content and work organization is one which managements are keen to reserve ultimately for unilateral regulation. In fact, employers receive powerful backing on this issue from the law of contract. In Britain the judge-made 'common law' of contract obliges employees, amongst other things, 'to be ready and willing to work', 'to obey orders', and 'to observe fidelity towards the employer's interests'. When individual employees enter the 'free' contract of employment, therefore, they agree to place themselves while at work under the command of the employer. For this reason, a leading authority in the field of labour law, Otto Kahn-Freund, has called the individual contract of employment 'a command under the guise of an agreement'.

THE COLLECTIVE AGREEMENT

Much of trade unions' activity since their inception has been concerned with modifying the command structure underlying the individual contract of employment, subjecting an increasing number of areas of working life to joint rather than unilateral employer regulation. The main method of achieving this has been by the negotiation, conclusion and administration of collective agreements.

These agreements are of two basic kinds, substantive and procedural. A substantive agreement, as the term implies, is concerned with the substance of the employment relationship, regulating basic terms and conditions of employment such as the amount of wages, number of working hours, amount of holidays, and so on. The advantage of such agreements for employers is that they provide for a degree of stability and regularity at work for the duration of the agreement. The advantage for employees is that collective agreements give them a degree of participation and influence in the issues which have a major effect on their working life.

Procedural agreements, less well known than substantive agreements, lay down joint procedures for avoiding and regulating disputes at work, and in Britain they also sometimes lay down the rights and obligations of employee representatives. They are not normally subject to regular renegotiation, and thus tend not to be in the public eye. In fact, though, they are the unsung heroes of much 'orderly' industrial relations. The vast majority of individual and collective grievances and disputes are resolved without recourse to stoppages or lock-outs, often through procedures established by collective agreement.

It should be stressed that different countries have different systems of collective bargaining and collective agreements. Some, such as West Germany, France and the USA, have a statutorily regulated system which defines the collective agreement as a legally enforceable contract, involving the parties in an obligation to abide by its terms under threat of legal sanction. Others, such as Britain, have a 'voluntary' system of collective bargaining, where agreements are binding in honour only, relying exclusively on the support of the parties for their enforcement.

It is likely that collective agreements, whether in a statutory or voluntary form, will remain a crucial element in the industrial-relations systems of most advanced capitalist societies. This is not only because the alternatives (such as statutory incomes policies or the individual negotiation of employment contracts) are often impractical, but because in democratic societies people demand the right to have a say in basic matters which affect their lives.

PROBLEMS AND ISSUES

Having examined some of the main elements of the subject of industrial relations, this chapter will conclude with a discussion of a number of problems and issues which are likely to feature prominently in the future.

Wages, Wage-Payment Systems and Low Pay

Wages or salaries are generally the main source of income for employees and their families, the means of subsistence and the means to achieve a certain quality of life. This is why employees have a fundamental interest in maintaining and improving their wages or salaries. For employers, on the other hand, wages and salaries are a cost, and costs must be kept as low as possible in the interests of maintaining and improving the efficiency of their organization. This conflict between wages as income and wages as a cost lies at the heart of the conflict between employers and employees in industrial relations. As we have seen, it is usual in industrialized societies to attempt to 'institutionalize' and reconcile this conflict by subjecting wages to some kind of regular process of negotiation or collective bargaining.

In the twentieth century managements have attempted to make this process more 'scientific' by devising more 'objective' wage-payment systems, such as time-and-motion study, method-time measurement (MTM) and, more recently, job evaluation. In the case of job evaluation, each job is given a numerical weighting according to predetermined criteria such as skill, responsibility, physical effort and working conditions. Nowadays, these criteria are often discussed and agreed with trade unions. Ultimately, though, the payment attached to various jobs is based on market forces (expressed in terms of bargaining power) and the dominant values in society rather than on objective or scientific standards. For example, there is no intrinsic reason why nurses, dustmen and assembly-line workers should be paid substantially less than university lecturers and lawyers. A combination of their bargaining power and the social value we place on their work determines their place in the overall 'earnings league'.

At a fundamental level, therefore, the overall structure of wages in a society reflects and reproduces the values and inequalities of that society (see Bain, 1983, Chapter 11). Perhaps this is best illustrated by the continued existence of low pay, which can be broadly defined as wages which fall below the lowest decile of male earnings (see Bain, 1983, Chapter 8). In Britain, well over one fifth of the employed labour force are low paid, and this is perhaps the most pressing problem in the area of wages and wage-payment systems facing society in the 1980s.

Working Practices and Productivity

For most managements, much of day-to-day industrial relations involves maintaining the uninterrupted flow of the organization's work and devising ways of increasing the efficiency of manpower within the organization. Increasing the productivity of labour can be accomplished in a number of ways, including introducing new equipment and running down or replacing unprofitable products or inefficient services. Such strategies clearly have industrial-relations implications, and require careful manpower and industrial-relations planning, but they are essentially strategies adopted on the basis of technical and commercial rather than social considerations. However, the productivity of labour can also be increased by devising new industrial-relations and personnel policies (for example, training schemes and new wage-payment systems and structures), by work study, and in particular by re-forming working practices.

In the 1950s and 1960s, many managements sought to regain control over working practices by 'productivity bargaining', grant-ing employees higher basic rates of pay, shorter hours and job security in return for greater flexibility of working. In recent years, though, this achievement of increased labour productivity and general competitiveness has often become synonymous with the introduction of 'new technology'.

The Introduction of Microelectronic Technology

Technological change has been a feature of work organizations for as long as recorded history. It achieved particular prominence during the industrial revolution, when the wide-scale introduction of machinery substituted mechanical for human labour power and thus massively increased labour productivity. However, many people argue that the development and application of micro-electronic technology since the 1970s represent a revolution as fundamental as that of the first industrial revolution. A detailed assessment of the nature of microelectronic technology cannot be given here, but its comparative cheapness and size, coupled with its reliability and efficiency, certainly make it a potent challenge to existing practices both in manufacturing and in clerical and office work.

Technological change has both procedural and substantive implications for industrial relations. In procedural terms, the crucial question is how far and at what stage managements involve employees and trade unions in the whole process, and whether this involvement means joint regulation by negotiation, consultation or simply by the provision of information. In substantive terms, the issues range from basic industrial-relations questions, such as pay, grading and working practices (the latter very much the prime concern of managements); through questions of health and safety, retraining, supervision, career structures and job security (the latter very much the prime concern of trade unions); to questions of corporate policy, such as investment and product strategy and choice of technology.

Recent research has concluded that the most successful introduction of technological change for all concerned within an organization comes about when management develop a clear and comprehensive strategy in the planning and implementation of change, and when employees and their representatives are informed of the proposed changes at the earliest opportunity, leading eventually, after discussion and consultation, to the conclusion of a joint 'new technology' agreement between management and unions. With its potential impact on overall employment levels as well as within work organizations, the introduction of microelectronic technology will clearly be one of the major issues in industrial relations and the wider society in the years ahead.

Industrial Democracy and Worker Participation

The introduction of new technology is part of a much wider question, namely the nature and extent of the influence of employees over their working lives. Industrial democracy, worker participation, employee involvement and employee co-determination all refer to this phenomenon which is considered in more detail in Chapter 10. Of course, in a democratic society, most people are in favour of employees having some degree of influence over their working lives, but what this actually means depends on the individual's own 'frame of reference'.

In a wide-ranging survey of directors, managers (middle-managers and supervisors) and employee representatives conducted in Britain in the mid-1970s by the Department of Employment, a sample of each of the three groups was asked what they thought worker participation should involve. The majority of directors opted for a 'consultation' model (that is, joint discussions with employees, but ultimate decision-taking by management alone) and the majority of employee representatives for a 'negotiation' model (that is, joint decision-making throughout between management and employees). In between were the managers, who were split evenly between the two models (Knight, 1979).

We can see from this survey that not only is there a basic conflict between the views of directors and the views of employee representatives, but that there is also a clear and systematic relation between the position of the individual within the organization and their views on industrial democracy and worker participation. It was because of this division between employer and trade-union views that, in Britain, the Bullock Committee of Inquiry on Industrial Democracy (1975–7) failed to produce a unanimous report.

Against the background of large-scale unemployment and economic austerity, the debates of the 1960s and 1970s on industrial democracy and worker participation appear to have been superseded by more pressing matters. But all those concerned with industrial relations would do well to heed the warning given to British management in the early 1980s by a leading article in the *Financial Times*: '[Managers] should not believe . . . that employees' more docile attitudes, which have been bred mainly by fear of unemployment, automatically indicate a permanent acceptance of economic realities or a permanent willingness to cooperate with management decisions . . . The tide that swept the Bullock proposals on industrial democracy into a major issue has not receded for ever, and in future managers must base their new found . . . authority on the involvement and support of their employees' (30 November 1981).

Unemployment, Working Hours and Working Life

Industrial relations are, as we argued at the beginning of this chapter, about the rules and processes governing relations at work. Many of these rules, and the assumptions we make about industrial relations, were developed in the thirty years following the Second World War against a background of full employment. Some of the assumptions of this background are coming to look increasingly fragile. It is as yet impossible to assess the significance of large-scale unemployment, nor whether it will become a permanent feature of the working landscape in the future. Some of the answers to these questions will depend on whether national and international strategies are developed to deal with the problem. In industrial-relations terms, various policies have been advanced, including the reduction of overtime, the progressive reduction of the working week, longer holidays, job sharing, early retirement and a shorter working life. Many of these policies would undoubtedly require political intervention and legislative support, but they could also be developed by employers and trade unions nationally and within organizations and companies. What is clear is that the long-term existence of large-scale unemployment causes not only economic and social, but also psychological and spiritual deprivation, challenging the very foundations of democratic society.

CONCLUSION

The alternatives for the future seem rather stark, and clearly go way beyond the traditional boundaries of industrial relations. Industrial-relations policies and practices are but part, albeit an important part, of the wider social and political fabric of industrial-capitalist societies. The essential choice facing us is whether to plan and implement the changes which inevitably lie before us with or without the positive consent and confidence of working people. Industrial relations are, in this as in so many other respects, a symbol of something much bigger, a symbol of the way we run our lives and our society.

CHAPTER 11

Employee Participation

WYNNE HARRIES

The literature on employee participation reflects the difficulties which writers have experienced in defining it. Numerous commentators have noted that the term has been used imprecisely; that a given writer fails to use it consistently; that the meanings differ significantly between writers; and at least one commentator has concluded that 'it means all things to all people'.

Some indication of the four differences may be gathered from the following quotations. Participation 'refers to influence in decision-making exerted through a process of interaction between workers and managers and based upon information sharing. The degree to which influence is extended determines the degree of participation which occurs given that such influence is exerted through a process of interaction and information sharing and is not solely dependent upon coercive power' (Wall and Lischeron, 1977). A number of students of industrial relations have defined participation in terms of upward-directed power on management decision-making. Participation 'is the *exclusive* control and management of productive organizations by their *full* active membership on a basis of equality of vote' (Vanek, 1975). Yet others have attempted to recognize the whole variety of types and forms of participation in their definition: 'Workers' participation in management occurs when those below the top of an enterprise hierarchy take part in the managerial functions of the enterprise' (Walker, 1974). 'I should like to include the entire spectrum of workers' power, from its most rudimentary form (receiving information from management) down to its opposite, complete worker determination' (Blumberg, 1968).

Various forms of participation have been identified.

1. *Workers' control.* A number of productive cooperatives exist in capitalist economies (e.g. the Kibbutz in Israel, and the Mondragon group of cooperatives in the Basque provinces of Spain). It is also the national form of economic activity in socialist Yugoslavia.

The main characteristic is that the workers are the owners of the cooperative enterprise. In Yugoslavia they are so viewed because all capital is 'socially owned'; in capitalist countries there is a membership fee on joining which forms either all or part of the capital of the cooperative. The owner-workers govern the enterprise through a committee or council of workers (or their elected representatives), which selects a management team. The management team is accountable to the workers for the profitability of this enterprise and may in certain circumstances be sacked. The emphasis on the workers' control on policy decisions and ownership of the means of production has tended to blind cooperatives to the considerations of employee participation in decisions at other levels in the organization.

2. *Worker directors.* In this situation shopfloor workers sit on the board of directors. There has been considerable argument as to whether the role of such worker directors should involve the full range of activities of conventional directors (that is, policy decisions covering the whole range of finance, including capital investment; marketing and other technical and professional areas); whether they should be limited to considering personnel issues only; or whether they are there merely to reflect the views of the workers. Questions have been raised as to why other kinds of workers are not to be represented (white-collar workers, managers, engineers, etc.). Disagreements have existed over whether workers should have parity of representation with management on the board, and whether interest groups outside the organization should be represented (e.g. consumers, ecologists). The methods of selection and election of worker directors have also been of concern. Are they to be selected by managers or unions? Alternatively are they to be elected by all shopfloor workers (or only those who are union workers) or all workers below the level of senior management? Are worker directors to hold the post for a certain period, and if so how long?

3. *Joint negotiation and bargaining.* This is the form which British unions have developed historically. The role of the union, as the representative of workers, is to confront management over issues which are central to the interests of their members (traditionally, these have emerged as wage increases, conditions of employment and the handling of workers' grievances). As part of their view

of themselves as 'permanent opposition parties' which confront managers, the unions have striven to remain independent of management and are wary of engaging in any activities which will make them jointly responsible with management for the economic success of organizations. For the unions participation and industrial democracy mean the organization of labour into powerful unions; the right to bargain, as representatives of labour, with management; the right to use the strike as the ultimate sanction. Within this view, increasing participation would be to extend negotiation and bargaining into other managerial decision-making areas. While European and Scandinavian unionists have been prepared to do so, and also adopt a more cooperative relationship with management, British unions have been reluctant to move away from their traditional role of confrontation.

4. *Joint consultation.* This consists of discussions and exchanges of information between workers and managers. Such discussions may take place either within a formalized and structured committee (elected worker representatives, committee meets regularly and has an agenda) or it may consist of *ad hoc* and/or informal meetings between all the members of a workgroup and their supervisor. In the UK topics for consultation have traditionally excluded those which are subject to negotiations with unions (e.g. wage increases). This has often led to consultation meetings discussing items of low interest to workers, or management informing workers of decisions which they have already made.

5. *Participative management.* Three practices have been traditionally connoted by this form: an organization-wide, formalized structure of interlocking decision-groups, which includes members from the adjacent levels in the organizational hierarchy and which is superimposed on the existing organizational hierarchy (e.g. System 4, Likert, 1961); productivity improvement teams, composed of managers and workers who may receive financial recompense in relation to the savings they achieve; or a style of supervising subordinates which emphasizes the approachability and frequent contact with the supervisor and the exchange of information. All three practices assume that cooperative, high-trust relations exist between superiors and subordinates.

6. *Job redesign.* Job design as exemplified by the work of F. W. Taylor (1947) emphasized the removal of planning and other

cognitive activities from shopfloor workers, and simplified the residual manual activities (e.g. deskilling), and generally routinized work content. But today job redesign seeks to reintroduce autonomy, variety, and cognitive challenge into people's jobs. Herzberg (1968) tackled this problem in relation to the design of individual jobs ('job enrichment'); the Tavistock Institute of Human Relations advocated autonomous workgroups, who could exercise a certain degree of control on their day-to-day immediate work activities (Trist et al., 1963).

Earlier attempts to describe participation consisted of a series of simple bi-polar characteristics. This was not very successful since so many criteria were identified and the typology tended to become too complex and cumbersome and did not advance understanding. The characteristics most often mentioned are:

1. *Formal versus informal.* Formality is judged to be indicated by the structures used for employee participation (e.g. a committee is set up, the membership is constituted, rules are made for the election of members, the agenda is determined, the frequency, and length, of meetings is specified).

2. *Integrative versus disjunctive.* Some forms of participation take place within a framework of conflict and consist of power-based bargaining between parties (disjunctive); other forms assume a cooperative relationship and emphasize the importance of influence and discussion (integrative).

3. *Direct versus indirect.* Some forms of participation enable the worker to communicate directly with the superior (direct); other forms require the election of representatives who will be the ones who communicate directly with the superior (indirect participation).

4. *Autonomous decision-making versus interactive decision-making.* Some forms of participation increase the area of discretion and autonomy of the worker at his job, which tends to reduce the need to interact with superiors (autonomy); other forms require interaction with superiors and/or subordinates and peers and, on balance, will increase interaction with these people (interactive).

5. *Management-instigated versus worker-instigated participation.* This self-evident categorization has been complicated by the tendency for governments to intervene and for participation to arise either from bipartite agreements between management and unions or

tripartite sponsorships (management, unions, government).

This approach did demonstrate some patterns. For example it was noted that management-instigated participative schemes were nearly always integrative and tended to be more often direct than indirect. In contrast trade-union forms of participation were more usually disjunctive, and almost always indirect. While these observations do not cover the full spectrum of participation, it moved analysis along to start considering how these differences could be accounted for, and if possible to extend the explanation to cover the whole range of forms of participation.

IDEOLOGY, MANAGERIAL PREROGATIVE AND EMPLOYEE PARTICIPATION

Bendix (1974) defined management ideologies as 'all those ideas which are espoused by or for those who exercise authority in economic enterprises, and which seek to explain and justify that authority'. Sutton, Harris, Kaysen and Tobin (1956) took ideology to be 'any system of beliefs publicly expressed with the manifest purpose of influencing the sentiments and actions of others'. Nichols (1969) took the view that 'business ideologies are about power and that they consist of those patterned and selective self and structural representations put forward by businessmen which pertain to its distribution'. Mannheim (1960) distinguishes two kinds of ideologies: 'those complexes of ideas which direct activity towards the maintenance of the existing order; and those complexes of ideas which tend to generate activities towards changes of the prevailing order'. For the purposes of this chapter we will identify the following characteristics (derived, directly or indirectly, from the above definitions) in our use of the term 'ideology'.

1. Ideologies are related to issues of *authority* and *power*.
2. Ideologies *justify* or *influence*, which implies that the ideas they contain may be concerned with maintaining or attacking a given system, or the position of those who govern it.
3. Following from (2), there is some degree of *conflict* about the present system or order.
4. Ideologies are espoused either by those who occupy certain

structurally defined positions, who can be said to have *interests* of both an economic kind and in the perpetuation of a given authority structure, or by those whose interests lie in changing the existing authority structure.

5. In addition to being concerned with interests, ideology may also represent efforts to define the roles of authority-holders and the purposes of the system in which they operate.

It will be seen from this list that ideology is bound up with power, interests and conflict, but that we recognize that it is also involved in solving problems to do with people's role identity in the system and the objectives of the system.

We must note that the presentations of ideas may take the form of an avowed ideological intent by the author, but it may be only one of the objectives and themes within the presentation. We must also recognize a distinction between the author's intent and the effect on the audience. For example, the author may intend an objective and 'scientific' treatise, but members of the audience may see it as supportive or threatening to their ideological stance. They may wish either to emphasize or to minimize its significance, and accept or question its objective validity, for ideological reasons.

Our reason for introducing the concept of ideology is that, while some writers have argued that participation is about cooperation and have discussed it in relation to those forms of participation which range from accepting the current authority structure to modifying it in very minor ways, other writers have considered participation forms which modify authority relationships in more significant ways, or, fundamentally changing that order, have tended to do so in terms of a basic conflict of interest between the parties they are discussing.

McGregor (1960), while agreeing with the traditional objectives of management (increasing profits, productivity, efficiency), disagreed with the traditional methods of controlling employees in attempting to achieve these objectives (authoritarian relationships between management and employees; the prerogative of all decision-making held by managers). He advocated employee participation in managerial decision-making in the sense of granting them the right to *influence* decisions. He based this proposal on an alternative view of human nature (which he termed 'Theory

Y') to the view of human nature which informed the approach to control employed traditionally by managers ('Theory X'). He identified four contrasting assumptions about human nature in the two theories.

Under Theory X managers assumed:

1. Employees inherently dislike work and, whenever possible, will attempt to avoid it.
2. Since employees dislike work, they must be coerced, controlled, or threatened with punishment to achieve management's goals.
3. Employees will shirk responsibilities and seek formal direction whenever possible.
4. Most workers place job security above all other factors associated with work, and will display little ambition.

He argued that these assumptions and the associated systems of management control resulted in conformity, mistrust and conflict; while the means of control which created these adverse characteristics were themselves costly to administer.

Under Theory Y it was assumed that:

1. Employees can view work as being as natural as rest or play.
2. People will exercise self-direction and self-control if they are committed to the objectives laid down for the company (employee participation in decision-making will lead to commitment to decisions).
3. The average person can learn to accept, even seek, responsibility (thus he or she should be given greater opportunity to experience both more autonomy and more participation).
4. Creativity in decision-making is widely dispersed throughout the population and is not necessarily in the sole possession of those in management positions.

Under this approach, McGregor claimed, employees would experience less conflict with managerial objectives, the quality of decisions would be improved, and a less complex (and expensive) managerial control system was required. These would lead to obvious positive effects on profit, efficiency and productivity.

Turning our consideration away from McGregor's ideas as a contribution to a theory of management, and viewing it in terms of its ideological implications for managers, we may note the following. McGregor's Theory Y does seek to change the role identity of subordinate employees and, to a lesser extent, that of managers. Managers should recognize the legitimate right of employees to seek to influence their decisions, which requires only a minor accommodation of the hierarchical structure of managerial authority. In return management would gain the consensus of employees to their objectives and their cooperation in achieving the objectives. It may be noted that McGregor makes no mention of organized oppositionary groups (e.g. trade unions) in his discussion.

Fox (1966) advanced the argument by advocating a pluralistic approach to industrial relations in the United Kingdom, and distinguished between the characteristics of the *unitary* and the *pluralist* frame of reference.

Unitary System

1. There is one source of authority and one focus of loyalty within the organization; members of the system owe allegiance to their appointed leaders (managers) and no others (e.g. trade union leaders).
2. There are no oppositionary groups, functions or leaders within or without the system (organization).
3. It is the duty of the leader to act in such ways as to inspire the loyalty he requires.
4. Morale and success are closely connected and rest heavily upon personal relationships.
5. Each member accepts his place and function in the system, gladly following the appointed leadership.
6. All members strive jointly towards a common objective, to the best of their ability.
7. Where unions have had to be accepted by the organization's leadership, their activities are limited to 'market relations' (that is, the terms and conditions of hiring labour) but *not* management relations (the exercise of authority over labour in the work situation *after* it has been hired).

We can equate Fox's unitary system to both Theory X and Theory Y if we assume that the major difference between Theory X and

Theory Y is that the former relies on the formal authority and charismatic character of the leader, while the latter relies on direct participation, as influence, in the form of leadership style or small group meetings.

Pluralistic System

In contrast, this view:

1. recognizes that rival sources of leadership and attachment exist within and without the system (through employees' memberships of unions and professional associations);
2. explicitly acknowledges the presence of social values in the system which recognize the right of different interest groups to combine and have an effective voice in decision-making;
3. involves trade unions not only in 'market relations', but also in the exercise of management authority in deploying, organizing and disciplining the labour force *after* it has been hired. Trade unions are viewed as legitimate representative institutions which participate with management. Participation is seen as a matter of achieving power equalization between management and workers. It is *not* a question of allowing labour to be the sole decision-makers (that is, workers' control).

This pluralist view of organizational management, the recognition of more than one interest group in the organization with legitimate claims for taking part in decision-making, clearly draws on the way governing a society is achieved within a pluralist democracy (different political parties representing different interests, elections of representatives, a government and opposition). One modification to this model, in terms of the organization, is that managers are not expected to be elected. This approach differs from Theories X and Y in that it is concerned with power (indeed power equalization) rather than influence. Instead of ignoring unions, it not only recognizes their existence but claims that they should be equal in power to management, and share in all the decision-making. The pluralist view constitutes a more direct challenge to the structure of managerial authority in organizations and demands a more drastic change in the way managers look at themselves and at the purposes of their organization.

Greenberg (1975) has covered a wider spectrum than that attempted either by McGregor (1960) or Fox (1966). Greenberg identified four 'schools of thought' which he labels management theorists, humanistic psychologists (e.g. McGregor, Likert), democratic theorists (Fox's pluralists) and the participatory left who, although following the basic tenets of Karl Marx's teachings, identify more with the philosophy of decentralization and autonomy advocated by Yugoslav leaders than with the philosophy of centralized planning followed in the USSR. His analysis suggests even more strongly the hypothesis that attitudes to participation may reflect the political orientations of individuals and interest groups and their associated ideologies. More specifically, that the more right-wing political view would be strongly related to Theory X, or management theory in Greenberg's terms; that centre-right and centre-left (social democrats and democratic socialists) would be more likely to take the pluralist view of participation; that a more left-wing orientation would advocate workers' control and self-management within a decentralized socialist, economic system; and that the extreme-left position would subordinate issues of participation and industrial democracy to the political authority and economic planning exercised through a centralized and bureaucratic structure by the state (e.g. the USSR).

Various forms of participation can be examined in relation to the concept of ideology, more particularly political ideology. Some early researchers examining behaviour in group discussions equated member participation with verbal activity; the more a member talked, the greater the participation. This view equated participation with the degree of passing of information to others. In the 1960s some researchers (French, Israel and As, 1960; Vroom, 1960) began to relate participation to '*decision-making*' between superior(s) and subordinate(s) and specifically related employee participation to the amount of influence the subordinate(s) had on the final decision. Some commentators began to include under the umbrella term of participation the work of researchers on job design, on both individual jobs (Herzberg) and the organization of tasks for groups where the emphasis is on increasing the autonomy of workers within their immediate job (Trist, Higgin, Murray and Pollock, 1963).

These researchers worked within a certain paradigm. They

assumed that the relationship between the superior(s) and sub-ordinate(s) was cooperative, that they shared a basic agreement over values and objectives, and that the aim of participation in decision-making was to establish the best technical decision or problem solution to which everyone who had taken part in the decision-making process strongly agreed. They also identified with managerial values and objectives, and the hypotheses they explored involved outcomes which management would view as important. Subordinate participation in decision-making was examined in relation to productivity, technical quality of decisions, lateness of employees and turnover, their job satisfaction and the degree to which they felt alienated from their work and their firm. This group of writers and researchers was predominantly American, academic and trained in either psychology or social psychology.

Two other groups of writers may be identified. They are pre-dominantly European and were either sociologists or students of industrial relations; politically they reflected the ideas of liberals, social democrats and socialists. In contrast to the consensus assumptions of the American psychologists both these groups viewed the typical relationship between worker and manager in a capitalist society as one based on deep-rooted conflict of interest. Organizations for them were not characterized by highly inte-grated cooperative interaction of members sharing the same values and aims, based on a hierarchy of control operated by managers who were concerned with the welfare of their subordinates, and who made decisions in a 'neutral' fashion based on their objectivity and expertise which legitimated their sole right (prerogative) to make decisions within organizations. One of the two groups of European sociologists we will label incremental-pluralists, the other group radical-socialists.

The incremental-pluralists may be termed pluralists (see Fox, 1966) because they view organizations (and society) as composed of opposing interest groups. They tend to simplify the situation by interpreting this view, in organizational terms, as composed of two permanently opposing groups: managers representing the interest of shareholders in profit-making and workers concerned with pro-tecting their jobs, and with improving their working conditions and income from work. Rejecting the view that organizations should be viewed as a cooperative unity, they argue that there is a second legitimate source of leadership within the organization, namely the union (its officials and shop stewards). This alternative leadership may often be latent, but it becomes manifest whenever the latent conflict crystallizes into specific and concrete issues. Cooperative relations between workers and management may, and often do, operate for much of the time, but they are always temporary and the result of negotiations leading to an agreement between management and unions. Cooperative relationships should be seen, therefore, as only part of a cycle consisting of the appearance of manifest and specific issues of conflict, followed by negotiation between management and unions (which may include power struggles involving strikes and lock-outs); then the establishment, by negotiated agreement, of a new order, this being followed by a period of peace until another issue appears to trigger off the next cycle. These cycles are seen as sustained by the fundamental conflict of interests which is inherent in the relationships between managers (concerned with profit generation) and workers (concerned with protecting, and increasing, their means of livelihood).

This group of writers rejects the view of employee participation as the granting by managers to subordinates of the opportunity to *influence* managerial decision-making, since such a view would still recognize the legitimacy of managers to the sole possession of the prerogative of decision-making. Granting workers influence on decision-making does not affect the managers' right to make the final decision and to decide to what degree they will be influenced by subordinates' suggestions and arguments. The authority of the manager remains unchallenged by a mode of participation which accords to subordinates only the possibility of influence. Given the central emphasis that pluralists place on conflict, their approach to participation is not concerned with influence but power, based ultimately on coercion (the ability to strike so that organizational activities are brought to a standstill with strong possibilities of adversely affecting the level of annual profits) to counterbalance management's coercive base (the right to sack and the lock-out). This group prefers the term 'industrial democracy'; the term suggests *upwardly exerted power* by workers (individuals and groups) and their representative institutions (the trade unions). For these writers participation is about mobilizing the power of workers so that there is a greater chance of power equalization between workers and management; for some, it is about extending rights of bargaining and joint negotiation between managers and unions into more areas of managerial decision-making. In the UK this pluralist position has been wedded to the view of unions as a 'permanent opposition party' to management, refusing to accept any joint responsibility with management for the running of organizations, and concerned solely with defending the interests of their members. In a number of European and Scandinavian countries this essentially confrontational view of the role of unions is not so strong, and examples have been established where unions have accepted relationships which reflect more of a joint responsibility with management (e.g. co-determination in West Germany).

This pluralist paradigm views the relationships between managers and unions as reflecting a struggle on the part of the unions to gain power parity with management and to use forms of participation which the workers and their representative institutions (unions) have evolved out of their own history and current experience in the UK (unionization of workers, joint-negotiation machinery backed by legislation, and the efficacy of the strike). The objectives of such industrial democracy are to increase the job security of workers, improve their working conditions, and increase their earnings.

The pluralists are neither radical nor revolutionary but take an evolutionary, incrementalist view of developments in the relations between workers and managers. They do not advocate large changes in organizational relationships which must be compressed into a very short time period. In contrast the radical democratic-socialists, as the term implies, do wish for radical changes and solutions as compared with current practices in organizations. They have been labelled 'democratic' because they prefer to identify with the highly decentralized political and economic institutions of socialist Yugoslavia with its concern for developing forms of self-management in organizations, and the concept of socially owned capital (which contrasts with the concept of state-owned capital in the USSR, with its attendant state bureaucracy emphasis on a state-planned economy and constriction on the autonomy of both workers and management). Thus while Yugoslavia is not a political democracy, as conventionally understood in Western capitalist countries, it is carrying out a radical, nationwide experiment in economic or industrial democracy. The platform for some pluralist advocates of industrial democracy is that all the various institutions in a democratic society should be democratic. Thus there should be political democracy (universal suffrage), social democracy (embodied in some form of welfare state) and economic, or industrial, democracy, with a democratic, capitalist economy reflected in a democratic management structure. Pluralists are interested in Yugoslavia, since it involves interpreting political democracy as decentralized governmental decision-making under a permanent communist government (which is to be understood as representing the will of the people) and a socialist attempt to develop a political, social and economic democracy. Of some interest to Western observers is the fact that their self-managed economic organizations operate in a free economy after the capitalist fashion, thus their viability is dependent on their ability to make profits. While confrontational pluralists look at managerialist forms of participation with suspicion, the radical socialists would dismiss such participation as manipulative and/or designed to divert the workers' attention away from the fact that such participation never includes the strategic decisions and seldom coordinative decisions. They would dismiss pluralists as conservatives, inadvertently preserving the status quo, because they fail to realize that power equalization will never be achieved through incremental development. For radical socialists industrial democracy must be based on removing the private ownership of capital – the workers must be the owners. Until socialism is achieved, worker-owned cooperatives provide a stop-gap. For them the main problem is that in capitalist economies the means of production are usually separated from the workers. They are the property of the capitalists, the shareholders, who do not contribute any skills, knowledge or physical effort to creating the profits yet gain wealth, dividends, from lending their capital to the organization. Following the writings of Marx they argue that workers should own the means of production and benefit directly from their efforts to increase surplus wealth (profits); workers should also be encouraged to take part directly in the control of the organizations and be educated and provided with relevant experiences so that they can do this effectively. In the radical-socialist view of organizations the workers will be making the strategic decisions, not managers who are primarily interested in producing profit for the shareholders.

Just as the radical-socialists have criticized the paradigms of the unitary-managerialists and of the incremental-pluralists, so in turn have their ideas been criticized. Managerialists have pointed to the skills, knowledge and experience required of managers to make decisions in financial, marketing, technical and coordinating areas of decision-making; where worker-directors had been tried, they were most involved when discussing personnel policies and seemed unable to contribute to technical areas of finance, marketing and engineering design. They argue that both by experience and interest workers are most effective and comfortable making suggestions in relation to their own immediate work tasks and that therefore this is where participation must be located. They also point out that not everyone is interested in power and control and that, for many workers, work is merely the means to earn money to enjoy their leisure and family pursuits. At work they value being left alone by their supervisors (see, for example, Goldthorpe et al., 1968), and could hardly be expected to welcome being asked by their supervisors to join in decision-making. If workers require participation so ardently, why, it is asked, is it not given higher priority by unions in joint negotiation. Or when greater autonomy on a job is introduced, by management, why does it become the basis for a claim by the unions for an increase in pay, rather than be valued by the worker for its own sake? Given the low level of research evidence available, ideological claim can be followed by ideological counter-claim, and readers must draw their own conclusions as to which of these various arguments carries the most force.

While Yugoslav self-management is the most obvious example congruent with the radical-socialist paradigm, a number of examples of worker control exist in the UK, not all of them based on Marxist–socialist theory.

Although none of these examples can claim to have become the dominant form of enterprise in our society, the following may be briefly mentioned. After the election of the Labour Party to power in 1945, certain key industries were nationalized. The Labour Party had considered two forms of nationalization: top management positions filled by trade union leaders, or given to managers selected for their managerial abilities but accountable to society for the performance of their industries. The latter model was adopted and implemented. It had been hoped that nationalization would make the workers feel that it was now their industry, and that conflicts characterizing management–worker relationships under private industry would disappear. Although nationalized industries have worked hard at setting up and maintaining joint-consultation machinery, and in the 1960s the steel industry and post office experimented very cautiously with worker-directors, there is no evidence that, over the years, either workers or trade unions have viewed, or related to, nationalized industries and private industry in any significantly different way.

There are also examples of worker-owned producer cooperatives (that is, engaged in manufacturing), not to be confused with distribution or consumer cooperatives (the 'Co-op in the High Street'). Cooperatives require that their members pay a capital sum on joining. In the UK, they have often been set up by workers in an attempt to keep their jobs when their factory has been closed by the owners. A number of these were established in the 1960s and received government funds (e.g. Meriden motorcycles, KME, the *Scottish Daily News*). One of the most famous and economically successful producer cooperatives is in the Basque provinces of Spain and commenced operations in 1956 (Oakeshott, 1973; Johnson and Whyte, 1977–8; Eaton, 1979; Bradley and Gelb, 1981, 1982). Equally well known is the Israeli kibbutz system (see, e.g., Barkai, 1975).

Examples also occur where private ownership has been modified into partnership or common ownership. The best known examples are the John Lewis Partnership (Flanders, Pomeranz and Woodward, 1968) and the Scott–Bader Commonwealth (Bader, 1975).

While there is some variation, most cooperatives have some form of workers' council or committee, which typically appoints a manager who in turn selects the management team. The performance of the management is accountable to the workers' council, which makes strategic decisions (probably advised by the management team), while the management team are responsible for coordination, planning and control at the organizational and task level. During the mid-1970s some of the larger cooperatives (Yugoslavia and Mondragon) began to give more serious consideration to involving the lowest levels of their organization more directly in decision-making at the task level through the introduction of some form of autonomous work groups. Up to that time there is some evidence that management had operated on a day-to-day basis in a conventional way, relying on authority, and had structured and engineered work following the principles of 'scientific management' which emphasizes removing cognitive activities (such as planning) from the shopfloor worker, creating narrow specialized jobs and deskilling them. This certainly had occurred in at least some of the Mondragon cooperatives.

CHAPTER 12

Internal Politics

BOB LEE

Recently a large manufacturing company announced that it was to close one of its major plants. This decision was taken by a handful of people with a great deal of power and we can only speculate about their motives: to safeguard profits, or for the long-term good of those who remain employed, or some combination of factors? Those who decided to close the factory had such power that many middle-managers would have implemented the decision unquestioningly. Some managers might have tried to bring about changes collectively, or to use their power to soften the blow for others and protect themselves, but most would simply comply. The press expected the major opposition to the plan to come from employees and their unions, who threatened a 'sit-in' and strikes at other plants.

Even this brief outline of an unfortunately commonplace social drama introduces some of the ideas which form the basis of organizational politics. Within an organization there are different interest groups whose goals may conflict and whose attitudes may differ. Coalitions can form to pursue particular courses of action, or strategies. Power enables interest groups to affect the behaviour of others. The political system of the organization results in different types and degrees of power for different interest groups.

Organizational politics, like management itself, has been practised ever since people began to work together. The formal study of management has a far shorter history however, with the major roots of political insight dating back only to the 1950s. The political perspective as a coherent respectable way of thinking about organizations is a phenomenon of the last decade. A most notable exception was Niccolò Machiavelli, who synthesized his experiences of sixteenth-century Italian politics into the classic *The Prince*. His brilliant observations and maxims are often quoted and many of them are just as relevant today:

The gulf between how one should live and how one does live is so wide that a man who neglects what is actually done for what should be done learns the way to self-destruction.

There are two ways of fighting: by law or by force. The first way is natural to men, and the second to beasts. But as the first way often proves inadequate one must needs have recourse to the second.

The following example of political behaviour in a contemporary organization is taken from the author's personal experience; it serves to show that 'the spirit of Machiavelli' lives on in modern companies.

A management trainee was asked by his Departmental Manager to investigate the possible implementation of a computerized work scheduling system. Neither the manager nor the employees who would be subject to it wanted a favourable report on the system. The manager pointed out how the change would reduce his flexibility and made it clear that anyone with the trainee's obvious talent and career prospects would be able to find many other problems which would make computer control inappropriate. The employees, many of whom were his friends, made it clear that the trainee would be held personally responsible for any unpopular change. The trainee's report was unfavourable.

This indicates that the conventional idea of the organization as a neat 'system' in which managers work as a team for the good of the company is over-simple. A conceptual framework is needed which employs concepts of sectional interests, conflict, coalitions and power.

BASIC POLITICAL CONCEPTS

Two distinct views of organizational politics can be identified in the literature. In the more common 'managerialist' approach, politics are recognized as a fact of life, but seen as undesirable. In the 'radical' approach almost all behaviour is viewed as political and the observer should not evaluate its desirability.

Compare the following definitions:

Company politics is the byplay that occurs when individuals (or groups of individuals) want to advance themselves or their ideas regardless of whether or not those ideas would help the company (Hegarty, 1976).

Political behaviour is defined as behaviour by individuals, or, in collective terms, by sub-units, within an organisation that makes a claim against the resource-sharing system of the organisation (Pettigrew, 1973*a*).

The first author takes a managerialist view that the organization is a unitary whole with its own objectives and represents the view that managers should not pursue their own interests to the detriment of the 'good of the company'.

The second author takes the radical view of different interest groups trying to get their own way and no single interest group, such as owners, managers, trade unions, competitors or suppliers, is given any predominant right to influence organizational activity.

The radical perspective avoids interminable arguments about 'Who says what the organization's goals should be?' 'What if there is disagreement within this group?' 'Where does this group get the right to set goals?' 'Do other groups have rights?' 'Are the goals made specific and fully communicated?' and so on. It is an enlightening exercise to view the board of directors as no more than one group amongst others trying to manipulate the organization in pursuit of its objectives. The radical perspective is descriptive rather than prescriptive and its very amorality, which some find unsettling, helps to focus attention on what really happens rather than what should happen. It is particularly valuable for explaining why events often occur which are clearly not in the interest of organizational profit, growth or sometimes even survival. It is also much more appropriate for explaining intraorganizational resource-allocation decisions than the widely recommended 'rational' decision-making models.

A basic radical model depicts the organization as a loose and dynamic 'coming together' of individuals and interest groups into coalitions. Each party pursues sectional objectives which often conflict. At one level the organization consists of a large number of competing, cooperating and compromising interest groups, while at another level it is itself an interest group.

The basic political model suggests two key questions:

1. Why do organizations not disintegrate with so many interest groups pulling in different directions?
2. What determines the things that happen in organizations and the directions they follow?

The answer to the first question centres on the stabilizing forces at work. Each party has a stake in the survival of the system and if the organization goes out of business nobody wins. The objectives pursued may be partly conditioned by what is seen as achievable within the political framework. An equally important stabilizer is the 'socialization' process whereby society builds itself into our personalities, teaches us specific ways of acting, thinking and feeling. People are brought up with a view of what the business should do, how people should act, and what they should expect which leads them not to 'rock the boat' but to accept the goals which they are 'supposed' to accept.

Perhaps the most important stabilizing factor in all business organizations is the extreme influence of one particular interest group: top management. They can create rules, systems, policies and procedures to ensure the general conformity of most people within the organization to their ideas. The recruitment system can be seen as a method of pre-vetting, only accepting those who support their view. Appraisal and promotion systems also ensure that only those who accept this view will be promoted to powerful positions; the training system informs people what is expected of them; and the payment system rewards them for staying in line. A wide range of control systems are used by managements to integrate the different sectional groups: budgets, MBO, policy statements and manuals, job descriptions, rules and regulations, and direct orders. These all help the organization to cohere, albeit in the direction favoured by one particular interest group. The top-management group, in political terms the 'dominant coalition', may well not be a united group although they may support the management-control systems described. Many of the most dramatic political battles take place as senior executives fight for promotion, or empires, or try to change the direction which the organization is taking.

Concentration of control into the hands of top management means that they create the 'rules of the game' which govern most political behaviour. Conflict occurs within these 'rules' and only rarely does some party try to 'change the system'.

POLITICAL MODELS FROM THE LITERATURE

In the 1960s, Andrew Pettigrew conducted observation studies of the struggle by a group of computer programmers trying to retain their status against the new breed of systems analysts. The programmers claimed that the analysts did not have their expertise in handling computers and tried to establish myths about the difficulty and indispensability of their work. They kept control of information and techniques by not keeping records or written descriptions, which prevented their work being routinized or transferred. They also fought to retain control of recruitment policies (Pettigrew, 1973a,b, 1974, 1975).

Pettigrew's fundamental guiding framework was as follows:

> The organization is here assumed to be a political system. Political processes evolve at the group level from the division of work in the organization and at the individual level from associated career, reward and status systems. Sub-units develop interests based on specialized functions and responsibilities; individual careers are bound up with the maintenance and dissolution of certain types of organizational activity and with the distribution of organizational resources. At various times claims are made by sub-units and individuals on scarce organizational resources. The scope of the claims is likely to be a reflection of the sub-units' perception of the criticalness of the resources to its survival and development. The success of any claimant in furthering his interests will be a consequence of his ability to mobilize power for his demands (1975, p. 192).

Iain Mangham analysed the social and psychological processes which underpin all human behaviour (Mangham, 1979). His viewpoint is of man as active, 'continuously anticipating, monitoring and justifying his actions to himself and others', an 'active initiator rather than passive reactor' (p. 27). He also notes man's ability to anticipate the behaviour of others and choose his own behaviour accordingly. Furthermore, people are seen as goal-seeking, pursuing personal goals which are not necessarily integrated with the goals of others. Conflict is a logical result of human social psychology: 'behaviour within organisations may be characterised as the struggle of reasonable men to have their own view of what is reasonable prevail' (p. 218).

This appreciation of the cognitive processes behind political behaviour is important because it is the point of departure from earlier approaches which tended to see people as passive, influenced by internal 'instincts', 'drives' or 'needs', or by external forces created by managers.

Ian MacMillan is perhaps the most ambitious of all the political theorists in the model he has developed (MacMillan, 1973, 1974, 1978). His ideas extend to the interorganizational level and usefully remind us that it is often as important for managers to be aware of political behaviour between organizations as within organizations. For our purposes, however, we shall focus on MacMillan's model of individual political behaviour and coalition formation within organizations.

Figure 1 represents MacMillan's framework. This starts with the individual who has a set of values and attitudes, some idea of his political capability, and also a personal set of current needs and goals which motivate his behaviour. He surveys the organization and perceives opportunities and threats which are relevant to his current motivation. On this basis the individual actively formulates personal strategies for satisfying needs and achieving goals.

The individual in a large organization can do little alone, and so seeks to increase influence by combining with others who would like to see the organization take similar directions. The wide variety of motivations brought to the organization by different individuals ensure that many coalitions will form and that each individual will tend to belong to several. Coalitions tend to be represented by agents who demand support for the group in return for support for the individual. The individual's boss for example can be considered to be an agent representing the dominant coalition and his shop steward represents the union.

Our acceptance of political activity is such that the process of bargaining may not be overt and indeed neither party may be directly aware of it. During this process of bargaining the individual may learn more about his political capability and the nature of his environment and this feedback may cause him to adjust his strategy

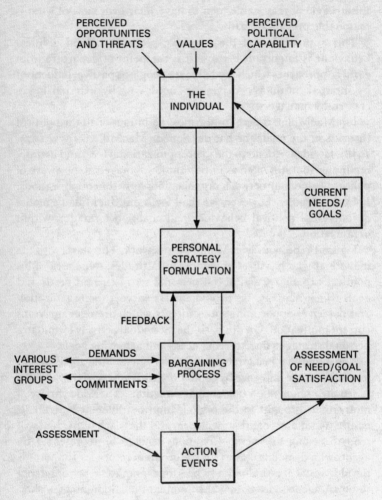

1 The political nature of individual action (adapted from MacMillan, 1978)

or reassess his goals. The outcomes of the bargaining process are commitments on both sides to certain activities in exchange for certain rewards. As time passes both the individual and the coalition assess each other's contributions. The individual feeds back his assessment of the coalition's performance when reconsidering his personal strategy. If his current strategy is successful he may become more adventurous and progressively increase his political capability and level of motivation.

Thus MacMillan's picture of the organization is built on the coalition. It is not usually possible for a coalition to satisfy all the demands of its members so they tend to develop a set of generalized goals. The larger the coalition, the more generalized its goals and the looser the commitment of the members. Large coalitions are usually combinations of smaller coalitions which have come together for specific mutual advantages. We can view the organization in terms of individuals, coalitions, 'super-coalitions' and, at the highest level, a 'dominant coalition'.

POWER

Power is the factor which binds the organization together and yet, paradoxically, pulls it apart. Without power there can be no movement, change or progress. It determines the direction of organizations and charts the course of events in all our lives. In traditional management theory a key variable is authority, often defined as the right to make people do things. Authority and power are related but by no means are they the same. A simple definition of power is the ability to make people do things. Many a manager has discovered that it is possible to have authority without power and power without authority.

Dahl (1957) provided the most quoted definition of power: 'A has power over B to the extent that he can get B to do something that B would not otherwise do.' This sounds straightforward enough but power is not a simple phenomenon. It is not purely a property of an individual. We tend to say that 'she has great power' but what we mean is that under these circumstances, for this type of decision, she has great power. A managing director may have great influence in the boardroom but none at all on the rugby field.

POWER: SOURCES, USES AND CONTEXT

The political view sees the manager not as a servant of the owners nor as a technocrat serving the system but as a manipulator trying to compete and cooperate with others in order to pursue his own ends.

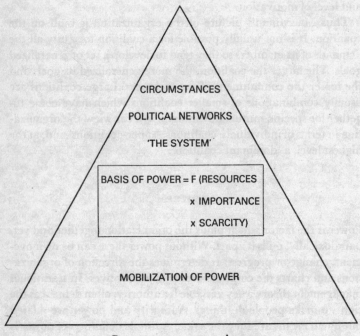

CIRCUMSTANCES

POLITICAL NETWORKS

'THE SYSTEM'

BASIS OF POWER = F (RESOURCES

x IMPORTANCE

x SCARCITY)

MOBILIZATION OF POWER

2 Power: sources, uses and context

Figure 2 represents three important and related aspects of this power. Power must have some source or basis, but a strong power base may be ineffective against a weaker one if it is not used or mobilized skilfully. All power interactions take place within particular circumstances or contexts such as the systems which management set up to control activity towards their ends. This context may place constraints on the alternatives open to the parties in a political struggle and may also influence their bases of power.

In the early literature we find several attempts to categorize the potential bases of power which may be used in organizations. French and Raven (1959) identified five such bases. Reward power is the ability to provide things which people want, the 'carrot'. People may do what their boss tells them because he offers them promotion or higher pay. Coercive power is the ability to punish or do things which people do not want, the 'stick'. A supervisor, for example, may be able to discipline, prevent promotion, or allocate unpleasant tasks. Legitimate power is the acceptance of the right of the power-holder by those being influenced. Subordinates may obey a supervisor because they believe he should tell them what to do, irrespective of his ability to reward or coerce. In some situations subordinates may give legitimate power to someone other than their formal boss, such as a shop steward or an informal leader. Referent power is based on people 'identifying' with the power-holder, feeling that he should act in that way, and that they would act like that. In the extreme, referent power would be hero worship, but may be comradeship or respect. Expert power is based on special abilities or knowledge. A supervisor may be obeyed because of respect for his technical expertise.

These bases of power may or may not be real, and in many situations it is enough that the person we are trying to influence believes that they are, or may be, real. In almost all situations there are power bases on both, or all, sides. Workers can reward a good supervisor by working well, and a technician may have more expertise than his boss. Beyond these simple 'vertical' relationships, much of organizational life involves managers interacting with other managers. Different power bases may be brought to bear in various situations: departments compete for a larger share of the budget; major projects such as new products or new factories; competition for promotion; or the introduction of new systems or machines.

David Mechanic (1962) has a slightly different way of looking at sources of power in a way which complements that of French and Raven. For him a person has power from control of or access to: information which people want; people who can get things done or who have power; and/or instrumentalities, things that people need or want. It follows from this that the same power base may be useful in some cases but not in others, depending on two factors: 'importance' and 'scarcity'.

The importance of a power source is the extent that it is needed by the parties we are trying to influence. This factor is sometimes called dependence. The scarcity (or irreplaceability or substitutability) of a power source relates to its availability elsewhere, because if there are several other sources of a particular reward or piece of information, then its usefulness as a power base diminishes. Emerson (1962) states: 'power derives from having something that someone else wants or needs, and being in control of the performance or resource so that there are few alternative sources.' Thus the power equation includes the resources at our disposal, their importance and their availability elsewhere.

For Pfeffer (1981) the power of any organizational sub-unit is related to the dependence of other sub-units upon it for action, information or other resources. He notes that: 'those sub-units or individuals within the organisation that can provide the most critical and difficult to obtain resources come to have power in the organisation. These include money, prestige, legitimacy, rewards and sanctions, and expertise, or the ability to deal with uncertainty' (p. 101).

The ideas that resources are central to the work of the organization and that coping with uncertainty leads to more power, are supported by Hickson et al. (1971). The importance of this model is demonstrated by the work of Pettigrew described earlier and also that of Crozier (1964). While researching in a French tobacco plant, he discovered that maintenance engineers appeared to possess inordinate power, which they exploited to their advantage. This was largely because the only major unpredictable uncertainty in the plant was machine breakdowns, as the rest of production was routine. The engineers kept their irreplaceability level high by refusing to allow documented repair procedures and by training new engineers orally.

It can be seen that there are two related broad groups of power bases: those due to membership of a formal functional group and those due to the individual. It is clear that these are interdependent since the members of a group influence its behaviour, and the group is an important influence on them.

Legge (1978) offers a useful summary of this type of framework:

A manager's power to implement the policies he believes are

appropriate depends on a range of inter-related factors. These include: the organisation's dominant ideology; the areas of contextual uncertainty it defines as being of crucial importance to resolve; how it defines, measures and evaluates sources; the manager's own level of expertise in the areas of activity he undertakes; his right of access to those he needs to influence and from whom he requires information in order to design and implement policy; his ability to establish credibility with those individuals he seeks to influence and from whom he seeks support; the resource power his position demands (p. 34).

The idea of a 'dominant ideology' relates closely to the idea of a 'dominant coalition'. It is a useful simplification but we must beware of assuming that it is a single, accepted, unchanging set of beliefs and attitudes. Nevertheless there are many ideas that most of us do agree upon: who should do what, who should make decisions, how they should be made, and who should have what power.

The context of the power process is the second major feature of the framework for understanding power in Figure 2. The context includes every aspect of the situation and the environment which is relevant to the power process. The game of chess can be used as an analogy. The most obvious source of power is the participant's possession of chesspieces in particular locations on the board. Power cannot be understood solely in terms of measurable and visible resources, and so strategies of the combatants have a great effect on the outcome of the game. One player achieves a 'powerful' position when he has a superior strategic position over his opponent. There is another unseen but extremely powerful force at work on both chess players which is easy to overlook. Thus 'the rules of the game' govern their entire thought processes and the resultant behaviour.

'Rules of the game' have a close analogy in organization which Steven Lukes (1974) calls the 'third dimension of power'. The first dimension, reflected in Dahl's definition quoted earlier, is the focus on behaviour in decision-making. The one-dimensional view involves observable conflict of interests. Awareness of the second dimension is seen by Lukes as a major advance: 'it incorporates into the analysis of power relations the question of the control over the agenda of politics and of ways in which potential issues are kept out of the political process.' It is often a simple matter for those in positions of power to prevent sensitive issues ever being raised. This two-dimensional view of power is still inadequate for it assumes that 'if men *feel* no grievances, then they have no interests that are harmed by the use of power'. Lukes's third dimension involves the things we do without question: 'A may exercise power over B by getting him to do what he does not want to do, but he also exercises power over him by influencing, shaping or determining his very wants.' Further, 'is it not the most insidious exercise of power to prevent people, to whatever degree, from having grievances by shaping their perceptions, cognitions and preferences in such a way that they accept their role in the existing order of things'. This is the process of 'socialization' that we all go through from our earliest days. We see the way things are and for the most part we accept it as the way they should be. Why do we accept that managers have the right to decide pricing policy, dividends, where to locate new factories, and so on? Is it because we have been socialized into such beliefs? The major weapon in a deliberate three-dimensional strategy would be propaganda, which many companies use. Management representatives may argue they work hard for the benefit of all, and they frequently describe the organization as a 'team' or 'family', to prevent their prerogatives being challenged. Company induction programmes may be considered as partly propaganda exercises to encourage new employees to accept the existing nature of the organization.

OTHER CONTEXTUAL FACTORS

Perhaps there is not much we can or would want to do about our own socialization except question our too-ready acceptance of 'the way we do things' or 'the system'. However, this is not to imply that we can ignore the environment within which power is exercised. Most power resources and strategies have to be related to the environment within which the process takes place. There is an existing configuration of power sources, relationships, coalitions, laws, systems and procedures which are the result of past activities. This configuration has resulted in some actors having access to particular resources and strategic options, which means that any future struggle will be much easier for them. The existing circumstances may also include the profitability of the company, the culture of the society or the development of a new production process. Circumstances may provide opportunities, challenges, threats and constraints.

Access to power in the past has resulted in the dominant coalition establishing 'systems' in an attempt to ensure that their goals are pursued: criteria for promotion, the selection process, a reward system, budgetary controls, company policies, rules, regulations and procedures. Drawing attention to the context of the power process serves to show that a political actor who understands the current situation is likely to be much more effective.

MOBILIZATION OF POWER

Two protagonists whose objectives conflict may have equal power, but one may be more successful than the other by mobilizing power more effectively. Consider the combatants in our chess game mentioned earlier: the outcome will be determined by the strategic ability of each player; furthermore a more skilful player who takes over a game in a weak position may still be able to win. So it is in organizations. Clever mobilization of apparently weak power sources may be more effective than poor mobilization from strength. This idea of power mobilization draws on the ideas of Handy (1976).

The most obvious method of converting a power base into action is the use of force. In organizations this rarely takes the form of physical bullying, and is more likely to be economic threat: 'do it or I'll fire you', 'pay us more or we'll strike', or 'promote me or I'll resign.' Force is a crude method which may be effective but tends to have long-term negative effects owing to built-up resentment. The defeated party may just be waiting for a chance to get even.

Perhaps a more desirable means of influencing people is persuasion. In its pure form this simply involves convincing people that a particular course of action is best, by relying on expertise and logic. Often, however, a manager who tries this method supports it implicitly with potential coercion or perceived legitimate or referent power.

A common strategy involves exchange of services or favours for the desired behaviour. In the case of union–management negotiations there may be a formal exchange of increased productivity for increased pay. Exchange between managers may take the form of favours, such as the personnel manager agreeing to support a production request to the capital expenditure committee in exchange for support on the job-grading committee. On a less obvious level a subordinate may be loyal to his boss in order to get a pay increase or a promotion.

The most subtle method of mobilizing power is to create the environment to make it difficult for people not to do what you want. This method is often used by the dominant coalition, but it is sometimes also possible for lower managers to create systems, rules and procedures within their own departments. Manipulating the situation may also take such forms as setting up a large committee to delay a decision, or loading it with people who support your view.

The author once witnessed a situation in which management set up the environment rather unwisely and had to pay the price. In order to save the wages of a number of craftsmen and reduce production costs they organized an entire foundry around the output of one machine operated by a small, cohesive group of semi-skilled workers. These workers soon discovered how important and irreplaceable they were and managed to acquire skilled rates and very favourable bonuses for their semi-skilled work.

AFFECTING THE DECISION PROCESS

Pfeffer criticizes the early approaches which focus exclusively on static sources of power: 'it is possible for a social actor within the organisation to have power because of his or her ability to affect some part of the decision process.' This reminds us that power is a contingent variable which must be reassessed for each particular decision or situation.

Any political strategy must consider possible actions and counter-moves by other parties, and the aftermath of any political activities. It could be better to lose, or to compromise, than to create a situation which may be undesirable later. Pfeffer indicates that the use of power is less obtrusive in good strategies. Nobody likes to be overtly influenced so it pays to be subtle. Effective strategies usually aim to legitimate or rationalize the decision and to increase support for the actor's position. The strategies of influencing basic decision premises, the alternatives considered and the information available are all unobtrusive. They are not always used in a deliberately political manner, and people tend to convince themselves of the correctness of a position which is in their own interests.

There are six major areas of the decision process which an actor may try to affect:

1. The Subject

The actual decision subject is the starting point. Does it have a history in which people have taken positions? Is it important or central in its implications? How important is the decision to you and to others, how much are you prepared to risk, how much will they fight? Can the decision be broken down into less obvious or less controversial decisions?

Bachrach and Baratz (1962) identified the prevention of decision issues from surfacing in the first place as an unobtrusive use of power. This strategy is usually used by those who profit from the status quo and it involves modification, or deletion, or failure to raise issues at formal meetings.

This strategy is used by managers to influence employees because if they are not involved in decisions such as salaries, product policy, recruitment, and so on, then they are unlikely to dissent. Companies often fear unionization because it brings into the open decisions which were previously management prerogatives.

2. The Nature of the Decision Process

It is critical to know who sets the time-scale, the decision-making procedure, and who makes the ultimate decision. Outcomes may be biased by influencing these characteristics, for instance if a speedy decision is required then unresearched alternatives are likely to be neglected. Can we load a committee with allies? Do we possess resources which are important for the decision-maker?

3. The Basic Premises of the Decision

Strategies, values and ideology set by the dominant coalition exert considerable influence on specific decisions. Discussion may take the form: 'our alternative is better than yours because it conforms more closely to organizational goals (or values).' Pfeffer also notes 'there are two ways to affect the premises of decision. The first way involves actually having laws, regulations, or pressure from some powerful actor imposed to impact constraints and values used in the choice process. The second involves asserting these constraints or value preferences.' The actor who can affect the objectives or constraints for a decision can influence its outcome. To do this of course he must be involved in some way with the decision process.

4. The Alternatives Considered

In most decisions the final range of choices considered is far smaller than the feasible options. There is much power in being able to affect the initial sifting process, for example in: the elimination of job candidates before the shortlist stage; the choice of projects for detailed investigation; or the creation of an agenda for a meeting, etc.

5. Information about Alternatives

A powerful role of providing information to the decision-makers is often delegated to lower-level subordinates. The participant armed with impressive information, jargon, facts and figures wields power which can be directed towards a favoured alternative.

6. The Parties to the Decision

Who decides on the parties to be involved? Can allies be pushed to the fore and potential opponents eliminated from the process? Can key participants be influenced in any way to elicit a favourable attitude? It is important to be aware of the different roles of participants: information providers, opinion leaders, one vote on a democratic committee? Who has the final say?

ANALYSING THE SITUATION

MacMillan's model described earlier assumes that individuals examine their circumstances before adopting a political strategy. The simplest form is a SWOT analysis (Strengths, Weaknesses, Opportunities, Threats). The political actor needs to identify trends in the existing situation and compare the likely future with his goals. It is wise to identify the key actors who are in positions to influence the future using an actor/issue matrix (see Figure 3).

Possible political actors

		A	B	C	D
Key issues	a				
	b				
	c				

3 Actor/issue matrix

For each issue or decision consider who is likely to be for, neutral, indifferent or against ($+$ o 1 $-$). This helps to identify chances of success and potential coalitions. Where can changes be made which will reduce opposition and increase support? What power resources are available for influencing the different parties involved? By repeating the process for several issues it is possible to look for trade-offs with different actors.

An ends/means analysis can help to clarify the actor/issue matrix by examining strategic options likely to be followed by each actor (see Figure 4).

Key actors	Probable goals	Means to achieving goals
A		(i) (ii) (iii)
B		
C		
D		

4 Ends/means matrix

A relationships matrix helps to identify the nature of the relationship, its strengths and weaknesses, and the functions it serves for each actor (see Figure 5).

Another exploratory device is a force field analysis which involves five stages (see Figure 6):

1. Define the target situation and the current situation.
2. List the forces (people, environment, system) for and against achievement of the target.
3. Evaluate the forces by describing them qualitatively and noting any relationships between them.
4. Represent the forces on a force field diagram, perhaps using a scale from 1 to 5.
5. Consider the opportunities for improving existing favourable forces and reducing unfavourable forces. Can new positive forces be introduced?

SIMPLE ADVICE

There are as many specific political strategies as there are political situations. Lists of strategic options which may be useful in different

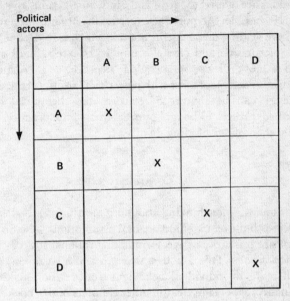

Political actors

5 Relationships matrix

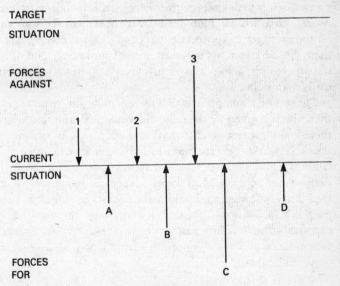

6 Force field analysis

situations are offered (Martin and Sims, 1956; Hunt, 1979). Much of this is sensible: 'Acquire the expertise the organization requires'; 'Join the leading department, not one which is in decline'; 'With-hold information and carefully time its release'; 'Build up useful relationships'; 'Increase people's dependence'; 'Acquire the behaviour patterns of those with power'; and so on. All these specific strategies can be shown to relate to the theoretical concepts described earlier, although putting them into practice may be harder than understanding them.

CONCLUSION

The framework for thinking about organizations embodied in this chapter is built on two fundamental assumptions. The first is that people are primarily active, formulating rational strategy towards their own ends. This is both a strength and a weakness. There is much more to individual behaviour and decision-making than rationality, as is made clear in other chapters of this book.

The political approach provides a useful counter to the over-simple view which characterizes people as responding to internal needs, being 'led' or 'motivated' by management. It is important for the manager to appreciate that people do not merely carry out their job descriptions, use their formal authority, and work in response to physiological and psychological drives which can be easily manipulated.

The second assumption is that there is no 'right' to power except that which is given by the actors in a political situation. Further, there is no 'greater good' towards which people in organizations should be working except that which they perceive themselves. This 'amoral' value position has been shown to be useful but it is just that, a value position. Most theories of organization are built on the idea that organizations should make profits, or at least have some purposeful existence. If we do not know what the organization is supposed to achieve how can we design it? How can we evaluate its performance and make 'improvements'? Upon what criteria can decisions be made?

CHAPTER 13

Ethics in Business

KEITH BLOIS

MEMO

TO: Mr Jones, Managing Director
FROM: Mr K. Day, Sales Director

THE HEATH CONTRACT

It is proving difficult to get this contract signed yet I am convinced that our offer is very competitive. However, Mr Tiles (their Purchasing Director) has stated on several occasions that he doesn't find our proposal attractive on 'personal grounds' and this (together with his constant references to his need for a holiday which he says he can't afford) I interpret as an indication that he requires some form of personal inducement to swing the contract our way. I guess that the cost to us would be no more than £1,000 which, in view of our desperate need for this job if we aren't to have redundancies, does not seem much. I appreciate that we have never gone in for this sort of thing before and therefore would like your approval, on behalf of the Board, to start 'negotiations' on this matter.

INTRODUCTION

The attempt to promote human happiness is the foundation of ethics (Kupperman, 1970). There are difficulties in providing an agreed definition of 'ethics'. Many writers on ethics do not provide a definition (that is, 'a statement of the precise meaning of the word') and definitions are not totally compatible amongst those who do provide them. The statement used here, while not receiving unquestioning acceptance from philosophers, would probably be tolerated. A further difficulty is that philosophers distinguish between 'ethics' and 'morality', although this chapter follows the convention of everyday language and uses the terms interchangeably.

The study of ethics is concerned with understanding what constitutes human welfare and identifying the type of conduct which will increase it. Thus ethics seeks to depict what is a desirable state to aim for and a desirable way of attaining it. This study is prescriptive: one should not do that which is judged to be ethically wrong but seek to do that which is ethically best.

Ethical behaviour is the application of the understanding provided by such study to life. This understanding may be specific knowledge but more typically the behaviour patterns developed by individuals through their upbringing, formal education and experience of life.

In so far as the purpose of ethical study is to guide action towards human welfare it does presume that individuals are free to make choices. This issue of freedom to choose makes ethical decision-making a different problem for individuals acting for themselves alone than when acting as part of an organization. Thus, to take an extreme example, an individual in the army is severely limited in freedom to make certain decisions. In industry and commerce the individual's freedom to make decisions is seldom as limited as in the armed forces, but there are situations where it is, and some would argue must be, so restricted (Nagel, 1978). Thus some organizations have procedures which provide individuals with minimal freedom in the placing of contracts with suppliers and in the recruiting of staff. This is seen as a mechanism for ensuring that the firm gets the best supplier or employee regardless of the personal interests and desires of the manager making the decision. Strict adherence to such procedures is usually demanded to ensure that a manager may not favour a friend but it also defends the manager from criticism when the friend or friend's firm is the best for the job.

The study of ethics in business is thus primarily concerned to help individuals operating in organizations to identify behaviour which will not be detrimental to human welfare and more positively to encourage behaviour which will benefit it. Ethics also helps to determine which organizational systems make the attainment of ethical behaviour more or less difficult for the individual.

Let it be clear, however, that modern ethical studies do not produce a neat set of rules to be followed in defined circumstances. These studies would contradict themselves unless they insisted that the ultimate responsibility for decision-making lies with the individual.

SOME GUIDELINES

How then can employees of a firm formulate their response to a situation which poses an ethical question? Examination of the opinions of those philosophers who study ethics and moral reasoning is not always helpful for the person unacquainted with their way of thought. The results of these studies show the thinking to be complex, some would say lacking in practicality, and often downright contradictory. Furthermore when dealing with 'practical' issues they seem to deal with either macro-problems (such as nuclear disarmament) or micro-problems (is it justifiable to sleep with my fiancé(e)), rather than those 'bite-size' problems which may occupy a manager's thinking, such as whether to withhold or tamper with information. However, there is a core of agreement among the experts. First, there are particular ethical decisions which it is best to regard for all practical purposes as predetermined. Second, to evade questions about the morality of one's actions is, at the best, a form of moral negligence (Lewis, 1972). Third, sound ethical thinking is based upon as full an understanding of the situation as it is possible to obtain in the specific circumstances (Fletcher, 1966). Fourth, statements like 'I know there are moral objections to it, but we must be guided by practical considerations' merely indicate that the speaker's fundamental basis of moral evaluation is the issue of expediency (Glover, 1970). Fifth, because of the impossibility of accurately predicting future events an ethically sound decision may produce undesired or unintended results (Schelling, 1981).

Although these five statements are not very specific their application to particular circumstances shows them to be of value. Consider the problem posed at the start of this chapter. Should Mr Jones allow Mr Day to 'negotiate'?

1. Predetermination

It would be a strange person who examined every decision to determine its moral content because there are simply too many decisions to be made each day for an individual to give each one separate consideration. Even if possible, it would be unnecessary, for most decisions do not have morally very significant effects. However, there are decisions which could have significant results but which also receive no conscious consideration. Prohibitions – on stealing and killing – and commandments – tell the truth, be kind to animals – are observed almost without thought. These are the general Judaeo–Christian precepts to which most Europeans and North Americans subscribe, but beyond these individuals develop their own 'lists' which depend upon background and experience. Thus an experienced purchasing manager may have rules to apply to himself about accepting a gift from a supplier. By comparison somebody not usually involved in a purchasing decision may never have seriously considered what his behaviour should be if a supplier offered a gift, inducement or bribe.

In Mr Jones's case a typical predetermined rule might be 'obedience of the law' which declares bribes to be illegal. This predetermined position is of value to him and he might only reject it because of peculiarly difficult circumstances. It makes it less likely that in the heat of the moment he will follow a policy which is contrary to his personal value system. If he decides to reject this predetermined view after due consideration, he will be clearly aware that his action represents a significant change in his behaviour patterns.

2. Moral Negligence

Mr Jones is guilty of moral negligence if without serious thought he decides to allow Mr Day to offer Mr Tiles an inducement. On the other hand, he is equally guilty of moral negligence if he foresees ominous consequences for his firm and its employees if he does not allow Mr Day to do this and yet, without serious thought, forbids Mr Day from taking any action. This may appear to demand masochistic behaviour as it seems to require a manager to impose upon himself the considerable strain and emotional turmoil of contemplating a decision which never has a 'right' answer. However, to avoid consideration of an issue which can directly affect the lives of others is a form of cowardice. Is it too much to ask that an issue with important consequences for others should be taken seriously? Indeed perhaps the ability to make such decisions is all that separates us from the animals.

This view of moral negligence does presuppose that the individual recognizes that the issue has a significant moral dimension. Obviously on some issues people disagree as to what is the ethically correct response. There are also many cases where some people apparently fail to see a moral issue in a situation which even their close friends would consider to have an obvious ethical dimension.

Such differences arise from the complex factors which contribute to the development of an individual's personality. One function of professional codes of practice and company codes of conduct (to be discussed below) is to attempt to make members of these bodies aware that certain categories of decision do involve moral aspects.

3. Full Understanding of the Situation

Mr Jones is likely to be more than fully occupied with running the firm so it would be frivolous to suggest that a massive investigation involving time and money could be undertaken. However the types of issues that he might be expected to consider include:

1. How has this situation arisen? If Mr Jones's company has 'never gone in for this sort of thing before' why has it arisen now? Has the company dealt with Mr Tiles before? If so, why does he appear to be making this suggestion now? If not, is he likely to be involved in future negotiations?
2. How would Mr Jones see this matter if he was involved in it in some other capacity, for example as Mr Tiles's managing director, or if he worked for one of Tiles's competitors? What about the reaction of his employees if they heard that he had agreed payments of this kind?

   Questions of this nature make Mr Jones aware that actions seldom affect only two parties. Others observe actions and adjust their behaviour in the light of them. Yet others may be affected more directly than at first appears to be the case.

3. Has the problem been defined accurately? Does Mr Jones have a full understanding of the legal aspects of the situation and the penalties of making a payment? Has Mr Day really understood Mr Tiles's intent and, more importantly, has he really established that they won't get the contract unless some payment is made? Are there any other ways in which they could get the contract without this action: for example, are there other managers in Tiles's firm who might be involved in directing the contract towards Jones's company?

The aim of this exercise is for Mr Jones to be aware of the consequences of allowing or forbidding Mr Day's 'negotiations'. This will take some effort but should result in Mr Jones taking whatever action he decides upon 'with his eyes open'. It may even open up some alternative policies which he had not previously considered.

4. Practicability

If Mr Jones wishes to be guided by 'practical considerations' then he must be prepared to state how these are to be judged. If it is expedient to provide Mr Tiles with an inducement then for whom is it expedient or advantageous?

Mr Jones is considering the basis of his choice, having previously listed their consequences. A decision which favours oneself is not necessarily unethical but most people are very good at rationalizing away their selfish behaviour.

5. Unforeseen Consequences

As the future is unknown there is always a possibility that any action may turn out in retrospect to be 'obviously' incorrect. However, decisions have to be made and are made in the knowledge of their uncertain outcome. It follows that where a person perceives a decision as being important they will take steps to try to make as informed a decision as possible (as suggested above). An essential part of the information sought is to provide an assessment of likely future outcomes.

So the five 'rules' do perhaps provide some guidelines within which Mr Jones may structure his decision. However, the major weakness of much discussion of ethical behaviour arises from the fact that it treats individuals as free to reach their own decisions, whereas operating within an organization limits their freedom of action.

Surprisingly, there is little discussion among writers on ethics of how individuals work out the conflicts which do arise when their personal views conflict with their organizational responsibilities on matters of ethical import. The next section attempts to throw some light on this very difficult and yet very important area of concern.

THE MORALITY OF ROLES

A fundamental problem to be considered is whether or not in a moral sense Mr Jones's actions as managing director are fully attributable to him as an individual? If an inducement is provided, what is Mr Jones's moral responsibility?

This issue combines two very difficult ethical problems: collective responsibility and the morality of role behaviour. As a member of a board of directors what is the individual's responsibility for 'the Board's' decisions?

It seems to be accepted in modern society that individuals occupying positions within an organization are insulated, both in their own view and the views of others, from what they do. For example: what is the mechanism which converts a person from a murderer to an executioner; from a kidnapper to a social worker taking a child into care? People take actions in their official capacity but often on their own initiative which they would never consider taking in their private lives. On the other hand, they often feel obliged to carry out instructions in their official capacity to which they personally cannot subscribe. Sometimes both types of action lead to much heart-searching and on other occasions they are excused because 'I was only doing my job'.

To understand the nature of this problem for anybody who takes on a role as a member of a formal organization it may be useful to consider the issue at three levels: the morality of the role itself; the morality of the role enactment; and the morality of the role acceptance (Downie, 1972).

1. Morality of the Role

People will pass moral judgements, both adverse and positive, on some roles in society. For example, many people would regard the role of the secret policeman as wrong and they would regard it as such no matter who fulfilled the role or within which society it existed. It must be questioned whether or not there are roles in British business which could unequivocally be classified as wrong, as distinct from wrongly enacted. Perhaps the 'asset stripper' would be one, but at once the argument moves to the delicate ground of identifying organizational systems which make the attainment of ethical behaviour more or less difficult.

Some people feel that the 'asset stripper' is a necessary role in the capitalist economic system, and they do not regard the system as immoral, and indeed argue that it is considerably more ethical than other forms of economic organization. However, for others the asset-stripper role is part of the 'unacceptable face of capitalism', and, for yet others, capitalism is based upon unethical behaviour. Thus in determining the moral worth of a role it is likely that a view of the moral worth of the system which creates that role will be needed. However, a businessman in a job today is part of an existing system and he must make decisions within that context. This, of course, in no way precludes him from critically examining the system and, if he so wishes, seeking to adapt it.

2. Morality of Role Enactment

Very few appointments are precisely specified in terms of their duties. Fewer still provide a precise interpretation of the way the duties are to be fulfilled and, even where such interpretations are provided, the personality of the individual filling the role will result in variable performance of the required duties. It follows that frequently there is considerable room for individual interpretation of role enactment and thus the possibility of a moral dimension. It might mean little more than thinking of the best timing of a redundancy announcement from the recipients' point of view. It could be more fundamental, like a decision whether or not to leak some misleading information about a competitor.

3. Morality of Role Acceptance

A person taking on a role adds the rights and the duties of that role to their rights and duties as a member of society. In accepting a role the individual must therefore consider the moral implications of both the rights and the duties. Some roles may be perceived as necessarily involving certain morally unacceptable aspects while others may appear to offer too little opportunity to benefit human welfare. Thus an anti-abortionist might refuse a job which would involve connection with abortion, while a member of the Friends of the Earth might reject a job which offers no opportunity to support constructive ecological policies. A role is often ill-defined initially, it may change, and unexpected 'expectations' with regard to duties may arise. Few personnel managers appointed in the mid-1970s expected to spend most of their time dealing with redundancy issues in the early 1980s.

How does this concept of the morality of roles assist Mr Jones? Firstly it must be assumed that Mr Jones did not perceive the role of managing director as morally offensive when he accepted it. Secondly, he did not perceive it to be wrong for him to accept the position which means that he felt he had the capability, in terms of both personal attributes and freedom of choice, of enacting the role in a morally acceptable way. If these two assumptions are correct then the issue centres on the morality of role enactment. Here two categories of concern determine the moral content of the issue: concern with outcomes and with actions, each of which will constrain the other. The difference between Mr Jones as a managing director and as an individual affects the balance struck between these two concerns.

As a managing director Mr Jones is acting for an institution designed to serve purposes larger than those of particular individuals. Because of these larger purposes Mr Jones's actions are likely to reflect a greater concern with outcomes than with actions.

A historical illustration may make the issue clearer:

In September 1665 the first death from the plague occurred in the Derbyshire village of Eyam. The two religious leaders persuaded the villagers to isolate themselves from the rest of Derbyshire in an attempt to halt the spread of the disease beyond the village. Fifteen months later 260 of the 350 villagers were dead but the plague had not spread. Was it ethical for these two men to persuade any one apparently healthy villager to stay on in that village?

The information is not available and it is not possible to know, but try to imagine the forms of pressure these two must have brought to bear on the villagers to persuade them to stay and consider the ethics of such behaviour. These leaders enacted their roles with a concern for the outcome and almost certainly, even in their own eyes, used unethical actions to achieve the outcome which history declares to be a good one.

As Mr Jones tries to work out the morality of his role enactment he must seek to identify the probable outcomes of those actions open to him. In many cases he will feel uncertain about the 'rightness' of whatever decision he takes, but he will know that the decision was reached in a morally responsible manner.

THE PROBLEM OF UNACCEPTABLE DECISIONS

What if the decision that Mr Jones feels is right for the firm is unacceptable morally for him as a person? As he considers this conflict he will become aware of a number of constraints which arise from his competence as a manager and his sense of loyalty and responsibility to a number of groups.

Consider first his managerial competence. As a managing director one part of his role is to coordinate and direct the activities of the various aspects of the organization. In this role Mr Jones necessarily has to exhibit trust in those reporting to him: trust in their competence; their honesty; their readiness to report unsatisfactory situations; and so on. Though as a managing director he might be expected to 'nose out' unsatisfactory situations, a modern organization can only run on mutual trust and respect.

Trust is a tenuous and complex asset because a colleague may be trusted for his technical competence but not for his business acumen. Furthermore, managers tend to trust each other unless they have good reason not to. This can lead a manager to act on a false assumption for quite long periods before he realizes that a colleague is not to be trusted, if only in the sense of being less competent in his role than is acceptable.

Loyalty and trust are mutually dependent but this raises difficulties as Mr Jones's loyalty to his immediate colleagues, his employees, his customers, the shareholders, his family and many other groups may be in conflict. Yet without the trust of these groups and his trust in them he may be unable to operate as managing director. It follows that Mr Jones may sometimes find that he cannot impose his own view because to impose it would so severely upset his working relationships with these groups as to make his job impossible. Nevertheless there may be issues on which Mr Jones feels or comes to feel so strongly that a decision is unethical that he will be obliged to put aside his feelings of loyalty, even to disregard appeals to his loyalty and ultimately to refuse to continue in the role of managing director.

When such situations arise the problem for Mr Jones is to decide how far to press his own views. Is this a resigning matter or is it a matter on which opinion is to be expressed but not pressed? In between these two positions are a multitude of possible positions. The action chosen by Mr Jones inevitably will be strongly and quite properly influenced by his personal as well as his business responsibilities. In addition Mr Jones must assess what effect his action will have on the firm's behaviour. This is never clear and certainly it must be asked whether resignation is a more effective mechanism for resisting a firm's unethical behaviour than continuing to influence the firm's policies from within (Hirschman, 1970).

CODES OF PRACTICE

It was suggested earlier that codes of practice have a contribution to make in making managers sensitive to areas where ethical issues might arise and to stipulate or suggest behaviour in specific circumstances. Codes of practice have been developed both by professional groups and by some companies. When a member of a professional group is found guilty of an infringement various penalties may be imposed. These can range from a public reprimand to ejection from the group (which in certain cases may make it impossible for the guilty person to practise the profession). In the case of company codes the consequences of proven infringements are less clear and vary from company to company.

These codes offer only limited support for a manager facing an ethical issue because they are usually formulated in general terms and some are so comprehensive in their generality as to be undemanding. Critical ethical issues often arise from unforeseen technological and social occurrences: thus major developments in information processing led to serious concern for the security of personal information. Members of organizations may come from a wide variety of cultural, educational, religious and political backgrounds and in consequence the code must be sensitive to a range of views. It is difficult to determine who are supposed to assist. Here the issue of 'practicality' arises again for, as Donaldson and Waller (1980) stated, the prime intent of most codes and the way they are administered is the maintenance of the profession or company's good reputation. The public (non-members of the group to which the code applies) interest is incidental ('occurring as a minor accompaniment') to this purpose. As a consequence ethical behaviour may not always be welcome if it exposes the profession or company to undesired publicity.

Thus codes of practice cannot be relied upon to ease the manager's moral burden of making ethical decisions. At their best they can offer the public certain safeguards – at their worst they can inhibit ethical behaviour.

COMMON ETHICAL ISSUES IN BUSINESS

It is obviously impossible to provide a comprehensive list of topics, issues or situations where ethical problems arise in business. Such a list could not be complete, nor could it indicate the multifacetedness of problems and decisions in business – and it is usually this multifacetedness which creates ethical dilemmas.

A further problem is that there are a number of issues which only arise within certain areas of business and as such are difficult for people not involved in these areas to appreciate. For example there is a Code of Conduct applicable to members of the Market Research Society and the Industrial Marketing Research Association. Some of the features of this Code can only be fully appreciated by persons acquainted with modern marketing research. The issue of misleading informants when conducting surveys is contrary to the Code. It would surprise people not familiar with market-research techniques to learn that 'We can certainly sometimes justify it [that is, misleading informants] on technical grounds' (Jowell, 1983).

In every specialism there are situations which appear unacceptable and inexplicable to the lay person and yet the professionals involved have clearly understood and evaluated the ethical implications.

There are a number of situations which commonly raise ethical problems for the individual in business. Indeed an international survey showed that senior managers view the relationship of their personal ethics and their business practices as a major issue (*International Management*, February 1983). This issue can be categorized in a number of ways but in this chapter a fourfold categorization will be used: bribery, withholding and falsification of information, law-breaking and delegation.

Should a firm offer bribes to a potential customer, a public servant with influence, etc.? Should managers accept bribes? What is a bribe? Is a free lunch a bribe or not? The survey showed that 38 per cent of a sample of 900 executives from sixteen industrial countries had recently been involved in making or being offered 'irregular' payments.

In the category of withholding and falsifying information it is well recognized that, while in a court of law the individual swears to tell 'the whole truth', in other parts of life the individual is only expected to tell 'the truth'. For example what an advertisement says must be true but it does not have to include information which harms its sponsor. Thus in law, withholding information is not always illegal, yet there are many cases where the deliberate withholding of information by a firm has adversely affected other firms and/or individuals. Even the timing of the release of information can, of course, significantly affect its impact on people.

Falsification of information is an equally troublesome and yet common issue. Obviously falsification is 'wrong' and yet it is not always clear what 'falsification' is. In the case of quantitative information the way it is presented can radically affect how it is understood; for example price increases can be made to look large or small by careful selection of the dates between which the price changes are measured.

A third category is that of law-breaking. While it is clear that to obey the law is not to guarantee ethical behaviour, there can be little doubt that in most Western European and North American countries the law is regarded as a fundamental basis of social stability. It follows therefore that breaking the law is a very serious matter, not because of the penalties which the law-breaker may incur, but because such acts may disrupt our social structures. Nevertheless firms do break the law and not infrequently do so knowingly and deliberately. The matters involved may range from opening shops on a Sunday through to major breaches of safety regulations. Reading reports of court cases where companies have been prosecuted makes it clear that not only do some companies break the law but only do so after very careful consideration of the issues involved and in the belief that their actions are justifiable despite being unlawful.

A final major category concerns delegation. Obviously managers necessarily have to delegate authority to their juniors on many occasions. Whatever the reason for delegation the manager must make clear what limits he is setting on his junior's authority and, when the junior acts within them, must accept responsibility for those acts. Failure to make clear what are limits of employees' authority is bad management. Failure to accept responsibility for juniors acting within their defined authority is unethical. However this again is difficult in practice if only because new and unforeseen circumstances are always arising and decisions must often be taken without there being time to refer them to higher authority.

These four categories – bribery, withholding and falsification of information, law-breaking and delegation – are not confined to business. In various forms they can be observed in any organization: central and local government; religious bodies; charities; universities; and so on. The consequences of ethically irresponsible decisions can be severe for individuals and communities which are affected by them. The damage done can be physical and/or psychological, as illustrated by Heilbroner (1972). For individuals who make ethically responsible decisions the consequences may also be severe: loss of job; blocked promotion; loss of colleagues' confidence; psychological stress; and damaged family relationships. Yet the *International Management* survey provides the encouraging evidence that, while 53 per cent of the managers had in the last five years faced at least one major conflict between their personal beliefs and their employer's requirements, 67 per cent of them resolved the problem by having the integrity to do what they believed was right. Furthermore 70 per cent of these believed they had suffered no disadvantage by acting according to their conscience with a further 8 per cent reporting themselves as merely having been reprimanded.

The frequency of the occurrence of the ethical dilemmas and the difficulty of providing guidance to those involved in any organization stresses that 'ethical problem-solving and decision-making are growing knottier all the time, with the "grey area" between black and white spreading' (Fletcher, 1966). This fact does not, however, excuse the decision-makers from attempting to make responsible decisions, be they manager, priest, social worker or teacher.

CONCLUSION

What then should Mr Jones do in response to Mr Day's memo? Contradictory though it might seem, to reply 'Only Mr Jones can decide' is not to avoid the issue. Others have the easily abused privilege of offering advice and opinions but the decision is Mr Jones's alone. Equally it will be Mr Day's decision whether or not to accept Mr Jones's decision.

What has been written above may help Mr Jones in two ways. First by reminding him that roles have moral aspects and the time to start to think about them is ideally prior to accepting them. Second, because many roles evolve and develop over time this is not a once and for all matter. The three aspects of role and the five guidelines concerning ethical evaluation begin the process of 'unfolding' the problem.

Finally the statement that 'because of the impossibility of accurately predicting future events an ethically sound decision may produce undesired or unintentional results' cannot be a source of comfort but may, perversely, provide some reassurance. Obviously it is little consolation for a manager who has agonized over a decision to find that undesired results arise because of unforeseen developments. It may, though, be some reassurance to know that because of the recognized difficulties of prediction he cannot be criticized for the results of a decision made in a responsible manner. He can however be legitimately criticized for not making a decision.

CHAPTER 14

Culture's Consequences

ARNDT SORGE

Most people do not associate management with the word 'culture'. They would think of opera, the theatre, museums or scholarly work. The notion of culture seems to fit the idea of a liberal education rather than the down-to-earth and efficiency-minded concerns of management. A complication is added by the fact that prevalent notions of culture are ambiguous and different from each other.

WHAT CULTURE IS ALL ABOUT

The word is derived from the Latin *colere*, 'to plant, grow'; and although it has come to denote a much larger area increasingly removed from planting and growing, the roots of the word are suggestive. It has the following shades of meaning:

1. It implies an interference with nature; natural objects can only be partly influenced, and the human skills involved are 'culti-vated' in the process, at the same time as cultivating the object. There is thus an interaction between human beings and the objects with which they are concerned.
2. On the one hand, nature is partly controlled, shaped, changed or even suppressed by cultural activity. Culture brings about artificial arrangements which would otherwise not be found in nature, at least not in the same place or pattern.
3. On the other hand, there are limits to the manipulation of the environment since outcomes are beyond human control because of complexity, levels of available skills and knowledge, or social customs, norms and taboos.

We thus find a dialectic interplay of *artefacts* and *nature*, which not only brings about conflict between them, but also an interpenetration by which people try to assimilate them. In most of central Europe, nature consists of plants which were introduced or 'allowed' to grow and artefacts are particularly appreciated for being 'natural' or blending into nature. This goes for houses, gardens, social norms of behaviour as well as modes of thinking. This idea of culture as distinct from nature, with their manifold interpenetrations, implies a wide definition. This follows from the anthropological approach of Berger and Luckmann (1971, pp. 63–99). In man, instincts do not give clear impulses to behaviour. In comparison with other species, man is particularly dependent on physical and social nurture for a long time. In the course of this learning process, man receives a behavioural repertoire from his intimate and wider social environment. This is not transmitted in a mechanical way, but is actively cultivated. The environment presents stimuli that the individual grapples with and learns the meaning of. Such stimuli may be toys or other artefacts, reprimands, inducements, pictures, stories and random aspects of other people's behaviour.

People experience different stimuli according to their social *collectivities*: families, parts of town, ethnic or linguistic groups, school forms, play groups, factory workforces, regional populations or nations. Collectivities cultivate particular behavioural repertoires and modes of thinking through day-to-day practice and individuals acquire the meaning of stimuli, and modify and transmit it to others. They actively select stimuli rather than waiting for them to occur. Hence, the repertoire is constantly in flux: it is transmitted from one individual to another, and it slowly changes and evolves in the course of transmission.

Man strives to survive in a hazardous environment through the development and use of a vast range of artefacts: tools, housing, forms of communication and transport. Behaviour is both stimulated and stabilized by social institutions. In this context, the word 'institutions' has a wider meaning than in everyday language; more than the Royal Lifeboat Institution or the Lord Mayor's Banquet. What we really mean by 'institution' is a stable pattern of social interaction. Humans habitually use behavioural and symbolic patterns in social interaction which make their meaning acceptable or not to members of a collectivity. Institutionalized patterns of behaviour are thus accepted or rejected for other than well-defined factual purposes. In this respect, social institutions are similar to the Lord Mayor's Banquet, which is much more than just an occasion to satisfy hunger.

Culture includes technical and social artefacts, which are cultivated to a large extent independently of known and immediately visible purposes and reasons. This is not to say that institutions are irrational; they are necessary for social coherence. Institutions are not always designed with a well-defined range of purposes in mind, and their original purpose is usually lost in history. They are ambiguous because they are generalized patterns, above and beyond the original rationale. Culture is the backbone of human life in social collectivities, but it is different from the natural backbone of an individual because it is man-made, artificial and evolves faster. The individual constantly contributes to institutional evolution in piecemeal steps, but at the same time cannot extricate himself from its influence.

Institutions thus imply something like a 'mental programming' of individuals (Hofstede, 1980, pp. 14–19) but human behaviour is not like that of even sophisticated computers (Sorge and Fores, 1979). There is an element of choice in institutionalized behavioural patterns (Child, 1972) so that humans constantly modify and re-construct their technical and social environment (Schreyögg, 1980).

The cultivation of institutional patterns does not mean that culture disintegrates into fragmented sub-cultures as the specialization in a society increases. To the extent that people live in different spheres at the same time, or come from one sphere and go to another, they will transmit patterns across spheres and maintain the cultural coherence of larger collectivities. Management is never just management *per se*, but the management of social units in particular domains (hospitals, schools, engineering, job-shops, chemical plants, banks, etc.), with people from particular social classes, ethnic backgrounds, work or educational careers, in particular areas of the world or a country.

Institutions are never precisely or rigidly fixed. They have to be ambiguous, and the 'mental programming' of individuals has to be imprecise and even contradictory, for otherwise the inventive spark of the human mind would not be triggered, and this is necessary for the species' psychic sanity and material and biological survival. An example will show the implications of cultural analysis for the day-to-day practice of management.

THE PREDICAMENT OF PRODUCTION MANAGER BAKER

John Baker runs the works of the Pipework & Vessels Division of a large engineering group. He is responsible for two shops: a 'heavy' shop with the foundry, presses, cold-rolling, welding and heat-treatment activities; and a 'light' shop with pipe-bending, turning, milling, drilling, grinding and light assembly. The plant is close to Newcastle, and produces primarily for the shipbuilding industry and the Central Electricity Generating Board. It had to change because of the demise of shipbuilding and stagnating investment in the CEGB. The Division had to try hard to win new customers, primarily in the chemical industry and North Sea oil exploration. At the same time, the owning group reinforced cost controls and brought in management changes. Management and the workforce were told that the group would be forced to close or sell the plant if they did not pull their socks up, increase productivity, meet delivery dates better than in the past, and win contracts from new customers.

Faced with gloomy prospects in December, the divisional board and the general manager speedily agreed to sign a contract which the sales manager was lining up. The production manager (Baker) agreed very reluctantly, grumbling to himself that 'people in sales always rush things through without giving me the time to check whether it's feasible, and the general manager always agrees in order to look good to head office, without giving me the resources because they want to reduce costs and don't like buying new machines if they don't have fantastic pay-back periods'.

John Baker has endless discussions with the engineering manager and the production engineering superintendent about the justification of investment into production plant. He thinks production engineering should be responsible to him, but head office do not. He feels that they are 'technical-college boffins without a real grasp of things like likely down-time, malfunctioning, reaction of operators, all sorts of hiccups in the organization and with the unions which cost a lot and everybody expects me to sort out'. In the eyes of production engineers, Baker is old-fashioned, does not know much about technology, and has not learnt much since he took his Diploma in Industrial Administration ten years ago, which did not increase his technical strength. He had served an apprenticeship and acquired an HNC previously, but then worked in production control and plant management.

Relitions with the unions are none too good, either. The boiler-makers' union is strong in the heavy shop, and it reacts sharply against infringements of demarcation rules, 'dilution of skills', and organizational or training changes. The Amalgamated Union of Engineering Workers is stronger in the light shop, but it is divided into shop stewards' groups from the pipe-bending section, the machinists and the toolroom. Foremen and technicians are repre-sented in bargaining by TASS, which does not always get on easily with the rest of the AUEW.

The new contract creates more work in the light shop, but hardly any in the heavy shop. To add to Baker's headaches, the Division budget for the next year provides for the acquisition of numerically controlled (NC) lathes and mills. Baker has doubts whether they come at the right time because he fears grave running-in and training problems which would jeopardize the achievement of delivery dates in the new contract. Additional qualified and reliable manpower, for an extra shift, is hard to come by; and possibilities of internal transfer and retraining, from the heavy to the light shop, are very precarious. Transfers would threaten carefully negotiated pay scales and job-evaluation criteria. This is a headache for the personnel manager who warns Baker not to do anything hasty. Baker thinks that he himself should be responsible for industrial relations.

In terms of cultural anthropology Baker's predicament is that everybody expects him to do something while he is hemmed in by institutional patterns which he can modify only marginally. The culture of the owning group keeps him locked into formal profitability, productivity and accounting routines. The Division allocates responsibility in fragmented form; he has no authority over production engineering and an unclear authority over indus-trial relations. The division of responsibility between production management and production engineering, linked with separate careers, is strongly rooted in his country's heritage of managerial careers, education, training and organization practice. Workforce representation in unions, job demarcation, bargaining arrangements and methods of payment are also rooted in national traditions and carefully cultivated company collective agreements.

Baker often wonders whether his colleague Hans Bäcker in West Germany is better off. He met him two years ago, and had found that Bäcker ran works very similar to his own, in terms of technology, products and size. He heard that Bäcker had all that he was longing for. Bäcker was firmly in control of production engineering and did not have much trouble with non-production people about choice and acquisition of equipment. After his apprenticeship, he had worked as a fitter for five years and took a part-time course in work study. He had then studied for a college degree in production engineering, worked as a production engineer, work planner and production controller, and eventually as a production manager. He has only one union to contend with, and the works council represents the whole workforce, whether unionized or not. There are more skilled people in the works since, as Bäcker explained, 'someone who has not at least served an apprenticeship is nowadays considered a layabout'. Apprenticeships are not longer than three-and-a-half years, apprentice wages are comparatively lower than in Britain, and the unions demand more apprenticeship places rather than fewer. The foremen are better trained, have more authority, and relieve Bäcker of a lot of trouble-shooting on the shop floor. His working day is calmer, less conflict-ridden and more conducive to a consistent production policy with a more long-term perspective. It is much easier for him to retrain and transfer labour internally, not only because of the union structure, but also because people respond to training opportunities more quickly.

On the other hand, Bäcker was rightfully daunted by the huge amount of social policy, industrial democracy, work protection and other legislation and court rulings which had to be considered, not to speak of complex collective agreements with unions and the works council. Bäcker commented: 'If people in Britain believe that their legislation has become difficult to bear in mind, they ought to come and see ours. You need your own lawyer by your side to run a place, but I think that's what the personnel department is there for. I suppose all this negotiation and legislation business makes the place predictable because everybody knows what they are up against and so you can make people move together in the direction which keeps all of us in business.'

Baker was convinced that there were cultural differences between his works and those of Bäcker in terms of company organization, manpower training and education, the structure of occupational careers, industrial relations and other fields. These differences were in the minds of people, in society as well as in the company as a microcosm of society. He concluded that this was what made them so difficult to pinpoint, get hold of and change, unlike a worn-out cutting-tip on a tool. He knew which direction he would like to move the company, but he also had to think of the old Irish joke: 'If I were you, I would not start from here.'

There was no systematic, well-planned solution to his predicament, as in management textbooks. A cultural revolution was the last thing he wanted. So what did he do? Nothing at first, besides urging the personnel manager to say that redundancies in the heavy shop were probably imminent, because of a lack of orders. Then the new NC machines arrived and, as he had predicted, their rate of utilization was abysmally low to start with, because of all the factors production engineering had not taken into account. This brought up fears that deadlines would again not be met. With the unions in despair because of the recession and possible redundancies, and the divisional board because of the threat of contractual penalties, loss of further orders and possibly worse to come from group head office, Baker felt that the time was ripe and told the divisional board and shop stewards that there were two alternatives: either to 'go to the wall' or accept his plan. This plan implied internal transfer of workers from the heavy to the light shop; more training, particularly for machinists in NC operation and programming; more shiftwork to increase machine utilization and integrate transferred workers in the light shop; integrated bargaining and wage scales for all shopfloor workers; and his own direct influence on production engineering. The plan was agreed.

In sociological terms, he had changed the culture of the factory substantially, by weakening job-territory demarcation, and altering payment systems, training arrangements, worktime patterns and organization structure, with long-term implications for union organization and possibly career paths. He had brought about this change by relying on the traditional cultural resources of his country: improvisation at the right moment when intense pressure brought received cultural patterns into an impasse. Compared with Bäcker's factory in Germany, there is convergence in some respects, such as in the greater uniformity of shopfloor workers and pay scales, and closer links between production management and engineering; but other industrial relations differences remain as they were, and to some extent they become larger.

It is characteristic that cultural change did not take place because the actors behaved in a self-consciously cultural way, like artists keen to cultivate their individuality. John Baker tried to find a practicable solution under intense economic pressure and power influences; he used power at the time when it came to him, and his tacit experience and intuition.

The difficulty of change arises because institutions in different spheres are linked: trade union organization is, for instance, linked with remuneration systems, vocational training practices, shopfloor organization, personnel policy and other factors. A cultural dialectic operates: change conflicts with stability, but is rendered possible because of it.

This story shows that cultural contrasts are particularly notable between nation states. The question now is how to relate different managerial practices and structures to properties of the wider culture. There are basically two ways of approaching the issue: to look at the institutional artefacts in a society and see how these relate to management; or to explore the mental programming of individuals to establish the link. The two perspectives are not mutually exclusive or contradictory.

Institutions cover a very wide ground, and consist of: statute and unwritten law; other social norms; and custom and practice in occupations, associations, organizations, kinship groups or larger collectivities. Studies have explored different institutions at the level of national collectivities (Maurice et al., 1980, 1982).

Institutions may be examined at different levels of abstraction. At a higher level of abstraction Crozier (1964) singled out the precariousness of face-to-face relationships as a long-term cultural trait. This explained the tendency to adopt bureaucratic patterns to achieve a form of central coordination and management which protected the autonomy of actors in the bureaucracy against exercise of authority by instituting impersonal formal mechanisms and norms.

If we consider what happened in Baker's situation from a more abstract perspective we see that change was possible because action was compatible with abstracted institutional patterns. These are company individualism in personnel policy and training arrangements, confrontation with some trade-union representatives in a less consensual system of industrial relations, the precarious authority of production management and ambivalence around the separation of production managements and engineering. Here, we have a more dominant cultural factor which is shown, for Germany from a British perspective, by Hutton and Lawrence (1981) and Lawrence (1980).

VALUES AND PREFERENCES

'Mental programming' approaches consider the individual person's values, beliefs, preferences or other attitudes. Studies of the implications of mental programs for management have usually applied the concept of values. This can be found in Child (1981) and in Hofstede (1980), probably the most important comparative study on culture's consequences for work-related values. Values are taken to be 'mental programs that are relatively unspecific' which 'are programmed early in our lives' through childhood socialization of the individual. Earlier studies of this type are reported in England (1975) and Weinshall (1977).

Hofstede (1980) isolated four dimensions of culture as dominant factors: power distance, individualism, uncertainty avoidance and masculinity. National cultures were shown to vary within these dimensions, which we could use to compare Baker and Bäcker's behaviour and values. There is a higher degree of individualism in Britain, while Germany emphasizes collective coherence to a greater extent. Baker has to play an individual power game, whereas Bäcker deployed his strategy within a social framework which tends to legitimize individual activity more on the basis of adequacy in view of a collectively expressed will.

Uncertainty avoidance is seen in the legalistic character of industrial relations in Germany whose function is to anticipate and regulate as many occurrences in working life as possible. It is also brought out by Bäcker's acceptance of a complicated legal framework because it makes life calculable, increases by allegiance of the workforce, and generally makes his work calmer and easier to do. Conflicting constraints on Baker's behaviour and the management structure increase uncertainty, although authority is formally laid down. Paradoxical as it may sound, Baker's conduct is geared to creating a collectively better result for the company, and reducing uncertainty over its future, by acting individually and not avoiding uncertainty.

It must be stressed that values or other forms of 'mental programming' may apply in different degrees to different social spheres. Uncertainty avoidance, for instance, is not always more emphasized in Germany than in Britain. In shops, at bus-stops and in other similar public places, the tendency to avoid uncertainty by orderly queuing is much stronger in Britain.

CULTURE'S LESSONS

The realization that management is not the same universal activity everywhere has a number of lessons to offer. They follow an analysis of management as a 'cultured' activity which is governed by similar underlying principles as art, agriculture, engineering or any other human activity including all forms of social behaviour.

A first lesson is that there is never a 'natural' way of managing, or one most appropriate to achieve a result, except in terms of a prevalent social definition or under particular conditions of the prevailing social environment of management. This is, however, not autonomously given but can be influenced. Answers about good or best managerial practice are therefore always culturally relative. Managerial recipes cannot necessarily be used outside the cultural context in which they originated. This lesson is particularly well brought out by Hofstede (1980, Chapter 9).

This point should not be understood as an attack against the transfer of managerial practice in principle. However, with the rise of multinational companies, increases of international trade and communication, and the overwhelming influence of an American management ethos and practice in the period after the Second World War, there has emerged an unprecedented tacit belief in universally valid best practice. This belief has been declining recently, and the time has come to abandon management fads and examine recipes much more carefully to see whether they fit into cultural patterns relating to social institutions and the mental 'programming' of social actors (Sorge and Fores, 1981).

Improvement and change are always possible. Social institutions and mental 'programs' are ambiguous and conflicting so as to permit, stimulate, enrich and possibly provoke change, while at the same time stabilizing social actors and institutions. Dialectic contradictions are distinctive for opposites which conflict and support each other at the same time. They are the spice of human life in society which keeps it going, much as the plus and minus poles are needed to keep electricity flowing.

Within a dialectic perspective, a manager would not ask if changes have to be made or not, or whether he has a choice or is constrained. Instead, the questions are: what has to change to assure stability? What has to remain stable to make change viable? Which constraints do I choose in making a choice?

This is the appropriate way of transferring experience and recipes from one culture to another. It does not involve imitation but ingenious and judicious tinkering. The concept, recipe or mental 'program' has to change at least marginally in order to fit into a different context. But even marginal changes are crucial, require a great deal of reflection and dedication, and are in no way inferior to supposedly radical changes. They require intuition at least as much as factual knowledge. If this cultural lesson is well learnt, the manager is not puzzled either by the variety of culturally relative concepts or the difficulty of adopting and realizing generally valid experience.

CHAPTER 15

The American Company in Britain

IAN JAMIESON

The fascination with how other countries organize their affairs has always been with us. From the earliest times we have listened to travellers' reports from far and wide about such diverse matters as family rituals, agricultural practices and economic customs. Trade between nations and the widespread development of industrial capitalism has meant that the focus of much recent attention has been on economic matters. Two questions have dominated: first, are other nations or other firms more successful than our own; second, if they are what is the secret of their success?

While Britain was the industrial leader up until about 1850 other countries scrutinized Britain and British firms for the secret of her success. What was it that allowed Britain to be so technologically innovative? What was it about the socio-cultural structure of Britain, about the management of its enterprises that allowed it to be so prosperous? By the middle of the nineteenth century however Britain had passed her economic zenith, and now it was the turn for British eyes to be cast on the economic features of other societies and for similar questions to be asked.

Although Britain's economic competitiors have been many and various, the USA has always held a special place. The American exhibits at the Great Exhibition of 1851 excited particular attention because of their industrial ingenuity. They were sufficiently startling to send large numbers of worried industrial commissioners across the Atlantic to report on the 'American system of manufacture'. These industrial commissioners were followed by an unending stream of travellers and officials right up until the 1950s. Most of the reports, no matter how technical their starting points, put great emphasis on the socio-cultural differences between the two nations as being a major factor explaining the greater productivity of American industry.

While the British were admiring the 'American system' in the

USA the Americans began to export it to the British mainland. In 1801 an American Chamber of Commerce was established in Liverpool to assist the cotton trade. By the 1830s a large number of American merchants were residing in Britain (Wilkins, 1970). In 1841 the American publishing firm of Wiley and Putnam joined a number of the earliest American investors in Britain – the life-insurance companies (Kindleberger, 1969). 1856 was a special date because it marked the first American factory in Britain. Five American partners in the US firm of J. Ford & Co. set up a vulcanized-rubber factory in Edinburgh. The factory was entirely American designed; key workers were brought from across the Atlantic and all the capital was subscribed by the US investors.

From such small beginnings in the nineteenth century direct American investment in the UK has grown apace. From the end of the Second World War until the 1960s the influence of American firms on the British economy has been considerable. American management and managerial methods have dominated the whole of the managerial culture of private industry. Just as from the late 1970s it is hardly possible to find a management journal that doesn't have an article about *Japanese* firms and management methods, so in the 1950s and 1960s American management was hegemonic. So powerful was the American presence that there were considerable fears as to whether the Europeans could survive the onslaught. Jean-Jacques Servan-Schreiber's book *The American Challenge* (1968) epitomized the worries, and *The American Takeover of Britain* (McMillan and Harris, 1968) expressed the sentiment exactly.

What is the extent and nature of the 'American challenge' in Britain? The various studies of the Economist Advisory Group (EAG, 1976) give us a clear picture. There are about 1,600 US affiliates operating in the UK, most of them in manufacturing, and particularly prominent in high-technology, capital-intensive industries. Six sectors – food, tobacco, metal manufacture, other machinery, other electronic apparatus and motor-vehicle manufacture – account for 53 per cent of total US affiliate sales and for 48 per cent of employment (EAG, 1976). In the manufacturing sector they sold goods worth almost £8,000 million in 1973/4, that is 12 per cent of the total production of all UK manufacturing enterprise. They employed 9 per cent of the UK labour force and accounted for 16 per cent of all UK manufacturing exports (EAG,

1976). American firms account for one sixth of the bank deposits in Britain.

The visibility of American firms in Britain is particularly high as the following selected list of firms indicates: Ford, Esso, Gallaher, Texaco, Rank Xerox, IBM, Mars, Heinz, Kodak, Hoover, Procter and Gamble, NCR, Kraft Foods, Kelloggs, Gillette, Black and Decker, Texas Instruments, Colgate-Palmolive, Avon Cosmetics, Johnson and Johnson, Quaker Oats, Ronson Products, American Express, Diners Club, CBS and Collier-MacMillan. Substantial penetration in certain economic sectors and high visibility are probably not enough to account for the worries about American influence that were so prominent in the 1960s and 1970s. Two other related factors need to be brought forward. In the first place, all the available evidence suggests that American firms operating in the UK are very successful. The Economist Advisory Group study in 1976 concluded that 'over the last 24 years the U.S. manufacturing affiliates have earned consistently higher rates of return on their capital than their UK competitors'. There are considerable accounting problems in comparing the profitability of one company with another, particularly when one of these companies is a foreign-owned affiliate (see the warnings regularly published in the Government publication *Economic Trends*). Transfer-pricing arrangements between American subsidiaries and their parents, as well as the effect of floating exchange rates, make the direct comparison of the profitability between American and British firms in the UK particularly hazardous (Jamieson, 1980). Despite these problems there does seem some general agreement among economists that, on average, American firms are more profitable than British firms. This has also been shown to be the case for American and British firms operating in third countries (Dunning, 1970), and so the overall conclusion of greater profitability seems safe enough.

Secondly, the greater profitability of American firms has been taken as prima facie evidence of the superiority of American management and American management methods. Management as a body of theory and methods was born and grew up in the USA. The classic writers on management and organization were nearly all American (Taylor, Follett, Barnard, Simon) and the more recent managerial gurus (Herzberg, Argyris, Likert, Drucker) have a similar origin. The first business schools had their home in the USA (the first was the Wharton School of Finance & Commerce, founded in 1881) and the leading schools are arguably still to be found there. When the Franks Report in 1963 argued for the setting up of British business schools it significantly talked of setting up a 'British Harvard'. American managerial methods came to Britain not only via the work of the American business schools and leading management writers, but also via management consultants and American subsidiaries which act as business schools (Thomas, 1969). People with experience in American companies, particularly those with well-recognized managerial strengths for financial management and planning like Ford, or for marketing and sales training like Mars, were much sought after by British firms.

What are the distinctive features of American management that have made it such a revered commodity? Is it just a series of techniques that can be taken up by any firm, or is it more like a philosophy – a way of looking at problems and solving them that lies embedded in the culture of the United States? It is important that we are careful in assessing the evidence when tackling these questions. Management is essentially a practical activity dominated naturally enough by practioners; such theory as exists would not be readily assented to by everybody. In such a situation myths and unfounded assertions find a ready home.

Fanciful stories about the differences between British and American management abound and pass readily as evidence. For example, it is widely asserted that American marketing methods are superior to British. To demonstrate this point anecdotes are commonly told at marketing conventions. A popular one goes something like this. 'An American went to Africa to sell shoes. A British salesman went there too. When the Brit got there he immediately sent a telegram back to his company in Northampton. It read "Coming back at once. Nobody wears shoes here." The American also sent a telegram. It read "Send two million shoes. Nobody wears shoes here."' Most importantly, because the management and organization of companies differ according to their size, the industry within which they are located, and their products, when one is comparing British and American management methods it is important to make sure that one is comparing like with like. It would hardly make sense to compare the management and organization of the Chase Manhattan Bank and British Leyland and then draw some conclusions about British and American management methods. However, a comparison between Ford and British Leyland would be illuminating, as would a comparison between the Chase Manhattan Bank and one of the British clearing banks. The very best methodology is offered by those studies which compare accurately matched companies by size and product (Richardson, 1956; Inkson et al., 1970; Jamieson, 1980).

The first distinctive feature of American management is that it is more formalized. When we talk of formalization we are referring to the organizational technique of prescribing how, when and by whom tasks are to be performed (Hall, 1962). American firms are more likely to have fixed procedures for a wider range of activities than their British opposite numbers (Richardson, 1956; Inkson et al., 1970; Granick, 1962; Jamieson, 1980; Turnbull, 1982). This stress on formal procedures amounts to a much greater use being made of the techniques of managerial control. This is especially noticeable in the field of financial and budgetary control, but it is also a distinctive feature of the personnel area. In personnel many commentators have remarked on the stress that American firms place on a range of formal procedures for management selection (e.g. American firms are much more likely to draw up proper job descriptions and person descriptions than British firms, as well as use some recognized interviewing programme). The American firms are then more likely to have a management-development programme to make full use of the talent they have recruited. These differences are variously supported by a wide range of researchers (Urwick, 1954; Acton Society Trust, 1956; Stewart, 1957; Seyfarth et al., 1968; Jamieson, 1980). In marketing the same pattern emerges: the Americans are much more likely to use a set of systematic techniques to assess the market, plan the campaign, and sell the goods (PEP, 1966; Chruden and Sherman, 1972; Permut, 1977; Jamieson, 1980).

Thus American firms have a large number of rules and procedures, of controls and techniques for regulating the work of the company. And yet anybody who has frequent contact with American firms will realize that this is a bit of a paradox. American firms tend to be rather open, informal institutions. It is common for researchers and journalists to comment that it is far easier to gain access to the world of the American company than to penetrate some of the closed citadels of British business (Dunning, 1970; Jamieson, 1980; Thackray, 1981). Indicators of this informality regularly turn up in the literature. American offices are more likely to be modelled on the open-plan system reflecting both the importance attached to communications in the organization and the smaller emphasis placed on status distinctions between members of the staff. The traditional distinction between the office and the works is also less symbolically marked in American firms. It is, for example, much more common to find managers and workers eating together in the same canteen in American companies than in their British counterparts. All of these features of workplace organization tend to make for a less formal 'feel' to the company and this is reinforced by the tendency to adopt a more informal mode of address.

Overall this mode of operation means that managers working for American firms are much less likely to view them as formal and bureaucratic despite the much wider range of fixed procedures in their organizations. But there is a deeper and rather more significant reason for this phenomenon. The clue is to be found in a classic work on organizations by the American sociologist Alvin Gouldner. In his work *Patterns of Industrial Bureaucracy* (1955) Gouldner found that the 'sheer degree of bureaucracy was not as important in eliciting complaints about red tape as was the *type* of bureaucracy'. In American firms the range of procedures for doing things are not regarded as constraining rules imposed from above. The procedures are rather seen as a set of managerial techniques that every *professional* manager should be able to use to further the good of the firm. Managers working for American firms tend to be better qualified and are more likely to have been on management training courses where such techniques can be acquired. In this sense, it might be legitimate to talk of American managers being more professional than their British counterparts – they have access to and are competent in a far greater range of managerial techniques. The decision-making process in American firms tends to 'combine informal interaction with formalized standard procedures' (Mallory et al., 1983).

Another feature of American firms in Britain contributes to their informal climate. They tend to be more decentralized than their comparable British competitors, in that the locus of authority to make decisions affecting the organization is not confined to the higher levels of authority (Ellis and Child, 1973). Thus, American firms tend to involve their managers more in the decision-making process of their organizations (Thomas, 1969; Stopford, 1972). In a study with an exemplary methodology – a comparison of British and American companies operating in Malaysia – Sim found that 'American subsidiaries tended to practice an open door policy and encourage their employees to participate in the planning process. British subsidiaries tended to confine their participation and information access to their top management personnel only' (Sim, 1977).

A variety of reasons can be offered for such a finding. There could be psychological factors at work deriving from the different set of cultural values to be found in America. For example, in a closely matched sample of American and British companies it was found that American managers tended to have more faith in their subordinates' abilities than British managers (Heller, undated). Structural factors are also likely to be involved. Formalized organizations tend to be relatively decentralized because detailed control from the top is unnecessary if the organization is managed by an elaborate system of procedures (Pugh et al., 1968, 1969; Hage and Aiken, 1967). In addition, the dominant ideology of the leading American management schools and the 'progressive' companies has been termed 'Theory Y' (McGregor, 1960). This stresses the importance of individuals realizing their own potential by being allowed to take a whole range of decisions that would normally be taken higher up the organization. At the managerial level of the firm this has led to the 'management by objectives' movement and MBO schemes are much more likely to be found inside American firms than British. (In this connection, see the chapter on 'Control' by Paul Finlay.) A relatively decentralized organizational structure is clearly consistent with the Theory Y view.

Economists would argue that for firms to make direct investments in a foreign country they must have specific advantages over local firms that can be profitably exploited. In addition to managerial professionalism, much of the American advantage initially lay in novel production techniques (the 'American system of manufacture'), which perfected large-batch and mass production.

Today, however, American firms are concentrated in two sectors of the British economy: science-based, research-intensive industries such as pharmaceuticals and computers; and consumer products.

Several studies show that American companies spend proportionately more than comparable British companies on research and development in the United Kingdom (Gruber, Mehta and Vernon, 1967; EAG, 1976), although not much of this is spent in the British subsidiaries (Dunning, 1970).

The comparative advantage of firms supplying consumer products tends not to lie in any 'technological lead' but in marketing expertise which has been long established. As long ago as 1880 the US pharmaceutical firm of Burroughs, Wellcome & Co. 'adopted aggressive sales techniques, making personal calls on doctors and handing out samples . . . They advertised extensively in medical and trade journals' (Wilkins, 1970). The importance of marketing in American firms continues to the present day. Jamieson (1980) has shown for a matched group of British and American firms operating in the UK that the American firms were more likely to concentrate their efforts on the marketing side of the business while the British firms tended to concentrate on production. This confirms previous work done on a large sample of firms by Political and Economic Planning (PEP, 1966).

The more traditional areas of British business have often suffered hardest at the hands of the American marketeers. A good deal of the quite remarkable penetration of American banks in the corporate market has been put down to the marketing factor. The other obvious source of the Americans' success is the greater sophistication of their procedures and services, such as on-line computer cash management programs (Turnbull, 1982).

Significant differences also exist between the British and American systems in industrial relations including a much lower rate of unionization in the USA, a more decentralized bargaining structure and finally a greater willingness on the part of American unions to fulfil Shaw's dictum that the unions are the 'capitalism of the proletariat' (Banks, 1974; Kassalow, 1969; Seyfarth et al., 1968; Evans, 1982).

Do American firms in Britain pursue distinctively different industrial-relations policies? There are several popular views: that American firms tend to be anti-union; that they are more ruthless in dealing with their employees; and consequently that American firms are more strike-prone.

It is certainly not difficult to find well-publicized examples of American firms that do not recognize trade unions, or who have got involved in protracted recognition disputes (IBM, Kodak, Mars, Heinz). Investigations have however suggested that 'non-recognition of manual-worker trade unions by foreign-owned firms is no worse than amongst domestic firms' (Steur and Gennhard, 1971). The evidence is more equivocal when it comes to white-collar unions, and the white-collar union ASTMS complained about the practices of American companies to the Royal Commission on the Trade Unions (Donnovan, 1968).

There is plenty of anecdotal evidence to support the view that American firms are more ruthless with their employees than British companies. Chruden and Sherman talk of the 'hire and fire' reputation of American firms in Europe (Chruden and Sherman, 1972). A comparative study of a large British and a large American firm sited in the UK noted the 'unusually high risk of becoming a casualty at some point' in the American firm, and the 'propensity to retain dead wood' on the part of the British firm (Sofer, 1970). These features are further supported, albeit impressionistically, by other writers (Farmer, 1968; Thomas, 1969), although a well-matched study by Jamieson (1980) could find no evidence of the difference.

What are the effects of these policies? There is some evidence to suggest that American firms in Britain are more likely to pursue their own independent line rather than conform to the practices of their industry. Many large and influential American firms have left their employers' federation to bargain separately. American firms were notable pioneers of productivity bargaining in the UK, being responsible for six of the first thirteen agreements (EAG, 1976). Furthermore, there is clear-cut evidence of American firms paying more than their British counterparts. In 1973/4 US affiliates, on average, paid 17 per cent more wages and salaries per employee than UK firms (EAG, 1976).

Two major studies conclude that American subsidiaries are *less* subject to strikes than domestic firms (Steur and Gennhard, 1971; Creigh and Makeham, 1978). Moreover the pattern of strikes appears to differ – foreign-owned subsidiaries are more likely to avoid the very short and the very long strike. Perhaps short strikes are largely avoided because of the streamlined company-based bargaining structures, while the higher capitalization of US firms may have led them to be wary of long drawn-out stoppages.

MANAGERS

A business organization is not only defined by its products and structure, but also by the people who create and work that structure, the management personnel. Are the managers who work for American subsidiaries in Britain distinctively different from those who work for British firms?

It is tempting to argue that the most obvious difference is nationality – American firms employ American nationals to run them. Although there are examples of this, one of the most distinctive features of American affiliates is the very absence of American managers in the organization. The US Chamber of Commerce in 1967 estimated that there were about 229 American managers working for US companies (Dunning, 1970); a sample survey by the Economists Advisory Group put the figure at 'less than 0.3% of those employed by U.S. affiliates' (EAG, 1976).

An unpublished study by the author of some nineteen senior US executives working for American companies in Britain suggests several reasons for their presence. First, there are a small group of senior managers working for firms which are (or were) primarily in the business of servicing other American companies operating in Britain. It is felt that this service is best provided by home-country personnel who understand the problems of American companies operating overseas. The most common reason given for the American presence was in terms of a 'managerial gap' – the American manager represented expertise that was not available (or at least not available to them) in the indigenous managerial labour force. Finally, one third of the respondents in the study, when asked about the circumstances leading up to their appointment, reported that there had been a crisis in the subsidiary. The crisis had usually taken the form of some sort of managerial failure at the top and/or a sharp decline in the company's performance. There is evidence to suggest that in times of crisis the parent company falls back on what it is certain of – the expertise and reliability of home-country business experience, but American firms in Britain do *not* have a policy of employing American managers if they can avoid it.

If American companies do not, by and large, employ American nationals as managers, do they recruit distinctively different personnel to manage their plants? Do they organize them differently?

One view that finds a lot of support in the literature is that American firms are committed to using talent without regard to any particular personal characteristic, like age or sex. In the USA all forms of age discrimination in employment have been forbidden by law since 1968. Using national data, it can be shown that there are greater proportions of women in administrative and managerial positions in the USA compared to the UK. Is this pattern carried over to American firms operating in Britain? Despite a good deal of impressionistic evidence, the only two studies with adequately matched samples failed to note any differences (Ellis and Child, 1973; Jamieson, 1980). It seems safe to conclude that American anti-discrimination practices have not been exported across the Atlantic.

The commitment to using high-talent manpower can take other forms, however, the most obvious being the commitment to employ highly qualified people as managers. Many commentators have cited the poor qualifications of British managers as one of the most distinctive features of British management (Leggett, 1978; DEP, 1983). A study using a matched sample of British and American firms found the following significant differences (see Table 1 below).

TABLE I *Percentage of managers in British and American firms with stated qualifications (Jamieson, 1980)*

Qualification	Managers in American firms		Managers in British firms	
	%	N	%	N
Post 'A' level qualifications	56.0	80	33.4	26
First degree or equivalent	36.5	53	29.0	23
Management training	66.9	97	48.7	38

The higher proportion of managers who had received some form of management training in American firms is one indication of the greater emphasis paid to management-development policies inside US subsidiaries. Another indication of this factor is the fact that working for an American firm means that the manager is more likely to be moved around a range of different jobs inside the company (Granick, 1962; Novotny, 1964; Inkson et al., 1970; Ellis and Child, 1973). If American firms had more branches in the UK we might see more evidence of the much higher geographical mobility required of those who work for American firms (it is not for nothing that IBM executives claim that IBM stands for 'I've been moved').

There is a widespread view that in some respects life is harder in American companies. We have already noted the 'hire and fire' policy of some American affiliates and there are some other indications. One of the most commonly cited findings is the intense pressure of work and longer hours to be found in American firms. The greater pressure of work has been noted by Granick (1962) and Jamieson (1980). It can largely be attributed to the fact that American firms impose a greater degree of structure on the managerial role, set targets and deadlines for jobs, etc. In terms of hours of work the evidence seems consistent with the inter-country comparison made by Child and MacMillan (1972) that 'managers as a whole in the United States work very much longer hours than their British counterparts'. This feature of the American way of work does seem to have been exported to the US affiliates (Jamieson, 1980).

EXPLAINING THE DIFFERENCE

We have argued that there is considerable evidence to suggest that the American firm operating in Britain is distinctive *vis-à-vis* its British counterparts. We have described in some detail how they differ but we have not said much about why they differ, or whether they will continue to exhibit such differences.

Several theoretical positions of varying degrees of sophistication are relevant to the discussion. At a simple level is the view that the American firm in Britain is a reflection of the different socio-cultural structure of American society. Thus, for example, it might be argued that the more informal, employee-centred structure of American companies can be explained by reference to the lack of status distinctions inside American society, and this can itself be explained by reference to the historical development of American society (Potter, 1954; Thistlewaite, 1955; McGiffert, 1970; Jamieson, 1980). The significance of culture is denied, or at least demoted, by those who stress that the differences can be accounted for merely because the USA is at a different stage of development. This complex thesis has many variants (Child and Tayeb, 1983). At its simplest (and most simplistic) it is the view that industrial development imposes its own pattern of constraints on society and that economic organizations gradually have to conform (Kerr et al., 1960). A particular version of this thesis is applied to firms, where it is argued that 'organisation building has its logic ... which rests upon the development of management ... and ... there is a general logic of management development which has applicability both to advanced and industrialising countries in the modern world' (Harbison and Myers, 1958). A more complex version of this thesis is that differences between British and American firms can be explained by the fact that Britain and the United States are at different stages of development – generally that American firms represent a more 'advanced' position (Hickson et al., 1974, 1979).

Whatever the merits of these rival views it is clear that the position of the American firm is not static. An interesting element of changing organizational structure which throws light on many of these broader issues is the changing nature of relationships between American companies in Britain and the parent company in the US. Although control relationships between parents and subsidiaries are extremely complex, some general features do emerge. Finance and production generally tend to be more tightly controlled in American subsidiaries than personnel (Jamieson, 1980; Mallory et al., 1983). Marketing tends to be tightly controlled if the product is a branded one and a homogeneous image is required. If the company produces a wide range of products for a variety of markets, a looser mode of control can be expected. The age of the subsidiary can also be a variable. In general the older the subsidiary the more likely that most of the major operating problems will have been solved, so tight control will be unnecessary. The corollary is that younger organizations will need stronger control, and this seems to hold true for subsidiaries that have been directly created by the American parent, although if the American firm acquires a subsidiary via takeover, then relatively loose control tends to be exercised over the organization in the early days. If the parent is centralized, then this will also spread to its subsidiaries. The relationship between size and control takes the form of an 'inverted U'. The relatively small subsidiary is often not regarded as important enough to warrant tight control, while the really big subsidiary is generally well organized enough to conduct its own affairs (Alsegg, 1971).

The control relationships can be fitted into the explanatory framework advanced by Perlmutter (1969). This is a three-stage evolutionary model of the multinational organization, where the minimum autonomy is allowed to subsidiaries. This form of organization gradually evolves into a polycentric type, where the parent company recognizes that local conditions are different from those faced by the parent company and those of other subsidiaries. Finally, at the top of the evolutionary tree is the geocentric company where there is the fullest cooperation between the subsidiaries and the parent on the basis of full equality. The guiding principle for decision-making becomes 'culture-free rationality'. At this stage, it is argued, the nationality of the firm and its managers is no longer of any significance. As the President of IBM World Trade Corporation puts it, 'For business purposes the boundaries that separate one nation from another are no more real than the equator. They are merely convenient demarcations of ethnic, linguistic and cultural entities.' The international executive has become a 'man for all countries' (Webber, 1969). There are some signs amongst the largest American multinationals operating in Britain that they are moving towards 'geocentric' structures.

GOODBYE AMERICA, HELLO JAPAN

Of all the changes that are occurring in the American company in Britain, the most significant is its declining influence on management culture. America herself has seen her economic position eroded. Her growth rate continued to decline while the rates of many industrialized countries continued to grow. In the seventies the Vietnam War channelled off funds and industrial capacity, the dollar was devalued, there was a balance of payments deficit. Watergate raised questions about the supremacy of 'the American way'.

Some commentators argued that the problems of the American economy were deep-seated. The boom decades of the 1950s and 1960s were built on the backlog of innovations from the two previous decades. These were held up because of the Depression and the Second World War. The question is whether American corporations and American management have the ability to compete successfully in the 1980s and 1990s. America has not made much of an impression in the new technologies, and many of its firms seem to be primarily engaged in a rearguard defence of older technologies (Thackray, 1981).

Successful European firms like those in automobiles (Fiat, Volvo, BMW, Renault, VW and Peugeot, and Michelin in tyres), Italy's ingenious appliance manufacturers (Zanussi, Indesit), and West Germany's Hoechst, Bayer and BASF have shown that European managers and managerial structures can more than compete with the Americans in the old industries and some of the new. It is Japan, however, that has done most to break the spell of American management. It has shown that it can compete in the old industries (cars, shipbuilding, steel) and virtually dominate the new. Its management structure and methods look radically different from the American model.

It is clear that American managerial methods are no longer hegemonic in the UK, but the influence of American companies is still very significant. And there are still areas in the economy where American companies can and have made swift inroads. Carpets and 'fast foods' are good examples in recent years, as well as banking which we have already mentioned. But even in banking there are unmistakable signs that the Japanese are coming!

CHAPTER 16

Japanese Management

MICHAEL WHITE

Japanese management provokes us to characterize its distinctiveness and to interpret its success. These two aspects of the 'Japanese question' are inseparable in a discussion which is directed towards management rather than more general cultural or social issues. It is not sufficient to consider what is 'different' about Japanese management, for without the unparalleled economic success of the large Japanese corporations the obsessive concern with Japan and its industrial methods would not exist. Equally, the success of the Japanese would not be so fascinating if it were based on the solid, traditional virtues of the West German economy. The study of Japanese management offers Western readers both the hope of practical gain and the intellectual fascination of a multidimensional puzzle.

Early studies tended to describe a medley of features of Japanese organizations and the distinctiveness of the observations spoke for themselves (Yoshino, 1968). At this stage – before 1970 – very few Japanese companies had developed international or multinational operations, and competition with the West was almost wholly in the form of direct exports. While it was easy for the early investigators and observers to point to remarkable features of the Japanese companies, it was equally easy for sceptics to argue that these features had no relevance for the West since they originated in and reflected a profoundly different society, and were unlikely to be assimilable elsewhere. Once the phase of Japanese multinational operations commenced, the terms of the argument were altered. If Japanese methods could be shown to 'work' in the West, then the practical relevance of Japan-watching would obviously be enhanced. Study of Japanese management is now concerned with what is distinctive, what is successful, and what is *transferable*, and the format of research designs and discussions is predominantly *comparative*.

THE NOTION OF SUCCESS

The notion of success is implicit in much that is written about management, and most managers probably subscribe to a belief in its importance. There are of course many possible criteria for success, not all mutually compatible, but there is in principle no difficulty in selecting *some* criteria, whether in terms of business accounting ratios, productivity measures or competitive advantages. The claim of the Japanese to some kind of pre-eminence in the 'league table' of industrialized nations over the past decade resides in their consistent achievement of success according to the criteria which *they themselves* regard as most important.

An interesting example is presented in a comparative study of the world motor-vehicle industry by Bhaskar (1980). This compares American, European and Japanese manufacturers in terms of their international operations. It is shown that in the years leading up to 1980, some European and American firms surpassed Japanese car makers in terms of profit margins and return on capital employed – accounting ratios which are dear to large Western corporations. Indeed, the most successful firm of this period, on these criteria, appears to have been Ford of Europe. However, Japanese companies do not place a heavy emphasis on profitability but give a much higher priority to market growth and market penetration (Balloun, 1981). On these criteria, Bhaskar shows Japanese car makers comprehensively outperforming American and European competitors.

According to strategic analysts, the Japanese competitive position in international markets has been to a substantial extent based on the unit-cost advantage derived from a large domestic market together with their pursuit of the market-share strategy in export markets (Gregory, 1982). Large volumes of production within short periods have permitted the leading Japanese manufacturers to move rapidly down the 'experience curve' of competitive cost advantage (Abernathy, 1974), widely popularized by the Boston Consulting Group – much of whose own experience, on which their strategic doctrine has been based, was gained in Japan. A particularly sophisticated version of the 'experience curve' hypothesis, combined with exchange rate and relative labour-cost considerations, has recently been proposed by Baxton Inc., and again notably applied to explaining the competitive advantage of Japanese international corporations (Kiechel, 1981).

But low unit costs of production, which give companies greater freedom of competitive manoeuvre, probably cannot be achieved without a conscious striving for higher productivity. And there is indeed ample evidence that improved productivity ranks high amongst the criteria by which Japanese industry assesses its own achievements.

Even at the level of the economy, Japanese government agencies place great emphasis on productivity improvement as a national objective. Economic performance up to the end of the 1970s has been briefly but impressively analysed in these terms by the International Trade Research Office of MITI (1980). The publication demonstrates a widening gap in productivity improvement between Japan and all major competitor countries over the period 1960–80. This difference became specially marked after the 'oil shock' of 1973. Growth of exports, both in terms of comparisons of national export performance, and in terms of the performance of Japanese industries relative to one another, has been strongly correlated with rate of growth of labour productivity.

From a management viewpoint, a particularly important message emerges from this analysis of the contributory factors of improved productivity in Japan, in the periods before and after the 'oil shock'. Up to the early 1970s, Japan's productivity growth depended chiefly on massive capital investment. From 1975 onwards, while capital investment *per se* remained important, its impact was reduced because (crudely speaking) there was less cash available in industry. However, the contribution to labour productivity of 'technological progress' remained at an unchanged level despite reduced capital investment; and this became by far the most important influence on productivity in the electrical sector, which is the spearhead of the Japanese economy. Technological progress is taken to include 'rationalization of capital facilities, improvement of production system, workers' skills, and advancement of technology' – what might broadly be termed a 'knowledge component'. So this strongly suggests the importance of management expertise in sustaining productivity growth.

The importance of labour productivity is perhaps most graphically seen in publications concerning that other well-known preoccupation of Japanese management – product *quality*. It is characteristic of Western management thought that unit labour cost and quality are seen as opposed to a degree and subject to trade-off. No such distinction is apparent in Japanese management thinking. From early stages in the Japanese 'quality movement', which has every right to that name in view of the massive scale of its institutionalization, quality has been partly conceived in terms of the elimination of *waste*, including the elimination of wasteful inspection tasks. In a recent publication of the Nissan Corporation a senior executive talking of the company's steps to improve the *quality* of products emphasized the goal of a 10 per cent annual improvement in labour *productivity* (Kanao, 1982). There are many other examples of Japanese discussions of quality programmes in which the concept of productivity is heavily emphasized (Nakaoka, 1981).

Strong performance in productivity (including quality-based productivity) can be regarded as one of the main means by which Japanese firms have realized the potential of large-volume, high-growth competitive strategies. But this would not have been possible without the continuous development of well-designed, attractive and (in some instances) innovative products. It is apparent that many Japanese themselves view product development and innovation as the key to the forthcoming stage of international competition. An analysis prepared by the influential Nomura Research Institute (Ohtsubo, 1981) argues that the distinguishing features of R & D expenditure in Japan have been, until recently, its extreme decentralization, its relatively small scale and its concentration upon product development and process improvement. In this sense, R & D has been (like quality improvement) inseparable from the Japanese preoccupation with productivity and unit cost of labour. However, the author of this paper argues that, since about 1979, the trend has been for R & D to be used in more fundamental product innovation and diversification, which has become by far the most important function of such investment. Larger scale R & D-based product innovation efforts are now increasingly being funded through inter-company cooperation to overcome some of the limitations of decentralized organization.

Japanese competitive success can therefore be summed up as a combination of business strategy emphasizing high growth and market penetration, if necessary at the expense of short-run profits; a long-term and continuing obsession with labour productivity and unit costs; a product-quality orientation which is not in any way divorced from the productivity obsession; and a continuous effort at product improvement which has been supported by small-scale R & D applied close to the cutting-edge of the business. In the future, there may well emerge a more intensive, large-scale type of research-based product innovation, but the emphasis on labour productivity and low unit cost is unlikely to alter.

This brief review puts us in a better position to examine realistically some of the main research findings or discussions concerning the role of Japanese management in the success of Japanese enterprises. Even though such research has not always been directly guided by the 'success criterion', it seems reasonable in sifting the available material to concentrate on those treatments which appear to shed light on Japanese competitive strength.

JAPANESE HUMAN RESOURCE MANAGEMENT

The most persistent and popular school of explanation of Japanese industrial success has emphasized the special qualities – or perhaps one should say, the *quality* – of the Japanese workforce. In one extreme version, this explanation takes away the credit for success from Japanese management, since it is argued that the virtues of Japanese workers are autonomous and socially derived. According to this view, Japanese firms merely had to develop a reasonable level of commercial and technical competence in order to start reaping the advantages of a workforce which Japanese society had rendered exceptionally industrious, capable and loyal. Such a viewpoint can, however, for all its popular currency, easily be refuted by reference to Japanese sources which describe the development of Japanese industry in the early post-war period (Japan Management Association, 1972). From such accounts, it is apparent that Japanese firms, drawing workers in from rural areas or from traditional craft occupations, faced all the customary difficulties of disciplining them to work regular hours, to restrict the time they spent making tea and socializing, and so on. Moreover, the 1950s were, in many of the growing modern industries, a time of severe conflict between management and workers, pursued fiercely on both sides with strikes, lock-outs and large-scale dismissals.

If Japanese workers are exceptionally industrious and committed, and if low levels of industrial disputes and reasonable wage demands have played an important part in Japanese competitiveness in recent years, then this must be recognized as the result of a learning process, to which Japanese management has presumably contributed. Also, if all or even most of the credit for Japanese success is attributed to the Japanese workers, it becomes difficult to explain how Japanese multinationals continue to succeed when manufacturing in Western countries with Western workers.

But *how*, then, did Japanese management shape its workforce? One long prevalent explanation concerns what has come to be known as 'the Japanese employment system': the formal methods and procedures, and the management tactics of working with those methods and procedures, in what British firms would call 'personnel and industrial relations'. In fact, Japanese firms tend *not* to recognize personnel as a separate 'professional' function, but this does not gainsay the importance which they attach to their 'employment system' (Trevor, 1983).

Three elements of the employment system are generally regarded as most distinctive: lifetime employment, seniority-based payment systems and unions organized on a corporate rather than an industry or occupational basis (Hanami, 1980). Certainly the combination of lifetime job security and steady if gradual advancement in pay for all workers offers a plausible explanation of the loyalty and corporate identification which seems to typify Japanese employees. Other features of the employment system may be no less important in other ways: the seriousness and meritocratic basis of recruitment, the continuous provision of both formal and on-the-job training and the opportunity for participation in some kinds of organizational decision-making – especially in relation to implementation of change (Sasaki, 1981).

This certainly constitutes a formidable package of distinctive practices and methods, yet it now seems very probable that the package has a superficial or symptomatic significance rather than affording a fundamental insight into Japanese management. It is international comparisons and the issue of transferability which reveals this. In the USA, Pascale together with colleagues compared Japanese subsidiaries with American companies in the same industries; they also reversed the process, comparing American subsidiaries in Japan with Japanese home companies (Pascale, 1978a,b). The general conclusion from these studies is that the country of location, rather than the country of origin, determines personnel practices; the Japanese do not export their employment system. The main exception to this is welfare and social provisions for employees, where the US-located subsidiaries appear to have spent massively. In Britain, the main European base of Japanese multinationals, studies have failed to detect the introduction of any substantial elements of the Japanese employment system in Japanese-owned subsidiaries. Instead, Japanese subsidiaries in Britain have shown themselves highly sensitive to local conditions, and have developed their personnel policies in a pragmatic and adaptive manner.

Perhaps, however, it is not so much the formalities of the Japanese employment system which matter, as the underlying management philosophy which has created it. With his article entitled 'Zen and the art of management', Pascale (1978) steered the debate in the USA towards a more impressionistic and speculative account of the Japanese management philosophy. He contrasted the individualistic, aggressive, 'make it happen' type of American manager with the group-centred, unassertive type of Japanese manager who shaped changes gradually and intuitively. By the time of the best-selling book by Pascale and Athos (1981), however, this focus had been widened through involvement in the 'excellent companies' project initiated by McKinsey, the American management consulting firm, partly in response to the pressing competitive challenge posed by Japan to American business. In Pascale and Athos's book, as in the book by Peters and Waterman (1982) which reports the 'excellent companies' study, the view proposed is that *all* the most successful companies, whether American or Japanese, are converging upon a common type of management – although this is perhaps more *characteristic* of large Japanese corporations as a whole than it is of American corporations.

What then is this type of management? The best grip on the argument is provided by the McKinsey 'seven S' schema of management which is used in both sources. The 'seven Ss' are:

strategy, structure, systems, style, skills, staff and superordinate goals; the last may be translated as 'organizational values'. One of the main claims being advanced is that the excellent companies, including the Japanese ones, emphasize the last four rather than the first three of the list. Moreover, according to Pascale and Athos, large Japanese corporations as a whole tend to be indistinguishable from large American corporations in terms of the first three (strategy, structure and systems) but to have a generally higher preoccupation with the last four (although the *best* American companies are level with them in this respect also). But – to continue the argument – it is these last four organizational attributes which concern the human management, rather than the technical-rational management, of the enterprise. In this sense, the position adopted by Pascale and Athos (and by Peters and Waterman) is concerned with the primacy of 'human-resource management'.

In many respects, the argument recalls that of the American 'human relations' school of management thinkers who were so influential in the early post-war period. Indeed Peters and Waterman explicitly accept the parallel, and acknowledge the indebtedness. Yet, as many critics have pointed out, there are deep weaknesses in the 'human relations' position (Fox, 1974). It is not clear that this new formulation avoids the old difficulties. For instance, there is no discussion of how conflicts of interest between employers and workers can be better handled by companies with strong emphasis on 'human relations' or 'human values'. There is no discussion, either, of why satisfaction of employees' needs should support corporate excellence; the literature of job satisfaction continually demonstrates a yawning gulf between the two. Pascale and Athos adopt a mystical view of Japanese management style, which emphasizes the religious and philosophical origins of an 'organic', gradualist and cooperative approach to decision-making and problem-solving. Yet strangely, the picture they paint of their main Japanese example, Matsushita, more clearly reveals a tough-minded, results-oriented rationalism, in which humanistic values are reduced to ritual observances.

Do the arguments of Pascale and Athos, or of Peters and Waterman, explain the competitive strengths of Japanese companies to which attention was earlier drawn? The 'human-resource management' ideas seem most readily applicable, in principle, to explaining Japanese strength in the continuous development of better products. The cadres of engineers, technicians or customer service specialists are presumably the object of much coaching, nurturing, encouraging, involving and inspiring, in companies which value product development highly. However, there is no indication that Pascale and Athos have studied product development processes in Japan; this remains *terra incognita*. The product-development strategy of Matsushita is well known, but the means by which this strategy gets implemented – and why other companies cannot equal them in such a strategy – remain mysterious.

On the subject of unit costs of production, or of the achievement of high levels of productivity and quality, these authors have little to say. Indeed, production is rarely mentioned. Their assumption that Japanese companies do *not* have distinctive manufacturing systems is directly contradicted by evidence which will shortly be described. Nor is their emphasis on gradualism and participative improvement of performance at all consistent with Kamata's (1983) recently translated diary of life on the Toyota production line. Toyota is not, of course, a 'typical' Japanese company, but it surpasses most others in precisely the respects which are here at question – concern for productivity and quality. Kamata leaves one in little doubt that Toyota's achievements in these respects come from an exceptionally hard-driving, disciplinarian and authoritarian system of work.

WORK, DISCIPLINE AND EQUALITY

There is indeed much to be learned about Japanese management by looking directly at production. Here we are fortunate to have one of the pre-eminent contributions to this or to any field of research in industry. The study in question is Dore's *British Factory – Japanese Factory*. Although published in 1973, and although limited (for most of its detailed evidence) to four factories – two each in Britain and Japan – Dore's book has no competitors either as a description or as an analysis of life on the Japanese shopfloor.

The main focus of the study was the Japanese 'employment system'. Dore was not concerned so much with the possibility of transfer (although he did regard it as possible that there would be some movement of British companies towards the Japanese employment model), as with the explanation of national distinctiveness in industrial relations. In exploring this theme, he went far beyond the formalities of lifetime employment or corporate unionism. The study discusses, albeit in a subsidiary way, work systems, attitudes to work, discipline and the role of supervision. The insightful observations in which the book abounds yield many hints about the foundations of Japanese industrial success, even though this was a topic which Dore did not address directly.

The picture which Dore paints of the Hitachi factories is of a meticulously organized and closely supervised world. The pace of work is not necessarily intense (although in Kamata's account of Toyota it is, to an extreme degree); but discipline shows itself through conscientious attendance, the use of the whole working day for production – without encroachment by slack timekeeping or slow starts after meal-breaks – and the acceptance by workers that the needs of the company take priority over their own wishes, even to the extent of sacrificing holidays. There were, proportionally, twice as many supervisors in the Japanese factories as in the British (which were closely matched in terms of product range and technology), and the supervisors had a far more dominant position in the system of communications and control, and in looking to the individual worker's welfare.

In another pioneering study, Takamiya (1979) examined four manufacturing plants located in Britain, and involved in the production of electrical consumer goods: two being Japanese subsidiaries, one a US-owned subsidiary and the fourth a leading British manufacturer. Takamiya argued that if 'employment systems' and 'human relations' really had the effect of creating happy, enthusiastic or committed workers, then this should be revealed through the workers' job satisfaction. But just as job satisfaction studies in the US had failed to reveal the expected differences, Takamiya also showed that the employees in the four companies which he studied had broadly similar levels of satisfaction. Yet on measures of productivity and quality, the Japanese plants were clearly outperforming the US-owned and British plant.

Takamiya suggested that the explanation for the superior performance of the Japanese firms resided in specific production-management practices, and in the way in which members of management were trained. At the British firm for example, quality-control problems were being tackled by introducing expensive computer-aided test equipment (without notable success), while at the Japanese factories the emphasis was on close examination by engineers at points on the production line where faults were occurring, followed by further instruction for the operators concerned, and assistance in eliminating faults by the design of small, inexpensive jigs or warning devices. The managers in the Japanese firms were much better informed about the whole production system, rather than just their own immediate responsibility within it, because they had been moved around the departments in the course of their training, and were expected to take a company-wide rather than a departmental viewpoint in problem-solving.

If the studies of Dore and Takamiya are put together, the suggestion is that understanding of Japanese success in production management is likely to come from closer observations of the details of management practice. This approach was followed in a study by White and Trevor (1983), which obtained the perceptions of British employees in three Japanese-owned factories and three Japanese-owned financial organizations in London. The study also compared the results, for the largest manufacturing plant, with a sample survey of industrial workers in the community where it was located.

Once again, the study found little evidence of differences either in job satisfaction or in evaluations of management from a human-relations viewpoint. But workers did perceive the Japanese firms as being 'different' from British employers, they particularly emphasized the difference in the approach of management, and they evaluated the working practices in their organizations in a highly distinctive manner. Meticulous organization, strict observance of rules and procedures, tight timekeeping disciplines, priority given to quality over quantity of production, double-checking to achieve quality, personal quality responsibility, and close involvement of managers in the details of work were among the significant responses of the British workers.

The more qualitative material from this study supports many of the observations made by Dore in Japanese plants, and hence suggests that Japanese practice, in certain essentials, is transferable to British industry. Strong discipline, careful use of time for production, and high supervisory ratios were all conspicuously present in the main case study. More important, perhaps, British production workers appeared to respond to these demands in a positive and enthusiastic way. The 'work ethic' referred to in the Japanese studies of Dore seems to be available in Britain if rekindled in an appropriate way.

One of the questions which White and Trevor raise is how, in fact, it is possible for Japanese companies to make radical changes in working practices, and particularly to introduce a more disciplinarian style of management, when the industrial-relations tradition of British manufacturing is strongly based on 'custom and practice' and on a high degree of worker control on the shopfloor. They argue that this is essentially a problem of authority, and of the basis on which authority is legitimized. Again, it is Dore who suggests an explanation. Modern Japanese society continues to show great respect for status and authority, yet at the same time is exceptionally egalitarian. Egalitarianism comes from meritocratic selection for upward mobility, combined with the post-war democratization of all social institutions, which took place in a wave of revulsion against the previous regime with its authoritarian and militarist inclinations. Thus nearly all Japanese regard themselves as 'middle class' (De Roy, 1979); and just as the sharp distinctions between middle class and working class, which persist in Britain, are impossible in Japan, so also there is no great divide in a Japanese company between managers and workers, but rather a subtle continuous gradation of status. According to Dore, it is this egalitarianism which accounts to a considerable degree, though there are other influences, for the Japanese workers' acceptance of work disciplines and, indeed, their close identification with the interests of the organization. It is relatively easy for the Japanese worker to see himself as being 'on the same side' as his management.

White and Trevor found that feelings of egalitarianism continued to play an important role in their British cases. Acceptance of Japanese management was largely based on perceptions that they were closely involved in production, treated workers on equal terms, wore the same uniform overalls, and ate at the same table with workers in the canteen. Although these comments applied to Japanese-trained British managers as well as to Japanese ex-patriates, there was some feeling that the British managers did not carry through the Japanese approach to management so fully, and there were fears of 'going back to the old British ways' when the expatriates pulled out.

It is worth stressing that Japanese 'egalitarianism' does not merely consist in symbols such as uniforms or single-status canteens, although these can be important. The Japanese practice of management appears to emphasize (in these cases at least) direct involvement in production, rather than a remote 'expert' role. While Japanese technical expertise was much admired, their willingness to impart information to workers made a powerful impression.

TECHNIQUES AND TACTICS OF JAPANESE MANAGEMENT

The ideas about work and authority which have just been described suggest that Japanese management is often highly 'production centred', in two senses: people (including management) are subordinated to the task of the enterprise, and the key to that task is seen as lying in the production line itself.

This may seem a somewhat 'old-fashioned' viewpoint. However, it is consistent with the emphasis on productivity and unit costs which has been referred to earlier. In the most recent phase of thinking about the Japanese business challenge, American manufacturing specialists have begun to recognize the exceptional character of Japanese management specifically in the production area. In his widely cited paper, Hayes (1981) has argued that the Japanese have achieved their advantage by persisting with precisely those 'old-fashioned' virtues of production management which American industry began to let slide in post-war years. In a parallel paper, Wheelwright (1981) has spoken of the strategic character of operations management in Japanese management thinking. Whereas American companies have assumed that strategy is concerned with acquisition and diversification, capital investment planning, or marketing postures, the Japanese have recognized that excellent methods of supply and manufacture create powerful leverage on the company's strategic position *vis-à-vis* its competitors. Accordingly, they give it much higher status, and devote more resources to it, especially management resources.

Schonberger (1982) takes a further step in this direction and argues that the leading Japanese manufacturers have developed fundamentally more effective techniques of production than Western industry. He concentrates on two, both of which have become widely known through the example of Toyota: the 'just-in-time' (JIT) production control and supply management system, and the 'total quality control' (TQC) procedures. In a sense Schonberger elaborates on knowledge which was already available, but there are two respects in which his treatment is an advance. First, his account is illustrated throughout by reference to a US-based Japanese subsidiary (Kawasaki); it seriously examines the transferability of Japanese production techniques (especially JIT) to US industry, and comes to a positive conclusion. Second, and more important, Schonberger discusses at considerable length the cumulative repercussions of JIT and TQC on other aspects of production (such as space and layout requirements, or the man-power in stores, inspection and other ancillary functions), and equally upon the behaviour of management and workers. The book is not based on any substantial body of research evidence; yet the observations and insights of a specialist in production engineering, who is also alive to the interactions between techniques and behaviour, repay close attention.

Schonberger illustrates his thesis not only through the formal systems of JIT and TQC, but by drawing attention to associated Japanese practices such as doing away with production conveyor systems, eliminating or minimizing the role of specialist staff in quality control, deliberately sending only vague and general com-ponent specifications to suppliers, dispensing with goods-inwards inspection, and (in some circumstances) only checking the first and last item in a production batch. In all these cases, the account he gives of the advantages bestowed by the policies suggests that Japanese management assesses the long-run adaptation of people (such as workers, inspectors and suppliers) to these policies, rather than merely the immediate effect.

The most fully illustrated case is the JIT system, as operated in Kawasaki. The JIT system controls production by 'pulling' batches of sub-assemblies through to final assembly on the demand of the latter; by then pulling parts through to sub-assembly on their demand; and so on. At the same time, production lot sizes are made as small as possible: the supposed advantages of long production runs are deliberately cast aside, and this is made economically feasible by concentrated efforts on minimizing set-up time between batches. The main financial effect of JIT production is to reduce work-in-process inventories to a substantial degree. But the effects on workers' behaviour are also considerable. Because lot sizes are so small, and because work on one section is only carried out when it is required immediately by the next section down the line, there is rapid and direct feedback concerning quality. Moreover, the presence of 'the customer' becomes much more real. Final assembly is producing only those items which are needed by sales; it is not separated from the customer by making for finished goods stock. Similarly, each section of production becomes a surrogate customer for the section or sections which supply it, for they too are not making for intermediate stocks.

In general, Schonberger observes, JIT production, in stripping away both buffer stocks and the delay-times of long production runs, tends to reveal weaknesses of production which would otherwise be hidden. Whether this effect was anticipated when JIT was first introduced is not known; but there seems little doubt that Japanese management working with this system is fully aware of it, and deliberately *intensifies* it. The Kawasaki system described by Schonberger includes the provision of yellow signal lights which operators can use when they run into trouble. When management notices that yellow lights are rarely in use, they take workers out of the production teams and put them onto other non-production activities. The de-manned sections then begin to run into difficulties in keeping up with production demands; yellow lights come on; and supervisors, production engineers and others must pitch in to overcome the troubles by honing production to a finer pitch of efficiency.

Schonberger's analysis is an important step towards developing a comprehensive understanding of Japanese production management, in which techniques and systems could be linked to worker behaviour, and to supervisory and management practices. However, the book also makes it apparent how little is yet known at this detailed level, especially about management practices. The techniques and systems are much easier to capture and describe than the day-to-day actions which management must take to operate them effectively.

It is also necessary to stress that JIT and TQC are only two of the production systems in use in Japan. They have been widely used in mechanical assembly, but in the electrical and electronics goods industries, or in shipbuilding and heavy engineering, for example, quite different systems – no less radical – have been developed. Western understanding of these systems has been hampered while they existed only in Japan, and were described only in Japanese-language publications. With the advent of more Japanese manu-facturing plants in the West, and with an increasing tendency for Japanese firms to produce technical summaries of their production and quality methods in English, the fertile originality of the Japanese in the development of production-management methods will become widely appreciated.

CONCLUSIONS AND DIRECTIONS

This review of Japanese management began with an outline of the features of its success in international competition. Before it can be claimed that Japanese management is understood – in any practical sense – it must be possible to explain the means by which success has been achieved, and to judge how far these means are transfer-able to enterprises in other industrial countries. This provides a standard by which our knowledge of Japanese management can be assessed.

The most solid progress, according to this criterion, has been made in the area of production management. The Japanese have demonstrated a persistent dedication to the reduction of unit costs and the achievement of continuous improvements in productivity of labour. The research conducted in Japan, the USA and Britain collectively yields many insights into the methods of management which have been involved. We can see radical departures in the design of production systems and techniques, which appear to have been devised with a particular insight into the long-term re-percussions on the behaviour of participants. We see management practices which stress the importance of direct involvement in production, and draw managers and technical experts into a cease-less improvement of fine details. We see quality consciousness given an overriding importance, and yet considered in many ways as merely the most powerful method of achieving high productivity. We see a hard-driving, dedicated and disciplinarian management which assumes that workers will respond to the demands made upon them – the 'assumption of virtue', as Dore calls it. And we see a natural 'egalitarianism' of management which, at least in Britain, seems capable of making the Japanese style of management accepted and respected.

At this point, the temptation to extract higher-level concepts from the evidence becomes strong. Yet this temptation should at present be resisted. Experience so far suggests that progress in understanding Japanese management has come from detailed observation and analysis, preferably as close to the point of production as possible, rather than from generalization or from more global views of Japanese corporations. This could be because the state of knowledge has not advanced sufficiently to enable higher-level concepts to be derived. Or it could be that Japanese management is not conformable to Western higher-level conceptualization, if indeed any management is, but will always be best appreciated by observing it at the detailed level, where the Japanese themselves seem to thrive.

It has to be admitted that, even at the detailed level and in regard to production, less is known than remains unknown. Even if we can describe some of the means by which Japanese management achieves its effects, we know very little about the process by which these approaches have been learned. Certainly, in the well-known case of Japanese quality-improvement methods, a long and painful path of learning had to be trod, and to appreciate this casts a quite different light on the problem of treading the same path of development in the West. On a shorter time-scale, virtually nothing is known of the design process for the new production plants, especially those established in the West, or more generally of how Japanese management assesses the requirements for setting up a new manufacturing operation.

And, of course, although the importance of production can justifiably be stressed, that is not the whole story by any means. Product design and development have, as earlier stated, played a major part in the Japanese competitive success. Although some case-study material is available in this area, it is couched in broad terms. The experience of studies in the production area suggests that there may be much to learn by conducting more detailed comparative studies of management practice in design-engineering and product-development departments. The same can be said of strategic planning and decision-making, although the difficulties of conducting research in that field, even in Western companies, are notorious.

Despite the obvious limitations on existing knowledge, some claim for the relevance and practical worth of studying Japanese management can already be made. The ability of the Japanese to devise methods of management totally at variance with Western assumptions, both technical and human, and yet to achieve outstanding results, has administered a refreshing shock to management thinking. It is not necessarily the case that Western management must follow where the Japanese lead, but at least the existing assumptions must now be seriously questioned in the effort to develop more competitive policies and practice.

SECTION C

MANAGEMENT OF FUNCTIONAL AREAS

Introduction

A powerful *raison d'être* for the present section is a continuation of the idea of context. Any manager in any functional area is disadvantaged, maybe emasculated, without a knowledge and understanding of at least the contingent functions: so they are all context for somebody, and in their totality they are the corporation itself.

While companies are structurally differentiated into these functional areas of sales, personnel, R & D, and so on, the way in which managerial activities are divided up is arbitrary and variable in real life. It is important to take on board the fact that there are no absolute boundaries because, *inter alia*, this is reflected in the perceptions of contributors in this section. In short, there are overlaps, especially between the chapters on marketing, production and purchasing.

Our idea of continuing context may be given a wider application in this section: that is, where it has seemed a good idea not to treat one of these elements solely and simply as a corporate function, we have not done so. Thus, for instance, with R & D and finance, contributions have explored the wider nature of the entity, or its professional manifestation, rather than just treating it as a department in business firms.

As editors we have also encouraged contributors to come up to date and indeed to 'lean into the future' in their accounts of these functional areas. Or, to put it another way, they have inclined to present a picture of best practice in these functional areas rather than to detail the (imperfections of the) all-firms average.

The section in a sense culminates with a chapter on corporate policy. While corporate policy is clearly not a functional area *comme les autres* it does represent the outcome of informative inputs from the other areas, and is the apotheosis of the company's desire to shape its future. Finally, the book concludes with some thoughts about the future, not a finite attempt to predict it, but some discussion of the way the unknown future relates to the experienced present.

CHAPTER 17

Marketing

DAVID FORD

THE NATURE OF MARKETING

Marketing is the process by which buyers and sellers come together
for a mutually satisfactory transaction. They seek each other out,
try to assess each other's requirements, interest the other party in
themselves, and jointly consummate a transaction. The resem-
blance to a mating ritual is not incidental.

We are conscious of our part in the process as buyers when we
deliberately search through brochures, visit stores, or discuss
products with friends. We also observe some of the marketing
activity which is directed towards us. For example, we see the
advertising and display of products and we experience sales efforts
by door-to-door salespeople, etc. However, we do not normally see
many of the other marketing activities which manufacturers engage
in: product development and testing, selection of distribution
channels, producing advertising, or even market research (except
when we are interviewed). Even these activities form only a small
sub-set of marketing. Most of the things which we buy as consumers
are the end result of a long and complex chain of transactions
between raw material producers and the manufacturers of finished
products, machinery and containers; and between wholesalers and
retailers. This is industrial marketing and is often contrasted with
consumer marketing by the close contact and relationship between
the buying and selling organizations.

This relationship is quite different from the kind of purchase that
we are typically involved in as consumers where the contact
between the buyer and producer is very impersonal. Many companies talk to us only through advertising and we rarely ever communicate back to them except perhaps through market-research
interviews or letters of complaint. Few of us have met Mr Kellogg
or Mr Mars. Despite what we may often think, consumer marketing

is based on trust. We buy products through mail order and usually expect that they will arrive. We pick a pack of cornflakes from the supermarket shelf and are reasonably confident that the pack will contain cornflakes and, if it says 500 grams on the side, that there will be 500 grams there. If this does not seem remarkable, it is interesting to contrast our style of transactions with those which may be found in a Middle Eastern market or in any other previous period of history in this country. Manufacturers create brands through advertising and the associations of features or quality which brands have for us is the basis of our trust. We should also note the vast scale of marketing by adding up the number of transactions that we are each involved in during a typical day: the purchase of television programmes through a licence payment, the purchase of bus tickets, of groceries, restaurant or taxi services, hairdressing, etc. When people say that we live in a market economy, this does not just mean that our economic affairs centre on the process of buying and selling. Marketing is an integral and major part of our activities, of our view of each other and of our way of living.

So far, we have talked of marketing in a general context. However, much of what we speak of as marketing is the set of activities that manufacturers carry out to get us to buy their products or services. This is 'managerial marketing' and for the rest of this chapter we will explore some of its techniques.

THE MARKETING CONCEPT

The marketing concept was introduced not as another managerial technique like work study or discounted cash flow, but rather as a way of thinking or an approach to business. We can understand the marketing concept by contrasting it with two other ideas which were said by marketers to be current before it arrived on the scene (King, 1965). The first of these is the production orientation in which manufacturers see their primary role as the production of goods or services. Products are produced in quantity, and the emphasis is on output, internally generated standards of quality and on product specifications determined by the manufacturers themselves. This is perhaps the orientation we would associate with

Victorian England; with rapidly expanding population and newly opening markets in the colonial world. Indeed, it also existed in immediate post-war Britain. These were the days of rationing, when goods were 'on allocation'. It was easy to sell the products which you wished to supply, because supplies were short. Customer requirements did not need to be thought of in any great detail. The reader may wish to consider the extent to which production orientation is still around in some of our companies, whether they produce what *they* think we should buy.

The world then moved into the era we refer to as that of sales orientation. We may think of this in the U K as being after rationing finished in the 1950s, when, perhaps for the first time for a long time, supply outstripped demand. This orientation is characterized by increased efforts by companies to sell their products; more sales people, more advertising and more promotion, but what was being sold remained constant. In other words, engineers designed products (after all, engineers know about design), production people produced products (they know about production), and *then*, and only then, did the sales force become involved in selling the product. This orientation means that, when sales are down, the company makes greater efforts to sell its products, to increase its advertising, or to reduce its price. We can also see much of sales orientation in the efforts of many manufacturers today.

Marketing contrasts with these previous approaches. It is not simply advertising or selling, although it may involve these activities. Marketing starts with three questions:

1. What do customers want (or need, of which more later)?
2. Where and when do they want it?
3. What are they prepared to pay for it?

Thus marketing is the beginning of the business process. After it has found the answer to these questions, the business must determine whether it can provide these requirements *profitably*. If this is so, then it is the designer's task to translate customer requirements into products or services and for the production department to produce them. The adoption of marketing thus involves a certain humility. Whereas the previous orientations involved the company believing that it knew what it should produce for the market, a marketing orientation means that the company only produces what the market requires (and what it can make a profit by producing).

PROBLEMS IN IMPLEMENTING MARKETING

Marketing is a very simple idea, but it involves a tremendous change in many companies, which a large number of them have been unable to achieve. Marketing involves the following beliefs:

1. The assets of a company have little value without customers.
2. A company's livelihood is based on providing customer satisfaction.
3. Customers are attracted through promises, but held by satisfaction.
4. Marketing can make the promises, but it is the whole company which creates the satisfaction.
5. Therefore, marketing must control, or at least influence, other departments (derived from Kotler, 1980).

This latter point means that marketing is far too important to leave to a marketing department. Production, finance, personnel, indeed the whole of an organization must be attuned towards providing customer satisfaction. However, frequently marketing fails to penetrate into companies. Especially in large companies, production and other departments don't have contact with the market; they don't see the importance of the market to their activities and delivery is far removed from promise.

The distinction between wants and needs which was made above is the key to another problem in implementing marketing. For example, if we asked a housewife in the early 1950s what she wanted to make her clothes washing better, she would not have said that she wanted an automatic washing machine. At that time they did not exist. However, the marketer may have said that she *needed* an automatic washer and may have set in train the design and production of such a machine. Having produced what is believed to be the customer's need the task is then that of making the customer *want* it through the whole process of advertising and selling. Thus, one uncharitable interpretation of marketing is that it is one group of people who believe that they know what we need better than we know ourselves. They then devote great efforts and money to make us believe them! For example, a major product introduction being planned at the time of writing is clothes and chairs which have speakers embedded in them so that we can 'feel' music as well as hear it. This is based on the marketing companies' view that we need this product, and they will spend large sums to make us want it (Garner, 1983). People do not like being told what they need. More generally, many of us have an ambivalent attitude towards the idea that our welfare must always be associated with the proliferation of new goods and services. Marketing is often associated in our minds with this materialistic ideal and this is a reason for its poor reputation.

Another problem is that marketing is an extremely difficult activity to carry out. Even if the company can determine customers' requirements, it may not be profitable for them to provide what the customer wants. Therefore, companies may resort to trying to get consumers to buy what is convenient or profitable for them to sell. In this way, it is easy for marketing to degenerate into a sales orientation, which may indeed be profitable in the short term.

Few companies nowadays would not claim to be market-oriented. Despite this, consumer advice bureaux, and consumer groups and associations have proliferated, all of which aim to protect consumers against the actions of companies supposedly trying to satisfy their every whim. This must lead to the conclusion that marketing is an ideal which may not always be implemented in practice.

WHY PEOPLE BUY

A tremendous range of factors may influence us to buy one or other product. We may buy new shoes because our old ones leak, or a microwave to save time spent in the kitchen. We may also buy a certain brand of jeans because our friends have that brand. In other words, we wish to be associated with these friends and seek to make ourselves similar to them through the clothes that we wear, the drinks we drink, and so on. Householders, similarly, will furnish their houses as a way of expressing their particular tastes or to show how wealthy they are. Often people of a different social class will purchase different products or services. Those who are, or aspire to be, of the upper middle class may spend their money on sending their children to the schools of the upper middle class, or living in the areas where the upper middle classes live. Although these factors are extremely complex, they are part of a process by which we say, 'What sort of car, or house, is bought by someone like me (or someone like the kind of person I would like to be)?' Thus, we express the kind of person that we think we are, or would like to be, through our purchases of goods or services. To illustrate how important this self-projection is, think how infrequently people buy things which do not fit with their range of purchases. For example, someone with a house full of Habitat furniture, would be unlikely to have a vase of plastic flowers in their window!

THE MARKETING MIX

The marketer really has very few things available to influence customers to buy products or services. Those influences we refer to as the marketing mix:

　　the product or service offered;
　　the price charged;
　　the way products are promoted;
　　the way products are distributed (McCarthy, 1978).

All other factors which may affect which brand of product we buy or whether we buy at all are beyond the control of the manufacturer. The most important thing about the marketing mix is that the combination of the four elements is vital, and they are clearly interrelated. For example, if a company spends a lot of money on product development and on massive advertising and promotion then it will find it difficult to reduce the price of its product. Companies within the same market vary in the type of mix which they adopt. Some place major emphasis on supposedly high-technology products at high price and restrict the distribution of their products to a number of selected outlets. Others may sell lower-technology products at low price, with extensive distribution and national advertising. Examples of differences in marketing mixes can be seen in such markets as consumer electronics.

Compare, for example, the marketing of Amstrad with that of Sony or Technics.

We can now examine each of the elements of the marketing mix in turn.

Product

When thinking of a marketing mix, the term product can be used to include not only tangible products, but also services. For example, a holiday company must consider the type of holidays which it offers, whether it distributes them conventionally through travel agents or by direct mail, the extent and nature of the promotion it uses, and the prices which it charges.

The product is obviously at the core of a company's marketing efforts and it will devote extensive resources to product development. Through this it seeks to translate its view of customer requirements into a tangible form. This process is both expensive and fraught with problems. It has been estimated that for every fifty-eight new product ideas only one will successfully reach the market (Booz, Allen and Hamilton, 1965). Companies try to reduce the expense of the process and the failure rate of their products during development by seeking out the maximum number of new product ideas and having procedures for assessing and, if necessary, rejecting them. Products should not be developed by R & D departments alone but under the control of a marketing department to make sure that during development they retain their relevance to the market. For example, research engineers may seek to 'improve' a product during its development process or they may even provide features which are not required by potential customers. This may make it impossible for the company to sell the product profitably at its target price. The importance of new product development can be stressed even more when we consider the rate of product failure after reaching the market. William Ramsey, Development Director of General Foods (US), concluded in 1982 that the success rate for major new grocery brands in the UK is around 3 per cent. Also, even successful products on the market have a limited life before they are rendered obsolescent by the introduction of products by competitors.

Price

The first thing to be said here is that the price of a product on the market bears no necessary relationship to the cost of producing it. If this appears an odd statement, the reader is invited to consider whether an exclusive French perfume would continue to be successful, if sold at a price of 50 pence per litre! Although cost information is an important element in price setting, the price of a product is much more than a measure of its cost to produce, or even its cost to buy. The price is one aspect of the product which we buy. Sometimes, we like to buy expensive brands to indulge ourselves. At other times, price is one of the few indicators we have of the quality of different brands and the marketing manager must bear this in mind when setting prices. The three main elements in a pricing decision are the company's cost of production; the market's perception of the value of the product; and the competition which the company faces in its markets.

Pricing solely on the basis of the company's cost is the most straightforward method. Essentially it involves the calculation of the variable cost per unit of product, e.g. materials used, direct labour input, together with an allocated amount for indirect costs or overheads. A percentage profit margin is then added to arrive at the price. Unfortunately, this approach negates the marketing concept by setting prices from the perspective of the company, rather than of the market. Thus the price determined may be higher or lower than the market requires. The method also suffers from the difficulty of deciding a correct allocation of indirect costs. Despite this, the use of standard mark-ups is simple and safe and is used widely in the building trade and even in sophisticated marketing organizations such as retailers. Here the large number of lines carried and the importance of fully recovering a store's overheads militate against other methods.

A manufacturing company is likely to use its cost structure as a basis for calculating the minimum price it could charge at different projected levels of demand, and still break even or achieve a minimum acceptable return on the product. Thereafter, its research will be directed towards determining the price which consumers will be prepared to pay for the product (or the likely demand at different price levels). Pricing a product which is new to the market will involve comparison with the prices of near equivalents. For example, a new snack food may involve price comparisons with potato crisps and instant soups.

The marketers of a new product often consider their pricing in terms of a 'skimming' or a 'penetration' strategy. Skimming involves setting a high price for the product. The company can then count on a high profit per unit from the less price-sensitive customers. Subsequently, and after, it is hoped, establishing a reputation for high quality or exclusivity, the price can be reduced to appeal to more price-sensitive buyers. This strategy largely depends on there being technological or other barriers to the rapid entry of competitors. Where these do not exist, then the manu-facturer may opt for a penetration strategy. This involves a low price with the aim of building up a mass market in a short time. It may also have the advantage of delaying competitive entry because this low price raises the break-even point.

The manufacturer of a brand which is already on the market faces different pricing considerations. Here, concern will rest heavily on the likely pricing actions of competition. The impor-tance of an integrated marketing mix is again emphasized here. By product improvement and promotional activity many marketers try to avoid having to sell their product solely on price. Marketers are aware that it is easy to make a 5 per cent reduction to achieve short-term sales, but realize that such a small price reduction may involve a 50 or 60 per cent reduction in profit.

Promotion

Promotion is one of the most visible aspects of marketing. It includes all of the activities carried out by companies in order to transmit a marketing message to potential customers. It includes media advertising, such as press and television; sales promotion by coupons, in-store displays, etc.; and direct sales effort involving door-to-door or telephone selling. In the same way that companies have a marketing mix, so they develop a promotional mix. This is the combination of the different means of promotion which they consider optimum in carrying out their strategy. For example, the

escalation in the cost of TV advertising has caused some manufacturers to change their promotions mix to other media, or to
increase promotional activity at the point of sale.

Advertising is usually subcontracted to outside organizations
who design and plan campaigns. These in turn will subcontract
such tasks as filming TV commercials. The high cost of national
advertising can be indicated by one example. Towards the end of
1982 Nestlé relaunched its existing Gold Blend Instant Coffee on
the proposition that: 'We believe you'll prefer it to fresh ground
coffee.' The media expenditure on this in just a few months was
£2.5 million which compares with an annual expenditure of £4.47
million on the company's Nescafé brand.

This cost can only be justified if the company is aiming for a large
share of a national market. For other companies, the nature of their
market and their limited resources mean that promotion is
restricted to direct mail (leaflets) to selected customers or sales
efforts to stores and distributors. This is in the hope that sales effort
will then be made by the stores to the final customer. This is known
as a push strategy. A pull strategy is one of media advertising to
customers, to pull the product through the stores.

Place

The distribution of a product often involves wholesalers, retailers,
shippers and agents in addition to the manufacturer, who together
comprise the marketing channel. The channel companies are
usually independent, and their own aims may conflict with those of
the manufacturer. Also, they are often larger than the manufacturer. For example, Asda, the Co-ops, Sainsbury and Tesco
together account for over 40 per cent of UK grocery sales. The
manufacturer must choose the appropriate channel for its products.
For example, the launch of a specialized product such as compact-
disc audio systems involves considerable consumer education, to
demonstrate its superior performance. Because of this, a manufacturer is likely to concentrate on distribution through specialist
hi-fi retailers. In contrast, widespread distribution is a crucial factor
in the success of many convenience products such as disposable
razors or chocolate bars.

An example of the importance of the distribution element of the marketing mix is provided by C. & J. Clarke, the shoemakers. Clarkes face competition from the British Shoe Corporation, which owns and controls most retail outlets – Dolcis, Saxone, etc. Clarkes must therefore sell their own shoes through the relatively small number of shops which they own, together with the independent shoe shops, which are only responsible for 17 per cent of total shoe sales. Clarkes must aim for a major share of these sales and also try to help these retailers develop their business. To do this they provide design advice to the shops and about twenty-five new shoe retailers open each year with the aid of loans from Clarkes, in return for an agreement to take a certain volume of Clarkes shoes (*Marketing Week*, 29 April 1983). In this way, Clarkes seek to develop and ensure adequate distribution for their products. It is a battle with their competitors, not just for the attention of the consumer, but also for the shelf space of the retailer.

Finally, in considering the marketing mix, it is worth noting that not only does it represent the combination of variables which comprise the market offering, it is also the combination which we buy. Thus, we do not buy just the physical product, but the product, with the symbolism which is created by advertising, with its availability through distribution and at a price which we are prepared to pay.

MARKETING OVER TIME

Developing a marketing strategy for a product is not a static activity as consumer tastes and competitors may change over time. Marketers use the product life cycle to describe this process (Figure 1).

The product life cycle is based on a biological analogy that all products go through a cycle from introduction onto the market, through rapid growth in sales, to maturity, associated with low or zero growth in sales, and finally of decline. It is important to note that the PLC is *descriptive* of a generalized process, rather than being predictive of the behaviour of all products. Nevertheless, it is a valuable aid to management thinking and an aid to the planning of marketing through a product's life.

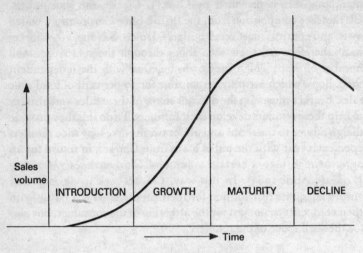

Sales volume

INTRODUCTION GROWTH MATURITY DECLINE

Time

1 The product life cycle

The Introduction Stage

Some of the major tasks of a company introducing a new product are to make the market aware of it, to educate potential customers as to how and when to use it, and to gain adequate distribution. Making customers aware of the product is likely to involve very heavy expenditure on advertising. This task has recently been faced by Black & Decker in getting across the message to consumers about its automatic painting device for DIY enthusiasts.

Following the period of intense marketing effort with the new product, sales growth (if it occurs at all) is likely to be rapid and the product moves into the growth phase. This brings a change in market conditions and the marketing tasks facing the manu-facturer. The success of the new product is likely to attract competition. Although competition will take a share of the avail-able business, its advertising efforts are likely to expand the overall market and thus take the market-development load off the shoulders of the initial manufacturer. The rapid expansion in the recently created market often means high profits for the many new members of the market. An interesting recent example was the multiplicity of small companies in the rapidly growing personal hi-fi market. Similar conditions existed many years ago in the growth phase of the market for black-and-white televisions.

Maturity and Decline

However, the market for black-and-white TVs (and subsequently colour TVs) moved into maturity – a period of slower growth or approaching saturation. This often leads to a weeding-out of the less competitive firms. Manufacturers in mature markets often seek to establish strength in a particular segment or segments of the market, that is, a group of customers which have distinct and different requirements. This may shield these companies from the price competition which is likely to increase in a mature market. Additionally, faced by successive introductions of newer and more up-to-date products, some manufacturers will 'relaunch' their product, with new advertising, packaging or features, e.g. 'New' Persil, etc.

In this way, the length of time that a product (or an individual manufacturer's brand) spends in the mature phase varies considerably. Despite this, there is an inevitability about the move from maturity to decline. This occurs as the product is overtaken by others based on more advanced technology, e.g. mechanical by electronic calculators; or where consumer purchases switch to other areas after saturation has been achieved, e.g. video recorders as compared to colour televisions. The marketing task is now that of managing this decline, that is, seeking to maintain sales as long as possible before the company itself launches a replacement product. An example was the Crusader range of Ford Cortinas aimed to bolster sales in the months before the launch of the Sierra.

The PLC also emphasizes the importance of planning for the life of a product and the necessity of maintaining investment in new products while existing products are still selling and before their decline in sales and profitability. A major factor in the decline of British Leyland and Chrysler (now Talbot) in the UK was that both companies did not keep up the pace of good new product development and hence found that much of their product range was in the decline phase. Both companies were then faced with the massive costs of a 'rescue' R&D programme to develop new products.

MARKET SEGMENTS AND MARKET POSITIONING

We have already mentioned how companies in mature markets may try to concentrate on one or more segments of the market. Market segmentation and positioning are key elements in a marketing strategy. Market segmentation is based on the premise that the requirements of all the potential customers in a market are unlikely to be the same. Therefore, a company must understand both what the different requirements of parts of the available market are and also how those requirements are distributed throughout the population. An interesting example of segmentation strategy is provided by Guinness.

Guinness has been described as a dying brand which has lost half its share of the total market (from 10 per cent to 5 per cent) in the past ten years as younger drinkers have changed from it to 'light' drinks such as lager. Guinness's famous and very entertaining advertising at the rate of £16 million per year in 1981 failed to arrest this decline. According to market research:

92 per cent of beer is drunk by men:
79 per cent is consumed by draught drinkers;
half of all beer is drunk by the 18–34 age bracket.

Among Guinness drinkers:

71 per cent is consumed by working people in the C2 and D social groups (people in skilled and unskilled 'blue collar' occupations).

However, this information on the importance of different segments by age, sex, social class, etc., does not provide all of the information necessary for the development of Guinness strategy. Further information is provided by segmenting the market into heavy users, light users and non-users of the product. Thus, Guinness could try to persuade heavy Guinness drinkers to consume even more. However, the company ruled this out as 8 per cent of their customers already consume 35 per cent of total volume. Similarly, they ruled out attempts to attract new drinkers as unlikely to produce much benefit in the short term. However, according to Guinness's advertising agency, Allen, Brady and Marsh, 'nearly 70% of those who drink Guinness, drink it only occasionally and they account for only 27% of the volume of Guinness sold.

About 1.7 million of these are below 35. If we could persuade each of the under 35's to drink just one extra pint of Guinness a week we could sell an extra 300,000 barrels a year.'

This segmentation analysis was the basis of a Guinness advertising campaign launched in early 1983. This campaign concentrates on the plight of the 'Guinnless' – those poor unfortunates who have been too long without Guinness. Through the help of the 'Friends of the Guinnless' it aims to bring these (infrequent drinkers) back to Guinness. The campaign also marks an important *repositioning* of the product. Previous Guinness advertising had emphasized the 'special' nature of the product. This was seen in its slow pouring ritual, its acquired taste, its almost 'precious' characteristics. Current advertising is aimed to 'take it off its pedestal and demystify it', by positioning it as a product suitable for frequent drinking. Whether Guinness's heavy advertising is successful or not, it has involved the company in the classic marketing activities of segmenting the existing market, concentrating on a worthwhile segment, and positioning the product appropriately, bearing in mind the competition and consumer requirements. More fundamentally, it has involved Guinness in the basics of marketing, 'a thorough understanding of the consumer and his needs, instead of a concentration on simply producing the product'. (This section has been based on Torin Douglas's report on Guinness in his column in *The Times*, 18 January 1983.)

INDUSTRIAL MARKETING

So far, most of our discussion has been in the context of consumer marketing. Industrial marketing is no less important and involves all of the sales of products between organizations. Thus, British Leyland buys tyres, glass, headlights, batteries, typewriters, computers, nuts and bolts, and food. The difference between industrial and consumer markets lies not so much in the products which are bought, as in the reasons for them being bought, the way they are bought, and the relationship between the buying and selling company. Nor should we believe that industrial marketing is a separate activity from consumer marketing. The two activities can be best thought of as part of a single channel, rather like the channel of distribution discussed earlier. Thus, glass manufacturers, seeking to introduce new 'wide-mouth' bottles for beer and soft drinks are involved in marketing *to* drinks manufacturers to use them. They market *with* drinks manufacturers to stores to accept them and, also, to consumers to like and to buy them.

Industrial marketing involves products and services which are bought, however indirectly, to further the production of a subsequent product or service, that is, they are bought for their *use utility*. Consumer marketing of course also involves products which are bought to be used. However, the sheer possession utility of products bought by consumers is often important. For example cars have important use utility for consumers, although their presence displayed on people's driveways testifies to their value as an ornament or a symbol of status. This is less likely to be important in the case of an industrial purchase, although there are many exceptions. Secondly, industrial marketers have to deal with professional buyers. Some of these are professional in the sense that their sole function involves buying, that is, the seeking and assessment of potential suppliers, often involving detailed analysis of supplier organization, finances, R & D and management resources, as well as the assessment of their products. Buyers also negotiate with suppliers over a price, product features and delivery as well as carrying out the more 'mechanical' activities of order processing. Some buying departments have responsibilities which extend into stores stock control and general materials management.

A buying department may be the sole group involved when a company is buying a relatively low-value, standardized product which it has purchased before, such as steel bars or shelving, etc. Marketers refer to this as a straight/re-buy or routine response behaviour. However, when the product is of major importance or has not been bought before, such as a large automated machine tool, then the process may be lengthy. Personnel from several other departments are likely to be involved, such as the users of the product (production management), those who influence the purchase through their expertise (R & D or design), and senior management who exercise overall control.

Industrial-marketing companies must be aware of who is likely to be involved in the purchase of their kind of product and also the nature of the process of purchasing. The group of individuals

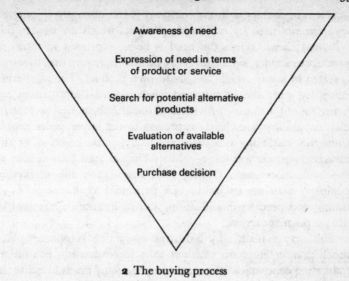

Awareness of need

Expression of need in terms
of product or service

Search for potential alternative
products

Evaluation of available
alternatives

Purchase decision

2 The buying process

involved are often referred to as the decision-making unit (DMU) and the process of buying can be seen to resemble a funnel, as shown in Figure 2. Thus, someone within a buying company becomes aware of a need for some new product or service. Their awareness of this may be raised by sales effort from a potential supplier or by a concern about the currently available facilities within the company. This need is then expressed in terms of a product or service. This expression may take the form of drawing up a specification and a particular supplier's product may be named as being the most likely purchase. This and alternatives will be examined and finally, through a process of negotiation with potential suppliers, a single product or service will be chosen.

The funnel analogy shows purchasing as a process of gradually reducing the alternatives for consideration. Also, different individuals or departments are likely to be involved at each stage; the awareness of need is likely to occur in the user department; the search for available suppliers is likely to be carried out by the purchasing department, although the evaluation of these alternatives may be carried out by both users and influencers. Also, the marketing company seeking to become a supplier must carry out different activities at each of the stages.

If it is in contact with the company it can often precipitate the awareness of need by explaining products which are new to this potential client. When the need is being expressed in terms of product or service, sales effort may be used to ensure that the need is stated in a way which favours its own product. The marketing company must also be involved when potential alternatives are being sought and may provide additional information so that its own capabilities are clearly expressed to the buyer. Sales people from the marketing company are likely to be involved at the awareness-generation stage, while technical staff have a role at the evaluation stage. During final negotiation the marketing company may use its production personnel to discuss issues of timing and product modification, and its finance department to discuss payment terms.

This may explain why industrial-marketing companies place much greater emphasis on their sales force than do consumer-marketing companies. The marketing company needs to maintain contact with the potential customer during the long periods between individual purchases of major equipment. Regular calls will mean that it is in contact at the appropriate awareness-generation stage. However, the marketing company is unlikely to be able to be in contact with all purchase influences in the buying company. Often the buyer acts as a gatekeeper and prevents the salesperson or sales promotion literature reaching others in the firm. The marketer must use advertising to reach these other influences.

Industrial-sales people often differentiate between being an 'in-supplier' and an 'out-supplier'. Their task is very different when they are the supplier who has been used for previous purchases, as opposed to one which has not been used previously. The repeat-purchase decision where the company is involved in consideration between previous and new suppliers is referred to as a modified re-buy or as limited problem-solving. It is interesting to think why sales people should place so much value on being the in-supplier. After all, if the buying company goes about its purchases in a rational and consistent manner then we could assume that it is able to assess its past experience with a supplier and evaluate this performance against the advantages offered by a new supplier. In fact, much of industrial marketing rests on such intangibles as the trust between buyer and seller and the informal arrangements over delivery and product changes which both sides make. It has been said that we never buy from strangers, only from friends. Much of industrial-marketing activity is involved in building trust, and in becoming and staying 'friends'. More accurately the relationship between buyer and seller is closer to that of marriage partners rather than friends. Unlike a marriage, however, this relationship depends on many individuals on each side.

MARKETING RESEARCH

If we think of companies having a relationship with their markets, advertising is the means by which they talk to these markets and marketing research is the means by which they listen. The nature of this relationship may be indicated by the fact that companies often spend many times more money in talking to (or at) their markets than they do in listening to them! Despite this, it is worth noting that UK expenditure on market research increased from £31 million in 1973 to £123 million in 1982 (*The Times*, 22 March 1983).

Marketing research involves many aspects and some are contracted to outside agencies in a similar way to advertising. It is useful to distinguish between the continuous monitoring of a company's markets and one-off special projects aimed at finding information about a particular aspect of those markets. The continuous monitoring of markets also involves the second important distinction in marketing research. This is between secondary and primary data. Secondary data refers to material already published, for example in trade directories, market studies in the press, by banks or research organizations, etc. The obvious advantage of such data is that they are cheap and reasonably readily available. The company may also subscribe to panel data on consumer purchase behaviour, or surveys on the ownership of products or use patterns, etc. Additionally, marketing research departments are involved in gathering much information on their own company's operations such as sales territory reports, delivery patterns, etc.

Much of this continuous monitoring forms part of regular management briefings and reports and is part of the company's management information system. One important aspect of this information system is the provision of forecasts. Forecasting is carried out in a variety of areas including the economy or the total market within which the company operates. An important regularly revised forecast is that of sales for existing or new products. These sales forecasts are the basis of the company's financial and production planning, and are also important in the company's corporate planning.

The company's marketing research department may also gather its own primary data, for example by operating its own consumer panel. However, it is likely to contract out larger studies involving extensive consumer interviews as these may be beyond its resources or expertise. The use of an outside agency does not remove responsibilities from the department. Effective marketing research depends on a clear brief to the researcher. This, in turn, means that the marketing research department must define the problem about which information is required and say exactly *what* information is required to enable management to solve the problem. For example, a small building society may be faced with the problem that more people are closing accounts with it than are opening new ones. Some of the early questions the building society may wish to ask are:

1. Is the problem confined to their society, or is it widespread? This may be found from secondary sources.
2. If the problem is particular to their society, what sort of people are closing accounts: the old, the young, etc.?
3. What do people know of the society and of its products and services?
4. What do people think of the society?
5. How do existing customers and non-customers compare this society with others?

Without this (and other) information, management action will be based on hunch and impression. Therefore, it cannot be over-emphasized how important it is for the company to have intimate knowledge of both its current and potential markets.

CONCLUSION

We have seen that marketing depends on awareness of the customers' requirements. Unfortunately, the more long established a company becomes, the less likely it is to retain its willingness to keep in touch with its markets and to remain aware of changes in customer requirements. It is more likely to become inward-looking and obsessed with its own organization and way of doing things, irrespective of their relevance to the world outside. Marketing is a department in an organization which involves activities such as pricing, advertising, selling, distribution and product development. Perhaps more importantly, marketing is the whole organization looking at itself, through the eyes of its markets, so that its activities continue to be relevant to those markets.

CHAPTER 18

Research and Development Strategies

JULIAN LOWE AND MICK SILVER

Technological advances are constantly reshaping private and public resource requirements and efficiency. Exhortations from government to industry are frequently concerned with the profitable development of new products and processes. In response to this, academics and management practitioners have written much on how best to manage technological change and innovation. It is not possible to cover all this and so this chapter will focus on the specific issue of research and development (R & D) strategy within the firm.

R & D can be initiated either to satisfy a particular market need such as the development of synthetic rubber ('demand pull'); or to find uses for technological advances such as the laser ('technology push'). There has been a considerable debate on whether the management of innovation should start with market needs or existing technological resources and strengths, though it is worth noting that the two sources might interact rather than be separate entities.

The earliest stage of the process of technical advance is commonly called 'basic research'. This is characterized by uncertainty of the principles involved and the eventual usefulness of the product. Once the principles have been discovered these are then used to create prototypes. This part of the process might be labelled applied research and is characterized by a focus on a specific market goal and the reduction of uncertainty regarding the technical feasibility at an economic cost. In the final innovation stage of development, design and commercialization, the product is fitted to specific consumer needs, in order to sell profitably. The extent to which one can precisely distinguish between the research and commercial development phases however is questionable (Ames, 1961; Jewkes et al. 1970; Arrow, 1969). Similar problems arise with process and product innovation where the distinction is important but ambiguous since the definition partly rests on who uses the innovation.

Expenditure on R & D takes place to increase the body of techniques or knowledge. The resulting 'technical knowledge' may be embodied in capital, labour and the way production is managed and organized. For example, in the case of robots in car manufacturing the technical knowledge for this new manufacturing process is contained in the robots, the skill of labour to use them, and the organization of the production process. Some technical knowledge may not actually be utilized but be available for use in the form of a 'book of blueprints' (to use Hay and Morris's (1979) terminology). For example, technical knowledge may exist as a design or as a working prototype for electrically powered motor vehicles aimed at a general consumer market. Some ideas may not be efficient in one period, but changes in relative prices of labour, raw materials and energy may increase the commercial value of this technical knowledge. The value may also decrease, as in the case of the vast R & D resources that were put into the manufacture of synthetic protein, which became obsolete as soya prices fell.

An important aspect of the innovation process is its diffusion through the system and so many firms are able to generate technical advances without getting customers to adopt them. The benefits of technological knowledge are clearly linked to the extent to which it is utilized. Diffusion is not static because products and processes are improved to meet the individual needs of firms and consumers (Gold, 1981). To increase technological knowledge, management must not only pay attention to the efficiency of research programmes in increasing technological knowledge but also to diffusion of innovations.

RESEARCH AND INNOVATION: SOME UK AND INTERNATIONAL EVIDENCE

Empirical evidence on the effects of R & D expenditures shows that the extent of R & D inputs *per se* are closely related to the rate of technological advance and innovation (Kennedy and Thirwall, 1972). This is probably true at both the individual firm and the country level and this section deals with the macro-background of

R & D management. This reflects the performance of firms in aggregate and also indicates the technological environment of specific management problems.

Changes in the inputs of R & D expenditure do not necessarily lead to commensurate changes in the output of technical knowledge in any period. The change in the physical volume of R & D work, or R & D real expenditure, may vary in a different manner from the costs of equipment and labour. Basic research expenditure in a given year is unlikely to lead to increases in the stock of knowledge in that same year and some applied research might also take a number of years to come to fruition. Not all R & D expenditure will successfully lead to any, or proportionate increases in, the stock of technical knowledge. The stock of technical knowledge is subject to depreciation or obsolescence just like expenditure on capital goods. The R & D manager has to take account of the impact on expenditure of changes in relative prices (costs), time lags, success rates and rates of obsolescence. All of these influence the conversion of R & D expenditure to its productive manifestation, the stock of technical knowledge.

There are many empirical problems involved in estimating the stock of technical knowledge, especially with regard to the rate of obsolescence, but some estimates are available for the UK (Bosworth, 1978, and Schott, 1978a). Schott (1976) found the stock of industrial technical knowledge in the UK to have increased at *annual* rates of 6.3 per cent between 1907 and 1931; 10.5 per cent between 1931 and 1950; 11.7 per cent in the 1950s; and 10.3 per cent in the 1960s. Substantial increases in R & D expenditure can be identified behind these increases, as the proportion of industrial R & D expenditure to the gross national product of the UK increased from 0.0025 in 1950 to 0.015 in 1960 and 0.017 in 1970.

Government financing of R & D expenditure is relatively important, accounting for 47 per cent of all R & D finance, over half of which is directed to defence (Bowles, 1981; and Business Statistics Office, 1978, for data).

While most Western countries have experienced rapid growth in R & D and been at the forefront of new technology, there has recently been a great deal of introspection as to whether, nationally and within companies, the resources devoted to R & D are sufficient and are being efficiently allocated. It should be noted that R & D is only part of the inputs leading to technical progress. One study found that on average 40 per cent of the cost of product innovation goes on tooling and the design and construction of facilities, while a further 15 per cent is absorbed in the costs of manufacturing and marketing strategy. In addition, in some industries corporate R & D is only responsible for a small proportion of significant advances (Mansfield, 1982). At the national and company level it is still likely however that innovation is related to expenditure on R & D.

Tables 1 and 2 illustrate the variability in R & D expenditure within UK industry and between countries. While R & D expenditure for UK manufacturing industry as a whole increased during the last decade, there are clearly areas where it was in decline and comparative decline with other countries in particular industries. Table 1 shows that certain sectors have suffered a significant decline in R & D expenditure, and Table 2 shows a comparative decline in R & D expenditure when compared to some of our close industrial rivals. The fall in the absolute value of R & D in real terms has, in the cases of the motor vehicle, aerospace and 'other manufacturing industries' been accompanied by a fall in R & D as a proportion of value added, and this must inevitably hasten the pace of industrial decline unless there have been substantial changes in productivity

TABLE 1   *Total UK industrial expenditure (intramural) on R & D (£ million, constant (1975) prices)*

	1964	1967	1972	1975	1978	Annual Growth Rate, per cent
All product groups	1,400	1,514	1,418	1,340	1,566	0.8
All manufactured	1,365	1,488	1,376	1,293	1,152	0.7
Of which:						
Chemical/allied	196	216	231	245	284	2.7
Mechanical engineering	115	155	94	103	118	0.2
Electronics	222	285	302	279	442	5.0
Other electrical	82	92	68	73	69	− 1.2
Motor vehicles	100	113	97	88	88	0.9
Aerospace	391	356	366	292	285	− 2.2
Other	260	272	219	213	226	− 1.0

Source: Business Monitor MO 14 Industrial R & D Expenditure and Employment, HMSO 1980, Table 1.

in R & D departments. Greatest concern should however relate to the level of outputs. These are difficult to measure, except in the terms of patents, etc., but there has clearly been a relative failure of research effort in certain key industries in the UK.

TABLE 2 *Per capita industry-financed expenditure on R & D by country ($1970)*

	1967	1975
Belgium	20.5	26.5
France	22.2	28.4
W. Germany	36.9	49.1
Italy	8.6	11.9
Japan	22.4	37.9
Sweden	30.3	50.2
Switzerland	45.5	62.0
United Kingdom	36.6	33.1
United States of America	46.7	52.1

Source: OECD Observer, 1980.

Lack of technical success has however been overshadowed by the failure of many technically successful products in the market. Concorde and the advanced gas-cooled nuclear reactor are two clear-cut examples of high technical sophistication which did not fit their markets.

R & D inputs are one way of measuring national performance in research and an alternative indicator is the level of global licensing payments. Licensing involves payment to the discoverer for the use of their innovation. In 1978 global licence payments amounted to $14 billion (Contractor, 1981). In the UK there was a fourfold increase in licensing royalties received between 1969 and 1979 and a similar growth in licensing payments (BSO, 1978). The UK currently has a surplus on its 'technology royalty' account of almost £150 million, and, apart from the UK, only the US, France and Switzerland consistently had a surplus. West Germany and Japan, who have been so successful in the post-war period, have only ever been able to cover half of their technology royalty payments with receipts from exported technology and know-how. Almost the whole of Japanese national technology policy has been based on technology licensing, following a policy of restrictions on foreign direct investment in all but exceptional cases.

Japan illustrates that R & D can be either performed in house or bought in; and this degree of choice has considerable managerial implications for firms. In addition, Japan has been in the vanguard of exceptional and explosive economic growth; but this has not led to technological dependence on other countries but to the establishment of an important technological platform on which the Japanese have been able to build. This is illustrated in Table 3 by an overall increase in the ratio of royalty receipts to payments during the last decade.

TABLE 3   *Japanese trade in technology 1970–80*

	Technology Exports royalty receipts (Yen, billions)		Technology Imports royalty payments (Yen, billions)		Ratio of Total Receipts to Payments
	Total	New	Total	New	
1971	27	N/A	135	N/A	0.202
1974	57	N/A	160	N/A	0.357
1976	83	N/A	177	N/A	0.47
1978	93	36	190	16	0.49
1979	122	47	192	38	0.63
1980	133	52	24	26	0.55
1981	159	74	239	27	0.66

Source: Survey of Research and Development (Prime Minister's Office, 1982).

This clearly reflects a growing independence of foreign sources of technology and a speeding-up of Japan's own research effort which has important implications for the R & D strategy of individual firms. In terms of new programmes the Japanese are now in surplus on their technology account. An indication of how they have used technology licensing to help them change not only their level of industrial growth but also their own in-house technological development can be seen from patents filed in the USA by the Japanese. Applications increased from 9,365 in 1976 to 12,951 in 1980, and they now account for almost 30 per cent of foreign patents filed in the USA, which exceeds the number of patent applications of all her major competitors.

R & D Effort and Productivity: The Theory

Just as the national picture has important implications for individual firms, lessons can be drawn from evidence on the efficiency of R & D at an industry level. There is a substantial body of literature about the conditions under which R & D input is likely to be most productive (Kennedy and Thirwall, 1972; Kamien and Schwartz, 1982; Gold, 1977; and Freeman, 1982). Evidence has generally focused on six relationships:

1. The impact of firm size on the efficiency of R & D activity.
2. The impact of firm size on the transference of research inputs to research outputs.
3. R & D participation levels between large and small firms.
4. The impact of competition and market structure on research inputs and outputs.
5. The impact of research on profitability and performance.
6. Internal managerial organization and successful R & D.

The seminal work of J. S. Schumpeter was the starting point for the majority of the studies (Schumpeter, 1950). His view was that major technological innovations are generated primarily by increasingly complex and heavily financed development programmes and that consequently large firms in monopolistic markets were likely to be the best vehicles for effective research investment. This Schumpeterian view of the research process has been challenged by those who claim that economies of scale are unimportant in many aspects of the efficient allocation and management of R & D. The key to successful research is argued to be a competitive market environment, which acts as a spur to firms to allocate their research effort in such a way as to meet consumer needs efficiently (Jewkes et al., 1970; Commanor, 1967; and Scherer, 1967).

Work has also concentrated on the extent to which different aspects of the process of technical advance may be affected. Particular questions are whether invention and innovation may respond very differently to firm and market conditions; and whether inputs and outputs are related in the same way across the whole size and industry spectrum or whether the relationship varies. The linkages between R & D as an input of technical knowledge to the production process and other factors of production have been established (Schott, 1978b). This view also identifies relative changes in the price of capital, labour, raw materials and

R & D to be related to the demand for R & D as an input into the production process. Considerable attention has also been devoted to the extent that successful innovation is linked to future profitability. This possibly holds the key to the sometimes apparently confused and conflicting nature of the evidence on R & D and the firm. The relationship between R & D and profits is likely to be two-way and R & D may either be the result of high profits or the cause of them. High profitability may enable the firm to build up its market position and defences against competition such that profits can be maintained in the long run (Koch, 1980).

R & D Effort and Productivity: The Evidence

R & D expenditure is highly concentrated in a few large firms; the five enterprises with the largest R & D expenditure in the UK in 1978 accounted for 41 per cent of all UK R & D expenditure and 76 per cent of all government R & D funds; fifty enterprises with the largest R & D expenditure accounted for 82 per cent and 96 per cent of expenditure and government funding respectively (Business Statistics Office, 1978, Table 16).

Studies of the relationship between size and inventive activity have suffered from a number of statistical problems. Indicators of 'inventive activity' are ambiguous, and the proxy variable of 'patents registered' ignores the variation of individual patents in terms of economic significance (Scherer, 1965; Schmookler, 1966; Taylor and Silbertson, 1973). Some patterns may be gleaned by using R & D expenditure as an input to a production function to identify how this is related to size of firms (Griliches, 1980). Evidence on the impact of various size-related and market-competition-related factors is sometimes conflicting but there are certain common strands.

While large firms sometimes have an advantage in the development of inventions to commercial success there is no evidence to suggest that this holds at the basic invention stages. Jewkes et al. (1970) emphasized the contribution of individual inventors in a study of fifty-one major inventions. Hamberg (1966) reported that only seven out of a total of twenty-seven 'major inventions' in the period 1947–55 came from the R & D units of large firms. Peck (1962) showed that less than 10 per cent of the major inventions in the aluminium industry came from major firms in that industry over the period 1946–57.

In some areas size is important in the effective development and commercialization of products but this relationship only holds up to certain levels; once firms become very large neither R & D inputs nor outputs increase in proportion to company size. In an important case the monopolies commission ruled against the merger of two pharmaceutical companies on the grounds that it would not aid the promotion of effective research effort.

R & D relationships may be industry-specific and technology-specific: chemicals and electronics for instance may relate far better to the Schumpeterian hypotheses of size and market control being important for effective R & D than do other industries (Scherer, 1967, and Freeman, 1982). In an exhaustive econometric study of US industry Griliches (1980) found that larger firms do not necessarily invest more in R & D relative to their size than smaller firms but that fixed capital-intensive firms, which may be larger and specific to certain industries, tend to be R & D intensive. The organization of R & D appears to have a significant impact. Project SAPPHO (Science Policy Research Unit, 1972) represents an important and systematic attempt to evaluate organizational and associated factors. In a statistical study of a large sample of firms, it found that successful innovation was related to: the firms' commitment to individual projects; the linkage between the firms and the outside scientific community working in related fields; and to the links within the firm of the marketing and R & D functions. There was little evidence that the use of planning and management techniques led to successful innovation (Rothwell, 1977). Other commentators have suggested that team research may suppress the originality of the creative scientist; and that when new ideas arise they require a powerful company champion to promote them through the various developmental stages (Hay and Morris, 1979).

A study of twenty major companies in the US concluded that: there were substantial interfirm differences in the management of R & D; the likelihood of success is enhanced if projects are subjected to early evaluation of potential market and profit; a close relationship between marketing and R & D increases the chance of success; and many firms carried out too many trivial projects with a high chance of technical success but with a low level of profit (Mansfield and Wagner, 1975).

The Management and Organization of R & D

Effective management and organization of technology involves the reconciliation of the various factors mentioned earlier. It is clearly concerned with developing the capabilities of individuals, as well as the characteristics of their institutions and the broader economic environment. In some ways the effective internal control of R & D can be based on those same organizational factors which are important in other areas of the firm, but R & D is also a special case, since it involves a longer time for the measurement of returns and the problems of the management of creative individuals.

The real difference arises because in many parts of the firm the organizational problem has been one of maintaining stability and the emphasis of many managers and other employees has been towards the perpetuation of the stability of the system. In contrast R & D is the vehicle of change and so the status quo may be quite inappropriate.

Management systems should change with changes in the technological environment, but even in research-intensive organizations flexible structures are the exception, particularly when management concentrate on hard information (command or control data) as opposed to soft information, as in the technical discussion of design (Hawthorne, 1978).

Burns and Stalker (1961) found that successful firms, experiencing rapid technological change, used committees as a mechanism for by-passing the formal functioning of the management structure because the number of factors became, at times, too great for the normal management information system to handle. A study of forty-two US firms found that a hierarchical organizational system, which focused on a rigidly defined organizational pattern, precluded cross-group and sideways communications. This worked when technical change was slow but not when it was rapid (McLeod, 1969).

The need for flexibility and not rigidity for innovation means that organizations pursuing proactive R & D policies must accept less internal control. In particular, hierarchical control in an innovative firm is a problem, as top decision-makers may become over-loaded owing to the substantial amount of information which they have to handle. One possible approach is that groups or teams must carry out decisions that would normally be dealt with higher up a traditional hierarchy. This may not be easy, since Linn (1983) notes:

> To convert a collection of individuals into a problem solving team requires interpersonal skills where there can be openness and trust. Hence, the interpersonal skills of supervisor and employee alike must improve if the firm is to successfully diversify. This necessity may be lost on supervisory personnel who were promoted to their present positions on the basis of technical (not interpersonal) competence.
>
> The success of an R & D department greatly depends on whether creative ideas are allowed to be introduced and implemented. This requires that management see that the proper creative atmosphere is established and maintained. Creative technologists flourish best when they are competent in skills required by the areas of technology involved and are appropriately stimulated and motivated. The continued success of any technological firm requires a stream of new products. Since new product development resides mainly in R & D personnel, any firm which does not insist on good personnel management within R & D flirts with failure.

Clearly the successful management of R & D entails the effective management and understanding of people, cash flows and customer needs. R & D requires planning which can only be effective when it is an integral part of management commitment. In addition the identification of technological opportunities is often a 'bottom up' process and consequently the management system must not contain too many filters as information is passed up through the organization. There is clearly a conflict between the need for freedom of action to stimulate creativity, and the requirement for the firm to be able to 'kill' projects that look as though they will not achieve either their technical or their commercial objectives.

B P has adopted a matrix form of organization to help meet the goal of creativity and the requirement for innovations to fulfil market needs. The organization of the BP research centre was described as follows (*Financial Times*, 1983):

The Sunbury Research Centre is organised on a matrix basis, with a large number of scientific disciplines – chemistry, solidstate, colloids, bio-sciences, etc. – each supported by several profit centres. Each of these sciences has the sponsorship of eight or nine BP businesses. BP is convinced that this intimate interaction of research with a great diversity of commercial interests is where the pay-off lies. 'Real discoveries are made "serendipitously". We don't allow demarcation disputes.'

Sunbury also has a long tradition of being able to assemble a task force for trials. The knack is not to pull people out of the mainstream but for the man appointed as task-force coordinator to nominate the people he wants to help him prepare for the trial. A big exercise this year is the preparation for BP's first trial of enhanced oil recovery.

Before a discovery reaches this stage, however, it has to survive a top-level technoeconomic appraisal by an independent group of scientists at Sunbury. BP insists that this group shall get access to any bright ideas very early, in order to justify spending more money.

The growth in subcontracting of R & D suggests that some firms are finding it increasingly worthwhile to run down their in-house facilities, because of the hierarchical and interest-group problems, and buy in their R & D from independent and specialist R & D companies (Globerman, 1980).

R&D STRATEGIES FOR THE FIRM

R & D is rarely a goal in itself but rather a means to more efficient production or the promotion of more marketable products, and so it has to be seen from a strategic point of view in the context of existing resources and marketing capabilities of the firm. Firms are exhorted to bring out new products. Kotler (1980) described them as the 'lifeblood of the company', while politicians of various hues see industrial R & D as a step on the road to economic recovery (Pavitt, 1983). There are considerable costs and pitfalls, however, for firms performing their own R & D. A major problem is the threshold level of expenditure necessary for R & D to be effective. This depends on the industry and stage of technology but some firms are unable to embark on their own research effort because of the high capital costs of equipment or the transience of the technology. In an evaluation of a large cross-section of firms and industries Freeman (1982) suggests that defensive and reactive strategies are in order for even some of the largest UK and European companies when faced with competition from the USA and Japan. A second problem is the probability of technical and product failure in certain industries. The pharmaceutical industry has to try out thousands of compounds before finding a successful one. Those same marketing texts which advocate an aggressive product policy also note the high proportion of product rejections and failures. A classic study by Booz, Allen and Hamilton (1965) looked at fifty-one major US companies and found that on average only 2 per cent of initial product ideas were commercially successful with almost 90 per cent failing prior to market testing. Schott (1976) in a study of eighty-one large British companies found the probability of *technical* success to be as high as 0.91, but no follow-up consideration was given to *commercial* success.

The third problem of R & D management involves the time-lags between technical development and commercialization. Mansfield (1968) showed that this lag could be substantial, as Table 19.4 illustrates.

TABLE 4   *Time-lags between invention and innovation*

Product	Lag between invention and innovation (*years*)
TV	22
Ballpoint pen	6
DDT	3
Nylon	11
Zip fastener	27
LP record	3

Source: E. Mansfield, *The Economics of Technological Change* (1968).

Even for developmental work, such as the introduction of a new model of motor car, the lag can still exceed four years, while for highly technical products, such as nuclear power plants, the time-lag may run into several decades. Clearly this presents a financing and cash-flow problem for the firm and it is a factor which might militate against substantial in-house R & D strategies for the smaller firm. Such long-term R & D projects are exceptional, however, as Schott's (1976) UK survey found 64 per cent of R & D projects were expected to be in use within one year and almost 80 per cent within two years.

Other factors shape and constrain company strategy. On the cost side, indivisibilities of equipment and manpower will affect the basic direction of strategies, while the persistent problems for cost control caused by engineers underestimating development costs have been well documented (Freeman, 1982). On the demand side, the reactions of rivals, the patent system and the law relating to the protection of other intellectual property may be crucial (Grabowski and Baxter, 1973; Freeman, 1982). Other factors are pertinent and in particular the firm's R & D strategy will clearly reflect management's attitude towards risk-taking, stability and growth. This might be fashioned by the external competitive environment or by specific key individuals within the organization. The short duration of R & D projects in large companies may, in fact, be a function of management's attitude to risk-taking. In addition to the firm's assessment of its own R & D strengths and weaknesses it is important that it should also relate to company strengths and weaknesses in marketing and production. Finally, questions of risk, rates of return and portfolio selection are central areas of R & D management where established management techniques may have a substantial role to play (Mansfield, 1982).

All these factors combine to determine and constrain firms of certain types, sizes and resources from undertaking an active and substantial R & D investment. Consequently the R & D strategy of the firm must be broadened to take account of alternatives to purely in-house research and development effort. Such strategies may include:

1. The (legal or illegal) imitation of innovation developed by others.
2. The purchase of patents under licence agreements.
3. The purchase of R & D and testing from contract specialist suppliers or other firms.
4. The joint development of R & D in collaboration with other organizations.

5. The hiring of personnel with scarce skills and knowledge of particular processes/techniques.
6. Merger with another organization with R & D resources compatible with own-company requirements.

These possibilities are not mutually exclusive and mixed strategies will often be required. There is a wide range of alternative policies to in-house R & D. Many projects may fall foul of the NIH (Not Invented Here) syndrome, whereby interest groups within a company obstruct and retard the incorporation of knowledge from outside, on the basis of it not stemming from their own (expert) sources. Additionally there is the real problem of technology transfer between organizations, although it is not clear whether this is any more difficult than the transfer of knowledge within an organization (Globerman, 1980). Ultimately the strategy or mix of strategies adopted by a firm will depend on the specific circumstances surrounding the technology and the company.

CONCLUSION

Various factors associated with the management and production of R & D and new products have been dealt with in this chapter. Ultimately R & D requires management to make financial, economic and organizational judgements but various external factors beyond the control of top management are also influential. Research evidence suggests that some of these external factors may be quite crucial in affecting the final effectiveness and output of R & D departments, but internal organization is also important and, especially within the large firms, problems of non-profit-related goals and bureaucracy stemming from a complex hierarchy may have to be solved.

While this chapter has identified the diversity of influences affecting the performance of R & D, we must always recognize the importance of R & D *per se*. Both in the UK (Kennedy and Thirwall, 1972) and in the US (Terleckyj, 1980, and Griliches, 1980) R & D has had a major and measurable impact on economic growth and private returns to individual companies. The importance of investing in R & D and its proper management are central to the successful progress of industry.

CHAPTER 19

Production/Operations Management

TERRY HILL

A business depends upon the products it makes or the services it provides, though companies differ in how much they produce internally or buy in from outside. Production management and operations management describe the same set of tasks. Both are concerned with managing those resources of an enterprise which are required to produce the goods (production management in a manufacturing company) or provide the services (operations management in a non-manufacturing company) to be sold. The separate terms, production management and operations management, that is, have developed because of the fact that, in most national economies, manufacturing activities have normally come before service industries. This has resulted in the emphasis being placed on the words 'production management'. The growth of service industries in more developed countries has brought with it the term 'operations management' as a more appropriate, general title. Throughout this chapter, therefore, the terms production management and operations management will be treated as being synonymous.

THE NATURE OF THE TASK

The role of the operations manager is to manage the transformation process, whereby materials or facilities become goods or services, and so manage all the support functions that this transformation requires. In most organizations, therefore, the size of the task is very large. It is usually responsible for the management of some 70–80 per cent of the company's expenditure, total assets and people. Consequently, the success of a business is underpinned, in no small part, by how effectively the operations task is performed.

MANUFACTURING ITEMS AND SERVICES

Goods are tangible items purchased so that they can be used. Services, on the other hand, are intangible, consumed at the time of being provided and with the customer taking away or retaining the benefit of that service. However, in many companies what is provided or produced is a mixture of both goods and services. For example, a person buys a new washing machine (goods) but also knows that included in that purchase are after-sales guarantees and maintenance (a service); similarly, you go into a restaurant to eat (a service) but this also embraces the food and drink you consume (goods). Figure 1 below, therefore, illustrates the mix between the goods and service content provided in a range of purchases.*

PURCHASE	MIX	
	100% GOODS	100% SERVICES
Vending machines		
Low-cost consumable goods		
Make-to-order, high-cost goods		
Meal in a fast-food restaurant		
High-quality, restaurant meal		
Regular maintenance		
Breakdown maintenance		
Computer bureau		
Management consultancy		
Health farm		

1 Different product/service mixes provided in a range of services
(Hill, 1983)

THE OPERATIONS PROCESS

The production/operations management (POM) task is concerned with the transformation process which takes inputs and converts them into outputs, together with the support functions required (see Figure 2). The transformation process will, in reality, be an inter-

* Figures 1, 2, 3, 5 and 6 are reproduced with permission of Terry Hill, *Production/ Operations Management*, Prentice–Hall International, 1983.

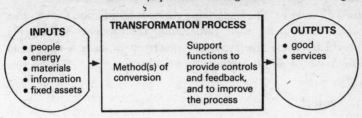

2 The operations function (Hill, 1983)

related set of different processes feeding into one another as part of the total transformation. Figure 3 below shows via a range of possibilities how inputs at one stage then become outputs from that stage and inputs into the next stage and so on.

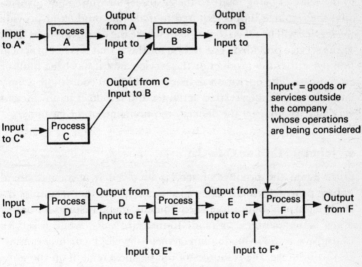

3 Interrelated processes (Hill, 1983)

CHOICE OF PROCESS

There are five basic ways which a company can choose to produce the goods or provide the services which are its business. Some of these will tend to be used only for certain products and not all are used for services. The underlying choice is based upon the volumes which have to be made rather than the product/service being provided. These five types are described in such a way as to emphasize the key differences between them.

1. Project

Organizations which are in the business of producing or providing large-scale products or services will normally choose the project process as the most suitable. Product examples include aerospace programmes or civil-engineering contracts. Service examples include consultancy assignments in corporate strategy (see the later chapter by Gerry Johnson), or supplying a large banquet to the customer's own premises. The product or service provided is unique in the sense of being made to the customer's requirements. Normally, the resource inputs required to make the product or provide the service will be taken to the point where the product is to be built or the service provided. The reason for this is that it is not practical to move either the product or the service once it has been built or established. The operation manager's task is to coordinate a very large number of interrelated activities and resources in an efficient way and also to meet the delivery requirements of the customer.

2. Jobbing, Unit or One-Off

Once again the product or service involved is of an individual nature provided to customer specification. Product examples include a purpose-built piece of equipment, metal castings for use by other manufacturers, or made-to-measure suits, while a service example is a tailor-made management-development programme. In this instance, the resources of the business remain on the same site and the product or services are flowed through them. On completion the product or service is then provided to the customer at the appropriate place.

3. Batch

This form of process is chosen once the volumes of the product or service increase and the product or service itself will be needed repeatedly. In batch operations the task itself is divided into a series of appropriate operations. An order quantity, in the sense of the required number, is then put through one set of processes until all items in the order quantity have been completed. The order quantity then moves on to the next stage where it will go through the next operation, and so on. Examples in manufacturing include such engineering processes as car-component production. On the service side typical batch processes include computer bureaux which process different clients' work, and some large clerical functions which handle many different tasks which have first been broken down in the way described here.

4. Line

With further increases in volume, investment is made to dedicate a process to the completion of one or a small range of products or services. Here again the demand for these products will have increased so that the company can justify investing in processes to make this stated range of products or services. Product examples include motor vehicles, while service examples include certain preparatory operations in fast-food restaurants (such as McDonalds).

5. Continuous Process

Yet again the volumes have increased to such an extent that an inflexible, dedicated process is now laid down to handle an agreed range of products (e.g. petrochemicals). The process is designed to run all day and every day with minimum shut-downs because of the high costs of starting up the process. The materials are transferred automatically from one part of the process to another with little labour input. The labour task is to monitor the systems and to take the required action where necessary. This type of process is not used in the provision of a service.

THE TASK

The complex nature of the production/operations task is illustrated in Figure 4.

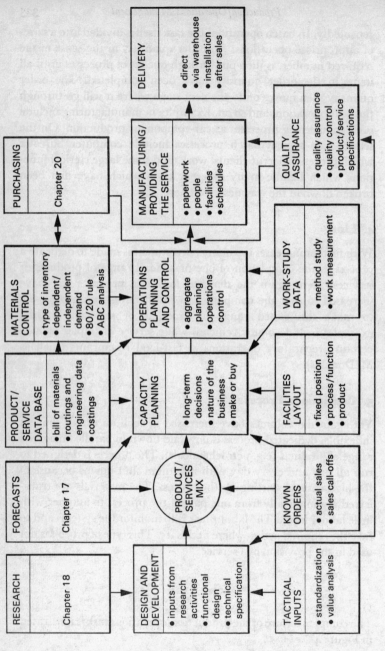

4 The production/operations task

DESIGN AND DEVELOPMENT

The design and development of the product/service is concerned with establishing the requirements of the item in line with given or anticipated market needs. It involves specifying in some detail the products or services to be provided. A product/service idea will often raise problems that call for research and development and which need to be solved before the design can be finalized. The organization, therefore, has two important inputs into the design phase. First is the degree of research and development activities in which the company is prepared to invest, and second a number of tactical, short-term activities aimed at improving the design process. These latter may be used as ways to help reduce costs and improve the design of the product/service.

Standardization

The principle of standardization is to reduce the number of components/materials which are required to provide the range of products/services the company sells. By doing this costs can be reduced by lower holdings of components and materials, longer production runs and bulk purchasing. On the process side, standardization of equipment should lead to a reduction in the spare parts kept on site in case of breakdowns and will simplify the maintenance task. In addition, it will provide for manufacturing an increase in flexibility in that all or more items can go on to more machines.

Value analysis*

Value analysis is another such important tactical activity. It provides a systematic approach to reducing the material cost of a product or service without impairing its function. Value analysis means noting the functions which a component, product or service is intended to perform, and then looking at the present design to try to provide these functions at a lower cost but without loss of quality. In this way value analysis may decrease material costs and perhaps

* Note: the application of value-analysis techniques at the design stage of a product/service is called value engineering.

labour costs through design changes. As Lawrence Miles, the man who developed these concepts in the immediate post-war period, said, 'On average, one fourth of manufacturing cost is unnecessary. The extra cost continues because of patterns and habits of thought, because of personal limitations, because of difficulties in promptly disseminating ideas and because today's thinking is based on yesterday's knowledge' (Miles, 1961). Note that in 1979 the cost of purchases made by all UK manufacturing industries totalled £91,233 million, so even a small percentage reduction would mean a considerable gain overall.

The value-analysis procedure takes each part of a product or service and looks, in detail, at each function. Every feature, tolerance, degree of finish or part of the service is vetted to ensure that none of these is adding cost to the product or service without providing a useful function, or that it cannot be substituted by something else that costs less but will do the job as well.

Capacity Planning

So far, the implication is that the design or service being sold by a company is its own design. In many situations, however, items are specified by the customer, and the company's task is to meet that customer need. Examples of this are referred to as make-to-order businesses: the item/service is made/provided to a customer order, often on a once-and-for-all basis. Companies providing standard products/services are referred to as make-to-stock businesses: they make standard, repeat, high-volume products/services to be sold in the market place. In both types of business, the next important step in the production/operations task is to plan adequate and appropriate capacity to meet the known or anticipated needs. Figure 4 again shows the interface between design, sales forecasts and known orders which provide essential inputs into the capacity-planning function.

In developing its objectives, a business needs to consider how it is to provide appropriate capacity in terms of both process capability and the volumes that can be handled. However, before discussing how organizations do this it is important to note some of the particulars.

First, capacity in planning terms will be measured by either labour or plant, depending on the process chosen. In most project, jobbing and batch processes, capacity is calculated by the number of people employed in the process (sub-process). But in line and continuous-process methods the factor governing capacity is plant.

Second, capacity in service industries has its own set of traits, including the facts that:

1. Many services are 'perishable' and cannot be turned into stock (for example, a seat on an aeroplane flight).
2. Because the consumer and producer interact in a service business, the consumer becomes a potential source of capacity (for example, in a self-service as opposed to a service-provided petrol station). The design of the service will determine the extent to which this takes place.
3. Defining a service in many businesses is difficult and as a consequence capacity is difficult to measure (for example, what constitutes serving a customer in a retail store?)
4. In most instances a service is provided and consumed at the same time (for example, dressing hair).

Third, larger orders will help to reduce the number of change-overs from making one product to another, which itself will lead to an increase in productive capacity.

The determination and control of capacity is at three levels:

1. Long-term capacity planning.
2. Aggregate planning – a medium-level planning activity looking ahead for periods of up to two years.
3. Operations control – monitoring production capacity in the short term.

Several decisions are involved in determining long-term capacity (see Figure 4 again), and the following factors impinge on them:

1. *Forecast demand.* Although this is difficult companies must try to do it, since the alternative is to have no plan at all.
2. *Characteristics of a make-to-order business.* In a make-to-order business a company is rarely able to produce anything ahead of known orders. So planning in this type of business means developing a capacity for the level and size of orders the company hopes its salesmen will get.

3. *Make-or-buy decision.* In theory, every component can either be made internally by the company itself or bought outside. Obviously, the more of a product or service which is provided internally, the greater the capacity has to be.

This attempt to forecast demand, and consider some of the issues involved in the exercise, is logically prior to decisions about the layout of manufacturing facilities.

FACILITIES LAYOUT

Facilities layout involves arranging such entities as the machines, equipment, workplaces, support functions, people, and so on within planned or existing buildings. The objective here is to reduce costs and provide for an orderly and efficient working arrangement.

The choice of process referred to earlier – project, jobbing, batch, and so on – has a fundamental influence on the design of the layout, as this choice dictates the flow of materials through what we have called the transformation process. There are three basic types of layouts which relate to the different choices of process.

Fixed Position Layout

Where a product is very large or needs to be provided in a particular location, then fixed-position layout is the appropriate way to locate all the necessary facilities. The situation is the normal layout for the project process where the resources needed to complete the task in the form of people, equipment and services are transported to the point where the product is being built or the service provided: for example, building a motorway, or on the service side organizing a lecture tour. The operations task is to reallocate these resources, once they have been used, to similar sites.

Process/Functional Layouts

A layout by process or by function brings together similar process capacities into the same geographical area. For example, all drilling machines will be positioned together, as would the invoicing checking section in a large administrative function. This layout reflects the fact that the business, in attempting to offer a wide range of products or services, has invested in people and plant capacities to meet these requirements. The demand for the particular product or service, however, is unlikely to be sufficient to warrant the dedication of a particular set of processes to making or providing that need. Consequently, different orders follow different paths through similar facilities. In order to increase the utilization of these facilities, and to facilitate specialization, similar facilities are grouped together as described. Each product or service is then routed through the appropriate facilities to complete the necessary operations (see Figure 5).

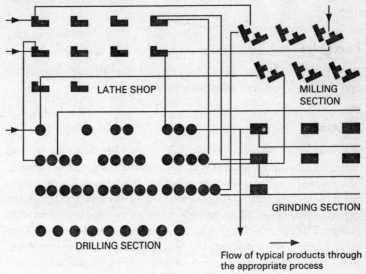

5 Typical product movement in a simplified process layout (Hill, 1983)

Product Layout

As volumes increase, the choice of process moves towards line or continuous process. High sales volumes are now sufficient to warrant dedicated plant, assigned to completing these products or items. The way the product is to be made or service provided is now determined and the facilities are laid down in a 'line' which reflects this. The product or service then flows down the line and is completed in this set of operations. It is unusual to find this product layout in service industries, but it is common in manufacturing, in the production of domestic appliances for instance.

PRODUCT/SERVICE DATA

An essential input into capacity planning, aggregate planning and operations control is the provision of adequate and accurate product/service data. These data include the materials, routings and costings associated with the products and services being provided.

Parts List

Parts lists are statements of the type and quantity of components and materials required to make a product or to provide a service.

Routings

An important feature of the production/operations task is to determine the different steps to make a product or provide a service, and the best way for these to be arranged. These routings then form the basis for completing the task and are an essential input into the capacity planning and operations planning and control referred to earlier. The information will include the task at each step, the time it takes (from work-study data), any machine setting-up involved, and other equipment required, together with details which will help the job to be completed more effectively.

Costings

Costing information derived from material, labour and overhead inputs will also be provided. Such information may be stored in this data-base or be provided by the accounting function.

OPERATIONS PLANNING AND CONTROL

A business, having obtained orders for its products/services, then has to provide them. To help achieve this it has to invest in the necessary procedures as well as processes, buildings and people. This section of the chapter concerns the investment in procedures to help control the work. These procedures span a long planning horizon as follows:

1. Long-term operations planning – this forms part of the capacity-planning procedure discussed earlier and generally looks five or more years ahead.
2. Aggregate planning – for periods up to two years ahead.
3. Operations control – monitoring the short-term activities involved in the production of goods or provision of services to meet customer orders or forecast sales (for example, to check that orders are on schedule).

Different processes, however, are controlled in different ways.

Project

The project process is selected by a business which provides products/services which are both one-off and of a large size. If there are few activities involved then the control approach is informal. Most projects, however, are complex and involve a large number of interrelated activities. Where this is the case, a formal control procedure needs to be developed. The generic name to cover these controls is network analysis. Various forms of network have been developed to provide different levels of control sophistication and to cover different control situations. The best known of these is critical path analysis (CPA). The network is drawn to present a picture of all the activities involved and show the interrelated nature of these activities to complete the task. The critical path is a key feature of this control procedure and refers to the set of sequential activities which together take the longest time to complete. Hence, if delays occur on these activities then the completion time will be extended.

Intermittent Processes: Jobbing and Batch

Jobbing processes are chosen to handle one-off, often large-scale, orders, whereas batch reflects the volume and product/service features of increased demand and the standard nature of the items sold. In operations-control terms the size of the task differs owing to the approach adopted in these two processes.

In a jobbing process, as much of the task is completed by one person, then the loading, sequencing and scheduling tasks are simplified. A typical scheduling solution is to use a bar chart similar to that in Figure 6 which provides an overall control picture of the

6 Bar chart representing assignment allocations to management consultants (Hill, 1983)

assignments loaded, the estimated completion of tasks and the availability of consultants (that is, capacity) to take on more work.

In batch processes, the key control is normally to provide information on the state of the numerous orders in the process against the delivery promises made to customers. A typical bar chart shows orders against process sequence on a time scale and Figure 7 provides an example. The increased uses of computers in these situations has enabled the high quantities of data to be managed more effectively and to provide that on-line, updated

PROCESS DESCRIPTION		ORDER SCHEDULING
	001	Order details should be shown in this section to a time-scale. The display of orders could be horizontal tabs, cards in preformed slots on the board, and so on. If this were a computer tabulation, the order descriptions might appear on the left of this area with the number of time-units (e.g. days/hours) shown to the right
	002	
SECTION 000 NC MACHINES	003	
	004	
	005	
	101	
	102	
SECTION 100 MILLING	103	
	104	
	105	

Time

7 Part of a scheduling plan in bar-chart form showing groups and the jobs loaded against each machine in the groups.

procedure so essential to the control of operations in batch processes.

Continuous Systems: Line and Continuous Processes

In these two processes, the loading and sequencing of jobs is built into the process itself as the plant is designed around the sequence of operations necessary to complete the product. The production-control task, therefore, is to monitor the flow of materials and components to the line or continuous process and then to monitor the products, once completed, in line with customer orders or ware-housing provision.

MATERIALS CONTROL

Inventory or stock comprises three main types, based upon the stage of an item's manufacture or provision:

raw materials and bought-out components;
work-in-progress (part finished items or services);
finished goods or items awaiting sale or dispatch.

In most manufacturing companies, the value of inventory is very high and usually is between 30 and 40 per cent of total assets. The advantages gained from this high investment include:

1. Raw materials and bought-out components allow the business to:
   (i) cope with the variability of supply; (ii) take advantage of quantity discounts; (iii) guard against uncertainty of supply; (iv) guard against price increases.

2. Work-in-progress inventory uncouples one part of the process from another part. Thus, one part feeds into an inventory holding and the next stage takes from this inventory holding at a later time. By doing this, it helps create greater flexibility and improves the utilization of the process.

3. Finished-goods inventory provides: (i) off-the-shelf customer service; (ii) some ability to cope with demand fluctuations; (iii) an insurance against process breakdowns or shortages.

The aim of materials or inventory control, therefore, is to provide these functions for a business while trying to minimize the value of the inventory holdings, not only because of the considerable investment involved but also the insurance, space and control costs associated with its provision. Two important perspectives underlying inventory control are the dependent/independent demand principle and the 80/20 rule.

To take first the dependent/independent distinction, separate items such as finished goods are classified as independent, whereas the components or sub-assemblies which go into these independent items are classed as dependent. This classification means that demand is forecast only for independent items, as the demand for the dependent items which go into them can be calculated automatically.

The 80/20 rule refers to the phenomenon that, in general, it can be said that 20 per cent of inventory accounts for 80 per cent of the total annual requirement value (unit value ($£$) for each inventory item × the annual usage in number of units = annual requirement value). Where this is so, the control implications for items will differ as explained later.

Another important set of information which is necessary to the planning and control function of the POM task is the provision of work-study data. This includes two main areas: method study and work measurement.

Method Study

'Method study is the systematic and critical examination of the ways of doing things in order to make improvements.' The key words in this British Standards (3138) definition are 'systematic and critical examination'. The systematic nature of this approach is exemplified by the steps to be adopted in a method study application. These are:

1. Select the work to be studied.
2. Record the relevant facts about the present method.
3. Examine the facts critically to seek improvements.
4. Develop the best way to do the job.
5. Record the new way and re-examine it.
6. Train those who need to do this job.
7. Install the new method as standard practice.
8. Maintain the new method with regular checks.

Work Measurement

'Work measurement is the application of techniques designed to establish the time for a qualified worker to carry out a task at a defined level of performance' (British Standards (3138)). Some of the techniques available are:

1. *Estimating:* using experienced people to determine the approximate time it would take to do the job.
2. *Time study:* a technique which requires a trained person to measure, on a stop-watch, the time it takes to do the job while

also assessing the rate at which the work is being carried out and adjusting the time allowed accordingly.

3. *PMTS:* predetermined motion time standards (PMTS) is a synthetic-based work-measurement technique where the time to complete a task is derived from predetermined tables of times for basic motions which have been based on many previous studies.

Once labour standards have been established, these then form an integral part of assessing capacity requirements, facilities layout provision, operations planning and control, and labour costs.

QUALITY ASSURANCE

The quality-assurance function embraces a range of activities which affect the quality of products or services. These include responsibility for specifying the quality characteristics of bought-out parts, and inspecting them on their arrival in the company, as well as responsibility for final inspection of the company's products, and in some cases intermediate checks at various stages of production.

MANUFACTURING AND THE PROVISION OF SERVICES TO MEET THE DELIVERY REQUIREMENTS OF THE CUSTOMER

In order to achieve the plan, the people, facilities, schedules and paperwork statements of what needs to be done have to be provided within the POM function, together with the schedules needed to be met in terms of the efficiency, cost, delivery and quality criteria appertaining to that business. The effective control of day-to-day activities is an essential part of the POM task. An hour lost is never regained without incurring additional costs and, as POM is usually responsible for the highest proportion of costs, then the effective control of these is a prerequisite to a profitable and successful business.

In addition, for some organizations, finished-goods warehousing, installation and after-sales support form part of the total provision and are administratively part of the POM task. As such these features are an essential part of what the business sells and, hence, has to provide.

CONCLUSION

The integration of schedules, bought-out parts, quality requirements, short-term and longer-term capacity issues, people, skill levels, process capability, absenteeism, breakdowns and more besides presents a difficult management job. Superimpose on to this the volume and numbers involved, together with the need to develop and improve this important area of expenditure and investment, and a task of considerable complexity is revealed. The internally derived dimensions and constituents of good performance are numerous. In addition, meeting schedules and the customer's review of quality and delivery performance constitutes another important perspective of what is meant by a 'good job'.

Operations management is then a function of considerable diversity and importance. It requires:

1. attention to detail, yet a need for long-term strategic thinking;
2. decisions based upon expediency, yet a need for continuous development; and
3. actions to meet today's priorities, yet the need to agree and meet future plans in an orderly and efficient manner.

The dimensions and skills of the task are many and span the whole business.

CHAPTER 20

Purchasing

JOHN STEVENS

PURCHASING AND ITS TERMS OF REFERENCE

In the last decade materials have become an ever-increasing proportion of the cost of producing an item for sale. The Bureau of the US Department of Commerce reported in 1980 that the average cost of fuel, components and raw materials exceeded 58 per cent of the value of finished products. The situation is similar in the UK and this percentage will probably increase as specialization increases. It can be appreciated, therefore, that the purchasing function is essential to the firm in the sense that purchasing is the life-blood of the production department, pumping in vital materials and supplies. Yet purchasing is often regarded as merely a subordinate service function. This is a serious mistake, as purchasing can make a positive contribution to profits and can provide considerable information which is vital to the forward planning of a company.

In view of the escalating cost of purchased items, the purchasing function plays a vital role in the profitability of the firm as a whole, and so it is essential that it should have the influence and power to perform this task effectively. Purchasing must also be integrated within the firm's organizational structure so as to facilitate the achievement of these objectives. The materials-management concept evolved in recognition of this need:

> Materials Management is the concept requiring an organisational structure which unifies into one functional responsibility the systematic planning and control of all materials from identification of the need through to delivery to the consumer.
> Materials Management embraces planning, purchasing, production and inventory control, storage, materials handling and physical distribution.
> The objectives of Materials Management are to optimise

performance in meeting agreed customer service requirement at the same time adding to profitability by minimising costs and making best use of available resources. (The Institute of Purchasing and Supply)

This concept of materials management puts the purchasing operation in context, and shows the wider activities with which it is necessarily associated.

PURCHASING LINKS WITH THE REST OF THE FIRM

Purchasing clearly cannot operate in isolation within the company and two-way lines of communication with other functions are just as important as communication with the supplies market (see Figure 1).

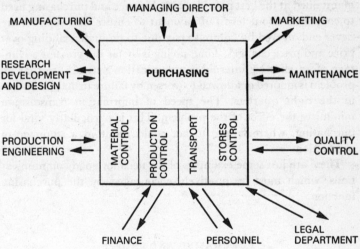

1 Materials-management organization

Purchasing can give vital information to top management about supplies, market price trends and possible shortages to assist in making top-level decisions. In return top management can give advance information about policy and so purchasing can assess the consequences and take appropriate anticipatory action.

If production and quality control are not satisfied with the quality performance of a supplier, purchasing can take the necessary steps to ensure improvement or to find an alternative supplier. Or again liaison with design and development is necessary when considering possible product innovations which may require new or specialist suppliers. Or marketing can advise of changes in demand for a product, and hence changed demand for its bought-out components.

Design and development, marketing, and purchasing, all involved at the initial stages of specifying the quality of material for a new product, can resolve the problems of price and availability versus technical perfection – thus enabling the company to obtain additional profits by the prevention of over-specifying by designers.

Purchasing can assist production with make or buy decisions by checking outside suppliers to ensure that constant supplies are maintained at the best possible price. Finance and purchasing need to cooperate about terms of payment to ensure that supplies are never endangered by failure to pay due to misunderstanding over price and price changes. Time-saving is by far the greatest advantage of an effective internal communication network, so that no problem is ignored or allowed to worsen by failure to make it known in the right quarters. The speed of information transmission minimizes the effect of the problem. This is particularly vital for purchasing, where failure to act could result in a stoppage of production.

These are just some examples of the need for good communications, which must be positively encouraged by the purchasing function.

PURCHASING AND PROFIT

If the average purchasing department spends over half of its company's income, it follows that purchasing can make a major contribution to profitability. Figure 2 shows the potential for its direct role in profit-making. If the largest cost element can be reduced then the net-income slice can be increased.

With this potential area for profit contribution the common approach to seeking increased profits from increased sales should be

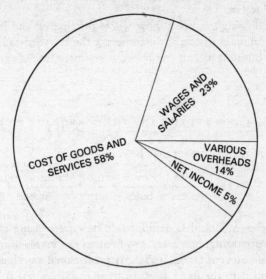

2 The purchasing pre-costs and profits as a percentage of sales

examined critically, and compared with opportunities for profit from purchasing and materials management.

Consider the example:

Sales volume	£100,000,000
Material costs	£ 50,000,000
Gross profit on sales	10%
A 25% increase in sales =	£25,000,000
Increased profit =	£ 2,500,000

How much has to be saved on purchases to give an equivalent £2,500,000 increased profit? In fact a 5 per cent saving on material costs gives a profit of £2,500,000 and it will normally be easier to get 5 per cent off the cost of materials than to increase sales by 25 per cent.

Such considerations will provide management with a guideline to making a balanced judgement about profit opportunities from selling and buying. This should result in a more balanced investment in skills and personnel employed in the functions of marketing and purchasing, something which has not been universally accepted so far.

The following examples show where purchasing and inventory control can make dramatic differences to the key yardsticks used to measure business success (return on investment, use of capital and profit).

PURCHASING, PROFITS AND THE CORPORATE PICTURE

The return on investment may be computed as:

$$ROI = \frac{Sales}{Assets} \times \frac{Profits}{Sales} \times \frac{100}{1} = \frac{Profit \times 100}{Assets}$$

Examples A, B and C demonstrate how purchasing can affect results. Purchasing, however, is sometimes not involved in capital purchases (Stevens, 1974, 1975). If professional purchasing had been applied to the fixed assets in these examples (A, B, C) then

Example A: Existing situation

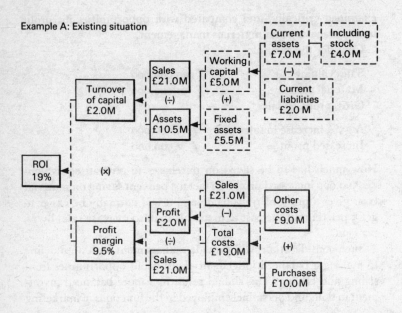

Example B Impact of savings of 5 per cent on purchases (= £500,000)

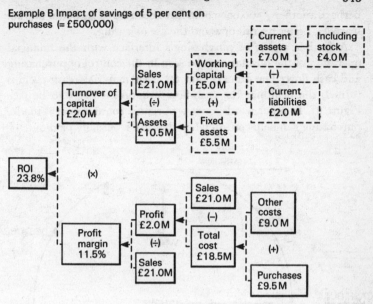

Example C Impact of stock reduction of £500,000

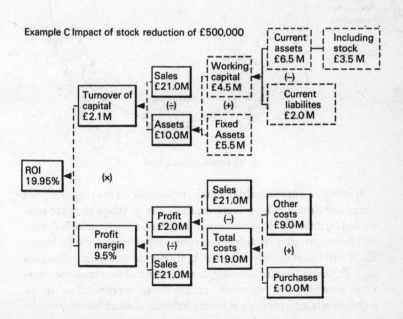

perhaps another £500,000 could have been saved by better market searches, better negotiation and the use of leasing.

A further aspect of purchasing's interface with the financial operation of the business can be seen in the control of purchasing and cash flow. The quicker that the cash–materials–cash cycle is turned, the healthier the cash-flow situation is likely to be (see Figure 3). In other words, once a purchase commitment is made, purchasing can help control when the cash is actually paid out.

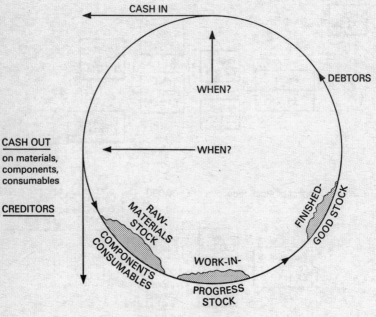

3 The cash/stock wheel

It is important to consider who is responsible for making decisions about the three stock pools shown in Figure 3. When they are controlled by different departments or functions decision-making times will be longer, and confidence in other departments will be lower. Each will build unduly high stocks if they do not trust colleagues in purchasing, manufacturing or marketing. The complete overview provided by materials management would allow quick adjustments and produce a better balance of stock levels over the

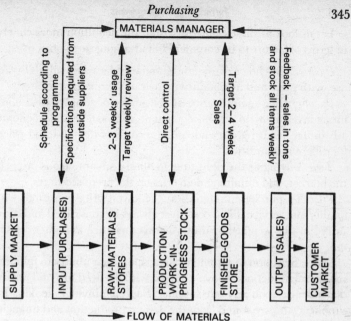

4 An integrated approach to materials control

three main stock holdings. Opportunities for buying ahead could be taken, financed perhaps by concomitant stock reduction in work in progress or finished goods. The model in Figure 4 shows an integrated approach to the control over materials which is the essence of materials management. Information would be gathered by the materials manager from both customer markets and supply markets.

But not all organizations have installed materials management on this integrated model and so its component parts may thus operate independently. When purchasing stands alone the following 'classic' definition summarizes its commonly accepted objectives.

> Purchasing is that function which aims to secure materials and services of the correct quality, in the correct quantity, at the right time, at the right price, from the right source, to be delivered as, when and where necessary.*

* Ironically no one remembers the source of this passage, regularly quoted in purchasing textbooks.

Let us look at these elements within the definition more closely, in terms of factors to be considered in attaining these objectives:

Quality. The choice of material standards, based on suitability for use, with price and availability related to the quality required.

Quantity. The maintenance of continuity of supply, with minimum investment in stocks, consistent with safety and economic advantage. This requires adequate records of demand and prices for different quantities.

Time. Buying at the right time to obtain advantageous prices in the market, and obtaining deliveries on the promised dates.

Price. To purchase materials at the lowest price consistent with quality and service. Final cost must always be considered and a low price must be weighed against other factors, such as higher costs in use.

Source. Selection of suppliers based upon their ability to fulfil the requirements defined above, coupled with the need to avoid unwise dependence upon any one supplier. Sourcing involves looking for suppliers who are sound from the design, production and financial points of view.

The terms of reference given to the purchasing function vary, and sometimes buying is carried out independently of inventory control and physical storekeeping. Here the term 'purchasing' is relevant. If some integration has taken place, a supplies organization may be said to exist, while total integration results in what we have called materials management.

Thus a purchasing department might carry out all or any of the following activities (see Croell, 1977, and Farrington and Wood-mansey, 1980):

1. Advising the board of directors on all matters relating to the organization's supply policy.
2. Giving assistance to consuming departments in determining the nature and time of need. Developing good liaison in the organization on all matters concerning materials.
3. Negotiating with and selecting suppliers, and fostering goodwill outside the organization and particularly in the supply market.
4. Progressing, or chasing suppliers to make sure they deliver on time.

5. Receiving and inspecting supplies delivered.
6. Checking invoices and approving them for payment.
7. Making inventory decisions and defining an inventory-management policy on bought-out materials.
8. Researching both new materials and alternative sources of supply.
9. Controlling in-bound transport requirements.
10. Disposing of scrap and surplus material.

The weight of importance given to this mix varies from one company to another; routine activities, nos. 4, 5 and 7, may sometimes be the predominant work of the department; in a weak purchasing department, no. 3 may mean merely placing orders where the supplier and specification has already been chosen by the user, say the design or production department. On the other hand a strong purchasing function might contribute substantially to nos. 1, 2 and 8, and would certainly be the key decision-maker in no. 3.

Evidence of purchasing's professionalism in source decision-making might be found in the degree to which pre-sourcing checks are carried out, and how objectively supplier performance is measured.

SUPPLIER CAPABILITY/SUPPLIER PRE-SOURCING CHECK

In order to secure satisfactory quality, price, timeliness, service and continuity of supply it is necessary for the buyer to have as much information as possible about present suppliers. This involves collecting information about actual or potential suppliers under the following headings.

Technical capability is concerned with the quality of the supplier's design and development facilities, production, and test and tool engineering. It involves establishing whether a source could ensure quality before, during and after production.

Production capability is the total capacity and efficiency of the supplier's production function and includes planning and control, manufacturing expertise, plant and equipment installed, inspection, stores and inventory control.

Financial capability refers to the supplier's financial stability and credit rating.

Management capability involves checking the effectiveness of the supplier's internal administration and systems, and their means of establishing and maintaining external relationships.

Purchasing capability involves checking the effectiveness of the supplier's own purchasing department.

A good start to a capability-analysis exercise is to keep an on-going record – a sort of 'identikit' of the suppliers. Key personnel should be noted, and any change in the management team might need a visit to check out the new person who may not fully understand the business if recruited from a different industry.

The sourcing decision is complicated and the purchasing department may have a range of options to choose from in some cases. All of the following may be simultaneously open to the buyer:

> Make *or* Buy
>> (Stevens, 1979; Jauch and Wilson, 1979)

> Use single *or* Multi-source
>> (Brooks, 1976)

> Use a manufacturer *or* Distributor
>> (Webster, 1975)

> Continue with old *or* Change to new supplier
>> (Buckner, 1967)

> Use small *or* Medium *or* large supplier
>> (Brand, 1972)

> Use customer *or* Free-agent supplier
>> (Bird & Shepherd, 1973; Ammer, 1962)

> Use home *or* Overseas supplier
>> (Newbury-Ecob, 1974; Davis, Eppen and Mattson, 1974)

> Use sister company *or* Free-agent supplier
>> (Swallow, 1976)

Use barter/counter/ *or* Normal purchase for cash
compensation trade   (Weigand, 1977; Lee, 1980; and Lattimer, 1980).

In considering these options a planned programme of supplier development is needed, continually seeking out, and recruiting, sources into the supply-market network (Leenders, 1965). Another question is the balance between purchasing becoming prone to excess supplier loyalty on the one hand, and the advantages of close and long-term supplier relationships on the other.

PURCHASING'S ROLE IN QUALITY DETERMINATION

Purchasing can make an input to the 'three Ds of Quality' (Determining, Defining and Directing Quality) by using a structured approach to arriving at descriptions or specifications. Users may not be able to move from a 'need' to writing the specifications themselves, and so the procedure in the flow diagram in Figure 5 below could be used.

Changes in organizational arrangements might also facilitate a better involvement of purchasing. Too often purchasing is at the

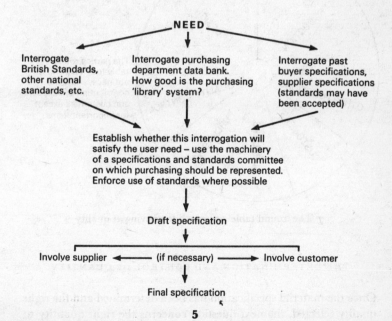

NEED

Interrogate British Standards, other national standards, etc.

Interrogate purchasing department data bank. How good is the purchasing 'library' system?

Interrogate past buyer specifications, supplier specifications (standards may have been accepted)

Establish whether this interrogation will satisfy the user need – use the machinery of a specifications and standards committee on which purchasing should be represented. Enforce use of standards where possible

Draft specification

Involve supplier ← (if necessary) → Involve customer

Final specification

5

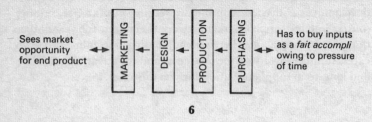

6

end of a long decision chain when quality and decisions are made (Figure 6, above). A better organization arrangement might be to adopt a 'round table' approach, so purchasing could make an input at the design stage, as shown in Figure 7, where Q represents quality, the topic for discussion which would produce consensus on technical versus commercial questions.

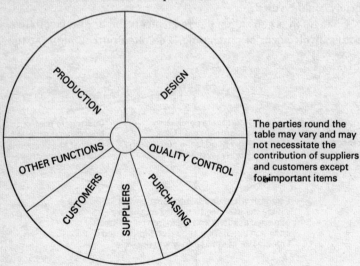

The parties round the table may vary and may not necessitate the contribution of suppliers and customers except for important items

7 The 'round table' approach to arriving at quality

THE DETERMINATION AND CONTROL OF QUANTITY

Once the material specification has been determined and the right quality selected, the next question concerns the right quantity to order. The fundamental responsibility of the purchasing department to meet the material needs of the factory and total requirements can usually be forecast fairly accurately from sales estimates, or the trend of incoming orders, or from production programmes and records. Although the ultimate objective of purchasing must be to satisfy the need for providing the total quantity required, it does not follow that the correct purchasing procedure is to buy or contract for the full quantity at one time. The 'right quantity' implies the determination by formula or policy of the particular quantity to be bought at any one time.

The manner in which quantities are determined varies with the type of production:

1. For special projects, quantities are based on specific needs.
2. For seasonal production, quantities are recurrent though not spread uniformly.
3. For continuous production, quantities are recurrent and uniformly spread.
4. For batch production, intermittent quantities are coordinated with the manufacturing programme.

If design or processing changes, or if revision of sales estimates are probable, then quantities may be provisional. Price trends also influence the ordering of quantities. Greater quantities may be bought on a rising market to take advantage of the cheaper rate when prices are rising, but buying is on a hand-to-mouth basis when prices are falling, particularly with high-priced materials which show wide price variations. Furthermore there are usually specific times in the year when a purchase will be more favourable from the negotiating point of view.

Other factors which will influence and in some cases determine quantities are the capacity of suppliers, rate of use, delivery time, storage costs and facilities, deterioration, transport costs, ordering costs and discounts. One of the following basic methods of determining order quantities might be selected after considering such factors:

1. Purchasing exact requirements and quantities based on specific needs.
2. Maintenance of agreed maximum and minimum quantities.

3. The use of the economic order quantity formula. This EOQ is the optimum trade-off between the cost of stockholding and the cost of acquisition: it is usually depicted in textbooks as the point where these two cost lines intersect.

4. The use of a periodic-review system. PRS is geared to time: basically the idea is that high-value items, say axles in a car factory, are bought in small numbers, held for only a short time, and the stock situation is reviewed frequently; whereas low-value items, say elastic bands, are bought in large numbers and held for a long time, with stocks being reviewed only infrequently.

5. Quantities varied according to price trend or availability.

6. Quantities based on forecast of probable demand and price fluctuations.

DETERMINING THE RIGHT PRICE

Sensitive commodities and capital goods are at opposite ends of the price characteristic spectrum. Methods of purchasing these items will be used to demonstrate this aspect of the purchasing task.

As far as price is concerned commodity items more nearly approach the economist's model. Most commodities are raw materials or foodstuffs produced in underdeveloped countries. The supply of such commodities may vary owing to climatic, economic or political factors. On the demand side, major nations stockpile or sometimes even release stocks of strategic materials, and so the interaction of supply and demand largely determines price. However, in many instances international agreements have modified the natural tendency for prices to vary according to demand/supply factors.

Capital items, on the other hand, are very often required as 'specials' by purchasing managers. The worth of the item is seen in its use within the purchaser's company, and buyers may be prepared to pay a premium according to this. Price, however, will be based on the cost of producing the item concerned, and the elements can be analysed. This approach to establishing price, known as price/cost analysis, can, with modification, be applied to things made for sale as well:

$$
\text{Price} = \begin{cases}
\text{Direct material cost} \\
\text{Direct labour cost} \\
\text{Design cost} \\
\text{R \& D cost} \\
\text{Factory overhead} \\
\text{Sales cost} \\
\text{General administrative expense} \\
\text{Profit margin}
\end{cases}
$$

Many materials are 'standard' in supply and are priced on the basis of various discounts. The table overleaf classifies these and indicates why sellers offer discounts, and what purchasers might do to prepare a counter-strategy in an attempt to improve discounts.

CONCLUSION

This chapter has underlined the advantages of professionalizing what is probably the last function in business which has been staffed by personnel with little education and training in the principles and techniques appropriate to it.

The profit potential in the effective operation of the purchasing and supply activity has been identified, together with the benefits of integrating purchasing, stock control, production control, inbound traffic, expediting and warehousing under the umbrella of materials management.

The role of purchasing in contributing to corporate policy-making and major decisions was outlined. The basic aspects of the task were described as getting the five rights: right quantity, quality, price, time and source. The emphasis here was to draw attention to the need for purchasing to make a positive approach to contributing fully in decision-making in all of these aspects of supply, if it wishes to gain acceptance as a key business function.

TABLE I *The buyer's price discount strategy*

Type of discount and commonest main supplier objective	Seller's strategy	Purchasing initiative
Quantity discounts Often offered as an inducement to purchase and take delivery of a larger lot. May be given when supplier has handsomely covered total costs. Discount given when supplier invoices for amount purchased and delivered.	1. Longer economic runs. 2. Sales protection. 3. Follow market leader. 4. To produce economic loads for transport. 5. To stock finished goods. 6. As a means of pushing through work-in-progress stocks.	Larger quantity to be balanced against increased stockholding cost, use of EOQ or use of opportunity cost in investing in extra quantity as compared with alternative use of money, and comparable return on investment.
Deferred rebates Given on cumulative value of business, usually at end of year's trading agreement.	As a defensive or positive marketing strategy?	Ensure a progressive discount structure. Examine the impact on sourcing strategy. What is the 'real value' of the deferred rebate?
Liquidity discounts Offered for prompt payment of accounts.	Is it for this ostensibly financial reason, or is it another marketing ploy?	*Weigh up* 1. Economics of paying early to gain discount. 2. Disruption costs of paying exceptions early.
'Trade' discounts To discriminate between distribution channels and ultimate users of the product.	The distributor's price differential-objective is to maintain distribution channels. To allow faster throughput as a manufacturer.	Evaluate the 'benefits' of the distribution link critically. Do we need them? Compare with sourcing ex manufacturer when a source choice exists. If justified in using the middleman, use to the fullest by:

	Physical distribution cost considerations. To allow manufacturers to dispose of low-value small orders.	consolidation of purchases via blanket orders; utilization of technical facilities, e.g. get stockholder to tailor original product (e.g. steel stockholders) and use his consultancy advice.
Specific incentives *Seasonal discounts* *Promotional discounts* *Containers, packages* *Price for scrap* or contaminated material supplied 'as new' in first instance. To recognize special supply circumstances.	To 'flatten' uneven demand to boost sales. An incentive to return containers promptly or incur a penalty, but perhaps a move to obtain extra profit? Used as a lever to maintain business for new material.	Buy in the off season. Take advantage if the purchase is a short-term requirement. Relate the cost of the package to the charge. Ensure good package control on site. Uncouple prices and negotiate them both. Net price paid may be the only yardstick in a difficult supply situation.
Discounts offered on 'group' contracts To recognize the existence of group-purchasing influences in customer organizations.	Where initiated by the supplier, to obtain wider business in-group or to defend business gained at factory level.	To make use of the strength of the group's purchasing power. Local purchasing management may be able to meet or beat global discounts if they can then examine the consequences of sourcing outside the group contract. Will it affect the contract and the discount structure agreed or not? If it does, what is the nett result on the corporate costs of supplies?

For further discussion material on price see Farrington, 1978, and Atkin and Skinner, 1976.

CHAPTER 21

Personnel Management: An Organizational Perspective

PAUL WINDOLF

PERSONNEL MANAGEMENT IN A HISTORICAL PERSPECTIVE

Personnel management is a product of welfare capitalism. As the factory system developed during the nineteenth century, working conditions became more and more intolerable. However, the excessive exploitation of the workforce proved to be counter-productive and so owners responded by developing techniques which eased working conditions. In Britain, Robert Owen was one of the first to introduce principles of welfare, education and 'mutuality' into a purely profit-orientated business (Briggs, 1968; Cole, 1925).

At this early stage personnel did not yet exist as a separate function. Mass production differed considerably from traditional handicraft methods. It required a new type of worker who had to be accommodated to unusual working conditions, the discipline of time and the loss of traditional autonomy. New techniques were needed to train a traditionally oriented workforce to new machinery and the division of labour (Pollard, 1965).

As migration from rural to industrial areas increased and the traditional family system broke down a new safety net had to be built up to protect workers against sickness and accidents. Social security had previously been organized by the family and the rural community. With rising social anomy, these traditional systems could no longer function and had to be replaced.

So, long before personnel became a recognized part of management, enlightened factory owners were aware of the importance of education, socialization and welfare for integrating the workforce into the production process. Thus, the predecessor of personnel management is the social worker rather than the scientific or business-oriented manager.

National differences in welfare capitalism were apparent even at an early stage. Whereas in Germany social welfare became a primary concern of state regulation, it remained the responsibility of firms and unions in Britain and the United States. Unemployment benefits and sickness payment were one of the important services unions had to offer to their members. Thus, the institutional framework for 'corporatist' solutions in Germany and the particular type of 'voluntarism' in Britain were already established in the last century (Flanders, 1974). These institutional arrangements had important and far-reaching consequences for the organization of personnel management and industrial relations.

Functions of personnel management evolved with changes in the social and cultural environment. Welfare and socialization figured among its most important tasks at the beginning of this century, whereas today welfare is organized by central state machinery (Atkinson, 1969). Personnel has become a highly specialized and professionalized management function at the centre of the conflict between capital and labour. Personnel managers hold boundary roles between the organization and the workforce, and serve as a safety valve for the organization. As collective bargaining and joint consultation replace the unilateral regulation of the work process, personnel departments become important in providing a procedural framework for joint job regulation.

In most organizations personnel functions develop through several stages. Initially personnel functions such as recruitment, training and redundancy are dealt with by line managers or foremen. Gradually personnel functions are centralized until a professionalized department has successfully monopolized all personnel functions as its own 'job territory'. Line managers in other departments are forced to abstain from personnel decisions because these come under the scope of a professionalized department. This process of functional differentiation is paralleled by a similar development of formalization and centralization of decision-making.

The contrast between traditional and professional personnel practice comes out well in a case study of a gypsum firm (Gouldner, 1954) describing the idiosyncratic decision-making of a foreman when hiring, firing, or promoting workers. Characteristics of the applicants such as appearance, their personal links to employees of the firm and arbitrary feelings of sympathy and dislike for particular workers were the main 'guidelines' used by the foreman. In contrast, professionalized personnel management should provide a barrier against such favouritism. Decisions are based on universalistic standards, they observe affective neutrality when hiring labour, and are oriented towards achievement rather than observable characteristics such as race or sex (Parsons and Shils, 1967, p. 77).

Furthermore, the rationality of personnel policy is not (or only to a minor degree) conditional upon the rationality of individual actors. It depends on the rationality of organizational structures with members acting in accordance with their role obligations.

CONTROL OF THE INTERNAL ENVIRONMENT

The term 'environment' is used as a shorthand label for a collection of variables which influence and are influenced by organizations. The differentiation between the 'internal' and 'external' environment (Duncan, 1972) proves particularly useful for the analysis of personnel management.

The 'external' environment of a business firm comprises product and labour markets, legal frameworks and political institutions, whereas the 'internal' environment is an analytical label for members of the organization, that is, the workforce of the firm. Though this connotation may seem rather odd, the reader is reminded that organizations are analysed in terms of abstract rules and roles rather than in terms of individual members. This distinction emphasizes the point that the *integration* of members into organizational roles is not taken for granted but is seen as an important objective for personnel management. The main function of personnel management is the control of the internal environment.

Environments and organizational structure influence each other. The implications of this for personnel management are that, on the one hand, the degree of specialization, professionalization and formalization of personnel policy is strongly influenced by environmental constaints; on the other, these organizational structures are instruments for controlling the external and internal environment.

This control implies negative as well as positive incentives. It requires training, moral persuasion and joint consultation. Generally speaking, personnel management has to achieve the compliance of the workforce with organizational goals. Ways of achieving this compliance vary considerably depending on the 'image of man' which personnel management adheres to. If the 'economic man' is the basic model, monetary incentives are the most important instruments of control. If, however, the 'responsible man' serves as a guideline, then co-determination and joint consultation are at least as important as a fair wage structure.

Functions of personnel management may now be defined more precisely: personnel is an active 'boundary department' charged with the control of labour markets; it has to influence educational institutions (as, for instance, schools and universities) and the legal framework as far as possible. At the same time, personnel departments have to adjust the work process to changing external conditions, such as a shortage of labour or a new strike strategy by unions. With respect to the 'internal' environment, personnel management has to integrate the workforce. Motivation, training, and enlarging the flexible capacity and skills of workers figure among the most important tasks of personnel.

THE POWER OF PERSONNEL MANAGEMENT

The concept of uncertainty has been used to generate hypotheses concerning power relationships within the organization (Hickson et al., 1971; Hinings et al., 1974). Basically, the concept refers to the 'unpredictability' of the firm's environment, and those departments which cope most successfully with uncertainty are the most powerful.

Specialized departments within the firm are largely concerned with particular segments of the environment which are of different importance for the success and survival of the firm. Those departments which have to cope with environments particularly important for the firm's survival are the most powerful. In most firms sales markets are more 'crucial' than markets for raw material, though in the petrol industry different priorities may be observed.

During times of high unemployment the labour market and the recruitment of skilled workers are less problematic compared with technical and product innovation. Occasionally, recruitment is not a problem and so personnel management ranks at the end of the prestige hierarchy of departments. Generally speaking, the labour market is a less crucial environment for most firms compared with problems of product innovation and sales. But in sheltered industries which enjoy a quasi-monopoly in the market (such as coalmining) the personnel department may be very powerful since the workforce and its integration is the most crucial problem facing the company.

Environments may be more or less 'turbulent', and so they are more or less predictable. In West Germany, for instance, the workforce seems to be more 'predictable' and their organized actions are less disruptive compared with Britain. The varying uncertainty of environments also holds true for different industries. Whereas in coalmining, the automobile industry and shipbuilding, personnel management has to cope with an active and organized workforce, industrial action is of less importance in textiles or banking. The unpredictability of the environment provides a further explanation for the relative power of personnel departments within the firm. The more difficult the environment is to organize, then the more power and organizational resources the department needs.

The uncertainty and importance of the environmental segment may both be high, but if the department is unsuccessful in coping with uncertainty, this failure may have negative consequences for the prestige and power of that department.

Finally, the extent to which a sub-unit's activity can be substituted influences its relative power. Departments whose special task may easily be taken over by other departments are less powerful compared with those departments exercising a functional monopoly. Personnel departments are particularly vulnerable because they may be substituted by *all* other departments. Each department head may become his own personnel manager. This decentralization of personnel functions is a constant threat for the professional status of personnel departments. They may come to be regarded as 'overhead costs' without which the company is better off. The tendency of devolving personnel functions back to first-line managers has often been observed in Great Britain during the economic crisis when most firms had to 'slim down' their overhead costs (Windolf, 1982).

Personnel management plays a crucial role in the 'social reproduction' of the firm when it is recruiting new members. Recruitment and selection may be used deliberately to stabilize the status quo of an organization or, alternatively, to bring about innovation and social change. The sociology of science has suggested that new ideas do not survive in scientific research unless the acolytes of tradition die out. This argument points to institutional rigidities which are difficult to overcome so long as the established membership remains. The conclusion can only be that new ideas require new members.

Regardless of whether personnel management is interested in preserving or changing the status quo it has to integrate new members into the organization by providing the required skills and attitudes. There is a trade-off between selection on the one hand and training and socialization on the other. 'All other things being equal, socialization and selectivity can frequently substitute for each other, on the simple ground that if the organization can recruit participants who have the characteristics it requires, it does not have to develop these characteristics through training or education. On the other hand, if the organization has to accept every individual who wishes to join, or every member of a specific but large and unselected group, it has to turn to socialization to produce the desired characteristics' (Etzioni, 1961, p. 158).

The degree of selectivity which organizations use when recruiting depends on environmental conditions (such as the labour market) and on the internal resources available. Firms which enjoy a monopsony (Bronfenbrenner, 1956) in a labour market may be much more selective compared with organizations which have to recruit labour under conditions of intense competition. Internal resources have a similar role in explaining the selectivity of the firm. The existence or not of specialized personnel departments with professional staff and elaborate instruments of personnel policy is of particular importance. The term 'organizational intelligence' is used here to denote the organization's capacity for processing information, integrating conflicting objectives, and inducing innovation and change (Wilensky, 1967).

Firms may be classified according to their labour-market power and their 'organizational intelligence'. Figure 1 shows these two dimensions. They are really continuous scales but arbitrary cut-off points are given to develop a classification system (taxonomy).

LABOUR MARKET POWER	HIGH	STATUS QUO	AUTONOMOUS
	LOW	MUDDLING THROUGH	FLEXIBLE
		LOW	HIGH

'ORGANIZATIONAL INTELLIGENCE'

1 A taxonomy of recruitment strategies

The taxonomy presents four ideal-type firms which differ with respect to their market power and their organizational intelligence. Each type of firm applies a different recruitment strategy in the labour market. A firm's recruitment strategy is defined by the following characteristics:

1. In the first stage the profile of an ideal candidate is defined. Some firms hammer out very precise profiles whereas others are content with a vague picture of the employee who is to be recruited.
2. In the second stage, the firm opts for one (or several) recruitment channels such as the Job Centre, newspapers, internal labour markets or the social networks of the workforce.
3. Next, the applicant has to pass several filters such as application forms, tests, interviews or medical checks.
4. Finally, the applicant has to pass a probation time which provides a last check on the preceding selective stages.

Thus, a recruitment strategy is the combination of different selective instruments such as recruitment channels, tests and interviews, references and medical checks. Firms which describe the profile of the ideal candidate only vaguely in advance, restrict their search activity to the social network and the internal labour market, and apply hardly any filter could be expected to recruit a different type of worker when compared with firms which lay down a precise skill profile and use all recruitment channels and filters.

STATUS-QUO FIRM

Firms operating a status-quo strategy are often found in rural areas where they enjoy a local monopsony. They use traditional production technologies and (depending on their size) have rudimentary personnel departments. The firm restricts its recruitment channels to friends and relatives of the employees and to the members of the local community. Thus the status-quo firm is oriented towards its traditional market segments (Manwaring, 1982). It tends to recruit workers with a similar level of skill and professional experience from the same social stratum, with a similar social background to those already employed with the company. In more technical terms, the firm tends towards an 'identical social reproduction' of its organization. This type of recruitment is strongly defended by an interest coalition of management and workers. Especially during times of high unemployment employees of the firm are interested in preserving the few vacancies for the members of their community. Management accepts this type of recruitment since it expects to engage a stable and reliable workforce. Moreover, workers thus recruited are controlled and disciplined by their relatives and friends.

The profile of the ideal applicant remains vague. Some minimum standards in terms of skill, health and age are required, but the main requirement for entry is the 'recommendation' of a friend. Personnel management 'consults' the workforce to get information on skills, stable work habits and family background of the applicant. As most applicants are known to somebody in the firm, filters such as tests, elaborate application forms or professional interviews are hardly used. The most important filter is the recruitment channel which excludes 'outsiders' and restricts recruitment to members of a closed social community ('extended internal labour market').

In firms classified as 'status quo', shop stewards (or the works council in a West German firm) exercise strong control over the recruitment process. Vacancies are offered as fringe benefits to the workforce and this privilege is strongly defended by workers' representatives.

The status-quo firm should not be mistaken for an unprofitable undertaking because it may, none the less, introduce advanced technology and new products. However, it is rarely a technological innovator, but rather adapts to changing conditions with a time-lag. Coalmining, for instance, illustrates the positive effects of the status-quo strategy in preventing accidents and reducing the training period. As new members are recruited from the same community, they are to some extent already familiar with the particular circumstances and the danger of the work.

THE AUTONOMOUS FIRM

The autonomous firm begins the recruitment procedure with a precise definition of the ideal candidate in terms of specific skills, age and experience. For most vacancies, detailed job descriptions exist specifying the requirements of the job and the profile of the applicant. Skills, age and job experience are usually specified within a small range so that, for instance, an applicant has to be in the age bracket 30–35, male, and qualified from a technical college with at least five years' job experience in the motor-car industry or a related industry.

The autonomous firm tends to impose its own internal structure on the labour market; it is not prepared to adapt its structure to prevailing market conditions. Neither unemployment nor full employment are likely to change the demand structure of those firms, although it is obvious that during times of full employment only market leaders are able to adopt the autonomous strategy. Only market leaders are so attractive to potential applicants that they can expect to achieve successfully their definition of an ideal candidate. They cream off the market because they are at the front of the queue of employers in the labour market. They accept neither poorly skilled nor overqualified applicants but insist on the profile of their ideal candidate.

In contrast to the status-quo firm the autonomous firm uses several, if not all recruitment channels. Its search activities are comprehensive and systematic. Hence, this type of recruitment comes nearest to the rational and professional recruitment activities which are prescribed by managerial textbooks as guidelines for practical purposes.

THE FLEXIBLE AND THE MUDDLING-THROUGH FIRMS

The flexible and the muddling-through firms are responsive to changing environmental conditions and adapt their internal structure to prevailing supply/demand relationships in the market. Most of them are small or medium-sized enterprises or, if they are larger than 1,000 employees, they are situated at the end of the waiting queue because of low wages and/or unpleasant working conditions. A lack of commuting facilities to a remote site can sometimes place the firm at the end of the queue.

The flexible/muddling-through firm does not usually enter the market with a precise profile of the ideal candidate; rather, it screens the market to 'see what is available'. After market information has been obtained the firm decides how to reorganize the division of labour and whether further training has to be given before workers available in the market could do the job. In times of full employment the firm has to manage personnel problems by 'muddling through'. In times of high unemployment it may be able to change the strategy.

The muddling-through and the flexible firm are in a weak labour-market position and they differ only in terms of more or less strategic thinking and personnel expertise in their market actions. Hence it is difficult to draw a clear-cut division between the two types of strategies.

The muddling-through firms runs the risk of bankruptcy because of a vicious circle which operates between the product and the labour market. The firm's weak position in the labour market means it has to produce with an unskilled and unstable workforce that is not motivated to stay on. A poorly qualified workforce has negative repercussions on product quality which affects the market image of the firm. The deteriorating position in the product market, then, weakens the firm's position in the labour market further.

The flexible firm is very often an integral part of a larger concern which offers professional expertise in personnel policy. This relative advantage makes adjustment to changing conditions in the labour market easier. Knowledge of the legal and financial framework allows the firm to exploit subsidies and institutional facilities.

Both these types of firm find a precise definition of the ideal candidate of little use since they seldom have the chance to attract a highly qualified labour force anyway. As the firm has to accept what remains in the labour market, filters are barely used. Thus, probation time is the most important filter to sort workers out who are unacceptable for the firm. Employment agencies are frequently used since they are the cheapest recruitment channels.

In conclusion it should be emphasized that firms may change their recruitment strategy with changing market conditions such that, for instance, a 'flexible' firm may opt for an autonomous strategy during times of high unemployment. A detailed analysis of strategies changing over time is given in Windolf (1982, 1983).

THE BUREAUCRATIC CONTROL OF THE WORKFORCE

As the influence of personnel management increases such instruments as personnel planning, job descriptions and appraisal schemes become more and more important in the administration of the workforce. These are bureaucratic instruments of control which are introduced for standardizing the work process. It seems difficult to give a stringent explanation for the widespread distribution of these instruments. They serve many purposes, have various side-effects, and are introduced for different reasons.

But the explanation which is developed here is closely related to industrial relations. Personnel management and industrial relations analyse the work process from different points of view. One reason for the rising use of bureaucratic instruments is co-determination and collective bargaining at the enterprise level. Regardless of the institutional shape that co-determination finally takes, it holds true that unilateral job regulation whether by unions or by management is gradually replaced by bilateral bargaining over pay and working conditions. The instruments of personnel management are bargaining devices. They help to standardize the work process and to make different workplaces comparable through the use of job descriptions. Job evaluations structure the internal labour market by laying down a hierarchical rank order of jobs; appraisal schemes provide measurements for individual performance; personnel planning determines present and future manning levels.

Without setting a precedent these instruments standardize bargaining objectives and are likely to supersede informal job regulations as well as custom and practice. Job descriptions, for instance, transform implicit rules of demarcation into an explicit system of work tasks and a rational division of labour. If the work process is organized mainly through custom and practice, it becomes extremely difficult for management to introduce change or to adjust the division of labour to new technology. Custom and practice is difficult to change since rules are implicit and their meaning 'fluid'. Very often they become obvious only as they are violated. Thus, the explicit structuring of the work process in terms of job descriptions and evaluation becomes a central precondition for effective collective bargaining.

TABLE 1   *Job description in British and West German firms*

	Britain	W. Germany	Ø
Large (1,000 +)	55%	30%	40%
Medium (100–999)	47%	19%	37%
Ø	51%	23%	38%

N = 130 firms

Figures give the proportion of firms which introduced job descriptions for at least three quarters of their employees.

TABLE 2   *Job evaluation in British and West German firms*

	Britain	W. Germany	Ø
Large (1,000 +)	98%	81%	90%
Medium (100–999)	76%	41%	58%
Ø	86%	55%	71%

N = 130 firms

Figures give the proportion of firms which introduced job evaluations for at least three quarters of their employees.

Tables 1 and 2 show that job descriptions and evaluations are more common in Britain than in West Germany. Both tables show an interaction effect between 'size' and 'country'. That is, the variable 'size', as well as the variable 'country', influences the incidence of job descriptions/evaluations. In West Germany the size-effect is larger. In small/medium-sized German firms job descriptions/evaluations are less frequently used than one would expect from the size-effect alone. For job evaluations the difference between large and medium firms amounts to 26 per cent in Britain but to 73 per cent in West Germany.

The sample represents some regions in both countries rather than the countries as a whole, so the data have to be interpreted with care. There is, however, no difficulty in interpreting the difference between large and small firms. The larger the organization, the more standardized the work process and the more bureaucratized the work control. This relationship between size and bureaucratic instruments of control has also been confirmed by other studies (Heydebrand, 1973, part 3).

It is also noteworthy that the differences between large and small firms is more important in West Germany than in Britain. This result is probably due to the influence which the works council in West Germany exercises in large enterprises. Two-tier negotiation with a first round at the national/regional level and a second round between the works council and personnel management is particularly important in these large enterprises. In small/medium-sized firms in West Germany managerial prerogatives are less frequently challenged. The works council is less powerful, and it may more or less be ignored by management. Because managerial control of the work process is taken for granted in such firms, job descriptions and evaluations are of little use. Management regards them as bureaucratic instruments which hamper the smooth functioning of production without strengthening the managerial position.

On the other hand the workforce may use job descriptions to introduce demarcation lines (which did not exist before) and job evaluations to stabilize income and internal promotion ladders (which had previously been controlled by management). But if shop stewards are the guardians of custom and practice, there is an incentive for management to introduce job descriptions in order to gain control of the work process.

A similar argument holds true for the wage-bargaining process. In Britain the fragmented union structure and competition of unions for membership leads to leapfrogging and wage drift. These centrifugal forces are less pronounced in West Germany. They figure among the main problems of personnel management as well as of industrial relations in Britain. In recent years joint negotiation at the level of the enterprise/establishment has been introduced to overcome the fragmented negotiation of workgroups (Brown, 1981). Job descriptions and evaluations are important instruments for replacing traditional wage differentials and establishing a rational wage structure which reduces the number of wage groups and cuts across traditional job territories. Job descriptions and evaluations are means of legitimizing wage differentials which are not based on traditional lines of demarcation.

A further explanation for those national differences which are shown in Tables 1 and 2 is found in national legislation. In Britain, anti-discrimination laws are more prohibitive compared with those in West Germany. Employers should pay equal wages for similar workplaces regardless of race or sex. This legal regulation is a strong incentive to structure the work process and wages according to 'objective' standards such as skill, responsibility and performance.

An additional instrument of management, namely personnel planning, has become more and more important in recent years. Most British firms which have had to administer large redundancy programmes during the recession introduced various forms of personnel planning. In West Germany, personnel planning was one of the main objectives of the Works Council Act of 1972. This Act made it obligatory for an employer to inform the works council of his manpower plans in 'full and good time'. This was expected to stabilize employment in the long run and to protect as many jobs as possible when redundancies have to be made. In industries with heavy demand fluctuations, peaks and troughs in employment would thereby be ironed out.

Yet during the recession personnel planning has become mainly a managerial instrument for administering redundancies. The number of workers to be made redundant and the sequence of redundancies were carefully planned in advance to 'slimline' the company (the most famous example being the British Steel Corporation).

It became obvious that personnel planning was strongly dependent on the contingencies of the product market. The stronger the fluctuations in the product market and the less predictable these fluctuations were, the less useful personnel planning was. Where markets are turbulent, personnel planning is useless. Only 'sheltered' industries, such as the public sector, can really base their policy on personnel planning. This argument is particularly well illustrated by the West German automobile industry. In April 1975, the Board of Directors of Volkswagen decided on a redundancy programme of 20,000 workers based on severance payments. In October 1975 Volkswagen employed 12 per cent fewer workers than in April. In November, the car market picked up, the recruitment ban was lifted and Volkswagen started to re-employ workers previously made redundant on severance payment.

Generally speaking, personnel planning is used by most firms to keep a 'quasi fixed factor' flexible (Oi, 1962). The quantity of labour has to be adjusted to fluctuations in demand. When methods of personnel planning are analysed in greater detail, it turns out that they vary considerably between different countries. There are at least two parameters which may be used for adjusting the workforce to fluctuations in the product market: hours and workers. The firm may either reduce/increase the hours per worker (through short-time/overtime) while the number of workers employed remains constant, or, alternatively, it may keep the hours per worker constant but reduce/ increase the number of workers. Most firms, of course, use both methods. However, there is empirical evidence to suggest that firms in the USA are more likely to adjust the amount of labour by laying off workers whereas in Britain and West Germany firms usually react by changing hours. The different reactions are explained by differences in the legal framework and by institutional rigidities. In Britain and West Germany, redundancies are extremely expensive. It is therefore cheaper to 'hoard' workers on short-time, whereas, in the USA, lay-off is the more appropriate instrument of adjustment. These differences in institutional arrangements explain different elasticities in national labour markets. Even if the economy picks up again, the effect will not immediately spill over into the labour market.

Employers in Britain and West Germany anticipate the risk of high redundancy costs and, therefore, prefer to stretch working time as far as possible by overtime while American firms are more likely to react by recruiting new workers (Hotz-Hart, 1983).

STRUCTURED CHARACTERISTICS OF PERSONNEL
DEPARTMENTS

A final remark concerns the structural characteristics of personnel departments in firms of different sizes, and the training of personnel managers.

TABLE 3 *Differentiation, professionalization and centralization in British and West German firms**

	Differentia-tion, per cent	Professionaliza-tion, per cent	Centraliza-tion, per cent
W. German firms	23	14	17
British firms	33	43	41
Large firms	56	47	42
Small/medium-sized firms	10	17	22
W. German large firms	61	30	26
W. German small/medium-sized firms	2	5	12
British large firms	53	59	53
British small/medium-sized firms	17	29	32
Average (all firms $N = 140$)	29	29	30

* Percentages give the proportion of firms with differentiated/professionalized/centralized personnel departments.

In Table 3 differentiation is defined as the number of positions in a personnel department with specific functions such as recruitment/dismissal, training and industrial relations. A firm is scored as highly differentiated and specialized if at least three sections with different functions exist in the personnel department. On average, 23 per cent of personnel departments in West German firms are highly differentiated, but in Britain the proportion is 33 per cent.

Professionalization is defined in terms of the formal education of personnel managers/officers. The personnel department is scored as 'professionalized' if the personnel manager and at least one officer passed through an institution of tertiary education (university, technical college, examination of I P M). A personnel department is scored as centralized if the majority of personnel functions (such as recruitment, training, negotiation of wages and working conditions) are centralized in the department.

In large (British) firms personnel departments are more differentiated, professionalized, and centralized compared with small (West German) firms (with the exception of differentiation, which scores higher in large West German firms (61 per cent) compared with British ones (53 per cent)). The interaction effect between size and country explains the difference between small British and small West German firms. As already emphasized, these figures should be interpreted with caution because they derive from a study by the author where the sample size was limited. Hence the following arguments are provisional pending more rigorous research.

Flanders characterizes British industrial relations as largely fragmented, informal and autonomous (Donovan Report, 1968, p. 18). Most negotiations on wages and working conditions are organized on the level of enterprises/establishments. There is no legal framework for co-determination obligatory for all firms. Hence, each establishment has to negotiate its own 'Work Council Act' (as, for instance, has been done in Ford's 'Blue Book'). This fragmented structure of industrial relations places a heavy workload on the individual firm.

Clegg (1980, p. 52) estimates that by 1978 the number of shop stewards probably exceeded 300,000 in Britain. He argues that industrial relations is a flourishing sector of economic activity. The number of shop stewards has to be matched – not in number but in bargaining capacity – by the enlargement of the personnel department. Hence, the fragmented character of British industrial relations provides an explanation for the higher professionalization and differentiation of personnel management in Britain, particularly in small/medium-sized firms. In large firms, there is probably no difference between Britain and West Germany since negotiation structures seem rather similar in both countries.

CHAPTER 22

Accountants and the Finance Function

JOHN BLAKE

In order to understand the position of the finance function in British management, it is necessary to understand how the accountancy profession in the UK has developed. Accountancy is the longest established management discipline in the UK, with a stronger system of professional training and organization than any other management function. Broadly, accountancy is concerned with:

1. Collection of data relating to the activities of an enterprise and its use of resources.
2. Analysis of data for decision-making purposes.
3. Control over the use of the resources.

To accomplish these objectives the accountant must draw on a number of disciplines. There is a strong link with economics. Accountancy theory uses concepts such as 'income' and 'capital', although in a different way from economics. Environmental factors such as inflation or foreign currency fluctuations have an impact on the enterprise which the accountant can only measure effectively given an understanding of the underlying economic causes. Law is another important related-discipline as the accountant operates within a framework of regulations which dictate the form and content of some reports. Many transactions can only be properly accounted for if their precise legal implications are understood. In recent years accountants have become increasingly aware of the importance of organizational behaviour. The accountant must understand the ways in which the people within an organization are likely to respond to information and control. The accountant's data-collection role requires a knowledge of data-processing systems. 'Double entry' bookkeeping has traditionally been used for data collection. Systems can be operated manually, by machine or by computer, and so an understanding of the various possible methods is necessary.

The accountant must also have a grasp of a wide range of quantitative techniques which can be used to provide an analysis of financial data.

This brief account indicates only the major overlapping disciplines. Accountancy is a subject area with very open boundaries and so the range of activities varies enormously between different cultures. For example, in West Germany there is no direct equivalent of our word 'accountant'; the world *Buchhaltung*,* translated most correctly as 'bookkeeping', describes a rather narrow function concerned purely with the data-collection system. By contrast in the UK accountants cover a wide range of functions.

A major function is the preparation of published accounts of an enterprise which are the financial reports presented to the outside world. In the case of limited companies these accounts are circulated to shareholders and filed with the registrar of companies.

The work of the auditor is linked to the preparation of published accounts. The external auditor verifies the accounts by evaluating the accounting system and by making a critical examination of the figures presented. A company may also employ an internal auditor, whose duties will be defined by management but will normally include a continuous review of the workings of the accounting system.

An area of work with which the general public tend to associate accountants is taxation advice. They are employed by companies, as well as individuals, to advise on how to arrange affairs so as to minimize tax liabilities while complying with the tax laws. Of particular importance to management is the provision of management information. Accountants are concerned with the design and operation of the management accounting system. They will also be involved in planning how to finance the company's operations and employ its resources. Work which attracts considerable publicity occurs when a large undertaking experiences difficulties leading to the employment of accountants as company liquidators and receivers. This work is also involved when a flourishing group of companies decides to close down part of its operations.

Company law and the Stock Exchange rules require companies to attach an accountant's report to documents, such as prospectuses, which public companies are required to publish in circum-

* I am indebted to my colleague Peter Lawrence for this observation.

stances such as a share issue. A company considering a major acquisition will normally employ accountants to report on the accounts and general financial position of the business being acquired. A wide range of organizations, such as banks, pension funds and credit protection agencies, require the services of accountants to advise on the interpretation of published accounts. Management will be involved in this process, both as consumers of information on other companies and as the subject of analysis themselves. In addition, because of their thorough professional training, accountants have often taken on a broader management role in a business enterprise.

THE ACCOUNTING PROFESSION IN THE UK

Most accountants are employed either by firms of accountants in public practice or directly by financial, commercial or industrial organizations. The latter employment is generally referred to as working 'in industry'. Most accountants are trained by one of the six major UK accounting bodies which, while maintaining their separate identities, have together formed the Consultative Committee of Accounting Bodies (CCAB). These are:

1. The Institute of Chartered Accountants in England and Wales.
2. The Institute of Chartered Accountants of Scotland.
3. The Institute of Chartered Accountants in Ireland.

These three bodies require their students to train in public practice, but their members are divided more or less evenly between those working in public practice and in industry.

4. The Association of Certified Accountants allows students to train either in public practice or in industry, while a majority of its members work in industry.

Under the Companies Acts members of each of these four bodies are permitted to audit the accounts of limited companies.

5. The Institute of Cost and Management Accountants requires its students to train in industry, and most of its members work in industry.

6. The Chartered Institute of Public Finance and Accountancy requires its students to train in the public sector, and most members are employed in local government.

Each of these bodies is of equal standing and all are incorporated by Royal Charter. They have a total membership in excess of 100,000 and more than 100,000 registered students. They have collectively set up the Association of Accounting Technicians, a 'second tier' body for junior accounting staff. In addition, there are several other small professional bodies, and some accountants do not belong to any professional body.

The external audit must be performed by an independent firm of accountants, but all the other accounting functions may be performed either by accountants employed directly by the enterprise or by firms of accountants in public practice. Normally, the larger the enterprise the more functions it will choose to have performed internally. Thus most businesses of any size will employ their own management accountants, while only a small number of companies employ their own tax specialists.

THE MANAGEMENT-INFORMATION SYSTEM

The accountant's role in the company's management-information system depends upon the size of the company and the nature of its business.

Cost accounting involves the analysis and allocation of costs to units of production or to areas of activity within the organization. Decisions on the allocation of costs between the activities of a business can have a significant impact on the apparent profitability of those activities, and can involve problems of judgement. Such decisions are particularly important where the enterprise is subject to some kind of external regulation based on the reported profit of individual parts. For example, to ensure that local-authority direct-labour organizations do not compete unfairly with private contractors, the Government requires that these organizations attain a specified minimum rate of return on capital employed. Consequently, the accountant's decision on the allocation of costs between different parts of a local authority may have an influence on whether or not these requirements have been met. When one part of a business supplies goods or services to another part, decisions on the appropriate 'transfer price' will have to be made, and this can involve the accountant in making delicate judgements about tax-planning considerations, cash flows within the business and the expected effect on the purchasing and selling pattern of the parts of the business. Decisions on such allocations of costs should be made by accountants who are independent of the management of the divisions of the business affected. Where the accountant's decision has an impact on the relationship of the business with third parties then such decisions should be scrutinized with particular care by the external auditor.

Preparing and monitoring budgets is an important aspect of management information. In drawing up the budget it will be necessary to coordinate data from all the functions of the business; often this is done by setting up a budget committee, including representatives from each of the management functions. During this process the accountant gains a view of the whole operations of the business, and this can be a valuable experience if the accountant progresses to a broader management role.

In the exercise of control over the use of the resources of the enterprise the accountant has a clearly defined role in keeping detailed records which show the various assets possessed by the business, and also for ensuring that the total resources tied up in various types of assets do not exceed the financial resources available to the business. This aspect of the accountant's role can be illustrated in relation to one type of asset: stock.

A manufacturing business will have a large part of its working capital tied up in stock and work in progress: raw materials, goods in the course of production and finished goods awaiting sale. In a business of any size it will be normal to maintain 'continuous' stock records, recording movements of stock and the balance of stock held. These records may be integrated into the double-entry book-keeping system, or be maintained separately by a separate stores record department. It is normal practice to verify the stock figure at least once in each year by means of a physical count which may take place on the date in the year to which the accounts are prepared, and where there is no continuous stock-recording system this 'stock-take' will be essential to establish the quantity of stock to be recorded in the Balance Sheet. Where a continuous stock-recording system is in operation, stock may be verified by counting a few items each day throughout the year in order to avoid disrupting production. Whatever method of stock counting is used, it will be necessary for the accountant to liaise with staff responsible for the custody of stock, and the internal and external auditors will both be interested in the procedures followed.

The accountant will have a view on the quantity of stock which the business can afford to hold, but other managers in the business will also have an influence on the stock level. The purchasing department will wish to acquire sufficient quantities of raw materials or bought-in parts to act as a buffer against disruption of supply, and take advantage of quantity discounts; the production manager will wish to avoid the risk of production being halted by shortage of any essential stock, and will wish to produce finished goods in sufficient quantity to permit an efficient production run; the marketing manager will wish to have sufficient stocks of each product line to ensure that all orders can be met, so as to avoid loss of sales. Good management involves reconciling these different objectives, with each department being aware of the needs of others.

The example of stock control demonstrates that the accountant cannot fulfil the responsibility to control the resources of the business in isolation from other managers. This is true of the accountant's role in all aspects of the management-information system, as an awareness of the meaning of the data supplied by other managers, and their information needs, is essential to the management accountant.

THE PUBLISHED ACCOUNTS: SOURCES OF AUTHORITY

The Companies Acts of 1948, 1967, 1976, 1980 and 1981 together impose detailed and extensive requirements on limited-liability companies about the content of the annual accounts. These have to be circulated to shareholders and debenture holders, and a copy must be filed with the Registrar of Companies where, on payment of a modest fee, it can be inspected by any member of the public. The Companies Acts also provide that the accounts of a limited company should be subject to an audit, and effectively provide that the auditor should either be a Certified Accountant or a member of one of three Institutes of Chartered Accountants. The Acts include transitional provisions allowing other auditors already in practice at the time of the relevant legislation to continue to practise, and provides certain other very minor exceptions.

Requirements about the form and content of company accountants also come from the accounting profession, in the form of Statements of Standard Accounting Practice (SSAPs) issued by the Accounting Standards Committee (ASC). The procedure for drafting these accounting standards includes provision for full and open consultation on the proposed requirements. The professional accounting bodies require their members, when acting as auditors, to include in the audit report a comment on any material failure to comply with SSAPs unless the auditors concur with the non-compliance. Because companies traditionally wish to avoid such comments in the audit report, and because the professional bodies in practice have a virtual monopoly of the audit of larger companies, this has been a powerful factor in inducing companies to comply with accounting standards. Nevertheless, because there is no legal requirement to comply with SSAPs it has been necessary for the Committee to be cautious in trying to impose unpopular requirements, and there have been several instances of controversial proposals being withdrawn or substantially amended under pressure.

A third source of authority, in the case of listed companies, is the Stock Exchange. The Stock Exchange listing agreement lays down a number of detailed accounting requirements, including a requirement for a half-yearly interim report.

THE EXTERNAL REPORTING ENVIRONMENT

The requirement to publish accounts is imposed upon limited-liability companies by law. Similar requirements are laid down for certain other bodies incorporated by law such as nationalized industries and building societies. The requirement to publish accounts is generally seen as originating in response to two needs:

1. It is necessary to have a mechanism whereby those who manage

a business (the directors of a company) account for their stewardship to the owners (the shareholders).
2. The concept of limited liability plays an important part in the development of an advanced industrial economy, but is fraught with danger for creditors. When published accounts are available, creditors are placed in a better position to assess risk and to observe any fraud.

While the Companies Acts do not specify the purposes for which accounts are required to be published, it is clear from the tone of legislation that shareholders and creditors of a company are regarded as the principal users of published accounts. For example, s. 19 of the Theft Act 1968 makes it an offence for an officer of a company to publish misleading, false or deceptive information about its affairs with the intention of deceiving shareholders or creditors.

Although traditionally accounting regulations have been designed to meet the requirements of these two user groups, there is undoubtedly a far wider range of users interested in the content of the published accounts. Committees on the development of accounting requirements set up both by the Government and by the Accounting Standards Committee have expressed the view that the interests of all potential users should be borne in mind when accounting regulations are drafted. One major group of users is shareholders. The financial reports give them an account of the way in which the directors have handled the resources entrusted to them. The Companies Acts specify detailed disclosure requirements relating to such matters as directors' emoluments, loans to directors and contracts in which directors have a personal interest, enabling shareholders to judge what personal benefits the directors derive from the company. The accounts may be expected to have a substantial influence on the way in which the shareholders exercise their voting rights, particularly on the appointment of directors. The accounts may also be expected to have an influence on individual investment decisions, when shareholders decide whether to increase, maintain, or decrease the amount of their shareholding in the company; and when potential shareholders decide whether to buy shares.

Creditors and lenders are another major group of users. They include such groups as debenture holders, banks providing medium-term and short-term loans, and suppliers who provide goods and services to the company on trade credit terms. Those providing short-term credit to the company will be primarily interested in assessing the solvency of the company: its ability to meet its liabilities as they fall due. Those providing longer-term credit will also be interested in assessing profitability and performance as an indicator of the company's prospects. All creditors may be interested in the company's ability to repay borrowings in the event of a liquidation.

A user group whose needs are becoming increasingly recognized is employees and trade unions acting on their behalf, who will be interested in using the financial reports to assess job security, future prospects and the company's ability to afford pay increases. It is important to bear in mind that employees are in a position to observe at their own place of work developments which may give a clearer view of the company's position than the published accounts.

The government is a major user of accounts as a basis for deciding the amount of taxation to be paid, as well as for other regulatory functions such as the regulation of mergers which might create monopolies. Governments have an interest in published accounts as a source of information about the state of the economy. Governments may also have a similar interest to that of shareholders or creditors when deciding whether to invest in individual companies.

Another type of user might be classified as 'trade contacts'. We have already seen that suppliers have an interest in company accounts as trade creditors, but they may also be interested in the published accounts of their major customers as a guide to their stability and future development. Similarly customers may examine the accounts of a major supplier to ensure that the company is financially sound, and can be expected to fulfil its commitments; for example, when placing contracts for a major construction project it is common practice to examine the published accounts of potential contractors.

Competitors are likely to be interested in how other companies in the same industry are performing. While some controlled exchange of information between companies in the same industry may be mutually beneficial, companies may wish to restrict the detail given in their published accounts in order to avoid giving an advantage to their competitors.

The activity of major companies in the economy is often a subject of public discussion, and so the published accounts of companies may be of interest to the general public. Each of the user groups considered above may be served, directly or indirectly, by advisers. For example, shareholders will be supported by stockbrokers, investment analysts and financial journalists.

The management of the business has not been included in this list because managers will base their decisions on internally generated data specifically designed for the purposes of the management-control system. Nevertheless, because each of the user groups we have identified may take decisions based on the published accounts and this will have a significant effect on the environment in which the company operates, the content of the published accounts will be of considerable interest to management. Managers can influence the content of the published accounts in three ways:

1. By taking advantage of those areas of choice permitted by accounting regulations. For example, the Accounting Standards Committee has issued an accounting standard (SSAP 13) which allows companies either to write off development expenditure against profit in the year it is incurred or, under strictly controlled conditions, to record the expenditure as an asset and to set it off against related income in future years. One factor which will influence management in choosing between these alternative accounting policies is whether they wish to increase or decrease the profit figure disclosed for the current year.

2. By making representations to those responsible for the issue of accounting regulations. In the UK an example of this arose when an accounting standard (SSAP 11) was issued requiring companies to include in their balance sheets as a liability the full amount of *potential* tax liabilities, even where, in practice, substantial amounts were unlikely to become payable. Many companies objected that such an approach would result in creditors becoming less willing to lend to businesses with apparently large liabilities, and under pressure the ASC issued a revised accounting standard (SSAP 15) which effectively permits companies to

restrict the liability for potential tax payments shown in the balance sheet to amounts which are likely to become payable.

3. By changing their behaviour in such a way as to present a different picture in the accounts. An interesting example of this arose in the US when an accounting regulation was issued requiring companies which acquired the right to use equipment under a long-term lease agreement to treat the transaction in the accounts as though the equipment had been acquired as a fixed asset financed by a loan. To avoid presenting accounts which show a high level of borrowings, many companies have negotiated a change in their lease agreements so that these do not fall within the official definition of long-term leases.

This effect of accounting regulations is known as 'information inductance'.

FINANCIAL PLANNING

The management of a business will be concerned with planning how the business is to finance its operations with advice not only from the business's own accountants but also from other professional advisers such as banks.

Broadly, a business can obtain finance either from its own proprietors (the shareholders, in the case of a limited company) or by borrowing. The more a business borrows, the higher the interest charges will be as a proportion of profit and the higher will be the risk that there may be difficulty in repayment. On the other hand, when a business is earning a return on the resources it employs higher than the rate of interest it pays, then the proprietors benefit to the extent of the amount of the excess return. A business is said to be 'high geared' if it has a high level of borrowing and 'low geared' if it has a low level of borrowing.

Whether a company is raising finance by an issue of shares or by borrowing, the range of methods available will depend on whether or not the company is listed on the Stock Exchange. A listed company is subject to certain regulations on the way in which it conducts its operations which do not apply to other companies, but a Stock Exchange listing gives access to raising finance from the general public by an issue either of new shares or of loan stock while other companies will have to obtain funds by private arrangement, often from institutions such as banks.

A company can increase the amount of finance from the proprietors by issuing new shares to either existing or new shareholders, or by retaining profits earned in the business instead of distributing them to shareholders. Borrowings may be long, medium or short term supported by a range of different types of security.

In choosing between the various types of finance, management will be influenced by the following factors:

1. The attitude of management and of the proprietors towards risk; thus a risk-averse management will avoid high gearing.
2. The costs of various forms of finance. These are not always obvious. For example, while the cost of using a bank overdraft is clearly the interest charge it is more difficult to quantify the cost of retaining profits in the business instead of paying a higher dividend.
3. The length of time for which finance is required. For example, it would be inappropriate to finance the purchase of a new building which will be retained in the company for many years by a bank overdraft repayable in the short term.

TAX PLANNING

The role of the accountant in the field of tax planning is the subject of much controversy, and is often misunderstood, so it is worth looking at in some detail. This work can be divided into two parts:

1. In compliance work the accountant will compute an estimate of the tax liability arising from the company's activities, and handle correspondence with the Inland Revenue settling the company's tax liability. The accounting system will be designed to enable the business to fulfil its obligations under the PAYE system and the VAT regulations, but once the system is designed it will not normally be necessary for the accountant to be involved any further in meeting these requirements.
2. In tax planning the accountant will advise the management of the business on how to arrange its affairs in such a way as to minimize the impact of taxation. On occasion, this role attracts

considerable publicity, and it is important to understand the accountant's role in this field.

All taxpayers have the legal right to arrange their affairs in such a way as to reduce their tax liability – this is known as tax avoidance. By contrast, it is illegal to misinform or to conceal information from the tax authorities so as to escape taxation on transactions – this is known as tax evasion. A further distinction that might be drawn is between tax-avoidance schemes which involve a genuine change in the way in which an enterprise conducts its affairs, and 'artificial' schemes whereby the commercial substance of the activities of the enterprise is unchanged and only changes in legal form are involved.

Four examples of tax planning will illustrate the issues involved:

1. When a business acquires equipment, the taxable profit can be reduced by a 'capital allowance' representing a percentage of the cost. Currently, in the year of acquisition a capital allowance of 100 per cent is allowed and so, in a year when high profits are expected, an accountant might advise that it would be an appropriate time to invest in new equipment in order to reduce the tax charge for that year.

   This example involves the enterprise in changing the way in which it conducts its ordinary activities. When the government introduced 100 per cent capital allowances the declared aim was to encourage companies to invest in new plant. Thus in this particular case the accountant's advice will result in the company behaving in a way that the government wishes to encourage.

2. Where a business consistently makes high profits, there may be no scope for the acquisition of additional equipment for use in the business. In order to secure the tax benefits of capital allowances, an accountant might advise setting up a subsidiary enterprise engaged in buying and leasing out equipment.

   This example involves the enterprise in developing a new line of activity in order to reduce its tax liability. In recent years there has been a considerable expansion in leasing activity for tax-planning reasons. Although the capital-allowance legislation was not originally envisaged as having these effects, successive governments have not acted to prevent this form of tax avoidance, perhaps because the economic effect is to increase purchases of plant.

3. Where a holding company has subsidiaries, then, under certain circumstances, a loss incurred by one subsidiary can be set off against the taxable profit of other subsidiaries. An accountant might advise setting off the loss against the profits of those companies with the earliest obligation to pay tax, so that while the total tax liability of the group remains the same the date of payment is deferred as long as possible.

   This example involves the exercise of choice permitted by tax legislation.

4. During the 1970s a particularly ingenious tax-avoidance scheme involving tax relief on interest payments was devised. To see how this works, imagine that company A wishes to avoid tax. Company A borrows a large sum of money from company X for one year, paying interest in advance. Shortly afterwards company A pays company Y a sum of money and company Y undertakes to discharge the liability to company X in one year's time. Because company Y enjoys the benefit of the borrowed funds for one year, the amount paid by company A will be less than the amount to be repaid. The interest paid to company X is likely to be similar in amount to the gain on disposing of the liability, since both are determined by current interest rates. It was argued that the interest paid was an allowable expense for tax purposes, while the gain on disposal of the liability was not subject to taxation. As soon as this scheme became widely known, legislation to block it was rapidly introduced!

   This example represents a case of totally 'artificial' tax avoidance. In practice, governments always act rapidly to close loopholes in tax law which make such schemes possible.

These four examples illustrate the range of tax planning, from an approach which results in the enterprise acting in accordance with government policy to an approach which is highly controversial. In practice, most tax planning is of the less controversial type. The ethics of artificial tax avoidance have been the subject of considerable public debate. Management may be attracted by the tax savings offered by artificial avoidance schemes; it may be useful to point out the following dangers:

1. Artificial avoidance schemes normally involve taking advantage of legal loopholes, and may involve prolonged and expensive litigation.
2. The outcome of such schemes is normally uncertain, and in pursuing an artificial scheme the company may lose the opportunity to take advantage of more modest tax reliefs which are legitimately available.
3. There are a number of areas of tax law where in practice individual inspectors of taxes can exercise discretion in their interpretation. Where a company has antagonized the inspector by involvement in a blatantly artificial scheme, such discretion is not likely to be exercised in the company's favour.
4. Artificial avoidance schemes are likely to involve the company in controversy, and to attract hostile publicity.
5. The conflicts in which the business is likely to be involved as a result of entering into an artificial scheme of tax avoidance are likely to absorb a lot of management time, to the detriment of the running of the business

CONCLUSION

Accountancy is a discipline with ill-defined boundaries. Those functions which involve helping the business to comply with external regulations, such as external financial reporting, tax planning, and auditing, are likely in the UK to remain firmly in the hands of accountants, particularly in view of the strength of the professional accounting bodies. There is, however, some controversy as to the role of the accountant in the management-information system, relating both to the appropriate training for this role and to the question of what influence this role should give the accountant within the organization. Traditionally many accountants have trained in public practice and then moved to employment with an enterprise in a management-accounting role. While this approach to training has in the past often been commended on the grounds that the accountant will have gained experience in the operations of a variety of types of enterprise, in recent years there has been growing concern at the possibility that accountants trained in this way do not have a sufficient appreciation of the working of the enterprise as a whole.

The accountant, in administering the management-information system, gains an insight into the activities of each of the departments of the business, and plays a central part in coordinating these activities. This insight, combined with the status that the accountant can derive from membership of a professional body with rigorous training requirements, puts the accountant in a powerful position to claim a broader management role. On the other hand, the emphasis on the issues of compliance with external regulations in the accountant's professional body can result in the accountant failing to identify with the ethos of the enterprise; at least one major multinational firm trains its own accounting staff and actually discourages them from seeking membership of any professional body.

As the calibre of recruits to the accounting profession is high, and the professional training they receive is thorough, so the accounting profession in the UK will continue to have a wide-ranging role in business. Whether or not experience in the accounting function will continue to form a sound basis for a broader management role will depend on the ability of the accounting bodies to give their members a more professional *management* training, and on the success of alternative management-development routes.

CHAPTER 23

Management Services

PAUL FINLAY

In all business organizations many people give a service to management: tea ladies, chauffeurs, messengers, telephonists, lawyers, parts of the personnel department, and so on. None of these would normally be part of a management-services department. So what service does such a management department give? Is it in any way special? Management-services departments are concerned with providing information systems for managers. This role involves primarily designing and implementing an amalgam of equipment, people and processes to permit the efficient performance of clerical tasks and to provide managers with the information needed for planning and controlling the use of resources. Secondly, a management-services department often helps managers to interpret the information they receive in order to improve their decision-making.

Currently, most staff in a management-services department are involved with computerizing clerical tasks, but this is unlikely to remain so as computers become more widespread and companies more mature in their use of them. These bread-and-butter tasks are exemplified by a customer-order-processing system. As its name suggests, this is designed to process orders sent to a company by its customers. The system has to be able to check the basic facts of the order: is the customer known, has he any outstanding debts to the company, does the company sell the goods he is ordering? It should also be able to check if the ordered goods are available from stock and, if so, to produce instructions to pick out of store for the order. If the goods are not available from stock, then the system should also produce a letter to the customer informing him of a delay. Invoices, dispatch notes and other documentation would also be expected to be produced automatically.

DATA-PROCESSING SYSTEM

Systems of this sort, carrying out clerical activities, are called data-processing systems: data are selected and processed to produce an invoice, a dispatch note, etc. The information produced by data-processing systems generally includes management information as well. While a single customer order is unlikely to be of interest to a sales manager, a monthly total of all sales is likely to be of great interest and will be one of the fundamental parts of the monitoring activity to ensure that the sales operation is under control. In this case, the processing of the data would entail the aggregation of all similar sales data for a month. Data-processing systems involve business processes that do not change much over time and so are used over and over again. Thus, almost irrespective of what the organization does, its data-processing systems remain basically unchanged: the systems are almost 'context independent'. As well as customer-order processing, typical data processing tasks are: stock recording, supplier order processing, ledger accounting and invoicing. These systems manipulate historic data according to fully predetermined rules.

THE SYSTEMS CYCLE

The development and maintenance of data-processing systems is achieved through following a set of activities that constitute the systems cycle. Its main stages are depicted in Figure 1.

Initially a view will have been taken within an organization that a new or changed data-processing system may be needed: for example, stock control may be poor and so sales staff are unable to respond quickly to customer queries. In stage 1, the system investigation would be undertaken with a view that improvements are required. A very broad-brush appraisal is made of the business requirement, and how the current systems are deficient, and possible solutions are enumerated. Each of these possibilities is then investigated for its technical, financial and operational feasibility. In testing technical feasibility, regard would be paid for example to such factors as whether transmission of the required quantity of data between two sites could be achieved, or whether the overall

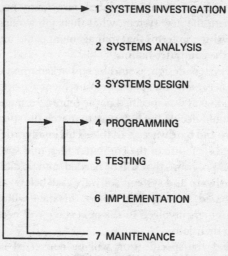

1 SYSTEMS INVESTIGATION

2 SYSTEMS ANALYSIS

3 SYSTEMS DESIGN

4 PROGRAMMING

5 TESTING

6 IMPLEMENTATION

7 MAINTENANCE

1 The systems cycle

processing speed of a given computer would be adequate. Financial feasibility would include considerations of the capital and running costs of the new system and a comparison of these with the benefits expected to be obtained. Operational feasibility would be concerned with whether the proposed system would be acceptable in operation: for example, would computer terminals in a warehouse be too much for the warehouseman? Would overnight processing be acceptable?

At the end of the systems investigation, a feasibility-study report would be prepared. This would restate the business requirement for a new system and outline the characteristics of the feasible solutions that had been investigated, their costs and organizational consequences. On the basis of this report, management would decide whether to proceed to the next stage, and if so to select the favoured option.

Stage 2 is the systems-analysis stage. The activities of stage 1 are repeated for the chosen option, but in much greater detail. The end-result of this stage is a systems-requirement report that describes very precisely what the new system will do, how it will do it, and how it will affect the business. For example, the report would contain details of how many computers there might be, where the computer terminals would be placed, how many people would be needed to run the new system, what their job would entail, etc. It would be written in terms that management could understand, not jargon for the computer boffins.

Stage 3, system design, would be embarked upon once management had accepted the systems-requirement report, namely that they wanted what was specified in the report. In stage 3, the system designer would decide the best way to match the specification with the software and hardware available. This involves determining the number and structure of the computer files, and specifying the set of computer programs that will be needed, and possibly also specifying the hardware and systems software (see below) that may need to be purchased. Among other things, this stage will specify all that the programmers involved in the next stage will need to know for them to do their job.

In stage 4 the specification will be converted into computer programs. These programs will need much testing before they will be suitable. A program will first be desk-checked, by running through the logic of it, and then tested with representative data. Later, in stage 5, the suite of programs that make up the system will be tested as an integrated unit. This testing should ideally be done by the people who are to use the system.

The testing will not affect the systems already being run in the company but will use specially prepared test data. In stage 6 (implementation), the new system will be run using 'live' data. Normally a period of parallel running is introduced whereby the new and old systems run side by side. While this calls for much more effort on the part of the staff involved, a direct comparison of systems can be made and faults discovered in the new system before they cause serious difficulties. The strain on staff during this time should not be underestimated as they will be running two systems where normally they run only one.

When the user is satisfied that the new system meets the needs as framed in the systems-requirement report, the system is accepted. The development side of the systems cycle is now complete, but as it moves into the maintenance stage possible reasons for it not working as intended could arise. For example, changes made by external organizations, such as VAT rate change or changes in the income-tax structure, would mean that the programs have to be altered accordingly. Thus there would be a cycling back to the programming stage to accommodate these changes. More significantly, deficiencies in the system may become apparent and theoretically the systems cycle would be started anew with a new system investigation, but, unless an error were a really major one, it is likely that the amendment would start lower down, at the systems-design or programming stages.

INFORMATION INTERPRETATION

While the development and maintenance of data-processing systems are generally the main activity in a management-services department, a further role is to help managers interpret quantitative information for decision-making. In all but the most trivial cases, a manager involved in planning has to consider many disparate factors: for example, if the problem were one of falling sales, the cause may lie in poor distribution, or be due to aggressive competition or the effects of production difficulties, and any course of action the manager takes to alleviate the problem is likely to involve many resources interacting in complex ways. As Ackoff (1981) succinctly puts it, managers are in a mess. In order to handle problems in this mess, managers need intelligence: not just in the sense of clear, rational behaviour, but in the sense of an overall picture of the situation. Murray (1979) defines intelligence as the outcome of the meshing and reconciliation of a set of information-carrying influences.

Just as data are the raw material from which information is produced through data processing, so information is the raw material from which intelligence is fashioned through information interpretation. As this definition of intelligence implies, it is not a one-dimensional quantity like information but multi-dimensional. For example, sales figures are one-dimensional in the sense that they have been obtained by adding like to like. Intelligence cannot be obtained solely through the application of preprogrammed routines. It is always context-dependent. A piece of information becomes more or less significant in the overall intelligence picture depending on the other pieces of information that are included.

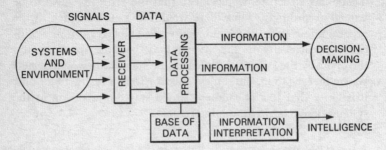

2 The purchasing pre-costs and profits as a percentage of sales

Figure 2 illustrates the way in which data, information and intelligence are associated in decision-making.

Modern Convergence

Until very recently the differences between data processing and information interpretation constituted the great divide in a management-services department. Sometimes the divide was seen as too great to encompass the two activities in the same department, and the information interpreters, primarily operation research analysts (see below), split off to form a separate group. However, with the extension of computers into very many company activities, there has been a coming together of the data-processing and information-interpretation personnel to produce integrated management-information systems. Managers can now use these systems much more readily and many of the bread-and-butter data processing activities produce much of the base information for management decision-making (including the advent of data bases, see below). Given this, a better name would be management intelligence systems.

THE JOBS AND EXPERTISE WITHIN A
MANAGEMENT-SERVICES DEPARTMENT

As one might expect, the number of people employed in a management-services department varies with the size of the organization it serves and the role that is perceived for it. To simplify explanation, the organization of a management-services department within a large company will first be described. This is a context where specialization is well developed, and this differentiation allows the roles of job-holders to be more easily explained. Later the differences between large and small organizations will be examined.

Management Services Departments in Large Organizations

A typical grouping is shown in Figure 3, headed by a management-services manager who often operates just below board level, reporting to the finance director. With a complement of about 1–3 per cent of the total company workforce, the department is likely to incur costs of around 1–2 per cent of the company's turnover. Its responsibility is to help the board decide on the strategy for information systems to be adopted by the organization: which computers to buy, which applications are tackled first, and so on. Techniques to help in this decision are termed business-systems planning and business-information-control study (Zachman, 1982). The department is likely to be split into six functional sections.

Data Processing

The data-processing section has two responsibilities:

1. To provide the facilities needed by the company as a whole to run established computer systems.
2. To provide the infrastructure for the other sections within the management-services department to carry out their functions.

To meet both responsibilities, the data-processing section needs computer operators to ensure that the computer is available for use and that systems are run as planned. Operators have to be familiar with the start-up and other necessary operations, and they need to be able to diagnose hardware faults and call in an engineer to correct them. As computers get more sophisticated they will be able to look after themselves, and so the requirement for operators will diminish. Microcomputers do not need anyone specifically designated as an operator and minicomputers need only a small amount of looking after.

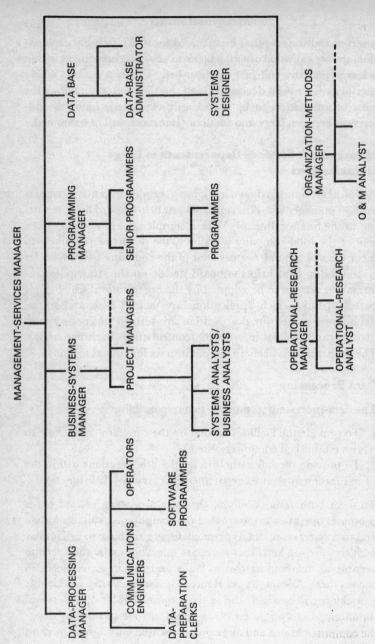

3 A typical organization for a management-services department in a large organization

To provide the facilities for running established computer systems, data-preparation clerks are required. With a general introduction of on-line data entry, such people are a dying breed, but they live on in organizations which are operating systems that rely on older-style batch entry. In on-line systems individual sets of data (such as the data in an order from a customer) may be input to the computer at any time and in any order because the system can check data as they are entered. With batch-entry systems, the sets of data are grouped into a batch and the whole batch input as one group. Customer-order processing was computerized early, and, unless resources have been found for conversion, many companies soldier on with it as a batch system. In such systems, customer orders are first checked by sales staff and then sent to a data-preparation area where clerks transfer the data on to some medium which the computer can read: cards, magnetic tape or disc. A process of verification is sometimes adopted whereby groups of data are keyed-in twice by different clerks and the data only accepted if the two versions are identical. This costly process is being replaced by the clerks in the main functional areas keying in their own data, which is verified by the clerk using sophisticated checking routines. While computer operators and data-preparation clerks run established computer systems, two further jobs are required when systems are being developed. Software programmers produce computer programs to support efficient systems development. A distinction must be made between software and applications programs. Software is programs that do not directly affect the running of a business operation, but act behind the scenes: such as the operating systems used by computers and the tools to help in the development of the applications. Applications programs, on the other hand, directly affect the operations of the company: such as a program to establish a new customer on the customer file and a program to perform an end-of-month accounting routine. Put another way, applications programs mimic the operations of the clerk doing the job before the introduction of the computer, whereas software mimics the overall departmental organization that allows him to do the job.

Software programming requires a detailed knowledge of the way the computer works; and thus a very different type of person from the applications programmer. The job appeals to computer buffs who are not necessarily very interested in the commercial application of their work. Much software is available from computer manufacturers and specialist firms, and so software programmers are only needed to meet unusual requirements.

As a result of the convergence of the technologies of communications, word processing and data processing into one vast unified technology, *communications engineers* are required. Great pressure to link up all word-processing and data-processing activities in an organization and to connect this system to others outside the organization calls for expertise on how to organize the flow of signals between the computer and the various input and output devices. The communications engineer provides this expertise.

The data-processing manager has to supervise the staff in the section, and has to keep abreast of developments in technology and software and know enough about the commercial requirement of the organization to be able to advise the management-services manager on hardware and software acquisition. The DP manager is responsible for the security of the computer installation, through control of staff entering the computer room, and by having back-up facilities in case of computer failure.

Business Systems

The business-systems section has two responsibilities:

1. To help maintain business systems currently in use.
2. To help develop new business systems.

To do this systems analysts carry out portions of the systems cycle: investigation, systems analysis, implementation and maintenance stages, and to some extent the design stage. An analyst's job, therefore, is to act as the primary 'face' of the management-services department to other departments: identifying, analysing, and defining the business needs for information systems and specifying this need in a form that facilitates the subsequent design and programming. Analysts are frequently grouped into teams of three to six members under a project manager who is responsible for information systems covering one functional area in an organization: typically, accounting systems, production systems, and so on.

Historically, systems analysts were concerned with computerizing clerical operations and thus dealt solely with data-processing systems. As such they had little to do with decision-making, and the overall company goals and information needs. With the development of management-intelligence systems, however, the need is for people who can analyse the business-information requirements at a higher level. They are called business analysts and are a hybrid between systems analysts and operational-research analysts (see below).

Programming

Central to the systems cycle are programming and testing, which are the areas of concern for the application programmer, who translates the specification prepared by the analysts and systems designer into a set of working computer programs. In business the computer language used is likely to be COBOL (short for Common Business Oriented Language) with a mainframe computer, or BASIC on a microcomputer.

Corporate View of Data

Historically, each new information-system application in an organization was developed with little or no regard for any other application. Although this disregard probably speeded up system implementation, it led to duplication of data, and to inconsistencies that prevented information being used for high-level decision-making.

To prevent these problems, the company has to take a company-wide view of data by analysis of data needs throughout the company, and organizing the creation of the separate information systems in such a way that data are only captured and stored once. For example, instead of allowing accounts and sales departments to capture and store similar but often critically different data on customers, the system has to ensure that one department captures the data both require in a form useful to both. Further analysis is then needed to define the structure of the files that will hold these data to allow suitable access. Data required speedily many times per day must be placed together in easily accessible files, while data needed only infrequently can be relatively inaccessible.

This corporate view of data highlights the need for systems designers. As the name implies, a systems designer designs the system of files and access methods to ensure that the company's information systems needs are met.

Data Base

An organization taking a corporate view of data can acquire a database-management system. This software is designed to manage data pertaining to the whole organization and not just to a specific department such as production or marketing. Cross-linkages between departments can then easily be made. Such systems are powerful tools and make life easier for both the user and the applications programmer, but they need to be managed for effective deployment by the data-base administrator – in effect a super-systems designer using sophisticated software tools.

Operational Research

Operational research may be defined as the application of mathematics and the scientific method to decision-making. Its origins were in military analysis during the Second World War and it became something of a vogue subject during the 1950s and 1960s. It fell from grace somewhat during the 1970s when rather over-elaborate mathematical models were seen not to help the manager in many practical situations. Operational-research analysts are now found generally in the head offices of large companies, where there is still scope for the full range of their very specialist skills.

Here they will be involved in activities such as devising the best method of scheduling lorries in a fleet, formulating methods for finding the cheapest mix of components to make a product to a given specification, and simulating the movement of steel around a mill to help identify the best way of operating.

Organization and Method

Organization and method are concerned to make clerical activities more efficient. These analysts predated the advent of computers and their function has now generally become part of the job of the systems analyst. In a large organization there may still be a role for the specialist in form design and the organization of paperwork that accompanies computer activities. This role will be further reduced by the introduction of the 'electronic office'.

MANAGEMENT SERVICES DEPARTMENTS IN MEDIUM-SIZED AND SMALL ORGANIZATIONS

In smaller organizations some of the jobs such as operational research, software programming and communications engineering are unlikely to be done. Other jobs will still need doing, although not necessarily by separate people. Business analysts will design the system they seek to implement, and often one person will be analyst, designer and programmer. The number of managers would also be considerably reduced: the roles of the business-systems manager, programming manager and data-base administrator might be carried out by one person. In the very smallest organization, there is no management-services department but merely a clerk operating a microcomputer with software and applications programs bought with the machine: any machine maintenance of programs is carried out by someone outside the organization.

THE FUTURE

The image of a single clerk running the computerized systems for a small firm gives a glimpse of what the future may be like. In many ways the present computer and systems industry must be like the car industry of seventy years ago: a multitude of keen enthusiasts building cars for themselves and for a few other people, with most owners having to 'get out and get under'. Now there are only a few companies producing cars and relatively few people do their own repairs. Few drivers know anything of substance about 'the works' except that it needs petrol, oil and usually water!

In ten years' time, it is likely that computer systems will have developed to a similar stage. Today, most smaller organizations do not attempt to build their computerized information systems from scratch but buy-in the software and applications programs (called computer packages), often with the computer itself in what is known as a 'turnkey system'. To continue the car analogy, you turn the key and away you go. Adaptation of the application programs to produce a special report is likely to be done by people with very little computer background. This will be possible because the computer languages will be very simple to use.

It may seem that management-services departments are destined to wither and die. It is likely that they will wither but it is unlikely that they will die. They will certainly change roles. For example, over the last fifteen years management-services personnel have been very active in financial planning. In that time their role has changed from one of doing much of the planning itself (together with the financial specialists) to helping with the procurement of computer packages through the intermediate stages depicted in Figure 4.

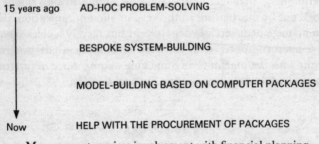

15 years ago   AD-HOC PROBLEM-SOLVING

BESPOKE SYSTEM-BUILDING

MODEL-BUILDING BASED ON COMPUTER PACKAGES

Now   HELP WITH THE PROCUREMENT OF PACKAGES

4 Management-services involvement with financial planning

The pure data-processing fuction is also likely to reduce in size. Expert systems are likely to grow. In these systems not only data but logic are manipulated. The development of such systems may call for organizations to employ knowledge engineers, who are able to 'capture' the expertise of experts and convert it into a computer system that mimics the expert. Such systems are currently available in the medical field.

CHAPTER 24

The Advent of Computerization: North and South

MATS BODIN AND PÄR LIND

NORTH: THE ECONOMICS OF COMPUTER USE

The Investment Calculus

Computers can be used to rationalize or increase the quality of the work performed in virtually every part of a company. In cases such as insurance companies, computer technology is now a fundamental requirement for their activities.

Although many instances of computerization are profitable, some are not, and so there is a need to determine whether the benefits outweigh the costs. A choice has to be made between projects, one of which may be the computer installation. The investment calculus is a quantitative prediction of the profitability of projects. The calculus serves as a basis for the decision on whether or not to go ahead with a project, and is often an important tool for project control. In the end, the evaluation of the projects is made by comparing the calculus figures with the actual project results. The most widely used methods are the pay-off and net present value.

Unfortunately the problems in using the calculus are such that its impact on computerization decisions is relatively low. Applied with caution it is useful, but it must be combined with other methods of project control and a set of qualitative objectives.

We shall discuss here the scope of the investment calculus and some of the reasons for its limited applicability in computerization projects.

An Example: Computerization of an Order-Entry Routine

A wholesale organization with twenty-five warehouses in various parts of Sweden wanted to update its stock-control system. With its existing system, when a sale had been made the stock inventory was updated, but this took some three weeks.

The sales and the purchasing departments felt that this time-lag ought to be eliminated, as neither knew the exact stock level. The company identified two primary goals for the system: increase the stock service level and decrease stock turnround time. The company considered switching to an on-line order-entry system which would enable salesmen to update the stock inventory data base immediately. When a salesman reserved an order for a customer, the system would immediately mark that batch as reserved, and the problems of two salesmen reserving the same batch for two customers would no longer occur. It would also be possible for a salesman to let a customer in a distant town know in seconds when he would get his shipment. When the sale was made, the salesman reserved a delivery from the warehouse as close to the buyer as possible.

An investment calculus was made. The costs identified were: the fee to the data-processing bureau; the new documentation needed; communication costs; and other costs closely related to the new computer system.

Profits were predicted from the reduction in data costs with the new system, and from the disappearance of labour-intensive tasks required by the old systems.

The calculus showed a positive balance, and the project was successfully introduced. The company stated, however, that the decision was not based solely on the calculus, which acted more as a guide and a quick test of the feasibility of the change. As the change would be profitable in terms of a rationalization in the data-processing budget, it was fairly safe to go ahead with it.

The most striking thing about this example, and with almost every investment calculus on computerization projects, is that it did not quantify those essential benefits that computerization was supposed to produce. The company was interested in knowing what could be gained, but the problems of predicting these effects in a precise, quantifiable way were so great that it was not seen as fruitful to spend very much time and effort on the investment calculation.

One of the main reasons for the change was to increase the efficiency of the warehouses. Clearly this was seen as a way of increasing the company's competitiveness, as salesmen would be able to give faster and more accurate answers to potential customers. Why was this not reflected in the calculus?

If we start at the department level, we can see that the computer was intended to be a tool with which the staff could work more efficiently. But merely to hand them the information faster would not automatically lead to their using it. The computer alone would not make staff change their methods of using the information. To what extent would an improvement of their efficiency be due to the computer? Many more changes were constantly occurring, some by intent, some by accident. How would changes in manning affect the department's capability? It was to be hoped that the staff would pick up new skills, contacts and insights, and even if the computer helped them in this it would be far from solely responsible for the staff's successes. A new manager could probably have a much greater impact than the computer. Furthermore, the sales department's results were affected by things it could not influence to any great extent: customers might change their demands and preferences; and competitors might make a technological breakthrough. For all we know, just to be able to maintain last year's sales figures might be an extremely good result.

In turning to a more general description of the problems affecting the calculus, we must distinguish between the reasons for computerization. To realize what the system is supposed to do is the key to understanding not only the possibilities of a precise investment calculus, but also to determining how the computerization process should be implemented.

Factors Influencing the Precision of a Calculus

In a company deciding on computerization there will be many opinions on what the system is supposed to do. Systems are described in different ways. The computing department will concentrate on its technical features, the directors will be interested in long-range planning, while the user department will be concerned with the functioning of the system.

This last issue of the computer system's immediate role is what interests us most. We must face the question: can the company increase its income by computerization, or will the computer just be doing what people did before, only faster?

Distinguishing between decreased costs or increased income may seem rather academic, but the possibility of determining to what extent an increase in income is due to the computer or to the market in general decreases with the greater separation between what the computer does and what the company sells.

A data-processing bureau selling computer time can easily see what new income a new system can generate. By buying a new machine it may acquire a new customer who is ready to pay a certain sum for a certain service. The income comes from selling computer time, so the link to larger sales is very short. But few companies actually sell computer services, and the majority use computers to support activities that seldom create income on their own. Reducing costs is thus in one way or another the main reason for computerization. This may be articulated as actually reducing staff, or as using computers in order to be able to increase the quality or quantity of work without increasing the staff. As this way of increasing profit is not directly linked to an increase in income, the calculus cannot be precise on anything but cost reduction – if that.

Turning from the benefit side of the calculus to the costs, we find that the degree of mechanization is the key characteristic. At one end of this scale, we find systems that do what people did before, but faster. A purely automatic system, such as a salary-computation system, requires few resources from outside the computer department. Formal procedures already exist, and the problems are mostly those of turning these routines into computer programs. The necessary personnel training is normally not very costly; those who are to use the system are old hands at what it is doing, but they must learn just how they will enter data. Calculating the total costs is thus pretty straightforward; few departments are involved (often only the user and the computer departments), and the activities required in the project are easy to identify and to define.

Other systems are required to achieve much more. In some cases they are necessary for the company's business. No bank would be able to operate as banks do today without computers. For them computerization has meant a fundamental change, and has even changed some of the notions of what is meant by 'profitable work'. In settings like these it is far more difficult to determine the costs of computerization. There are still the programming and computer-training costs that dominate other projects, but an extensive organizational analysis has to precede the actual implementation. Furthermore, staff training is much more extensive and not easily predicted. For example, new methods of purchasing must become part of staff thinking, and managers must turn their attention and energy towards new areas. It is very hard to predict how long it will take to achieve these changes that are at least as important as the computer system for reaching the overall target.

Non-stringent methods of internal pricing complicate cost predictions in systems of this kind. For example, personnel training and organizational changes are necessary, but if the department that is introducing computers does not have to pay for these, then they are not considered as a cost. The reasoning goes: 'We already have a management-services department, so it won't cost us anything to use it.' This is of course quite wrong. The user department will eventually pay for the help, but if the payment is hidden as a 'company overhead' it is frequently overlooked.

Internal pricing is not the only example of a lack of a 'company view' on computerization. Rationalization is often regarded as decreasing or, it is hoped, eliminating the slack in a department. Redundant capacity is seen as negative, and efforts are made to eliminate it. Computerization should lead to a reduction in workload, but the computer department faces an increase. Two questions should therefore always be raised: has the total slack in the organization been reduced? And do we now have sufficient slack left to cope with increases in workload or a sudden lack of manpower?

Why are Computer Investments Difficult to Calculate?

Cost reduction was not a primary objective in the sales-warehouse example cited earlier. In addition, it was not easy to predict the impact on sales of this change. In these respects it is representative of cases of computerization which are very often difficult to quantify. In order to understand why economic assessment of them has become more difficult with time we will look briefly at the history of computers.

Computerization on a wider scale can be said to date back to the early 1960s. Large companies expecting an increase in sales realized that not only would the production department need to expand, but that the increase in sales would also mean a greater workload for the finance department. As the administration of invoices and salary computations were (and are) not seen as increasing the company's profit, a process of rationalization was started.

Although technology then available was far from being as effective as that of today, it was still identified as a powerful tool for handling the increasing number of invoices without employing as many new people as manual procedures would require. Saving personnel costs and mechanization of existing procedures are the most important characteristics of such computerization. The investment calculus performed was straightfoward and could actually depict and quantify the true reasons for computerization – reduction of costs.

Ten years later a number of innovations in computer technology had emerged. Mini-computers, new structures in large or all-purpose computer systems and on-line and real-time features paved the way for an increase in computerization. Small and medium-sized companies could now afford computers, and started off in the same way as the largest companies a decade earlier. Invoice handling, salary computations and other administrative tasks found in the finance department were the prime targets for computerization.

Larger companies had already reaped many of the benefits in this field, and used the new technologies to bring computers into other parts of their organizations. Computers started emerging as tools for organizational change: printing companies could use computers in their production and thus become more competitive; grocery retailers could order goods by direct access to the wholesaler's data base, which increased the efficiency of both – and created a stronger link between them. Mechanization of existing procedures was replaced by formulating quite new procedures and using computers as one tool among many in designing the new activities to be performed. The investment calculus became very difficult, as cost reduction was no longer the main reason for investing money in computers, and extensive organizational changes resulted.

This 'aggressive' way of using computers as a tool to change the fundamentals of the activities has continued to be important. It seems likely that, in the future, computers will be regarded as most valuable when they open up quite new business possibilities.

Applying the Investment Calculus in Modern Systems

Using the investment calculus when the main goal of computerization is to help increase income requires that great care be taken because the calculus has difficulty in handling long time and distance consequences.

The advantages are said to be those of reducing data-processing costs and of reducing the number of people who work at the task that is to be computerized. But the real reasons are to be found elsewhere, and the computer system is only a small part of the changes needed to achieve these goals. It is therefore not possible to quantify to what extent achievement of them is due to the computer as such.

Moreover, data-processing costs can actually increase, because of the physical hardware, application software, maintenance costs and the new cost of administering the computer. One of the main reasons for this is the frequent lack of stringent internal pricing within companies already referred to.

The investment calculus tends to regard a computerization project as finished once the system is up and running. Costs for future alterations to the system are not represented, but are implicitly counted as operating costs. Because it is not known how long the system will last, we do not know for how many years it will be able to increase income or reduce costs.

The scope of the investment calculus is clearly limited. It mostly quantifies pure mechanization effects where the work is not seen as being changed in any dramatic way, so it is not very surprising that few managers use an investment calculus as the sole basis for their decisions.

Thus an investment calculus cannot be the only basis for a decision between several projects. As it does not depict the fundamental reasons for computerization, it cannot evaluate which project is likely to be the most profitable. It can, however, be used as an indication of whether a particular project is profitable. If we enumerate all the costs, including organizational analysis, training in new professional sales methods, and so on, and find that the effects of computerization alone make the project profitable, we can feel reasonably convinced that the project will be worthwhile.

Obviously the investment calculus cannot act as the only or even the main tool for project control. As the calculus quantifies mainly those side-effects that do not form the reasons for the project, using it as the main control mechanism would involve distortions. The main thrust of the first half of the chapter has been the illumination of these other considerations which are the context of the investment calculus.

SOUTH: COMPUTERS FOR DEVELOPMENT

Background

A similar pattern can be observed in the introduction of computers into developing countries. The booming world economy in the 1950s and 1960s that created a need for computers to increase productivity has been replaced by a stagnating economy. In developing countries the interest in adopting computer technology has therefore been tempered by other challenges confronting these less-developed countries (Muller, 1979).

A number of developing countries have nevertheless gained considerable experience from the use of computers. The first computer appeared in India in 1960, in 1962 in Indonesia and Egypt, and in 1965 in Malaysia, to mention just a few. The growth rate increased during the 1970s and towards 1980 540 computers were installed in India, 420 in Malaysia and 190 in Egypt. As a comparison, the numbers of computers installed in Europe in 1975 and 1980 were 172,000 and 465,000 respectively.

Studies of computer installations in developing countries reveal some basic concerns. Lack of application software designed for developing countries leads to inappropriate computer utilization. Focus on computer science in education at the expense of application-oriented education leads to a discrepancy between theory and practice, and between technological opportunities and social understanding. The marketing activities of computer vendors with their priority on fulfilling their business objectives are far from consistent with the most urgent development issues of the country. This will also hamper the selection of criteria for beneficial computer usage, and the development of indigenous computer policies.

It is natural in this context that computers are evaluated and viewed as an attractive form of advanced technology, but basic conditions of an economic, social and technical nature have a significant impact on their successful use.

The Users

In developing countries computers are mostly found in banks, insurance companies, government institutions and the bigger enterprises, in more or less the same way as when computerization started in the developed countries, and for very much the same reasons.

The public sector is by far the biggest computer-user. This is partly the result of a relatively small private sector with an industry infrastructure that is still in its initial phase, but also of the fact that military applications represent a significant proportion of public-sector computerization. Industrial applications are rare.

The picture of computer-users in developing countries would not be complete however without mentioning the subsidiaries of multi-national companies. Their production facilities are tightly bound to their headquarters and follow company standards in the use of computers. Their levels of data processing are normally significantly higher than those of the rest of the industry, and this is significant for the transfer of new ideas on and concepts of computerization into developing countries.

Characteristics of a Computer System

Computers introduced in developing countries are devoted to transaction-oriented types of applications, characterized by routine work, large volumes of data and relatively simple calculations. These include payroll, accounting routines and basic logistics.

Again, this choice is understandable in the light of the general nature of these applications, as every organization has accounting and payroll requirements. In addition, software packages and applications knowledge for these basic applications are often straightforward and general enough to fit most types of computers.

The next step in the application hierarchy is in areas such as order entry, stock control, purchasing and material-requirement planning. These routines are generally on-line with direct user–computer communication. Systems are now designed and developed to be integrated in communication networks and thus rely heavily on external factors such as telephone lines, technical specialists and vendor support.

Technical and socioeconomical constraints found in developing countries do, however, reduce the potential benefits of computers in on-line operation. Poorly functioning telephone lines, for instance, result in unreliable data communication. The computer cannot be integrated with other external functions and thus increase the overall performance simply because the interfaces between the computer and those external functions have not been (and cannot always be) appropriately specified.

There are therefore only a few organizations which have been able to move towards on-line-oriented systems where transactions are stored and retrieved in dialogue with a remote computer with simultaneous data processing.

With the recent developments in microcomputer technology it is, however, likely that small on-line systems will be available for a variety of applications, these systems requiring less integration to be efficient and their limited capacity providing limited solutions (Kline, 1982).

Computers are frequently adopted by central governments to provide ministries and international organizations with statistical data on which to base development policies and economic strategies. There is a growing concern about those nationwide information systems. The computer models as such are often rigid when compared to a constantly changing environment and do not respond to fluctuations in society. In addition, there are questions about the accuracy and the relevance of data fed into the computer models.

The ambition current among computer manufacturers and many computer professionals to develop systems aiming at more and more integration on a higher and higher infrastructure level has very limited relevance to the identified needs of most developing countries. In addition, different attitudes concerning the concept of efficiency ('time is not necessarily money, labour is not always expensive') and different needs should lead to different systems.

Specification of Needs

When considering the need for computer-based information systems it becomes clear, as with most advanced technology, that this kind of need differs substantially from the more basic human requirements: food and housing. Needs may be created in marketing campaigns or through the adoption of lifestyles from different socioeconomic systems. In addition, basic needs, as well as needs for most advanced consumption, are directly affected by changes in income level. The need concept is a relative one, difficult to define and probably strongly related to the development level of a region or a country.

The transfer of computer technology and the attempts to discern relevant levels of ambition as to its use have led to the current situation in a majority of developing countries being more influenced by marketing considerations among computer suppliers than of indigenous computer policies and strategies. A UNIDO report (1982) thus states that suppliers of computers set out to conquer the market by imposing products for which there was no local demand and offering solutions to problems which they, the suppliers, identified. For example, potential computer applications to benefit rural regions are rare. Kuhn and Kaiser (1982) report from India that in spite of numerous proposals concerning applications to food/agriculture, education and health/family planning, remarkably little has been done.

Different perspectives give different specifications of needs. The vendor/supplier/manufacturer of computer systems is apt to specify needs which do not deviate too much from the marketing plans, compiled at corporation headquarters in a developed country. The current computer-users in a developing country, probably a bank, government office or a big industrial enterprise, tend to subordinate their needs to application software already in use in developed countries.

Most developing countries are also very distant from the R & D and production sites of the computer manufacturers both in a geographical sense and in the possibility of influencing the development of computer systems and strategies. As a result, there is no real channel for feedback of information about specific needs and demands. The dialogue between manufacturer and user that influenced systems and applications in developed countries has never occurred in the underdeveloped countries. As a consequence, in India 50 per cent of all computer applications are total failures and only 20 per cent are successful (Kuhn and Kaiser, 1982).

In addition, the rapid development of computer technology results in new generations of hardware long before previous generations have become obsolete. Computer manufacturers' best people are devoted to future product development rather than the improvement of current products. The motivation to improve current products and to make adaptations to user requirements is weak since new products/ generations are 'just around the corner'. In the most advanced countries installations tend to get a certain amount of support from the suppliers, for goodwill reasons, and to bridge gaps between computer generations, but developing countries seem to be very much left alone in these situations.

So it is important to distinguish between appropriate and inappropriate computer technology and also between relevant and less-relevant levels of ambition in use.

The three following parameters should therefore be regarded as fundamental in the process of acquiring a computer system in a developing country:

1. The true availability of computer technology in terms of hardware, application software and consultancy support.
2. The influence of the technical environment on the system operation.
3. The influence of the socioeconomic environment and the possibility of a socioeconomically feasible implementation.

Computers in a Socioeconomic Perspective

Nationwide planning systems tend to be out of phase with the society they set out to describe, thus widening the gap between the macro-perspective of governments and the micro-perspective of man, with the consequence that 'one of the ironies of history is that citizens are usually left out of the issues that involve them most. As a result they feel a sense of helplessness and neglect and become indifferent to the actions of governments' (Perinbam, 1982).

The impact of computer technology is an issue of general importance and concern that is and has been debated with growing interest in developed and developing countries alike. In India 'there is a need to increase the awareness of people to the relatively new areas of technology such as microcomputers. Such an awareness is the necessary precondition of any social control over technology' (*Business India*, 1983). Abdus Salan, a former Nobel Prizewinner, commented that 'our [developing] societies have become consumers of technology, not technology-minded' (*Arabia*, 1983).

It is important to distinguish quantitative and qualitative effects. In quantitative terms: 'The impact [of microelectronics] has been less on developing countries than had been anticipated. There is little evidence that microelectronics technology has been widely used in developing country industrialization; and only limited evidence that developing country export of manufactured goods is being replaced in developed countries by domestically produced products manufactured cheaper (and hence now competitive) as a result of the use of new microelectronics based technology' (Oldham, 1981).

Unfortunately, this distinction between qualitative and quantitative impact does not help much since the *nature* of the problem is often qualitative ('who is to judge whether this consequence is good or bad'). We are thus faced with the problem of assessing qualitative consequences, a problem involving social as well as psychological aspects. To assist in this, models have been developed which distinguish between possible and probable impact, and between technical and socioeconomic environmental conditions (Lind, 1982).

A cultural aspect of computerization has relevance in this context, namely that: 'It is generally admitted that information is not culturally neutral. By considering programming languages, it can be seen that they are largely based on the English language. Above all current information is a reflection of a certain way of thinking and of a certain economic and social organization; it is the product of a rationalist and western culture. Is this cultural dependence inevitable and must developed countries resign themselves to it?' (Kalman, 1981).

This opens up a new and fundamental set of questions concerning the cultural aspects of computerization. For instance: if technical processes are products of culture, is it feasible to evaluate the impact of computers in different cultures without a thorough knowledge of local conditions? Do languages of different cultures possess the same abilities (words, expressions) to express a rational computer language? It is claimed that the Chinese language, for example, tends to counteract extreme formalization and abstraction in a reified logic. The tendency to argue and analyse phenomena in terms of a dialectical logic is reinformed in the language. Rigid 'A or not-A' categorizations are avoided (Elzinga, 1981).

Languages are reflections of culture and so are traditional rites and myths, being 'examples of mental activities of people and treated as communication in an unknown language' (Yalman, 1967). Together with the observation made by Lévi-Strauss, the anthropologist, that the structure of myths belongs to a different level of mental activity from that of language (Douglas, 1967), one is led to believe that the so-called 'software crisis' is far from merely a technical problem but comprises fundamental issues of a semantic as well as a sociocultural nature. Computer language as a narrow sub-set of common language offers a one-dimensional description of the multidimensional faces of man.

CHAPTER 25

Corporate Strategy and Strategic Management

GERRY JOHNSON

By 1980 Marks and Spencer had become Britain's largest retailer with stores in prime locations in most towns and cities. The network of stores together with the St Michael brand name attracted fourteen million shoppers each week. Another side to their domination, however, was that they were nearing saturation point in Britain, and so they decided to take their retailing skills into Europe to increase sales volume. They initially opened three stores in Paris, Brussels and Lyons which allowed them to experiment with the product range before placing large orders with suppliers. Once the product range was finalized and the stores had proved profitable, Marks and Spencer were well placed to mount a much larger assault on the European market.

In 1970 Jute Industries (Holdings) Ltd had been in the business of importing and processing jute, mainly for the carpet industry, for fifty years. In the decade up to 1970 it became increasingly clear that this traditional business was under threat. With a new chairman in 1970 the company reassessed its position. By 1981 the company, redesignated Sidlaw Industries Ltd, had rationalized production facilities and reduced overheads in their textile business; and half the company's turnover and virtually all the profits came from North Sea oil servicing, a totally different activity from its traditional business.

By 1980 unemployment in the West Midlands had reached 12 per cent and was rising. At the County elections in 1980 the Labour group had pledged active intervention by the County Council to help local industry and foster restructuring of the industrial base of the West Midlands. By 1982 the Labour-controlled Council had introduced an Economic Development Unit to assess which firms in the area might benefit from additional investment to expand profitably, provide a return on the investment, and create jobs. To raise funds attempts were made to allocate a proportion of the

Council's pension fund for local investment. The West Midlands County Council had always been concerned about local industry; by 1982 that interest had taken the form of an investment agency for local firms.

These three examples of quite different organizations are illustrations of *strategic* decisions which are the most important for organizations. In the long run success is not determined by the energy of a sales force, the efficiency of an accounting system, the productivity of a manufacturing plant or good labour relations. These are certainly important, but long-term success is the outcome of the strategies adopted.

THE CHARACTERISTICS OF STRATEGIC DECISIONS

What sort of decisions are strategic, and what distinguishes them from other sorts of decision? The characteristics of strategic decisions are:

1. They are likely to be concerned with the *scope of an organization's activities*. Does (and should) the organization concentrate on one area of activity, or many? Sidlaw, referred to at the beginning, although historically rooted in one business area moved to others, and one of these became its major profit-earner. The scope of activity is concerned with the way in which the management of the organization conceive of its boundaries, and what they want the organization to do and to be like.

2. Strategy involves *matching the activities of an organization to the environment* in which it operates. The examples at the beginning of this chapter illustrate changes to take advantage of an opportunity or deal with a threat in the environment. Marks and Spencer ventured into Europe to move outside a saturated market and into one offering new opportunities. The West Midlands County Council attempted to alleviate local business decline and growing unemployment. Sidlaw reduced its investment in a textile industry under threat to take advantage of a growing industry off its shores.

3. Strategy also involves *matching the activities of an organization to its resource capability*. There would be little point in trying to take advantage of new opportunities if the resources needed were not

available or could not be made available. So Marks and Spencer might have felt reasonably happy that their skills in retailing would be transferable to Europe, while Sidlaw might well have been apprehensive about their capability to move into North Sea oil servicing. Both had to assess the extent to which sufficient resources could be provided to take advantage of the opportunity.

4. Strategic decisions usually have *major resource implications*. These may involve acquiring new areas of resource, disposing of others, or fundamentally reallocating others. The West Midlands County Council along with other councils in the early 1980s faced major resource acquisition and reallocation tasks to carry through their intended strategy of economic intervention. Experts in investment appraisal had to be recruited and a special unit set up to carry out company appraisals. Funds were sought for investment purposes from the Council's pension fund, giving rise to legal and political debate. Similarly, Sidlaw's venture into the North Sea oil service industry had major resource implications. The traditional jute operations were cut back severely and the remainder modernized to make it more competitive: synthetic fibre companies were acquired; Peterhead harbour was redeveloped as a servicing base for the North Sea; and hotels around Aberdeen were developed. This involved fundamentally restructuring the physical, financial and manpower resources of the business.

5. Strategic decisions usually affect the *long-term direction* of an organization. They have longer time horizons than day-to-day operating decisions. Marks and Spencer's management knew that a major presence in Europe would take years to achieve. Similarly, supporters of the Labour group's economic initiative in the West Midlands knew that any substantial change in the nature of West Midlands industry and the employment levels in the region was a long-term aim.

6. Strategic decisions are usually *complex in nature* because they involve many considerations from within and from without the organization and have many ramifications. Sidlaw's decision to change the nature of its business had wide effects both inside and outside the company. It affected manpower planning, the financial structure of the business, the planning of production facilities and plant, negotiations with investors and unions, changes in organization structure, and so on.

LEVELS OF STRATEGY

Strategies are likely to exist at a number of levels in an organization. Clearly individuals may have a strategy: for example, to do with their career. This may be relevant when considering influences on strategies adopted by organizations but it is not corporate strategy. Corporate strategy can be considered at three levels. There is the *corporate* level where strategy concerns the scope of the organization's activities: the business interests of Sidlaw; the geographical spread by Marks and Spencer; the services offered by West Midlands County Council. Strategic decisions of the most general sort concern changes in the range of activities which are taken by senior management of large conglomerates with many diverse business interests. Most organizations face this kind of strategic decision at some time, however, when they begin to consider widening a range of products or services or moving their geographical area.

The second level is *competitive or business strategy* and involves competing in a particular market. So, whereas corporate strategy involves decisions about the organization as a whole, competitive strategy is related to a unit within the organization. How should the textile division of Sidlaw compete in its increasingly hostile market? How should new ventures, such as European operation by Marks and Spencer or the North Sea servicing operations of Sidlaw, position themselves in relation to competitors to secure their share of the new markets?

The third level of strategy is at the operations level where *functional strategies* are concerned with how the different functions of the enterprise – marketing, finance, manufacturing, and so on – contribute to the higher levels of strategy. Functional strategies will influence how an organization seeks to be competitive. Competitive strategy may depend to a large extent on decisions about market entry, product offer, financing, investment, and so on, but these decisions are made, or at least strongly influenced, at functional level.

STRATEGIC MANAGEMENT

How does strategy come about? What processes take place that lead to strategic decisions? These questions can be dealt with in two ways. There are views about how strategy *should* be formulated; these are the normative views expressed in most of the books on business policy (e.g. Uyterhoeven, Ackerman and Rosenblum, 1977; Glueck, 1980). There are also views based more on empirical evidence about how strategy is *actually* formulated which provided a somewhat different perspective.

A Normative View of Strategic Management

The traditional view of strategy formulation is of a logical and rational process, typically illustrated as in Figure 1, with the following seven steps:

1. First, *strategic objectives* are established at an appropriate level of generality. So, for example, objectives at a corporate-strategy level might concern the overall financial return and the general scope of the organization; whereas competitive-level (or business-level) objectives might be about market share, levels of profitability and operating efficiency. Without clear objectives it is difficult to make sensible strategic decisions since there is no yardstick against which to assess alternatives.

2. A *strategic analysis* involves understanding the strategic situation of the organization. Such an analysis might consider, for example, what changes have occurred and are likely to occur in the environment and how they will affect the organization. The analysis would also assess the resource strength of the organization in the context of these changes. Does the organization have the physical, financial and management capabilities to deal with the changes that are occurring? Tools and techniques of analysis recommended for such analysis are: examining environmental trends (Neubauer and Solomon, 1977); projecting future environmental changes (Linstone and Turdoff, 1975); resource-audit checklists (Buchele, 1962); and methods of financial analysis (Rowe, Mason and Dickel, 1982). Strategic analysis involves collecting, examining, and interpreting information to form a view of the key influences that will affect the choice of strategy.

3. *Strategic options* are then generated. A popular model of strategic options proposed by Ansoff (1965) and shown in Figure 2*a* is known as the growth vector. Organizations have the choice

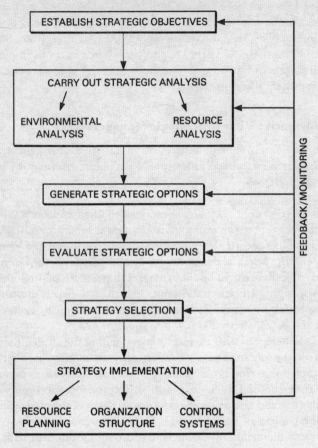

1 A normative model of strategic management

of: (i) *market penetration*, continuing to operate within their existing markets with their existing products or services; (ii) *market development*, continuing to concentrate on their existing products or services but launching them into new markets; (iii) *product development*, remaining within their existing market but moving into new products or services; and (iv) *diversification*, moving into new markets with new products or services.

The growth vector can be adapted to provide a more specific model. Staying within an existing market with present products

(a)

MARKETS

	EXISTING	NEW
EXISTING	MARKET PENETRATION	MARKET DEVELOPMENT
NEW	PRODUCT DEVELOPMENT	DIVERSIFICATION

PRODUCTS

(b)

MARKETS

	EXISTING	NEW
EXISTING	CONSOLIDATION OR MARKET PENETRATION	MARKET DEVELOPMENT
NEW	PRODUCT DEVELOPMENT	RELATED OR UNRELATED DIVERSIFICATION

PRODUCTS

2 Strategic options: *a* the growth vector; *b* a model of strategic options

may not necessarily involve penetrating that market further in terms of increasing market share, but could involve *consolidating* the existing position by, for example, becoming more cost-effective and thus more profitable. Two aspects of diversification can be identified: *related diversification* – moving into product markets related to existing operations; and *unrelated diversification* – moving into entirely new types of operation in which the organization has virtually no experience. Figure 2*b* refines the basic growth vector in these ways.

This model helps to categorize the types of strategy adopted by the organizations used as examples. Marks and Spencer used a strategy of market development. The West Midlands County Council sought a strategy of product (or service) development. Sidlaw adopted unrelated diversification while embracing a consolidation strategy in their textile division.

4. An *evaluation of strategic options* follows. Management is able to examine a set of options in terms of their strategic analysis and weigh one option against another. Some options might not make sense: the West Midlands County Council was already committed to helping its local industry and it could not have moved out of its own area to help industry elsewhere. Other options might be very risky. For Sidlaw to rely on market penetration in the jute-based textile industry as the main plank of their development would have been very risky indeed. Others build on strengths or overcome clear threats: so Marks and Spencer might have viewed European expansion as building on their experience in retailing while overcoming the threat of an almost saturated UK market.

5. A *strategy selection* among the available options then takes place. Which option should be chosen or should more than one be adopted? It is a complex choice as the number of considerations is very great. For a rational decision to be made the chosen option would need to be: (i) reconciled with the points recognized in the strategic analysis; (ii) be demonstrably workable; and (iii) be acceptable to the various parties with interests in the organization such as shareholders, managers and unions. In the end, the most rational decision would be to choose the option which meets these criteria *and* is likely to achieve the objectives laid down in the beginning.

6. The chosen strategy or strategies must then be implemented. *Strategy implementation* should not be thought of simply as putting into effect a strategic decision. Implementation involves developing a generalized decision into specific plans. Taking a decision to expand into Europe is one thing: but Marks and Spencer's management then faced detailed planning to achieve this. They had to consider what *resources* would be needed: financial, manpower, merchandise and property implications. They would also have to consider how the company as a whole should be organized for the new venture. Could the existing *organization* structure cope with the addition of the European business or would there have to be some reorganization? In either event, what *systems of control* would be needed to manage the new venture?

7. Throughout this series of strategic management activities and considerations there would be a continual process of *feedback* and *monitoring* from one stage to another. Consideration of options

would in itself raise points which would contribute to strategic analysis; and implementation planning would be an examination of the feasibility of a strategy and, hence, a means of evaluating it. So when a strategy is put into effect, there is continual feedback on the effectiveness of the plans so that decisions can be taken to amend or even change course altogether.

The normative view has much to commend it as a logical step-by-step approach to strategic management. It is neat, rational, understandable and provides managers and students of management with a sensible approach to strategic decisions. There are, however, dangers in thinking of strategic management in this way which hinge on the question as to whether or not this actually happens in organizations.

A DESCRIPTIVE VIEW OF STRATEGIC MANAGEMENT

The words 'strategy' and 'planning' have become almost inextricably intertwined. Students are likely to think that strategy arises out of the step-by-step planning process. Managers often talk as if the strategy of their organization is formed as the result of a 'corporate plan'; or they might apologetically say their company should really 'do more planning' as if this is a worthy endeavour in itself. There is increasing research evidence to show that the neat, logical, strategic planning approach does not happen in organizations; and, what is more, that very successful organizations manage well without it.

THE ROLE OF OBJECTIVES

The neatness of the normative model is challenged by evidence which questions the central role of objectives. Texts on management science state that managers should have objectives which are specific, unambiguous and measurable (Drucker, 1974). Different courses of action can then be assessed in terms of their likelihood of achieving these objectives. There is little empirical evidence to suggest that objectives perform this role, however, but they are often ill-defined, diverse and not agreed upon (Norburn and Grinyer, 1973/4), post-rationalized (Mintzberg, Raisinghani and Theoret, 1975), unstated, not explicit or very generalized (Quinn, 1980). It probably makes more sense to think of objectives as:

1. different according to the various interest and influence groups in an organization;
2. one of the many influences on a strategic decision; and
3. a product of the value systems of individuals and groups in an organization.

THE INFLUENCE OF VALUE SYSTEMS

The idea that strategy is a product of matching an organization's resources to its environment is over-simple. The perceptions and values of managers play a significant part in deciding how environmental opportunities and threats are interpreted. Two organizations, in the same industry and facing similar environments with similar resources, will not necessarily opt for similar strategies because of the different values and expectations held by people who influence strategic choice (Child, 1972).

Miles and Snow (1978) studied value systems predominant in organizations and found that different strategies, and indeed the management practices, can be understood in terms of value systems. Defender-type organizations in which conservative, defensive, cautious values predominate tend to opt for strategies concentrating on a secure market niche, specializing in terms of what they offer to that market, and ensuring that the organization is run as efficiently as possible. At the other extreme, prospector-type organizations value innovation and always being first onto the market with new products or services, and are likely to be continually looking for new products or new markets. They emphasize the innovative rather than the control aspects of management. Such differences in ideology within an organization play a part in the formulation of strategy. The dominant organizational ideology is built up over time and cemented in the power base. Miles and Snow show how in a defender-type organization the inclination towards efficiency and control is institutionalized through the predominance of senior levels of management with training and experience in control aspects of the business. In a prospector-type organization, on the other hand, senior management tend to be experienced in more innovative, venture management.

THE GENERATION OF STRATEGIC ACTION

The idea that strategic decisions are taken as a result of systematic analysis of the environment and of the resource position of the organization does not receive much support in research. A more accurate picture is that successful organizations appear to be sensitive to changes in their environment (Miller and Friesen, 1978; Norburn and Grinyer, 1973/4). This is likely to be because of the sensitivity of individual managers to an accumulation of stimuli over time (Lyles, 1981; Mintzberg, Raisinghani and Theoret, 1975), rather than to formalized analysis within a planning system.

This approach involves:

1. Managers becoming aware that 'something is amiss' as a result of a growing number of signals, usually from outside the organization, typically from customer or competitor action and technological change (Norburn and Grinyer, 1973/4), or changes in the economy (Glueck, 1980).
2. A point is reached where this accumulation of stimuli combined with a trigger, such as a downturn in company performance, confirms that there is a problem to be tackled.
3. A period of activity then follows to identify the nature of the problem at an organizational level. This may involve data collection but, even if it does not, a process of 'diplomacy' occurs as managers check how other, and particularly senior, managers perceive the problem (Lyles and Mitroff, 1980; Soelberg, 1967).
4. The organization may find great difficulty in proceeding beyond defining the nature of the problem, but clear identification of the problem may be passed over and more attention given to generating an agreed or acceptable course of action.

THE SELECTION OF STRATEGY

Just as there is little evidence of systematic analysis of strategic problems, so there is little evidence of systematic evaluation of strategic options. Managers are more likely to try to employ a solution to a problem in line with what they have tried or experienced before (Mintzberg, Raisinghani and Theoret, 1975). This is very much in line with what Spender (1980) describes as strategic 'recipes'. He argues that managers, in dealing with a strategic problem, bring to bear 'an accepted set of beliefs about what is consistent, realistic and which outcomes will follow the commitment of resources to specified actions' (Grinyer and Spender, 1978). This recipe is likely to be fairly similar within an industry but different between industries, and helps the manager understand environmental changes, or changes in performance of his own and other organizations. It will also contain guidance on appropriate action to be taken when things go wrong.

One of the main influences on the choice of strategy is matching a problem against the strategic 'frame of reference' of managers (Rumelt, 1979). The recipe or strategic frame is very important for understanding and selecting strategy, but it is also potentially very constraining as it is likely to lead to a perception of action required only in terms of past experience.

STRATEGY MAKING AS AN INCREMENTAL PROCESS

All this might seem a terrible muddle. How can organizations formulate successful strategies in such circumstances? Some do not, of course, and one of the major arguments for the formal approach is that it helps to utilize managers' individual abilities while demanding a rigorous, methodical approach. As Steiner and Miner (1977) say: 'At the very least, the formal system should give managers more time for reflective thinking ... But formal planning cannot be really effective unless managers at all levels inject their judgements and intuition into the planning process.'

It can also be argued that the activities described above are not as random and chaotic as they might appear. It is perfectly sensible to think of strategy as a 'pattern in a stream of decisions' (Mintzberg, 1978). The proponents of this 'incremental' view say that strategy comes about as a result of:

1. Many relatively small decisions over a period of time leading to a readjustment of strategy.
2. These decisions and changes take place within different parts of the organization at an operational level, rather than at the centre as strategic planning.
3. The process provides a continual testing of alternatives open to the organization. This evaluation through action can be activity in the market or proposals canvassed within the organization to see if they receive support. So, when Marks and Spencer moved into Europe they moved incrementally by opening three stores to test the most sensible approach to European operations and to evaluate their likely success. At the same time other strategies were tried out, for example, new product ranges were tested in U K stores.

Quinn (1980) summarizes incremental strategic management as:

> The most effective strategies of major enterprises tend to emerge step by step from an iterative process in which the organization probes the future, experiments, and learns from a series of partial (incremental) commitments rather than through global formulations of total strategies. Good managers are aware of this process, and they consciously intervene in it. They use it to improve the information available for decisions and to build the psychological identification essential to successful strategies. The process is both logical and incremental. Such logical incrementalism is not 'muddling', as most people understand that word. Properly managed, it is a conscious, purposeful, proactive, executive practice.

This incremental approach is appropriate when the environment of an organization is continually changing. Incremental change is a sensitive mechanism to ensure that the organization's strategic posture continually adapts to its changing environment. If incremental change fails to keep pace with changes in the environment then it may be necessary to make more fundamental changes in strategy. In these circumstances it is necessary to re-think the strategy at the corporate level as with Sidlaw Industries: failure to adapt to the increasingly threatening environment of their textile business required a much more fundamental re-think of the overall scope of the business. Mintzberg (1978) argues that these more fundamental strategic changes, which he calls 'global', are the sort that are more often 'intended' in the sense of being more systematically planned.

STRATEGIC MANAGEMENT: A REVISED MODEL

No one would suggest that because managers act in a particular way, it is necessarily good and sound practice. Research into strategic management leads to questioning of the traditional, normative view of strategic management. Some sensible amendments might be made to create a model which managers can better relate to the reality of their organizations. The salient points to consider are:

1. Objectives might better be thought of as an extension of the values and expectations of managers or interest groups rather than pre-determined criteria by which to assess performance.
2. Neither objectives nor value systems are the predominant influence on strategic decisions. Strategy is not simply a reconciliation of organizational resources and the environment but the reconciliation of resources, environmental influences and value systems.
3. Strategic decisions, particularly to do with competitive strategy, do not commonly come about through an intellectual process of analysis but through action, often incremental action. Thus strategic changes are continually tested out through implementation or through the canvassing of courses of action. Thus strategic analysis, choice and implementation are in continual interaction rather than being iterative as in Figure 1.

Figure 3 is a redrawn model of the strategic management process in these terms, which recognizes that there may be different, equally sensible, ways of arriving at strategic decisions. It might be quite sensible to test out possible strategic development through a process of incremental implementation. On the other hand it might be sensible to stand back and take a more analytical approach starting with a rigorous analysis of the strategic position, through an evaluation of options, to planning strategy implementation.

Whichever approach is taken, the different stages are not discrete. The strategic-management process involves understanding the strategic position of the organization ('analysis'), while continually re-thinking options ('choice'), and putting strategy into effect ('implementation').

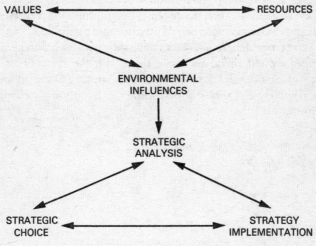

3 Strategic management: a revised model

CONCLUSION

This chapter has sought to achieve two aims: to provide an understanding of corporate strategy, in terms of the sorts of decisions that are called 'strategic' and why they are important; and to describe the process of 'strategic management', that is, how strategic decisions are made.

The emphasis has been on questioning traditionally held views about strategic management and suggesting that these views have not been sufficiently rooted in the reality of management. There has been an unrealistic emphasis on the importance of objective formulation and too little attention to the influence of organizational value systems. There has also been a preoccupation with the need for strategic decision-making to be a rational, step-by-step, 'intellectual' process when, in fact, it may be an incremental action-based process.

There are differences in emphasis which are significant, not least because readers may well be seeking to understand what management is about. They may understand that strategic decisions are of vital importance but think that, if the strategy of an organization does not appear to have come about through some rigorous, overt process of analysis, then management is unprofessional or lacking in strategic-management capability. It is more sensible to consider the extent to which management have shown an ability to perceive changes around them, reconcile these with the capabilities and values of the organization, and adapt the strategy of the organization, regularly and almost imperceptibly, to a continually changing environment.

CHAPTER 26

Thinking About Change

KEN ELLIOTT and PETER LAWRENCE

Between 1 p.m. and 4 p.m. on 8 November 1520 eighty-five persons were beheaded in Stockholm by order of Kristian II, the Danish king who also exercised overlordship in Norway and Sweden. Hundreds of others were publicly broken on the rack. The bodies were burned in three huge pyres on Södermalm hill, today a four-minute subway ride from Stockholm's central station.

These victims were supporters of Sten Sture, a popular but unsuccessful challenger to the powers that were. The Sture party were against Danish rule and the power and pretensions of an alien church, and for themselves. Our concern, however, is with neither the magnitude nor the causes of this atrocity, but with the light it throws on the relativity of time. A mere few years later, in the reign of 'good King' Gustav Vasa, a Swede for the Swedes, people congratulated themselves on their good fortune in living in a modern and civilized age.

It is important to underline this point since the later twentieth century has become obsessed with its own modernity. Somehow or other the feeling has grown up that this is an age like no other. With our megabytes and moonwalks, our earth satellites and electronic fund transfers, our cable TV and our flexitime, we have a faster rate of change and a more poignant consciousness of this change than any previous epoch has enjoyed. This conviction is not especially harmful, just wrong, and any sixteenth-century Swede could have put us right.

Again it is important to advance this corrective viewpoint. This way of writing about what is to come is so tremulous, so daunted by the presumptive acceleration of change, that it is able to say nothing about the future, except that it will be unrecognizable. Where the future of management is concerned we doubt this very much. Certainly there will be some changes by, say, the year 2000: there will be more of this and less of that; some trends we are presently aware of will have moved faster than we expect, while others will have U-turned; and there will be some things no one has thought of so far.

Yet management will still be about getting things done through people; it will have a past and a future as well as a present. There will still be a premium on social and political skills, a need for leadership and opportunities to shape outcomes rather than observe them.

None of this is to deny that change is occurring, only to rationalize our understanding of this change. Indeed this book has been about change in management, or at least has had change as an implicit sub-plot. Individual contributions have highlighted changes in several spheres – social, technical, cultural and economic. Particular chapters, for example, have documented the pressure for employee participation, the effects of computer acquisition, developments within particular management functions, the growing awareness of the need for ethical controls, the crescendo of government involvement in the private sector economy, and the increasing sophistication of organizational controls. The several chapters dealing with culture and the different management styles in other countries are again essays in change, raising tantalizing questions about the future. Will economically successful and managerially distinctive countries exert an influence on management practice beyond their borders, or will the year 2000 produce a homogeneous hodge-podge in what was once called 'the global village'?

The contemplation of on-going change raises, of course, the question of prediction. We do not want, in this short final chapter, to engage in prediction as much as to characterize the predictive enterprise. Three general points may be made about the future of management.

First, the answer to the question 'Can we predict the future of management?' is both yes and no. This paradox reflects the difference between continuous and disjunctive change. The range of continuous change trends will continue, with a few pluses and minuses. So that management in, say, the year 2000 will not be less sophisticated than it is today; it will be better qualified and more trained, have greater control resources and yet wider horizons, be involved in ever more complicated deals, and take account of ever more multifarious contingencies. On the other hand, there will be unknowable, unpredictable disjunctive changes as there were in the past. Those that have happened can be rationalized with hindsight and fitted into a development pattern, yet few people saw them coming and it will be the same with those yet to come.

Second, it may again be helpful to make a distinction between first-order and second-order influences on management. First-order influences are those which impinge directly on the task and those who manage it – the advent of computers for example – whereas second-order influences may be changes in society's values or people's expectations, or in, say, the education system. Ideas about work, or what is a reasonable working day, or about sharing within marriage, or about the individual's rights to the good life, may be more potent in their effects on management than changes in, say, accountancy conventions or profit reporting.

Third, and this consideration is perhaps different in kind, it is worth noting both the difference, and the difference in emphasis, between innovation and development. Both the technical-change and the futurology literature highlight innovation – an often unpredictable and always creative act that makes a portion of the world different from what it was before. What is more, innovation, especially scientific and technical, is popularly held to be a British strength. We do not mean to deny any of this, but to put in a 'good word' for the corresponding art of development. The process, that is to say, whereby brilliant ideas are translated into something that can actually be made and sold and piloted through a business organization with all its dynamic conservatism is at least as important as the antecedent creative act.

We will end these brief remarks by returning to the starting point, Södermalm hill in Stockholm, with a story about the unreliability of circumstantial indicators. One of the writers was ensconced on a bench in the square on top of the hill (contemplating the future of management) when a particularly scruffy tramp hove into view and headed for a dustbin in the corner of the square. It should be said straight away that tramps are not especially thick on the ground in Scandinavia, and the idea of seeing a tramp rifle through a dustbin in that country with the world's most comprehensive welfare provision is really rather disturbing. The tramp lifted the dustbin lid, painstakingly removed various bits of crumpled paper from several pockets, put the lot neatly into the bin, and sidled off.

The story has two morals. Prediction will always be incomplete, even when based on circumstances and what Konrad Lorenz calls 'intention movements'. But perhaps more important is that it serves to raise the question: who wants to live in a world with no surprises?

Further Reading

Chapter 1: Management: Science or Activity?

Many books deal with the historical background of management as set down in writing. A good synopsis is in: STEWART, R. (1970), *The Reality of Organisations*, London, Macmillan, which has been reprinted in the Pan Management Series.

A useful treatment of the particular British perspective is in: CHILD, J. (1969), *British Management Thought*, London, Allen and Unwin.

The next ideas of a variety of writers, including some whose work could not be dealt with in this chapter: PUGH, D. et al. (1964), *Writers on Organisations*, London, Hutchinson, which has been reprinted in the Penguin Modern Management Texts.

There is a good discussion of the clash between American and continental European ideas about running businesses in the chapter on 'The Character of German Management' in: LAWRENCE, P. (1980), *Managers and Management in West Germany*, London, Croom Helm.

A good idea of the condition of the USA when the idea of a separable 'management' arose is given by: BOORSTIN, D. (1966), *The Americans: The National Experience*, London, Weidenfeld and Nicolson; MORISON, S. E., COMMAGER, H. S., LEUCHTENBURG, W. E. (1969), *The Growth of the American Republic*, 6th edition, New York, Oxford University Press, Vol. 2.

Chapter 2: The Real Work of Managers

The three musts are the three books most extensively quoted in the present chapter: the pioneering study by CARLSON, S. (1951), *Executive Behaviour*, Strombergs, Stockholm; the American study by MINTZBERG, H. (1973), *The Nature of Managerial Work*, New York, Harper and Row; and the British study by STEWART, R. (1967), *Managers and Their Jobs*, London, Macmillan.

The second study by Rosemary Stewart discussed in the penultimate section of the chapter is written up in STEWART, R. (1976), *Contrasts in Management*, London, McGraw-Hill. It is an excellent book, but it is demanding reading.

The author's own studies of the work of British and West German production managers are written up in detail in reports for the Department of Industry and the Science and Engineering Research Council (see Bibliography). A lot of the ideas from the study are also present in LAWRENCE, P. (1984), *Management in Action*, London, Routledge and Kegan Paul.

Chapter 3: Self-Management

Practical applications of ideas presented in this chapter are given in detail in: PEDLER, M., BURGOYNE, J., and BOYDELL, T. (1978), *A Manager's Guide to Self-Development*, Maidenhead, McGraw-Hill.

A different approach presents 'a proven formula to radically improve [*sic*] your ability to manage your business by managing yourself more efficiently ... how to slash paperwork, avoid office bottlenecks and eliminate timewasting ... make lightning fast decisions and master the arts of communication' (from publicity material): SERIF, M. (1981), *How to Manage Yourself*, 2nd edition, New York, Fell.

Chapter 4: Management of Organizations

The following are textbooks which offer reasonably broad views of thinking on organizations. The emphasis of the first is especially practical: CHILD, J. (1977), *Organisation: A Guide to Problems and Practice*, London, Harper and Row; ETZIONI, A. (1964), *Modern Organizations*, Englewood Cliffs, New Jersey, Prentice-Hall; HALL, R. S. (1978), *Organizations: Structure and Process*, Englewood Cliffs, New Jersey, Prentice-Hall; MINTZBERG, H. (1979), *The Structuring of Organizations*, Englewood Cliffs, New Jersey, Prentice-Hall; PERROW, C. (1972), *Complex Organizations: A Critical Essay*, London, Scott Foresman.

The next four books contain readings on most aspects of organizational life. The first focuses on the comparative study of organizations. The second contains several extracts from the classics on organization and management. The concerns of the third are control and values. Those of the fourth are advanced but important and particularly up to date: LAMMERS, C. J., and HICKSON, D. J. (eds.) (1979), *Organization Alike and Unalike*, London, Routledge and Kegan Paul; PUGH, D. S. (ed.) (1971), *Organization Theory*, Harmondsworth, Penguin; SALAMAN, G., and THOMPSON, K. (eds.) (1980), *Control and Ideology in Organizations*, Milton Keynes, Open University Press; WARNER, M. (ed.) (1977), *Organizational Choice and Constraint: Approaches to the Sociology of Enterprise Behaviour*, Farnborough, Saxon House – Teakfield.

For a broad overview of the origins, concept and study of bureaucracy, see: ALBROW, M. (1970), *Bureaucracy*, London, Macmillan.

The systems versus action debate can be quite thoroughly understood by reading the following: MOUZELIS, N. P. (1970), *Organization and Bureaucracy: An Analysis of Modern Theories*, London, Routledge and Kegan Paul; SILVERMAN, D. (1970), *The Theory of Organizations*, London, Heinemann.

Chapter 5: Communication in Organizations

A very good comprehensive review of research on communication in organizations is provided in the chapter by PORTER, L. W., and ROBERT,

K. H. (1976), entitled 'Communication in organizations' in DUNNETTE, M. D. (ed.), *The Handbook of Industrial and Organizational Psychology*, Chicago, Rand McNally.

The chapter by GUETZKOW in MARCH, J. G. (1968), *Handbook of Organizations*, Chicago, Rand McNally, also provides a useful review of much of the earlier work.

The Penguin book of readings (PORTER, L. W., and ROBERTS, K. H. (eds.) on *Communication in Organizations* provides a more complete description of a number of the research studies mentioned in this chapter.

The reader who is interested in the nature of communication processes in the broad context might usefully consult SCHRAMM, W., and ROBERT, D. F. (eds.) (1971), *The Process and Effects of Mass Communication*, Chicago, University of Illinois.

Chapter 6: Leadership

The literature on leadership is voluminous. As a result, the first port of call should be some general reviews of the literature which will provide further references. Most of the following deal with important perspectives on leadership which it has not been possible to deal with in this chapter, such as the Michigan and the Vroom–Yetton decision-making approaches. In addition to the Schriesheim and Kerr (1977) paper cited in the bibliography, the following can be usefully consulted: BARROW, J. C. (1977), 'The variables of leadership: a review and conceptual framework', *Academy of Management Review*, 2, 231–51; HOUSE, R. J., and BAETZ, M. L. (1979), 'Leadership: some empirical generalizations and new research directions' in STAW, B. M. (ed.), *Research in Organizational Behavior*, Volume 1, Greenwich, Conn., JAI Press; VROOM, V. H. (1976), 'Leadership' in DUNNETTE, M. D. (ed.), *Handbook of Industrial and Organizational Psychology*, Chicago, Rand McNally.

For a detailed summary and analysis of some of the main leadership measures see: COOK, J. D., HEPWORTH, S. J., WALL, T. D., and WARR, P. B. (1981), *The Experience of Work*, London, Academic Press, Chapter 9.

Chapter 7: Control

A much fuller and very readable account of financial-control systems in everyday use is that given by Professor Sizer in his book: SIZER, J. (1979), *An Insight into Management Accounting*, Harmondsworth, Penguin.

Zero-based budgeting is further described by Pyhrr in his book: PYHRR, P. A. (1973), *Zero-Based Budgeting: A Practical Management Tool for Evaluating Expenses*, Chichester, Wiley.

For further reading on the topic of management by objectives, the reader is referred to: BECK, A. C., and HILLMAR, E. D. (1976), *Making MBO/R Work*, Reading, Massachusetts, Addison-Wesley.

Chapter 8: Ownership, Management and Strategic Control

The whole area of the ownership and control debate is reviewed in: SCOTT, J. P. (1979), *Corporations, Classes, and Capitalism*, London, Hutchinson.

General reviews of much of the background material are contained in: HANNAH, L. (1976), *The Rise of the Corporate Economy*, London, Methuen; CHANDLER, A. D. (1962), *Strategy and Structure*, Cambridge, Massachusetts MIT Press.

The most important empirical studies are: BERLE, A. A., and MEANS, G. C. (1932), *The Modern Corporation and Private Property*, New York, Macmillan; FLORENCE, P. S. (1951), *Ownership, Control and Success of Large Companies*, London, Sweet and Maxwell.

Some of the recent extensions to the debate are discussed in: GOSPEL, G., and LITTLER, C. (eds.) (1983), *Managerial Strategies and Industrial Relations*, London, Heinemann.

Chapter 9: Government Policy and the Economic System

General

THOMAS, R. E. (1982), *The Government of Business*, 2nd edition, Oxford, Philip Allan.

STEEL, D. R. (1982), 'Government and industry in Britain', *British Journal of Political Science*, *12*.

MORRIS, D. (1979), *The Economic System in the UK*, 2nd edition, Oxford, Oxford University Press.

BRITTAN, S. (1977), *The Economic Consequence of Democracy*, London, Temple Smith.

CROUCH, C. (ed.) (1979), *State and Economy in Contemporary Capitalism*, London, Croom Helm.

GRANT, W. (1982), *The Political Economy of Industrial Policy*, London, Butterworth.

VERNON, R. (ed.) (1974), *Big Business and the State: Changing Relations in Western Europe*, London, Macmillan.

Government and Multinational Companies

HOOD, N., and YOUNG, S. (1979), *The Economics of Multinational Enterprise*, London, Longman.

DOZ, Y. L. (1979), *Government Control and Multinational Strategic Management*, New York, Praeger.

Competition Policy and Consumer Protection

Department of Prices and Consumer Protection (March 1979), *A Review of Restrictive Trade Practices Policy*, Cmnd 7512, London, HMSO.

Department of Prices and Consumer Protection (May 1978), *A Review of Monopolies and Mergers Policy*, Cmnd 7198, London, HMSO.

Selective Intervention

WHITING, A. (ed.) (1976), *The Economics of Industrial Subsidies*, London, HMSO.

PAGE, S. A. B. (Sept. 1981), 'Protection and its consequences for Europe', *Journal of Common Market Studies*.

LEVACIC, R. (1980), *Selective Intervention*, Business Economics Course Unit 15, Milton Keynes, Open University Press.

STOREY, D. (1980), *Job Generation and Small Firms Policy in Britain*, London, Centre for Environmental Studies, Policy Series No. 11.

Industry Case Studies

BHASKAR, K. (1979), *The Future of the UK Motor Industry*, London, Kogan Page.

GARDYNE, J. BRUCE (1976), *Meriden: The Odyssey of a Lame Duck*, London, Centre for Policy Studies.

YOUNG, S., and HOOD, N. (1977) *Chrysler UK: A Corporation in Transition*, New York, Praeger.

PRYKE, R. (1981), *The Nationalised Industries: Policies and Performance Since 1968*, Oxford, Martin Robertson.

Government–Industry Relations

COOMBES, D. (1982), *Representative Government and Economic Power: Problems of the Government/Industry Relationships in Britain*, London, Heinemann.

Chapter 10: Industrial Relations

The major up-to-date textbook on British industrial relations is the collection: BAIN, G. S. (ed.) (1983), *Industrial Relations in Britain: Past Trends and Future Developments*, Oxford, Basil Blackwell.

An alternative written by just two authors is FARNHAM, D., and PIMLOTT, J. (1983), *Understanding Industrial Relations*, 2nd edition, London, Cassell.

For a shorter general introduction to British industrial relations since 1945 see CROUCH, C. (1983), *The Politics of Industrial Relations*, 2nd edition, London, Fontana.

On the question of industrial conflict and strikes, see the comprehensive but rather dry study by SMITH, C. T. B., et al. (1978), *Strikes in Britain*, London, HMSO, or the livelier, Marxist study: HYMAN, R. (1977), *Strikes*, 2nd edition, London, Fontana.

For a critical analysis of modern labour law see CLARK, J., and LORD WEDDERBURN (1983), 'Modern labour law: problems, functions and policies', in WEDDERBURN, LEWIS and CLARK (1983), *Labour Law and Industrial Relations: Building on Kahn-Freund*, Oxford, Oxford University Press, pp. 127–242.

Finally, for theory and policy discussion on industrial relations, see the well-written and influential 'pluralist' essays of FLANDERS, A. (1975), *Management and Unions*, London, Faber and Faber, and the wide-ranging historical survey of FOX, A. (1974), *Beyond Contract: Work, Power and Trust Relations*, London, Faber and Faber.

Chapter 11: Employee Participation

The two most useful sociological discussions of the meaning of employee participation are BLUMBERG, P. (1968), *Industrial Democracy: The Sociology of Participation*, London, Constable, especially chapters 1 and 7, and BRANNEN, P. et al. (1976), *The Worker Directors: A Sociology of Participation*, London, Hutchinson, especially pp. 1–59.

The most comprehensive survey of attitudes and practices in employee participation in Britain is KNIGHT, I. (1979), *Company Organisation and Worker Participation*, London, HMSO.

For a discussion of the law and practice of employee participation in Europe see BATSTONE, E., and DAVIES, P. L. (1978), *Industrial Democracy: European Experience*, London, HMSO.

Chapter 12: Internal Politics

PFEFFER, J. (1981), *Power in Organizations*, Boston, Pitman.
MACMILLAN, I. (1978), *Strategy Formulation: Political Concepts*, St Paul, Minnesota, West.
MINTZBERG, H. (1983), *Power In and Around Organizations*, Englewood Cliffs, New Jersey, Prentice-Hall.
BACHARACH, S., and LAWLER, E. (1980), *Power and Politics in Organizations*, San Francisco, Jossey-Bass.

Chapter 13: Ethics in Business

The following suggestions fall very roughly into three categories of which only the first is explicitly concerned with ethics in business. The other two – corporate social responsibility and the organization of business – are included because many ethical problems arise in determining what is a socially responsible action for a firm and because the way an economy is organized has moral implications. Indeed the way an economy is organized determines for some people their interpretation of the term 'corporate social responsibility'.

It is suggested that readers should take note of the geographical source of any writing in these areas. Although there are exceptions, the Americans are far more defensive than Europeans of business practices and, in particular, of the capitalist economic system.

Ethics in Business

BOWIE, N. (1982), *Business Ethics*, Englewood Cliffs, New Jersey, Prentice-Hall.

DONALDSON, J., and WALLER, M. (1980), 'Ethics and organisations', *Journal of Management Studies*, *17*, 34–55.

DRUCKER, P. (1981), 'What is "business ethics"?', *The McKinsey Quarterly* (Autumn), 2–15.

EVANS, W. A. (1981), *Management Ethics*, Boston, Martinus Nijhoff.

FRENCH, P. (1979), 'The corporation as a moral person', *American Philosophical Quarterly*, *16*, 207–15.

International Management (1983), 'Managers wrestle with ethical problems worldwide", *38*(*2*).

MACINTYRE, A. (1979), 'Corporate modernity and moral judgement' in Goodpaster, K. E., and Sayre, K., *Ethics and Problems of the 21st Century*, Indiana, University of Notre Dame Press.

MANNING, F. V. (1981), *Managerial Dilemmas and Executive Growth*, Reston, Virginia, Reston Publishing Co.

NASH, L. L. (1981), 'Ethics without the sermon', *Harvard Business Review*, *59*(*6*), 79–90.

POWERS, C. W., and VOGEL, D. (1980), *Ethics in the Education of Business Managers*, Hasting on Hudson, New York, Institute of Society, Ethics and the Life Sciences.

WILLMER, M., and KEISON, D. (1982), 'The ethics of deviousness', *Manchester Business School Review*, *6*, 11–15.

Social Responsibility

BEESLEY, M., and EVANS, T. (1978), *Corporate Social Responsibility*, London, Croom Helm.

GOODPASTER, K. E., and MATTHEWS, J. B. (1982), 'Can a corporation have a conscience?', *Harvard Business Review*, *60*(*1*), 132–41.

HEILBRONER, R. L. (1972), *In the Name of Profit*, New York, Doubleday.

MORGAN, E. J. (1977), 'Social responsibility and private enterprise in the UK', *National Westminster Bank Quarterly Review*, (May), 55–67.

SCOTT-ARMSTRONG, J. (1977), 'Social irresponsibility in management', *Journal of Business Research*, *5*, Sept., 185–213.

Market Structure

DWORKIN, G., BERNARD, G., and BROWN, P. G. (1977), *Markets and Morals*, New York, Wiley.

SEN, A. (1983), 'The profit motive', *Lloyds Bank Review*, *147*, 1–20.

WUTHROW, R. (1982), 'The moral crisis in American capitalism', *Harvard Business Review*, *60*(*2*), 76–84.

Chapter 14: Culture's Consequences

Those interested in a further introductory text that is not very difficult to read, with many vivid examples, may refer to: WEINSHALL, T. W. (ed.)

(1977), *Culture and Management: Selected Readings*, Harmondsworth, Penguin.

A more detailed discussion is provided by the three articles (by CHILD, J., JAMIESON, J., and SORGE, A.) in: *International Studies of Management and Organisation*, Winter 1982/83.

An empirically very rich and theoretically representative book for the 'values' approach is: HOFSTEDE, G. (1980), *Culture's Consequences: International Differences in Work-Related Values*, Beverly Hills/London, Sage Publications.

Another handy and readable selection of readings is in: *International Studies of Management and Organisation*, *10(4)*, (Winter), 1980/81, on 'Organisations and Societies'. The paper by Maurice, Sorge and Warner (pp. 74–100) characterizes the institutional approach.

Chapter 15: The American Company in Britain

There are a number of works that summarize the main differences between British and American firms: Economists Advisory Group (1976), *U.K. Industry in Britain*, London, Wilton House Publications; INKSON et al. (1970), 'A comparison of organisational structure and managerial roles, Ohio, USA and Midlands, England', *Journal of Management Studies*, 7(3), 347–63. JAMIESON, I. M. (1980), *Capitalism and Culture: A Comparative Analysis of British and American Manufacturing Organizations*, Farnborough, Gower; RICHARDSON, S. A. (1956), 'Organizational contrasts in British and American ships', *Administrative Science Quarterly*, *1(3)*, 189–207.

More popular accounts are contained in the following: GRANICK, D. (1962), *The European Executive*, London, Weidenfeld and Nicolson; MCMILLAN, J., and HARRIS, B. (1968), *The American Takeover of Britain*, London, Leslie Frewin; SERVAN-SCHREIBER, J. J. (1969), *The American Challenge*, Harmondsworth, Penguin.

Good historical accounts of the development of industry and business in Britain and America are contained in the following: BAGWELL, P. S., and MINGAY, G. E. (1970), *Britain and America: A Study of Economic Change 1850–1939*, London, Routledge and Kegan Paul. HABAKKUK, H. J. (1967), *British and American Technology in the Nineteenth Century*, Cambridge, Cambridge University Press.

The economic arguments about the role of the American firm in Britain are well summarized in: DUNNING, J. H. (1970), *Studies in International Investment*, London, Allen and Unwin.

Chapter 16: Japanese Management

The outstanding and indispensable book is: DORE, R. P. (1973), *British Factory, Japanese Factory*, London, Allen and Unwin.

The perspective of Dore's book is industrial relations, and behaviour and relationships in the work group. A contrasting perspective, emphasizing systems and techniques of management, but with useful behavioural insights, is: SCHONBERGER, R. J. (1982), *Japanese Manufacturing Techniques*, New York, Free Press.

There are two books available concerning Japanese management in Britain: TREVOR, M. (1983), *Japan's Reluctant Multinationals*, London, Pinter; WHITE, M., and TREVOR, M. (1983), *Under Japanese Management – The Experience of British Workers*, London, Heinemann.

To obtain the American 'human resource' view of Japanese management, there is: PASCALE, R. T., and ATHOS, A. G. (1981), *The Art of Japanese Management*, New York, Simon and Schuster.

Chapter 17: Marketing

A good general textbook in the area is KOTLER, P. (1980), *Marketing Management: Analysis Planning and Control*, 4th edition, Englewood Cliffs, New Jersey, Prentice-Hall. A UK textbook is BAKER, M. J. (1979), *Marketing*, 3rd edition, London, Macmillan.

A useful book on market and product policy is BAKER, M. J. (1983), *Market Development*, Harmondsworth, Penguin.

An interesting introduction to industrial marketing is HUTT, M. D., and THOMAS, W. SPEH (1981), *Industrial Marketing Management*, New York, Holt Saunders.

The relevance of marketing in the non-commercial field is illustrated by KOTLER, P. (1982), *Marketing for Non Profit Organization*, Englewood Cliffs, New Jersey, Prentice-Hall.

Chapter 18: Research and Development Strategies

General Texts

FREEMAN, C., *The Economics of Industrial Innovation*, Harmondsworth, Penguin, 1974, and 2nd edition, 1982.

GOLD, B. (1975), *Technological Change: Economics, Management and the Environment*, Oxford, Pergamon Press.

ROSEGGER, G. (1980), *The Economics of Production and Innovation: An Industrial Perspective*, Oxford, Pergamon Press.

Data Sources

For the UK: Business Monitor MO14. Industrial Research and Development Expenditure and Employment London, HMSO, 1981.

International statistics: the Organization for Economic Co-operation and Development (OECD), Paris, have occasional papers and reports on international comparisons of R & D spending.

Case Studies

JOHNSON, P. S. (1975), *The Economics of Invention and Innovation*, London, Martin Robertson.

PAVITT, K. (ed.) (1980), *Technological Innovation and British Economic Performance*, London, Macmillan.

The Diffusion of Technology

CONTRACTOR, F. (1981), *International Technology Licensing*, Lexington, Massachusetts, Lexington Books.

HILL, C. T., and UTTERBACK, J. M. (1979), *Technological Innovation for a Dynamic Economy*, Oxford, Pergamon Press.

The Organization and Management of Technology

BURNS, T., and STALKER, G. M. (1961), *The Management of Innovation*, London, Tavistock.

HAWTHORNE, E. P. (1978), *The Management of Technology*, London, McGraw-Hill.

Some useful journals
R & D Management
Research Management
'OMEGA', The International Journal of Management Science

Technology Strategies

KAMIEN, M. I., and SCHWARTZ, N. L. (1982), *Market Structure and Innovation*, Cambridge, Cambridge University Press.

Chapter 19: Production/Operations Management

There are, broadly speaking, two basic types of textbook in the area of production/operations management. The first type is those which cover the techniques involved and are biased towards a mathematical, operational-research-based solution to the POM task. These include: ADAM, E. E., and EBERT, R. J. (1978), *Production and Operations Management*, Prentice-Hall (USA-based textbook); BESTWICK, P. F., and LOCKYER, K. (1982), *Quantitative Production Management*, Pitman (UK-based textbook); BUFFA, E. S. (1977), *Modern Production Management*, Wiley (USA-based textbook); WILD, R. (1979), *Production and Operations Management*, Holt, Rinehart and Winston (UK-based textbook).

Recently, there has been a move away from this direction towards an approach that reflects the essential managerial aspects of the POM task and which aims to distinguish between the useful and less useful approaches of the techniques, and operative and research-orientated approaches. These include: CONSTABLE, C. J., and NEW, C. C. (1976),

Operations Management, Wiley (UK-based textbook); HILL, T. (1983), *Production/Operations Management*, Prentice-Hall (UK-based textbook); LAWRENCE, P. A. (1984), *Management in Action*, Routledge and Kegan Paul (UK-based textbook); SCHMENNER, R. W. (1981), *Production/Operations Management*, Science Research Associates (USA-based textbook).

Chapter 20: Purchasing

ALJIAN, G. W. (1982), *Purchasing Handbook*, 4th edition, McGraw-Hill.

AMMER, D. S. (1980), *Materials Management and Purchasing*, 4th edition, Homewood, Illinois, Irwin.

BAILY, P. J. H. (1978), *Purchasing and Supply Management*, 4th edition, London, Chapman and Hall.

BAILY, P. J. H., HARTWELL, J., and FARMER, D. J. (1981), *Purchasing Principles and Management*, 4th edition, London, Pitman.

COMPTON, H. K., *Supplies and Materials Management*, 3rd edition (1984), Plymouth, Macdonald and Evans.

ENGLAND, W. B., and LEENDERS, M. R. (1975), *Purchasing and Materials Management*, 6th edition, Homewood, Illinois, Irwin.

HEINRITZ, S. F., and FARRELL, P. V. (1981), *Purchasing: Principles and Applications*, 6th edition, Englewood Cliffs, New Jersey, Prentice-Hall.

LAWRENCE, P. A., and LEE, R. A. (1984), *Insight into Management*, Oxford, Oxford University Press.

LEE, L., and DOBLER, D. W. (1977), *Purchasing and Materials Management*, 3rd edition, Maidenhead, McGraw-Hill.

LYSONS, C. K. (1981), *Purchasing*, Plymouth, Macdonald and Evans.

STEVENS, J. M. (1978), *Measuring Purchasing Performance*, London, Business Books.

STEVENS, J. M., and GRANT, J. P. (1975), *Purchasing/Marketing Interface*, London, Associated Business Programmes.

WESTING, J. H., FINE, L. V., and ZENZ, G. J. (1976), *Purchasing Management – Materials in Motion*, 4th edition, New York, Wiley.

Chapter 21: Personnel Management: An Organizational Perspective

HICKSON, D. J., et al. (1971) 'A strategic contingencies' theory of intra-organizational power', *Administrative Science Quarterly*, *16*, 216–29.

HININGS, G. R., et al. (1974) 'Structural conditions of intraorganizational power', *Administrative Science Quarterly*, *19*, p. 22.

LEGGE, K. (1978), *Power, Innovation, and Problem-solving in Personnel Management*, Maidenhead, McGraw-Hill.

PERROW, C. (1979), *Complex Organizations – A Critical Essay*, Glenview, Illinois, Scott Foresman.

Chapter 22: Accountants and the Finance Function

The management-information system is discussed thoroughly, and at the same time very readably, in: SIZER, J. (1980), *An Insight into Management Accounting*, Harmondsworth, Penguin.

External financial-reporting practices are explained in: PARKER, R. H. (1982), *Understanding Company Financial Statements*, Harmondsworth, Penguin.

Financial planning is thoroughly covered in: SAMUELS, J. M., and WILKES, F. M., *Management of Company Finance*, 3rd edition (1982), Walton-on-Thames, Nelson.

An interesting collection of views can be found in: CARSBERG, B. V., and HOPE, R., *Current Issues in Accounting*, Oxford, Philip Allan.

Chapter 23: Management Services

Texts on computer-system development abound. Three good ones are: O'BRIEN, J. A. (1979), *Computers in Business Management: An Introduction*, Homewood, Illinois, Irwin; CLIFTON, H. D. (1978), *Business Data Systems*, London, Prentice-Hall International; OLIVER, E. C., and CHAPMAN, R. J. (1979), *Data Processing*, Winchester, DP Publications.

The role of operational researchers and the techniques they use are well described in: TAFFLER, R. J. (1979), *Using Operational Research: A Practical Introduction to Quantitative Methods in Management*, New Jersey, Prentice-Hall International.

Chapter 24: The Advent of Computerization: North and South

Virtually nothing has been written on the link between how a computer was intended to be used, and how an economic prediction of its profitability could be made, apart from some reports in Swedish of which Mats Bodin is the author or joint author.

For a description of the investment-calculus method, any textbook in microeconomics should do.

For those not acquainted with how complex the interaction between computer and company structure is, the following books may give some understanding: GRUENBERGER, F. (ed.) (1972), *Information Systems for Management*, Englewood Cliffs, New Jersey, Prentice-Hall; KANTER, J. (1972), *Management-Oriented Management Information Systems*, Englewood Cliffs, New Jersey, Prentice-Hall; VERZELLO, J. R., and REUTTER, J. (1982), *This is Data Processing: Systems and Concepts*, New York, McGraw-Hill.

A collection of papers giving a good picture of computers for development is: BENNET, J. M., and KALMAN, R. E. (eds.) (1981), *Computers in Developing Nations*, Amsterdam, North-Holland Publishing.

Of relevance also are: RADA, J. (1980), 'Microelectronics, Information Technology and its Effects on Developing Countries' in Bertings, J., Mills, S. C., and Wintersberger, H., (eds.), *The Socio-economics Impact of Microelectronics*, Oxford, Pergamon Press; BOGOD, J. L. (1979), *The Role of Computing in Developing Countries*, London, British Computing Society, Lecture Series No. 2; SIMMONS, R. A. (1973), *Guidelines for the Use of Computer Technology in the Developing Countries*, National Bureau of Standards Interim Report NBSIR Dec. 1973; KALMAN, R. (ed.) (1984), *Regional Computer Cooperation in Developing Countries*, Amsterdam, North-Holland Publishing.

A report, prepared for COSTED (Committee on Science and Technology in Developing Countries), giving a critical review of computerization in India is: KAISER, H., and KUHN, M. (1982), *Computer Applications – Prospects for Developing Countries*, Madras, Indian Institute of Technology.

A standard textbook on the transfer of technology to developing countries is: STEWART, F. (1978), *Technology and Underdevelopment*, London, Macmillan.

Chapter 25: Corporate Strategy and Strategic Management

For an overall approach to strategic management the following books are recommended. A good, clear example of the traditional approach: UYTERHOEVEN, H. E. R., ACKERMAN, R. W., and ROSENBLUM, J. W., (1977), *Strategy and Organization*, revised edition, Homewood, Illinois, Irwin. A text which adds research-based readings and papers to a basic idea: MCCARTHY, D. J., MINICHIELLO, R. J., and CURRAN, J. R. (1979), *Business Policy and Strategy*, 3rd edition, Homewood, Illinois, Irwin. For advice on techniques of analysis: ROWE, A. J., MASON, R. O., and DICKEL, H. (1982), *Strategic Management and Business Policy*, Addison-Wesley. A text with largely UK examples building on the framework outlined in this chapter: JOHNSON, G., and SCHOLES, K. (1984), *Exploring Corporate Strategy*, Englewood Cliffs, New Jersey, Prentice-Hall. A systematic approach to the formulation of competitive strategy is: PORTER, M. E. (1981), *Competitive Strategy*, West Drayton, Collier Macmillan.

The process of strategic management in organizations: QUINN, J. B. (1980), *Strategies for Change: Logical Incrementalism*, Homewood, Illinois, Irwin.

A text showing how value systems affect strategy: MILES, R. E., and SNOW, C. C. (1978), *Organizational Strategy: Structure and Process*, New York, McGraw-Hill.

References

ABERNATHY, W. J., and WAYNE, K. (1974), 'The limits of the learning curve', *Harvard Business Review*, *52*(*5*), 109–19.

ACKOFF, R. L. (1981), 'The art and science of mess management', *Interfaces*, *11*(*1*), 20–26.

ACTON SOCIETY TRUST (1956), *Management Succession*, London, Acton Society Trust.

ADAMSON, J. (1980), 'Corporate long-range planning must include procurement', *Harvard Business Review*, *58*, 25–32.

AGUILAR, F. J. (1967), *Scanning the Business Environment*, London, Collier Macmillan.

ALSEGG, R. J. (1971), *Control Relations between American Companies and Their European Subsidiaries*, New York, American Management Association.

AMES, E. (1961), 'Research, invention, development and innovation', *American Economic Review*, *51*(*3*), 370–80.

AMMER, D. (1962), 'Realistic reciprocity', *Harvard Business Review*, *40*, 116–24.

ANSOFF, H. I. (1965), *Corporate Strategy*, Harmondsworth, Penguin.

ARROW, K. J. (1969), 'Classificatory notes on the production and transmission of technological knowledge', *American Economic Review: Papers and Proceedings*, *59*(*2*), 29–35.

ASHBY, W. R. (1970), *An Introduction to Cybernetics*, London, Methuen.

ATCHISON, T. J., and HILL, W. W. (1978), *Management Today*, New York, Harcourt Brace.

ATKIN, B., and SKINNER, R. (1976), *How British Industry Prices*, London, Industrial Market Research.

ATKINSON, A. B. (1969), *Poverty in Britain and the Reform of Social Security*, Cambridge, Cambridge University Press.

BACHRACH, P., and BARATZ, M. (1962), 'The two faces of power', *American Political Science Review*, *6*, 947–52.

BACHARACH, S. B., and AITKEN, M. (1977), 'Communication in administrative bureaucracies', *Academy of Management Journal*, *20*, 365–77.

BACK, K., FESTINGER, L., HYMOVITCH, B., KELLEY, N., SCHACHTER, S., and THIBAUT, J. (1950), 'The methodology of rumour transmission', *Human Relations*, *3*, 307–12.

BADER, E. (1975), 'From profit sharing to common ownership', in Vanek, J., *Self-Management*, Harmondsworth, Penguin.

BAIN, G. S. (ed.) (1983), *Industrial Relations in Britain: Past Trends and Future Developments*, Oxford, Basil Blackwell.

BALDAMUS, W. G. (1961), *Efficiency and Effort*, London, Tavistock.

BALLOUN, J. S. (1981), 'Real lessons from Japan', *Speaking of Japan*, *13*.

BANKS, J. A. (1974), *Trade Unionism*, London, London, Collier-Macmillan.

BARKAI, H. (1975), 'The kibbutz: an experiment in microsocialism', in Vanek, J., *Self-Management*, Harmondsworth, Penguin.

BATESON, G. (1973), *Steps to an Ecology of Mind*, St Albans, Paladin.

BEARDON, R. A. (1983), 'Materials management – making it work', *Purchasing and Supply Management*, April, 41–2.

BENDIX, R. (1974), *Work and Authority in Industry*, Berkeley, California, University of California Press.

BENNIS, W. (1976), 'Leadership: a beleaguered species?', *Organisational Dynamics*, *5*, 3–16.

BERGER, P. L., and LUCKMANN, T. (1971), *The Social Construction of Reality*, Harmondsworth, Penguin.

BERLE, A. A., and MEANS, G. C. (1932), *The Modern Corporation and Private Property*, New York, Macmillan.

BHASKAR, K. (1980), *The Future of the World Motor Industry*, London, Kogan Page.

BIRD, M. M., and SHEPHERD, C. W. (1973), 'Reciprocity in buying and selling – a study of attitude', *Journal of Purchasing*, *9*, 26–35.

BLAKE, R. R., and MOUTON, J. S. (1964), *The Management Grid*, Houston, Texas, Gulf Publishing.

BLAU, P. M. (1956), *Bureaucracy in Modern Society*, New York, Random House.

BLAU, P. M. (1970), 'A formal theory of differentiation in organizations', *American Sociological Review*, 35, 201–18.

BLAU, P. M., and SCOTT, W. R. (1963), *Formal Organizations*, London, Routledge and Kegan Paul.

BLUMBERG, P. (1968), *Industrial Democracy: The Sociology of Participation*, London, Constable.

BLUMBERG, P. (1975), *The Megacorporation in American Society*, Englewood Cliffs, New Jersey, Prentice-Hall.

BOORSTIN, D. (1966), *The Americans: The National Experience*, London, Weidenfeld and Nicolson.

BOOZ, ALLEN AND HAMILTON, INC. (1965), *The Management of New Products*, New York, Booz, Allen and Hamilton.

BOSWORTH, D. L. (1978), 'The rate of obsolescence of technical knowledge – a note', *The Journal of Industrial Economics*, *26*, 273–9.

BOWLES, J. R. (1981), 'Research and development: expenditure and employment in the seventies', *Economic Trends*, No. 334, 94–111.

BRADLEY, K., and GELB, A. (1981), 'Motivation and control in the Mondragon experiment', *British Journal of Industrial Relations*, *19*, 221–31.

BRADLEY, K., and GELB, A. (1982), 'The replication and sustainability of the Mondragon Experiment', *British Journal of Industrial Relations*, *20*, 20–33.

BRAND, G. T. (1972), *The Industrial Buying Decision*, London, Cassell/Associated Business Programmes.

BRAUN, G. (1983), 'Grundbedürfnisse and Weltzivilisation', *Entwicklung und Zusammenarbeit*, 7, Bonn.

BRAVERMAN, H. (1974), *Labour and Monopoly Capital*, New York, Monthly Review Press.

BRIGGS, A. (1968), 'Robert Owen', *International Encyclopedia of the Social Sciences*, *11*, 351–3.

BRONFENBRENNER, M. (1956), 'Potential monopsony in labour markets', *Industrial and Labour Relations Review*, *9*, 577–8.

BROOKE, M. R., and REMMERS, H. L. (eds.) (1977), *The Strategy of Multi-national Enterprise: Organisation and Finance*, London, Pitman.

BROOKS, R. (1976), 'Single sourcing of stationery', *Industrial Purchasing News*, February, 36–8.

BROWN, W. (1981), *The Changing Contours of British Industrial Relations*, Oxford, Basil Blackwell.

BRYANT, C. G. A. (1970), 'In defence of sociology: a reply to some contemporary philosophical criticisms', *British Journal of Sociology*, *21*, 95–107.

BUCHELE, R. B. (1962), 'How to evaluate a firm', *Californian Management Review*, *5*, 16.

BUCKNER, H. (1967), *How British Industry Buys*, London, Hutchinson.

BULOW VON, A. (1982), 'Die wissenschaftliche Zusammenarbeit mit Entwicklungsländern ist eine kleine aber sehr fruchtbare Pflanze', *Entwicklung und Zusammenarbeit*, *1*.

BURCH, P. H. (1972), *The Managerial Revolution Reassessed*, Lexington, Massachusetts, Lexington Books.

BURGOYNE, J. G., BOYDELL, T., and PEDLER, M. (1978), *Self-Development: Theory and Applications for Practitioners*, London, Association of Teachers of Management.

BURGOYNE, J. G., and STUART, R. (1976), 'The nature, use and acquisition of managerial skills and other attributes', *Personnel Review*, *5*, 19–29.

BURNHAM, J. (1941), *The Managerial Revolution*, New York, John Day.

BURNS, T. (1955), 'The reference of conduct in small groups', *Human Relations*, *8*, 467–86.

BURNS, T. (1961), 'Micropolitics: mechanisms of institutional change', *Administrative Science Quarterly*, *6*, 257–81.

BURNS, T., and STALKER, G. M. (1961), *The Management of Innovation*, London, Tavistock.

BURTON, J. (1979), *The Job Support Machine: A Critique of the Job Subsidy Morass*, London, Centre for Policy Studies.

BUSHAN, B. (1983), 'The computers are coming', *Business India*, January.

BUSINESS STATISTICS OFFICE, Business Monitor No. 14, (1978), *Industrial Research and Development Expenditure and Employment*, London, HMSO.

CALDER, B. J. (1976), 'An attribution theory of leadership', in Staw, B., and Salancik, G. (eds.), *New Directions in Organizational Behavior*, Chicago, St Clair Press.

CAMPBELL, D. T., DUNNETTE, M. D., LAWLER, E. E., and WEICK, K. E. (1970), *Managerial Behavior, Performance and Effectiveness*, New York, McGraw-Hill.

CAMPBELL, D. T. (1958), 'Systematic error on the part of human links in communication systems', *Information and Control*, *1*, 334–69.

CAPLOW, T. (1946), 'Rumours in war', *Social Forces*, *25*, 298–302.

CARLSON, S. (1951), *Executive Behaviour*, Stockholm, Strombergs.

CARLSON, S. (1978), 'Knowledge, information and language', in FORES, M., and GLOVER, I. (eds.), *Manufacturing and Management*, London, HMSO.

CARTER, C. (1968), *Wealth*, Harmondsworth, Penguin.

CHANDLER, A. D. (1962), *Strategy and Structure*, Cambridge, Massuchusetts, MIT Press.

CHANDLER, A. D. (1978), 'The United States: evolution of enterprise', in Mathias, P., and Postan, M. M. (eds.), *The Cambridge Economic History of Europe*, Cambridge, Cambridge University Press.

CHANG, Y. N., and CAMPO-FLORES, F. (1980), *Business Policy and Strategy*, Hemel Hempstead, Goodyear.

CHANNON, D. F. (1973), *Strategy and Structure of British Enterprise*, London, Macmillan.

CHECKLAND, P. (1981), *Systems Thinking, Systems Practice*, London, Wiley.

CHEVALIER, J.-M. (1970), *La structure financière de l'industrie américaine*, Paris, Cujas.

CHILD, J. (1972), 'Organization structure, environment, and performance: the role of strategic choice', *Sociology*, *6*, 1–22.

CHILD, J. (1973), 'Predicting and understanding organization structure', *Administrative Science Quarterly*, *18*, 168–85.

CHILD, J. (1973), 'Organization: a choice for Man', in Child, J., *Man and Organization*, London, Allen and Unwin.

CHILD, J. (1977), *Organization: A Guide to Problems and Practice*, London, Harper and Row.

CHILD, J. (1981), 'Culture, contingency and capitalism in the cross-national study of organizations', in Cummings, L. L., and Staw, B. M. (eds.), *Research in Organizational Behavior*, vol. 3, Greenwich, Conn., JAI.

CHILD, J., FORES, M., GLOVER, I., and LAWRENCE, P. (1983), 'A price to pay? Professionalism and work organization in Britain and West Germany', *Sociology*, *17*, 63–78.

CHILD, J., and KIESER, A. (1979), 'Organization and managerial roles in British and West German companies: an examination of the culture-free thesis', in Lammers, C. J., and Hickson, D. J. (eds.), *Organizations Alike and Unlike*, London, Routledge and Kegan Paul.

CHILD, J. and MACMILLAN, B. (1972), 'Managerial leisure in British and American contexts', *Journal of Management Studies*, *9*, 182–95.

CHILD, J., and TAYEB, M. (1983), 'Theoretical perspectives in cross-national organizational research', *International Studies of Management and Organization, 12*, 23–70.

CHIPLIN, B., and STURGESS, B. (1981), *The Economics of Advertising*, London, Holt Rinehart and Winston.

CHRUDEN, H. J., and SHERMAN, W. W., JR. (1972), *Personnel Practices of American Companies in Europe*, New York, American Management Association.

CLARK, J., and LORD WEDDERBURN (1983), 'Modern labour law: problems, functions and policies', in Wedderburn, Lewis and Clark, *Labour, Law and Industrial Relations: Building on Kahn-Freund*, Oxford, Oxford University Press.

CLEGG, H. A. (1980), *The Changing System of Industrial Relations in Great Britain*, Oxford, Basil Blackwell.

CLEGG, S., and DUNKERLEY, D. (1980), *Organization, Class and Control*, London, Routledge and Kegan Paul.

COHEN, A. M., ROBINSON., E. L., and EDWARDS, J. L. (1969), 'Experiments in organizational embeddedness', *Administrative Science Quarterly, 14*, 208– 21.

COHEN, M. D., MARCH, J. G., and OLSEN, J. P. (1972), 'A garbage can model of organizational choice', *Administrative Science Quarterly, 17*, 1–25.

COLE, G. D. H. (1925), *The Life of Robert Owen*, London, Macmillan.

COLLINGWOOD, R. G. (1946), *The Idea of History*, Oxford, Oxford University Press.

COMMANOR, W. S. (1967), 'Market structure, product differentiation and industrial research', *Quarterly Journal of Economics, 81*, 639–57.

COMMITTEE ON INFORMATION TECHNOLOGY (1982), *A Programme for Advanced Information Technology: The Report of the Alvey Committee*, London, HMSO.

CONTRACTOR, F. (1981), *International Technology Licensing*, Lexington, Massachusetts, Lexington Books.

CREIGH, S. W., and MAKEHAM, P. (1978), 'Foreign ownership and strike proneness: a research note', *British Journal of Industrial Relations, 16*, 369–72.

CROELL, R. C. (1977), 'Measuring purchasing effectiveness', *Journal of Purchasing and Materials Management, 12*, 3–4.

CROUCH, C. (1983), *The Politics of Industrial Relations*, London, Fontana.

CROZIER, M. (1964), *The Bureaucratic Phenomenon*, London, Tavistock.

CYERT, R. M., and MARCH, J. G. (1963), *Behavioral Theory of the Firm*, Englewood Cliffs, New Jersey, Prentice-Hall.

DAHL, R. A. (1957), 'The concept of power', *Behavioral Science, 2*, 201–15.

DAHRENDORF, R. (1973), *Homo Sociologicus*, London, Routledge and Kegan Paul.

DALE, E., and MICHELON, L. C. (1966), *Modern Management Methods*, Harmondsworth, Penguin.

DALTON, M. (1951), 'Informal factors in career achievement', *American Journal of Sociology, 56(5)*, 407–15.

DALTON, M. (1959), *Men Who Manage*, New York, Wiley.

DANCE, F. E. X. (1970), 'The "concept" of communication', *Journal of Communication, 20*, 201–10.

DAVIES, O. (1974), 'A marketing approach to purchasing', *Long Range Planning, 7*, 2–11.

DAVIS, H. L., EPPEN, G. D., and MATTSON, L. G. (1974), 'Critical factors in world-wide purchasing', *Harvard Business Review, 52*, 81–90.

DAVIS, K. (1953), 'Management communication and the grapevine', *Harvard Business Review, 31*, 43–9.

DAVIS, K. (1959), 'Making constructive use of the office grapevine', Davis, K., and Scott, W. G. (eds.), *Readings in Human Relations*, New York, McGraw-Hill.

DEPARTMENT OF EMPLOYMENT (1983), 'Qualifications and the labour force', *Employment Gazette, 91*, 158–64.

DE ROY, S. R. (1979), 'A one-class society?', *Japan Quarterly*, April–June.

DERMER, J. (1977), *Management Planning and Control Systems: Advanced Concepts and Cases*, Homewood, Illinois, Irwin.

DESSLER, G., and VALENZI, E. R (1977), 'Initiation of structure and subordinate satisfaction: a path analysis test of path–goal theory', *Academy of Management Journal, 20*, 251–9.

DONALD, M. J. (1959), 'Some concomitants of varying patterns of communication in a large organization', *Dissertation Abstracts*, 19:3392.

DONALDSON, J., and WALLER, M. (1980), 'Ethics and organisations', *Journal of Management Studies, 17*, 34–55.

DONOVAN, LORD (1968), *Royal Commission on Trade Unions and Employers' Associations 1965–1968*, London, HMSO (Cmnd 3623).

DORE, R. P. (1973), *British Factory – Japanese Factory*, London, Allen and Unwin.

DOUGLAS, M. (1967), 'The meaning of myth' in Leach, E., *The Structure of Myth and Totemism*, London, Tavistock.

DOWNIE, R. S. (1972), 'Responsibility and social roles', in French, P. (ed.), *Individual and Collective Responsibility*, Cambridge, Massachusetts, Schenkman Publishing.

DRUCKER, P. F. (1955), 'Management science and the manager', *Management Science, 2*.

DRUCKER, P. F. (1974), *Management: Tasks, Responsibilities, Practices*, London, Heinemann.

DRUCKER, P. F. (1979), *Management*, London, Pan.

DUBIN, R. (1962), 'Business behaviour behaviourally viewed', in Stother, G. B. (ed.), *Social Science Approaches to Business Behavior*, Homewood, Illinois, Irwin.

DUBIN, R. (1970), 'Management in Britain – impressions of a visiting professor', *Journal of Management Studies, 7*, 183–98.

DUBIN, R. (1979), 'Metaphors of leadership: an overview', in Hunt, J. G., and Larson, L. L. (eds.), *Crosscurrents in Leadership*, Carbondale, Southern Illinois University Press.

DUBRIN, A. (1978), _Fundamentals of Organizational Behavior_, New York, Pergamon Press.

DUNCAN, R. B. (1972), 'Characteristics of organizational environments and perceived environmental uncertainty', _Administrative Science Quarterly_, _17_, 313–23.

DUNCAN, S. (1969), 'Non-verbal communications', _Psychological Bulletin_, _72(2)_, 118–37.

DUNNING, J. H. (ed.) (1971), _The Multinational Enterprise_, London, Allen and Unwin.

DUNNING, J. H. (1970), _Studies in International Investment_, London, Allen and Unwin.

DYAS, G. P., and THANHEISER, H. T. (1976), _The Emerging European Enterprise_, London, Macmillan.

EATON, J. (1979), 'The Basque workers' cooperatives', _Industrial Relations Journal_, _10_, 32–40.

ECONOMISTS ADVISORY GROUP (1976), _US Industry in Britain_, London, Wilton House Publications.

EILS, L. C., and JOHN, R. S. (1980), 'A criterion validation of multiattribute utility analysis and of group communication strategy', _Organizational Behavior and Human Performance_, _25_, 268–88.

EISENSTADT, S. N. (1958), 'Bureaucracy and bureaucratization', _Current Sociology_, _7_, 99–164.

EL-SAYED NOOR, A. (1981), 'Computing in Kuwait', _Datamation_, _27(13)_, 157–60.

ELLIS, T., and CHILD, J. (1973), 'Placing stereotypes of the manager into perspective', _Journal of Management Studies_, _10_, 233–5.

ELZINGA, A. (1981), _Cultural Components in the Scientific Attitude to Nature: Eastern and Western Models_, Technology and Culture Report Series No. 2, Lund, Research Policy Institute.

EMERSON, R. M. (1962), 'Power-dependence relations', _American Sociological Review_, _27_, 31–41.

EMERY, F. E., and TRIST, E. L. (1960), 'Sociotechnical systems' in Churchman, C. W., and Verhulst, M., _Management Science Models and Techniques_, Vol. 2, Oxford, Pergamon Press.

ENGLAND, G. W. (1975), _The Manager and his Values: An International Perspective from the United States, Japan, Korea, India and Australia_, Cambridge, Massachusetts, Ballinger.

ETZIONI, A. (1961), _A Comparative Analysis of Complex Organizations_, New York, Free Press.

ETZIONI, A. (ed.) (1961), _Complex Organizations: A Sociological Reader_, New York, Holt, Rinehart and Winston.

ETZIONI, A. (1964), _Modern Organizations_, Englewood Cliffs, New Jersey, Prentice-Hall.

EVANS, A. J. (1982), 'Britain and the United States: a comparison of human resources strategies', _Personnel Journal_, _61_, 656–62.

FARACE, R. V., and MACDONALD, D. (1974), 'New directions in the study of organization communication', *Personnel Psychology*, *27*, 1–15.

FARMER, D. H., and MACMILLAN, K. (1976), 'Voluntary collaboration vs. disloyalty', *Journal of Purchasing and Materials Management*, *12*, 3–8.

FARMER, D. H. (1973), *Some Aspects of Source Decision-Making vis à vis Corporate Plans in UK Based Multi-National Companies*, Unpublished Doctoral Thesis, University of Bath.

FARMER, R. N. (1968), *International Management*, California, Dickenson Publishing.

FARNHAM, D., and PIMLOTT, J. (1983), *Understanding Industrial Relations*, London, Cassell.

FARRINGTON, B. (1978), *Industrial Purchase Price Management*, Unpublished Ph.D. Thesis, Brunel University.

FARRINGTON, B., and WOODMANSEY, M. (1980), 'The purchasing function', *Management Survey Report*, 50, British Institute of Management/ Institute of Purchasing and Supply.

FEARON, H. E. (1973), 'Materials management – a synthesis and current review', *Journal of Purchasing*, *9*, 28.

FELDMAN, M. S., and MARCH, J. G. (1981), 'Information in organizations as signal and symbol', *Administrative Science Quarterly*, *26*, 171–86.

FESTINGER, L., SCHACTER, S., and BACK, K. (1963), *Social Pressures in Informal Groups: A Study of Human Factors in Housing*, Stanford, California, Stanford University Press.

FIEDLER, F. E. (1965), 'Engineer the job to fit the manager', *Harvard Business Review*, *43*, 115–22.

FIEDLER, F. E. (1967), *A Theory of Leadership Effectiveness*, New York, McGraw-Hill.

FIEDLER, F. E. (1971), 'Validation and extension of the contingency model of leadership effectiveness: a review of empirical findings', *Psychological Bulletin*, *76*, 128–48.

FIEDLER, F. E. (1972), 'Predicting the effects of leadership training and experience from the contingency model', *Journal of Applied Psychology*, *56*, 114–19.

FIEDLER, F. E. (1977), 'A rejoinder to Schriesheim and Kerr's premature obituary of the contingency model', in Hunt, J. G., and Larson, L. L. (eds.), *Leadership: The Cutting Edge*, Carbondale, Southern Illinois University Press.

FIEDLER, F. E., and CHEMERS, M. M. (1974), *Leadership and Effective Performance*, Glenview, Illinois, Scott Foresman.

FIEDLER, F. E., CHEMERS, M. M., and MAHAR, L. (1976), *Improving Leadership Effectiveness: The Leader Match Concept*, New York, Wiley.

FILLEY, A. C., HOUSE, R. J., and KERR, S. (1976), *Managerial Process and Organisational Behavior*, Glenview, Illinois, Scott Foresman.

FLANDERS, A. (1974), 'The tradition of voluntarism', *British Journal of Industrial Relations*, *12*, 352–70.

FLANDERS, A. (1975), *Management and Unions*, London, Faber and Faber.

FLANDERS, A., POMERANZ, R., and WOODWARD, J. (1968), *Experiment* in *Industrial Democracy: A Study of the John Lewis Partnership*, London, Faber and Faber.

FLEISHMAN, E. A. (1973), 'Twenty years of consideration and structure', in Fleishman, E. A., and Hunt, J. G. (eds.), *Current Developments in the Study of Leadership*, Carbondale, Southern Illinois University Press.

FLEISHMAN, E. A., and PETERS, D. R. (1962), 'Interpersonal values, leadership attitudes and managerial success', *Personnel Psychology*, *15*, 127–43.

FLETCHER, J. (1966), *Situation Ethics*, London, SCM Press.

FLORENCE, P. S. (1961), *Ownership, Control and Success of Large Companies*, London, Sweet and Maxwell.

FORES, M. (1982), 'Francis Bacon and the myth of industrial science', *History of Technology*, 7, 57–75.

FORES, M. (1983), 'Science and the "Neolithic Paradox"', *History of Science*, *21*, 141–63.

FORES, M., and SORGE, A. (1978), *The Rational Fallacy*, Berlin International Institute of Management, Discussion Paper 78–84.

FORES, M., and SORGE, A. (1981), 'The decline of the management ethic', *Journal of General Management*, *6*, 36–50.

FORSYTH, D. J. C. (1973), 'Foreign owned firms and labour relations: a regional perspective', *British Journal of Industrial Relations*, *11*, 20–28.

FOX, A. (1966), *Industrial Sociology and Industrial Relations*, Research Paper No. 3, Royal Commission on Trade Unions and Employers' Associations, London, HMSO.

FOX, A. (1974), *Beyond Contract: Work, Trust and Power Relations*, London, Faber and Faber.

FREEMAN, C. (1982), *The Economics of Industrial Innovation*, Harmondsworth, Penguin.

FRENCH, J. R., and RAVEN, B. (1959), 'The bases of social power', in Cartwright, D., and Zander, A., *Group Dynamics*, New York, Harper and Row.

FRENCH, J. R. P., JR., ISRAEL, J., and AS, D. (1960), 'An experiment in participation in a Norwegian factory', *Human Relations*, *13*, 3–19.

FRIEDMAN, A. (1977), *Industry and Labour*, London, Macmillan.

GALBRAITH, J. K. (1967), *The New Industrial State*, London, Hamish Hamilton.

GARNER, R. (1983), 'Good vibrations from Japan?', *Financial Times*, 28 April 1983.

GEHLEN, A. (1977), *Urmensch und Spätkultur*, Frankfurt/Main, Athenaion.

GLOBERMAN, S. (1980), 'Markets, hierarchies and innovation', *Journal of Economic Issues*, *14*, 977–98.

GLOVER, I. A. (1978), 'Executive career patterns: Britain, France, Germany and Sweden' in Fores, M., and Glover, I., *Manufacturing and Management*, London, HMSO.

GLOVER, I. A. (1979), *Managerial Work: The Social Scientific Evidence and its Character*, unpublished Ph.D. thesis, London, The City University.

GLOVER, I. A. (1980), 'Social science, engineering and society', *Higher Education Review*, *12*, 27–41.

GLOVER, J. (1970), *Responsibility*, London, Routledge and Kegan Paul.

GLUECK, W. F. (1980), *Business Policy and Strategic Management*, New York, McGraw-Hill.

GOLD, B. (1977), *Research, Technological Change, and Economic Analysis*, Lexington, Massachusetts, Lexington Books.

GOLD, B. (1981), 'Technological diffusion in industry: research needs and shortcomings', *Journal of Industrial Economics*, *24*, 247–69.

GOLDSMITH, R. W., and PARMELEE, R. (1940), *The Distribution of Ownership in the 200 Largest Nonfinancial Corporations*, Monographs of the Temporary National Economic Committee, Number 29, Washington, D.C., Government Printing Office for the US Senate.

GOLDTHORPE, J., LOCKWOOD, D., BECHHOFER, F., and PLATT, J. (1968), *The Affluent Worker*, Cambridge, Cambridge University Press.

GORDON, R. A. (1945), *Business Leadership in Large Corporations*, Washington, D.C., Brookings Institution.

GOSPEL, H. (1983), 'Managerial structure and strategies', in Gospel, H., and Littler, C. (eds.), *Managerial Strategies and Industrial Relations*, London, Heinemann.

GOULDNER, A. W. (1954), *Patterns of Industrial Bureaucracy*, Glencoe, Illinois, Free Press.

GOULDNER, A. W. (1955a), 'Metaphysical pathos and the theory of bureaucracy', *American Political Science Review*, *49*, 496–507.

GOULDNER, A. W. (1955b), *Patterns of Industrial Bureaucracy*, London, Routledge and Kegan Paul.

GRABOWSKI, H. G., and BAXTER, N. D. (1973), 'Rivalry in industrial research and development: an empirical study', *Journal of Industrial Economics*, *21*(*3*), 209–35.

GRABOWSKI, H. G., and VERNON, J. M. (1977), 'Consumer protection regulation in ethical drugs', *American Economic Review*, *67*, 359–64.

GRANICK, D. (1962), *The European Executive*, London, Weidenfeld and Nicolson.

GRANT, W. (1982), 'The government relations function in large firms based in the United Kingdom: a preliminary study', *British Journal of Political Science*, *12*, 513–16.

GRANT, W., and MARSH, D. (1977), *The CBI*, London, Hodder and Stoughton.

GREENBAUM, H. H. (1974), 'The audit of organizational communication', *Academy of Management Journal*, *17*, 739–54.

GREENBERG, E. S. (1975), 'The consequences of worker participation: a clarification of the theoretical literature', *Social Science Quarterly*, *56*, 191–209.

GREENE, C. N. (1975), 'The reciprocal nature of influence between leader and subordinate', *Journal of Applied Psychology*, *60*, 187–93.

GREENE, C. N. (1979), 'Questions of causation in the path–goal theory of leadership', *Academy of Management Journal*, *22*, 22–41.

GREGORY, G. (1982), 'Asia's electronics revolution', *Euro-Asia Business Review*, *1*, 1.

GRELLER, M. M. (1980), 'Evaluation of feedback sources as a function of role and organizational level', *Journal of Applied Psychology*, *65*, 24–7.

GRILICHES, Z. (1980), 'Returns to research and development in the private sector', in Kendrick, J. W., and Vaccara, B. Z. (eds.), *New Developments in Productivity Measurement and Analysis*, Studies in Income and Wealth, 44, Chicago, University of Chicago Press.

GRINYER, P., and SPENDER, J.-C. (1978), *Turnaround – Managerial Recipes for Strategic Success*, London, Associated Business Press.

GRUBER, W., MEHTA, D., and VERNON, R. (1967), 'The R and D factor in international trade and international investment of US industries', *Journal of Political Economy*, *75*, 20–37.

GUETZKOW, H. (1968), 'Communications in organizations', in March, J. G. (ed.), *Handbook of Organizations*, Chicago, Rand McNally.

HAGE, J., and AIKEN, M. (1967), 'Relationship of centralization to other structural properties', *Administrative Science Quarterly*, *12*, 72–92.

HALL, R. S. (ed.) (1972), *The Formal Organization*, New York, Basic Books.

HALL, R. S. (1972), *Organizations: Structure and Process*, Englewood Cliffs, New Jersey, Prentice-Hall.

HAMBERG, D. (1966), *Essays in the Economics of Research and Development*, New York, Random House.

HANAMI, T. (1980), *Labour Relations in Japan Today*, London, John Martin.

HANDY, C. (1976), *Understanding Organisations*, Harmondsworth, Penguin.

HANSARD SOCIETY (1979), *Politics and Industry – The Great Mismatch*, London, Hansard Society.

HARBISON, F. J., and MYERS, C. A. (eds.) (1958), *Management in the Industrial World: An International Analysis*, New York, McGraw-Hill.

HARE, R. M. (1963), *Freedom and Reason*, Oxford, Clarendon Press.

HARRE, R., and SECORD, P. F. (1972), *The Explanation of Social Behaviour*, Oxford, Basil Blackwell.

HAWTHORNE, E. P. (1978), *The Management of Technology*, London, McGraw-Hill.

HAY, D., and MORRIS, D. (1979), *Industrial Economics: Theory and Economics*, Oxford, Oxford University Press.

HAYDEN GREEN, G., and NORDSTROM, R. D. (1974), 'The rewards from being a disloyal buyer', *Journal of Purchasing and Materials Management*, *10*, 33–40.

HAYES, R. H. (1981), 'Why Japanese factories work', *Harvard Business Review*, *59*(4), 57–66.

HEGARTY, E. (1976), *How to Succeed in Company Politics*, New York, McGraw-Hill.

HEILBRONER, R. L. (1972), *In the Name of Profit*, New York, Doubleday.

HELLER, F. A. (undated), *A Study of British and American Managerial Skills*, unpublished paper, Tavistock Institute of Human Relations.

HERZBERG, F. (1968), 'One more time: how do you motivate employees?', *Harvard Business Review*, *46*, 53–62.

HERZBERG, F. (1968), *Work and the Nature of Man*, London, Staples Press.

HEYDEBRAND, W. (1973), *Comparative Organizations – the Results of Empirical Research*, Englewood Cliffs, New Jersey, Prentice-Hall.

HICKSON, D. J., HININGS, C. R., LEE, C. A., SCHNECK, R. H., and PENNINGS, J. M. (1971), 'A strategic contingencies theory of intra-organizational power', *Administrative Science Quarterly*, *16*, 216–29.

HICKSON, D. J., HININGS, C. R., MCMILLAN, C. J. and SCHWITTER, J. P. (1974), 'The culture-free context of organisational structure: a tri-national comparison', *Sociology*, 8, 59–80.

HICKSON, D. J., MCMILLAN, C. L., AZUMI, K., and HARVARTH, D. (1979), 'The grounds for comparative organization theory: shifting sands or hardcore?' in Lammers, C. J., and Hickson, D. J., *Organizations Alike and Unalike*, London, Routledge and Kegan Paul.

HILL, T. (1983), *Production/Operations Management*, Hemel Hempstead, Prentice-Hall International.

HILL, W. A., and HUGHES, D. (1974), 'Variations in leader behavior as a function of task type', *Organizational Behavior and Human Performance*, *11*, 83–96.

HININGS, G. R., HICKSON, D. J., PENNINGS, J. M., and SCHNECK, R. E. (1974), 'Structural conditions of intra-organizational power', *Administrative Science Quarterly*, *19*, 22–44.

HIRSCHMAN, A. E. (1970), *Exit Voice and Loyalty*, Cambridge, Massachusetts, Harvard University Press.

HOFFMAN, L. R. (1965), 'Group problem solving', in Berkowitz, L. (ed.), *Advances in Experimental Social Psychology*, Vol. 2, New York, Academic Press.

HOFSTEDE, G. (1978), 'The poverty of management control philosophy', *Academy of Management Review*, *3*, 450–61.

HOFSTEDE, G. (1980), *Culture's Consequences, International Differences in Work-Related Values*, Beverly Hills, Sage.

HOLLAND, S. (1976), *The Socialist Challenge*, London, Quartet.

HOSKING, D. M. (1981), 'A critical evaluation of Fiedler's contingency hypothesis', in Stephenson, G. M., and Davis, J. M. (eds.), *Progress in Applied Social Psychology*, Vol. 1, New York, Wiley.

HOSKING, D. M., and SCHRIESHEIM, C. A. (1978). 'Review essay: improving leadership effectiveness: the leader match concept', *Administrative Science Quarterly*, *23*, 497–505.

HOTZ-HART, B. (1983), 'Der Effekt von Unterschieden in der Arbeitsverfassung auf die Beschäftigungspolitik von Unternehmungen', Paper presented to the Verein für Sozialpolitik, Basel.

HOUSE, R. J. (1973), 'A path-goal theory of leadership effectiveness' in Fleishman, E. A., and Hunt, J. G. (eds.), *Current Developments in the Study of Leadership*, Carbondale, Southern Illinois University Press.

HOUSE, R. J., and DESSLER, G. (1974), 'The path–goal theory of leadership: some post-hoc and a priori tests', in Hunt, J. G., and Larson, L. L. (eds.), *Contingency Approaches to Leadership*, Carbondale, Southern Illinois University Press.

HOUSE, R. J., and MITCHELL, T. R. (1974), 'Path–goal theory of leadership', *Journal of Contemporary Business*, 5, 81–94.

HOWELL, J. P., and DORFMAN, P. W. (1981), 'Substitutes for leadership: test of a construct', *Academy of Management Journal*, 24, 714–28.

HUNT, J. G., OSBORN, R. N., and SCHULER, R. S. (1978), 'Relations of discretionary and non-discretionary leadership to performance and satisfaction in a complex organisation', *Human Relations*, 31, 507–23.

HUNT, J. W. (1979), *Managing People at Work*, London, McGraw-Hill.

HUTTON, S. P., and LAWRENCE, P. A. (1979), *The Work of Production Managers: Case Studies at Manufacturing Companies in West Germany*, Report to the Department of Industry, London.

HUTTON, S. P., and LAWRENCE, P. A. (1981), *German Engineers: The Anatomy of a Profession*, Oxford, Clarendon Press.

HUTTON, S. P., and LAWRENCE, P. A. (1982), *The Work of Production Managers: Case Studies at Manufacturing Companies in Great Britain*, Report to the Science and Engineering Research Council, Swindon.

HYMAN, R. (1977), *Strikes*, London, Fontana.

ILGEN, D. R., FISHER, C. D., and TAYLOR, M. S. (1979), 'Consequences of individual feedback on behavior in organizations', *Journal of Applied Psychology*, 64, 349–71.

INKSON, J. H. K., PUGH, D. S., and HICKSON, D. J. (1970), 'Organization context and structure: an abbreviated replication', *Administrative Science Quarterly*, 15, 318–29.

INKSON, J. H. K., SCHWITTER, J. P., PHEYSEY, D. C., and HICKSON, D. J. (1970), 'A comparison of organisational structure and managerial roles, Ohio, USA, and Midlands, England', *Journal of Management Studies*, 7, 347–63.

INTERNATIONAL MANAGEMENT (1983), 'Managers wrestle with ethical conflicts worldwide', *38(2)*.

JAMESON, B. (1979), 'Management by uncertainty', *Management Today*, February, 61–3, 138.

JAMIESON, I. M. (1980), *Capitalism and Culture: A Comparative Analysis of British and American Manufacturing Organizations*, Farnborough, Gower.

JAPAN MANAGEMENT ASSOCIATION (1972), *Sixty Years of Management*, JMA.

JAUCH, L. R., and WILSON, H. K. (1979), 'A strategic perspective for make or buy decisions', *Long Range Planning*, 12, 56–61.

JENKINS, D. (1978), 'The supervisor solution', *Management Today*, May, 75–7, 144, 147.

JENKINS, D. (1983), 'Half-trained managers', *Management Today*, May, 86–90.

JEWKES, J., SAWERS, D., and STILLERMAN, R. (1970), *The Sources of Invention*, 2nd edition, New York, Norton.

JHA, L. (1982), 'Economic strategies for the '80's'.

JOHNSON, A. G., and WHYTE, W. F. (1977), 'The Mondragon system of worker production cooperatives', *Industrial and Labour Relations Review*, *31*, 18–30.

JONES, R., and MARRIOTT, O. (1970), *Anatomy of a Merger: A History of GEC, AEI and English Electric*, London, Jonathan Cape.

JOWELL, R. (1983) (Conference Report), *Market Research Society Newsletter*, No. 206, 30.

JUCH, B. (1983), *Personal Development: Theory and Practice in Management Training*, Chichester, Wiley.

KALMAN, R. (1981), 'Eight strategies for informatics', in Bennet, J., and Kalman, R. (eds.), *Computers in Developing Nations*, Amsterdam, North-Holland Publishing.

KAMATA, S. (1983), *Japan in the Passing Lane*, London, Allen and Unwin.

KAMIEN, M. I., and SCHWARTZ, N. L. (1982), *Market Structure and Innovation*, Cambridge, Cambridge University Press.

KANAO, K. (1982), 'How does Nissan define a quality product?', *Nissan: Who We Are*, Nissan Motor Company Ltd.

KASSALOW, E. M. (1969), *Trade Unions and Industrial Relations*, New York, Random House.

KEEGAN, N. J. (1974), 'Multinational scanning: a study of information sources utilized by headquarters executives in multinational companies', *Administrative Science Quarterly*, *19*, 411–21.

KEENAN, A. (1976), 'Effects of the non-verbal behaviour of interviewers on candidates' performance', *Journal of Occupational Psychology*, *49*, 171–6.

KEESING, R. M. (1974), 'Theories of culture', *Annual Review of Anthropology*, *3*, 73–97.

KENNEDY, C., and THIRWALL, A. (1972), 'Surveys in applied economics: technical progress', *Economic Journal*, *82*, 11–73.

KERR, C. (1973), *Industrialism and Industrial Man*, 2nd edition, Harmondsworth, Penguin.

KERR, C., DUNLOP, J. T., HARBISON, F. H., and MYERS, C. A. (1960), *Industrialism and Industrial Man*, Cambridge, Massachusetts, Harvard University Press.

KERR, S., and JERMIER, S. (1978), 'Substitutes for leadership: their meaning and measurement', *Organizational Behavior and Human Performance*, *22*, 375–403.

KERR, S., SCHRIESHEIM, C. A., MURPHY, C. J., and STOGDILL, R. M. (1974), 'Towards a contingency theory of leadership based upon the consideration and initiating structure literature', *Organization Behavior and Human Performance*, *12*, 62–82.

KIECHEL, W. (1981), 'Playing the global game', *Fortune*, *104(10)*, 111–26.

KINDLEBERGER, C. P. (1969), *American Business Abroad*, New Haven, Connecticut, Yale University Press.

KING, R. L. (1965), 'The marketing concept', in Schwartz, G. (ed.), *Science in Marketing*, New York, Wiley.

KLINE, D. (1982), 'The micro comes to Pakistan', *Datamation*, *28*(*9*), 86–92.

KNIBER, A., RICHARDSON, C., and BROOKES, H. (1974), 'Deposit of Poisonous Wastes Act 1972: government by reaction?', *Public Law*.

KNIGHT, I. (1979), *Company Organisation and Worker Participation*, London, HMSO.

KOCH, J. (1980), *Industrial Organization*, Englewood Cliffs, New Jersey, Prentice-Hall.

KOHLER, P., and LEVY, S. J. (1973), 'Buying is marketing too', *Journal of Marketing*, *37*, 54–9.

KOHN, M. L. (1971), 'Bureaucratic Man: a portrait and an interpretation', *American Sociological Review*, *36*, 461–74.

KOLB, D. A., RUBIN, I. M., and MCINTYRE, J. M. (1971), *Organizational Psychology: An Experimental Approach*, Englewood Cliffs, New Jersey, Prentice-Hall.

KORMAN, A. K. (1966), '"Consideration", "initiating structure", and organisational criteria – a review', *Personnel Psychology*, *19*, 349–61.

KOTLER, D. (1980), *Marketing Management*, 4th edition, Englewood Cliffs, New Jersey, Prentice-Hall.

KROHN, R. G. (1971), 'Conflict and function: some basic issues in bureaucratic theory', *British Journal of Sociology*, *22*, 115–32.

KUHN, M., and KAISER, H. (1982), *Computer Applications – Prospects for Developing Countries*, Report for Committee on Science and Technology in Developing Countries (COSTED), Madras.

KUPPERMAN, J. J. (1970), *Ethical Knowledge*, London, Allen and Unwin.

LAMMERS, C. J. (1976), 'Towards the internationalization of the organizational sciences', in Hofstede, G., and Kassem, M. S. (eds.), *European Contributions to Organization Theory*, Assen, Van Gorcum.

LAMMERS, C. J., and HICKSON, D. J. (eds.) (1979), *Organizations Alike and Unalike*, London, Routledge and Kegan Paul.

LARNER, R. J. (1966), 'Ownership and control in the 200 largest non-financial corporations, 1929 and 1963', *American Economic Review*, *56*, 777–87.

LARNER, R. J. (1970), *Management Control and the Large Corporation*, New York, Dunellen.

LARSON, L. L., HUNT, J. G., and OSBORN, R. N. (1976), 'The great hi–hi leader behavior myth: a lesson from Occam's razor', *Academy of Management Journal*, *19*, 628–41.

LATTIMER, A. (1980), 'Will counter purchase deals bring economic suicide?', *Purchasing and Supply Management*, December, 25.

LAWLER, E. E., PORTER, L. W., and TANENBAUM, A. (1968), 'Managers' attitudes towards interaction episodes', *Journal of Applied Psychology*, *52*(*6*), 432–9.

LAWRENCE, P. A. (1980), *Managers and Management in West Germany*, London, Croom Helm.

LAWRENCE, P. A. (1983), *Operations Management: Research and Priorities*, Report to the Social Science Research Council, London.

LAWRENCE, P. A. (1984), *Management in Action*, London, Routledge and Kegan Paul.

LAWRENCE, P. A., and LEE, R. A. (1984), *Insight into Management*, Oxford, Oxford University Press.

LAWRENCE, P. R., and LORSCH, J. (1969), *Developing Organizations: Diagnosis and Action*, Reading, Massachusetts, Addison-Wesley.

LAWRENCE, P. R., and LORSCH, J. (1967), *Organization and Environment*, Cambridge, Massachusetts, Harvard University Press.

LEE, A. G. (1980), 'Counter purchase deal brings benefits to buyers', *Purchasing and Supply Management*, September, 17–18.

LEENDERS, M. R. (1965), *Improving Purchasing Effectiveness Through Supplier Development*, Cambridge, Massachusetts, Harvard University Press.

LEGGE, K. (1978), *Power, Innovation, and Problem-Solving in Personnel Management*, Maidenhead, McGraw-Hill.

LEGGETT, T. (1978), 'Managers in industry: their background and education', *Sociological Review*, *26*, 807–25.

LENSKI, G., and LENSKI, J. (1974), *Human Societies. An Introduction to Macrosociology*, New York, McGraw-Hill.

LEWIS, H. D. (1972), 'The non-moral notion of collective responsibility', in French, P. (ed.), *Individual and Collective Responsibility*, Cambridge, Massachusetts, Schenkman Publishing.

LIEBERSON, S., and O'CONNOR, J. F. (1972), 'Leadership and organizational performance: a study of large corporations', *American Sociological Review*, *37*, 117–30.

LIKERT, R. (1961), *New Patterns of Management*, New York, McGraw-Hill.

LIND, P. (1982), 'Computerization in developing and developed countries – a model for comparison', in Baark, E. (ed.), *Comparative Technological Change*, Technology and Culture Report Series No. 5, Lund, Research Policy Institute.

LINN, R. (1983), 'A sectoral approach to strategic planning for R & D', *Research Management*, *26(1)*, 33–40.

LINSTONE, H., and TURDOFF, M. (1975), *The Delphi Method: Techniques and Applications*, Reading, Massachusetts, Addison-Wesley.

LITTLECHILD, S. C. (1978), *The Fallacy of the Mixed Economics: An 'Austrian' Critique of Conventional Mainstream Economics*, London, Institute of Economic Affairs.

LOWE, J., and LEWIS, D. (1980), *The Economics of Environmental Management*, Oxford, Philip Allan.

LOWIN, A., and CRAIG, J. R. (1968), 'The influence of level of performance on managerial style: an experimental object-lesson in the ambiguity of correlational data', *Organization Behavior and Human Performance*, *3*, 440–58.

LOWIN, A., HRAPCHECK, W. J., and KAVANAGH, J. J. (1969), 'Consideration and initiating structure: an experimental investigation of leadership traits', *Administrative Science Quarterly*, *14*, 238–53.

LUHMANN, N. (1975), 'A general theory of organized social systems', in Hofstede, G., and Kassem, M. S. (eds.), *European Contributions to Organization Theory*, Amsterdam, Assen.

LUKES, S. (1974), *Power, A Radical View*, London, Macmillan.

LUPTON, T. (1963), *On the Shop Floor*, Oxford, Pergamon Press.

LUPTON, T. (1971), *Management and the Social Sciences*, Harmondsworth, Penguin.

LYLES, M. A. (1981), 'Formulating strategic problems: empirical analysis and model development', *Strategic Management Journal*, *2*, 61–75.

LYLES, M. A., and MITROFF, M. (1980), 'Organisational problem formulation: an empirical study', *Administrative Science Quarterly*, *15*, 109–19.

MACMILLAN, I. (1973), 'Business strategies for political action', *Journal of General Management*, *2*, 51–63.

MACMILLAN, I. (1974), 'Business strategies for political action', *Journal of General Management*, *2*, 51–63.

MACMILLAN, I. (1978), *Strategy Formulation: Political Concepts*, St Paul, Minnesota, West Publishing.

MCCALL, M. W., and LOMBARDO, M. M. (1978), 'Where else can we go?', in McCall, M. W., and Lombardo, M. M. (eds.), *Leadership: Where Else Can We Go?*, Durham, N.C., Duke University Press.

MCCARTHY, E. J. (1978), *Basic Marketing*, 6th edition, Homewood, Illinois, Irwin.

MCGIFFERT, M. (1970), *The Character of Americans*, Homewood, Illinois, Dorsey.

MCGREGOR, D. (1960), *The Human Side of Enterprise*, New York, McGraw-Hill.

MCLEOD, T. (1969), *The Management of Research, Development and Design in Industry*, London, Gower.

MCMILLAN, J., and HARRIS, B. (1968), *The American Takeover of Britain*, London, Leslie Frewin.

MACHIAVELLI, N. (1514), *The Prince*, Translated by G. Bull, Harmondsworth, Penguin (1961).

MAGNET, M. (1982), 'Managing by mystique at Tandem Computers', *Fortune*, *28*, 84–91.

MALINOWSKI, B. (1931), 'Culture', in *Encyclopaedia of the Social Sciences*, Vol. 4, New York, 621–45.

MALLORY, G. R., BUTLER, R. J., GRAY, D., HICKSON, D. J., and WILSON, D. C. (1983), 'Implanted decision-making: American owned firms in Britain', *Journal of Management Studies*, *20*, 191–211.

MANGHAM, I. (1979), *The Politics of Organisational Change*, London, Associated Business Press.

MANNHEIM, K. (1960), *Ideology and Utopia: An Introduction to the Sociology of Knowledge*, new edition, London, Routledge and Kegan Paul.

MANNING, P. K. (1977), *Police Work: The Social Organization of Policing*, Cambridge, Massachusetts, MIT Press.

MANSFIELD, E. (1968), *The Economics of Technological Change*, New York, Norton.

MANSFIELD, E. (1982), 'How economists see R & D', *Research Management*, 25(4), 23–9.

MANSFIELD, E., and WAGNER, S. (1975), 'Organizational and strategic factors associated with probabilities of success in industrial R & D', *Journal of Business*, 48, 179–98.

MANT, A. (1977), *The Rise and Fall of the British Manager*, London, Macmillan.

MANWARING, T. (1982), *The Extended Internal Labour Market*, Berlin, International Institute of Management, Discussion paper 82–29.

MARCH, J. G., and OLSEN, J. P. (1976), *Ambiguity and Choice in Organizations*, Oslo, Universitetsforlaget.

MARCH, J. G., and SIMON, H. A. (1958), *Organizations*, New York, Wiley.

MARGLIN, S. (1976), 'What do bosses do?', in Groz, A., *The Division of Labour*, London, Harvester.

MARTIN, N. and SIMS, J. (1956), 'Power tactics', *Harvard Business Review*, 34, 25–36.

MARX, K. (1867), *Das Kapital* (Vol. 1), Hamburg, Meissner (published in English in 1887 as *Capital*, London, Sonnenschein and Co.).

MASLOW, A. H. (1954), *Motivation and Personality*, New York, Harper and Row.

MAURICE, M., SELLIER, F., and SILVESTRE, J.-J. (1982), *Politique d'éducation et d'organisation industrielle en France et en Allemagne. Essai d'analyse sociétale*, Paris, Presses Universitaires de France.

MAURICE, M., SORGE, A., and WARNER, M. (1980), 'Societal differences in organizing manufacturing units: a comparison of France, West Germany and Great Britain', *Organization Studies*, 1, 59–86.

MEADE, J. E. (1975), *The Intelligent Radicals' Guide to Economic Policy*, London, Allen and Unwin.

MECHANIC, D. (1962), 'Sources of power of lower participants in complex organizations,' *Administrative Science Quarterly*, 7, 349–64.

MERTON, R. K. (1952), 'Bureaucratic structure and personality', in Merton, R. K., et al., *Reader in Bureaucracy*, Glencoe, Illinois, Free Press (this paper was originally published in 1940).

MERTON, R. K. (1968), *Social Theory and Social Structure*, New York, Free Press.

MICHELS, R. (1967), *Political Parties*, New York, Collier Books (first published as *Political Parties: A Sociological Study of the Oligarchical Tendencies of Modern Democracy*, 1915, Hearst's International Library).

MILES, L. D. (1961), *Techniques of Value Analysis and Engineering*, London, McGraw-Hill.

MILES, R. E., and SNOW, C. C. (1978), *Organizational Strategy: Structure and Process*, New York, McGraw-Hill.

MILLER, D., and FRIESEN, P. H. (1978), 'Archetypes of strategy formulation', *Management Science*, 24, 921–3.

MILLER, J. G., and GILMOUR, P. (1979), 'Materials managers: who needs them?', *Harvard Business Review*, 57, 143–53.

MINISTRY OF INTERNATIONAL TRADE AND INDUSTRY, International Trade Research Office (1980), *Japan's Labour Productivity*, MITI.

MINTZBERG, H. (1972), *The Nature of Managerial Work*, New York, Harper and Row.

MINTZBERG, H. (1978), 'Patterns in strategy formulation', *Management Science*, 24(9), 934–48.

MINTZBERG, H. (1979), *The Structuring of Organizations*, Englewood Cliffs, New Jersey, Prentice-Hall.

MINTZBERG, H., RAISINGHANI, D., and THEORET, A. (1975), 'The structure of unstructured decision process', *Administrative Science Quarterly*, 21, 246–75.

MONOPOLIES AND MERGERS COMMISSION (1972), *Beecham Group Ltd, and Glaxo Group Ltd.; Boots Group Ltd. and Glaxo Group Ltd.: A Report of a Proposed Merger*, London, HMSO.

MORAN, M. (1981), 'Finance capital and pressure group policies in Britain', *British Journal of Political Science*, 11, 381–404.

MORRIS, J. F., and BURGOYNE, J. G. (1973), *Developing Resourceful Managers*, London, Institute of Personnel Management.

MORRISON, A. M. (1982), 'Trying to bring GE to life', *Fortune*, 25, 50–59.

MOSCA, G. (1884), *Sulla Teoria dei governi e sul governo parlamentare*, Rome, Leoscher.

MOSCA, G. (1939), *The Ruling Class*, New York, McGraw Hill.

MULLER, M. (1979), 'Effective statistical computing in an environment of changing policies and technology', Manila.

MURRAY, T. J. (1979), 'Data information and intelligence in a computer-based management information system', *Journal of Applied Systems Analysis*, 6, 101–5.

NAGEL, T. (1978), 'Ruthlessness in public life', in Hampshire, S. (ed.), *Public and Private Morality*, Cambridge, Cambridge University Press.

NAKAOKA, T. (1981), 'Production management in Japan before the period of high economic growth', *Osaka City University Economic Review*, No. 17.

NEUBAUER, F. F., and SOLOMON, N. B. (1977), 'A managerial approach to environmental assessment', *Long Range Planning*, 10(2), 13–20.

NEW, C. C. (1973), *Requirements Planning*, London, Gower.

NEWBURY-ECOB, D. (1974), 'Substantial benefits from buying abroad', *Procurement*, 35, 37, 43.

NICHOLS, T. (1969), *Ownership, Control and Ideology*, London, Allen and Unwin.

NOBLE, D. W. (1965), *Historians Against History*, Minneapolis, University of Minnesota Press.

NOBLE, D. W. (1981), *The Progressive Mind 1890–1917*, Minneapolis, Burgess.

NORBURN, D., and GRINYER, P. (1973), 'Directors without direction', *Journal of General Management*, 1, 37–48.

NOVOTNY, O. (1964), 'American versus European management philosophy', *Harvard Business Review*, 42, 101–8.

NYMAN, S., and SILBERSTON, A. (1978), 'The ownership and control of industry', *Oxford Economic Papers*, 30, 1.

NYSTROM, P. C. (1978), 'Managers and the hi–hi leader myth', *Academy of Management Journal*, *21*, 325–31.

O'REILLY, C. A. (1980), 'Individuals and information overload in organizations: is more necessarily better?' *Academy of Management Journal*, *23*, 684–96.

OAKESHOTT, X.-R. (1973), 'Mondragon: Spain, oasis of democracy', in Vanek, J., *Self-Management*, Harmondsworth, Penguin.

OHTSUBO, T. (1981), *Research and Development Trends in Japan*, London, Nomura Research Institute (mimeo).

OI, W. (1962), 'Labour as a quasi-fixed factor', *Journal of Political Economy*, *70*, 338–55.

OLDHAM, G. (1981), 'Summary', in Granstrand, O., and Sigurdsson, J. (eds.), *Technology and Industrial Policy in China and Europe*, Technology and Culture Report Series No. 3, Lund, Research Policy Institute.

ORGANISATION FOR ECONOMIC COOPERATION AND DEVELOPMENT (1981), *Transborder Dataflows and International Business – A Pilot Study*, Paris, OECD.

ORLICKY, J. A. (1975), *Materials Requirements Planning*, New York, McGraw-Hill.

OTLEY, D. T., and BERRY, A. J. (1980), 'Control, organisation and accounting', *Accounting Organisations and Society*, *5*, 231–46.

PARSONS, T., and SHILS, E. A. (1967), *Toward a General Theory of Action*, Cambridge, Massachusetts, Harvard University Press.

PASCALE, R. T. (1978*a*), 'Zen and the art of management', *Harvard Business Review*. *56*(2), 153–62.

PASCALE, R. T. (1978*b*), 'Personnel practices and employee attitudes: a study of Japanese and American-managed firms in the United States', *Human Relations*, *31*, 597–616.

PASCALE, R. T., and ATHOS, A. G. (1981), *The Art of Japanese Management*, New York, Simon and Schuster.

PASCALE, R. T., and MAGUIRE, M. A. (1980), 'Comparisons of selected work factors in Japan and the United States', *Human Relations*, *33*, 433–56.

PAVITT, K. (1983), 'Patterns of technical change – evidence, theory and policy implications', *Papers in Science Technology and Public Policy*, No. 3, Science Policy Research Unit, Sussex University.

PECK, M. (1962), *Competition in the Aluminium Industry*, Cambridge, Massachusetts, Harvard University Press.

PEDLER, M., BURGOYNE, J., and BOYDELL, T. (1978), *A Manager's Guide to Self-Development*, London, McGraw-Hill.

PERINBAM, L. (1982), *Towards a New Interdependence of Nations*, IDRC Reports, Ottawa.

PERLMUTTER, H. V. (1969), 'The tortuous evolution of the multi-national corporation', *Columbia Journal of World Business*, *4*(1), 9–18.

PERMUT, S. E. (1977), 'The European view of marketing research', *Columbia Journal of World Business*, *12*(3), 94–104.

PERROW, C. (1970), *Organizational Analysis: A Sociological View*, Belmont, California, Wadsworth.

PERROW, C. (1972), *Complex Organizations: A Critical Essay*, Brighton, Scott Foresman.

PETERS, T. J. (1979), 'Leadership: sad facts and silver linings', *Harvard Business Review*, 57, 164–72.

PETERS, T. J. (1980), 'Putting excellence into management', *Business Week*, 21, 196–205.

PETERS, T. J., and WATERMAN, R. H. (1982), *In Search of Excellence*, New York, Harper and Row.

PETTIGREW, A. (1973a), 'Occupational specialisation as an emergent process', *The Sociological Review*, 21, 255–78.

PETTIGREW, A. (1973b), *The Politics of Organizational Decision-Making*, London, Tavistock.

PETTIGREW, A. (1974), 'The influence process between specialists and executives', *Personnel Review*, 3, 24–31.

PETTIGREW, A. (1975), 'Towards a political theory of organizational intervention', *Human Relations*, 28, 191–208.

PFEFFER, J. (1977), 'The ambiguity of leadership', *Academy of Management Review*, 2, 104–12.

PFEFFER, J. (1981), *Power in Organizations*, London, Pitman.

PICKERING, J. E., and COUSINS, D. C. (1982), 'The benefits and costs of voluntary codes of conduct', *European Journal of Marketing*, 16(b), 31–45.

POLITICAL AND ECONOMIC PLANNING (1966), *Attitudes in British Management*, Harmondsworth, Penguin.

POLLARD, S. (1965), *The Genesis of Modern Management*, Harmondsworth, Penguin.

PONDY, L. R. (1978), 'Leadership is a language game', in McCall, M. W. and Lombardo, M. M. (eds.), *Leadership: Where Else Can We Go?*, Durham, N.C., Duke University Press.

PORTER, L. W., and ROBERTS, K. H. (1976), 'Communication in organizations', in Dunnette, M. D. (ed.) *Handbook of Industrial and Organizational Psychology*, Chicago, Rand McNally.

POTTER, D. (1954), *People of Plenty; Economic Abundance and the American Character*, Chicago, University of Chicago Press.

PUGH, D. S., HICKSON, D. J., HININGS, C. R., and TURNER, C. (1968), 'Dimensions of organization structures', *Administrative Science Quarterly*, 14, 65–105.

PUGH, D. S., HICKSON, D. J., and HININGS, C. R. (1969), 'An empirical taxonomy of structures of work organizations', *Administrative Science Quarterly*, 15, 115–26.

PYHRR, P. A. (1977), 'Contemporary issues in cost and managerial accounting: a discipline in transition', in Anton, H. R., Firmin, P. A., and Grove, H. D., *Contemporary Issues in Cost and Managerial Accounting*, 3rd edition, Boston, Houghton Mifflin.

QUINN, J. B. (1980), *Strategies for Change: Logical Incrementalism*, Homewood, Illinois, Irwin.

RAMSEY, W. (1982), 'The new product dilemma', *Marketing Trends, 1*, 4–6.

RICHARDSON, S. A. (1956), 'Organizational contrasts on British and American ships', *Administrative Science Quarterly, 1*, 189–207.

ROBERTS, D. R. (1971), 'The nature of communication effects', in Shramm, W., and Roberts, D. F. (eds.), *The Process and Effects of Mass Communication*, Rev. ed., Urbana, Illinois, University of Illinois Press.

ROETHLISBERGER, F. J., and DICKSON, W. J. (1939), *Management and the Worker*, Cambridge, Massachusetts, Harvard University Press.

ROTHWELL, R. (1977), 'The characteristics of successful innovation and technically progressive firms' (with some comments on innovation research), *R & D Management, 7(3)*, 191–206.

ROWE, A. J., MASON, R. O., and DICKEL, W. E. (1982), *Strategic Management and Business Policy: A Methodological Approach*, Addison-Wesley.

RUMELT, R. (1979), 'Evaluation of strategy: theory and models', in Schendel, D., and Hofer, C., *Strategic Management*, Boston, Little Brown.

SAHAL, D. (1978), *Structure and Self Organization*, Berlin, International Institute of Management, Discussion Paper 78–87.

SAHAL, D. (1980), 'Technological progress and policy', in Sahal, D., *Research, Development, and Technological Innovation*, Toronto, Lexington Books.

SALAN, A. (1983), 'Today's pure is tomorrow's applied – an Islamic case for basic science research', *ARABIA, the Islamic World Review*.

SALANCIK, G. R., and PFEFFER, J. (1977), 'Constraints on administrator discretion: the limited influence of mayors on city budgets', *Urban Affairs Quarterly, 12*, 475–98.

SASAKI, N. (1981), *Management and Industrial Structure in Japan*, Oxford, Pergamon Press.

SCHEIN, E. H. (1978), *Career Dynamics: Matching Individual and Organizational Needs*, Reading, Massachusetts, Addison-Wesley.

SCHELLING, T. C. (1981), 'Analytical methods and the ethics of policy', in Caplan, A. L., and Callahan, D., *Ethics in Hard Times*, New York, Plenum Press.

SCHERER, F. M. (1965), 'Firm size, market structure and opportunity and the output of patented innovations', *American Economic Review, 55*, 1097–1125.

SCHERER, F. M. (1967), 'Market structure and the employment of scientists and engineers', *American Economic Review, 57*, 524–31.

SCHERER, F. M. (1980), *Industrial Market Structure and Economic Performance*, Chicago, Rand McNally.

SCHILIT, W. K., and LOCKE, E. A. (1982), 'A study of upward influence in organizations', *Administrative Science Quarterly, 27*, 304–16.

SCHILLER, H. (1981), *Who Knows: Informatics in the Age of the Fortune 500*, New York, Abler.

SCHMOOKLER, J. (1966), *Invention and Economic Growth*, Cambridge, Massachusetts, Harvard University Press.

SCHONBERGER, R. J. (1982), *Japanese Manufacturing Techniques*, New York, Free Press.

SCHOTT, K. (1976), 'Investment in private industrial research and development in Britain', *Journal of Industrial Economics*, *25*, 81–99.

SCHOTT, K. (1978a), 'The rate of obsolescence of technical knowledge: a comment', *Journal of Industrial Economics*, *26*, 281–3.

SCHOTT, K. (1978b), 'The relations between industrial research and development and factor demands', *Economic Journal*, *88*, 85–106.

SCHREYÖGG, G. (1980), 'Contingency and choice in organization theory', *Organization Studies*, *1*, 305–26.

SCHRIESHEIM, C. A., HOUSE, R. J., and KERR, S. (1976), 'Leader initiating structure: a reconciliation of discrepant research results and some empirical tests', *Organization Behavior and Human Performance*, *15*, 297–321.

SCHRIESHEIM, C. A., and KERR, S. (1974), 'Psychometric properties of the Ohio State leadership scales', *Psychological Bulletin*, *81*, 756–65.

SCHRIESHEIM, C. A., and KERR, S. (1977), 'Theories and measures of leadership', in Hunt, J. G., and Larson, L. L. (eds.), *Leadership: The Cutting Edge*, Carbondale, Southern Illinois University Press.

SCHRIESHEIM, C. A., and VON GLINOW, M. A. (1977), 'Tests of the path–goal theory of leadership: a theoretical and empirical analysis', *Academy of Management Journal*, *20*, 398–405.

SCHRIESHEIM, J. F., and SCHRIESHEIM, C. A. (1980), 'A test of the path-goal theory of leadership and some suggested directions for future research', *Personnel Psychology*, *33*, 349–70.

SCHUMPETER, J. S. (1950), *Capitalism, Socialism and Democracy*, New York, Harper and Row.

SCIENCE POLICY RESEARCH UNIT (1972), *Success and Failure in Industrial Innovation*, London, Centre for Study of Industrial Innovation.

SCOTT, J. P. (1979), *Corporations, Classes and Capitalism*, London, Hutchinson.

SCOTT, J. P. (1982a), 'Property and control', in Giddens, A., and Mackenzie, G. (eds.), *Social Class and the Division of Labour*, Cambridge, Cambridge University Press.

SCOTT, J. P. (1982b), *The Upper Classes*, London, Macmillan.

SCOTT, W. R. (1981), *Organizations: Rational, Natural and Open Systems*, Englewood-Cliffs, New Jersey, Prentice-Hall.

SEEMAN, M. (1957), 'A comparison of general and specific leader behavior descriptions', in Stogdill, R. M., and Coons, A. E. (eds.), *Leader Behavior: Its Description and Measurement*, Columbus, Bureau of Business Research, Ohio State University.

SELZNICK, P. (1943), 'An approach to a theory of bureaucracy', *American Sociological Review*, *8*, 47–54.

SELZNICK, P. (1957), *Leadership in Administration*, New York, Harper and Row.

SERVAN-SCHREIBER, J.-J. (1969), *The American Challenge*, Harmondsworth, Penguin.

SEYFARTH, SHAW, FAIRWEATHER and GERALDSON (1968), *Labor Rela-*

tions and the Law in the United Kingdom and the United States, Program in International Business, Graduate School of Business Administration, Ann Arbor, University of Michigan.

SHAW, M. E. (1964), 'Communication networks', in Berkowitz, L. (ed.), *Advances in Experimental Social Psychology*, New York, Academic Press.

SHERIDAN, D. (1976), 'Be a today's buyer', *Procurement*, June, 15–17.

SHERIDAN, J. E., DOWNEY, H. K., and SLOCUM, J. W. (1976), 'Testing causal relationships of the path–goal theory of leadership effectiveness', in Hunt, J. G., and Larson, L. L. (eds.), *Leadership Frontiers*, Kent, Ohio, Kent State University Press.

SHIFLETT, S. (1973), 'Contingency model of leadership effectiveness: some implications of its statistical and methodological properties', *Behavioral Science, 18*, 429–40.

SHOTTER, J. (1975), *Images of Man in Psychological Research*, London, Methuen.

SILVERMAN, D. (1970), *The Theory of Organizations: A Sociological Framework*, London, Heinemann.

SIM, A. B. (1977), 'Decentralised management of subsidiaries and their performance', *Management International Review, 17*, 45–51.

SIMON, H. A (1954), 'Staff and management controls', *Annals of the American Academy of Political and Social Science*, No. 292, 95–103.

SIMON, H. A. (1957), *Administrative Behavior*, New York, Macmillan.

SMIDDY, H. F., and NAUM, L. (1954), 'Evolution of a "science of managing" in America', *Management Science, 1*, 1–31.

SMITH, C. T. B., et al. (1978), *Strikes in Britain: A Research Study of Industrial Stoppages in the United Kingdom*, London, HMSO (Department of Employment Manpower Papers, 15).

SMITH, P. B. (1975), 'Controlled studies of the outcome of sensitivity training', *Psychological Bulletin, 82*, 597–622.

SOELBERG, P. O. (1967), 'Unprogrammed decision-making', *Industrial Management Review, 8*, 19–29.

SOFER, C. (1970), *Men in Mid Career*, Cambridge, Cambridge University Press.

SORGE, A. (1977), 'The cultural context of organization structure: administrative rationality, constraints and choice' in Warner, M., *Organizational Choice and Constraints: Approaches to the Sociology of Enterprise Behaviour*, Farnborough, Saxon House.

SORGE, A. (1978), 'The management tradition: a continental view', in Fores, M., and Glover, I., *Manufacturing and Management*, London, HMSO.

SORGE, A. (1980), *Cultured Organization*, Berlin, International Institute of Management, Discussion Paper 80–9.

SORGE, A. (1982), 'Cultured organization', *International Studies of Management and Organization, 12*, 106–38.

SORGE, A., and FORES, M. (1979), *The Fifth Discontinuity*, Berlin, International Institute of Management, Discussion Paper 79–84.

SORGE, A., and FORES, M. (1981), 'The decline of the management ethic', *Journal of General Management*, *6*, 36–50.

SORGE, A., and WARNER, M. (1980), 'Manpower training, manufacturing organization and workplace relations in Great Britain and West Germany', *British Journal of Industrial Relations*, *18*, 318–33.

SPENDER, J.-C. (1980), *Strategy-Making in Business*, Unpublished Doctoral Thesis, Manchester Business School.

STEINER, G., and MINER, J. (1977), *Management Policy and Strategy*, West Drayton, Collier Macmillan.

STEUR, M., and GENNHARD, J. (1971), 'Industrial relations, labour disputes and labour utilization in foreign-owned firms in the UK', in Dunning, J. H., *The Multinational Enterprise*, London, Allen and Unwin.

STEVENS, J. M. (1974), 'Buying capital plant', *Procurement*, September, 22–4.

STEVENS, J. M. (1979), 'Purchasing's role in the make or buy decision', 14th European Technical Conference BPICS.

STEVENS, J. M (1980), 'A come back for value analysis', *Industrial Purchasing News*, *15*, 43–6.

STEVENS, J. M., and GRANT, J. P. (1975), *The Purchasing/Marketing Interface*, London, Associated Business Programmes.

STEWART, F. (1976), *Technology and Underdevelopment*, London, Macmillan.

STEWART, R. (1957), 'Management development: some American comparisons', *The Manager*, January.

STEWART, R. (1967), *Managers and Their Jobs*, London, Macmillan.

STEWART, R. (1976), *Contrasts in Management*, London, McGraw-Hill.

STEWART, R. (1982), *Choices for the Manager*, London, McGraw-Hill.

STINSON, J. E., and TRACY, L. (1974), 'Some disturbing characteristics of the LPC score', *Personnel Psychology*, *27*, 477–85.

STOGDILL, R. M. (1948), 'Personal factors associated with leadership: a survey of the literature', *Journal of Psychology*, *25*, 35–71.

STOKMAN, F. N., ZIEGLER, R., and SCOTT, J. P. (1984), *Intercorporate Structure: A Comparative Study of Ten Countries*, London, Sage.

STOPFORD, J. R. (1972), 'Organising the multinational firm. Can the Americans learn from the Europeans?', in Brook, M. R., and Remmers, H. L., *The Strategy of Multinational Enterprise: Organisation and Finance*, London, Pitman.

STOREY, J. (1983), *The Managerial Prerogative and the Question of Control*, London, Routledge and Kegan Paul.

STRAUSS, G. (1962), 'Tactics of lateral relationship: the purchasing agent', *Administrative Science Quarterly*, *7*, 161–86.

STREETEN, P. (1981), *Development Perspectives*, New York, St Martin's Press.

SUTTON, F. X., HARRIS, S. E., KAYSEN, C., and TOBIN, J. (1956), *The American Business Creed*, Cambridge, Massachusetts, Harvard University Press.

SUTTON, H., and PORTER, L. W. (1968), 'A study of the grapevine in a governmental organization', *Personnel Psychology*, *21*, 223–30.

SWALLOW, S. A. (1970), 'Industrial marketing: the buyer's viewpoint', in Coram, T., and Hill, R., *New Ideas in Industrial Marketing*, Staples.

SWALLOW, S. A. (1976), 'Intra-company purchasing', *Industrial Purchasing News*, *12*, 74–8.

TAKAMIYA, M. (1979), *Japanese Multinationals in Europe: Internal Operations and Their Public Policy Implications*, Working Paper, Berlin, International Institute of Management.

TANNENBAUM, A. S., and COOKE, R. A. (1979), 'Organizational control: a review of studies employing the control graph method', in Lammers, C. J., and Hickson, D., *Organizations Alike and Unalike*, London, Routledge and Kegan Paul.

TAVERNIER, G. (1974), 'The rising importance of the purchasing manager', *International Management*, September, 43–52.

TAYLOR, C. T., and SILBERTSON, Z. A. (1973), *The Economic Impact of the Patent System. A Study of the British Experience*, University of Cambridge, Department of Applied Economics Monograph 23, Cambridge, Cambridge University Press.

TAYLOR, F. W. (1911), *The Principles of Scientific Management*, New York, Harper and Row, reprinted 1947.

TERLECKYJ, N. E. (1980), 'Direct and indirect effects of industrial research and development on the productivity growth of industries', in Kendrick, J. W., and Vaccara, B. N. (eds.), *New Developments in Productivity Measurement and Analysis*, Studies in Income and Wealth, No. 44, Chicago, University of Chicago Press.

THACKRAY, J. (1981), 'America's technology gap', *Management Today*, June, 68–73.

THISTLEWAITE, F. (1955), *The Great Experiment*, London, Cambridge University Press.

THOMAS, D. (1969), 'The Anglo-American manager', *Management Today*, February, 60–63.

THOMAS, P. S. (1974), 'Environmental analysis for corporate planning', *Business Horizons*, *17*, 27–38.

THOMAS, R. E. (1982), *The Government of Enterprise*, Oxford, Philip Allan.

THOMPSON, J. D. (1967), *Organizations in Action*, New York, McGraw-Hill.

TINNIN, D. B. (1982), 'The American at the wheel of Porsche', *Fortune*, *5*, 78–87.

TOSI, H. J. (1982), 'Toward a paradigm shift in the study of leadership', in Hunt, J. G., Sekaran, U., and Schriesheim, C. A. (eds.), *Leadership: Beyond Establishment Views*, Carbondale, Southern Illinois University Press.

TREVOR, M. (1983), *Japan's Reluctant Multinationalists*, London, Pinter.

TRIST, E. L., and BAMFORTH, K. W. (1951), 'Some social and psychological consequences of the longwall method of coal-getting', *Human Relations*, *4*, 3–38.

TRIST, E. L., HIGGIN, G. W., MURRAY, H., and POLLOCK, A. B. (1963), *Organizational Choice: Capabilities of Groups at the Coal Face Under Changing Technologies*, London, Tavistock.

TUNDER, J., and WIDING, J. W. (1965), 'Vendor rating by computer', *Electronic Procurement*, May, 23–7.

TURNBULL, P. W. (1982), 'International aspects of bank marketing', *European Journal of Marketing*, *16*, 102–5.

UNITED NATIONS INDUSTRIAL AND DEVELOPMENT ORGANIZATION (1982), *Implication of Microelectronics for the ECLA Region*, Vienna, UNIDO.

URWICK, L. (1954), 'The American challenge in industrial management', *British Management Review*, *12*, 3.

UYTERHOEVEN, H. E. R., ACKERMAN, R. W., and ROSENBLUM, J. W. (1977), *Strategy and Organization*, Homewood, Illinois, Irwin.

VANEK, J. (1975), *Self-Management: Economic Liberation of Man*, Harmondsworth, Penguin.

VROOM, V. H. (1960), *Some Personality Determinants of the Effects of Participation*, Englewood Cliffs, New Jersey, Prentice-Hall.

VROOM, V. H., and YETTON, P. W. (1973), *Leadership and Decision-Making*, Pittsburgh, University of Pittsburgh Press.

WALKER, K. F. (1974), 'Workers' participation in management – problems, practice and prospects', *International Institute for Labour Studies Bulletin*, *12*, 3–35.

WALL, T. D., and LISCHERON, J. A. (1977), *Worker Participation: A Critique of the Literature and Some Fresh Evidence*, London, McGraw-Hill.

WATERMAN, R. H., PETERS, T. J., and PHILLIPS, J. R. (1980), 'Structure is not organisation', *Business Horizons*, 14–26.

WATSON, T. J. (1980), *Sociology, Work and Industry*, London, Routledge and Kegan Paul.

WEBB, S., and WEBB, B. (1894), *History of Trade Unionism*, Longman.

WEBBER, R. A. (ed.) (1969), *Culture and Management*, London, Irwin.

WEBBER, R. A. (1970), 'Perceptions of interactions between superiors and subordinates', *Human Relations*, *23*, 235–48.

WEBER, M. (1947), *The Theory of Social and Economic Organization*, translated by Henderson, A. M., and Parsons, T., Glencoe, Illinois, Free Press.

WEBER, M. (1948), *From Max Weber: Essays in Sociology*, translated and edited by Gerth, H. H., and Mills, C. W., London, Routledge and Kegan Paul.

WEBER, M. (1981), *General Economic History*, translated by Knight, F. H., New Brunswick, New Jersey, Transaction (reprint of the 1927 edition, published by Greenberg, N. Y.).

WEBSTER, F. E. (1975), 'Perceptions of the industrial distributor', *Industrial Marketing Management*, *4*, 257–64.

WEICK, K. E. (1976). 'Educational organisations as loosely coupled systems', *Administrative Science Quarterly*, *21*, 1–19.

WEIDENBAUM, M. (1981), *Business, Government and the Public*, 3rd edition, Englewood Cliffs, New Jersey, Prentice-Hall.

WEIGAND, R. E. (1977), 'International trade without money'. *Harvard Business Review*, *55*, 28–42 and 166.

WEINSHALL, T. D. (1977), *Culture and Management. Selected Readings*, Harmondsworth, Penguin.

WHEELWRIGHT, S. C. (1981), 'Japan – where operations really are strategic', *Harvard Business Review*, 59, 67–74.

WHITE, M., and TREVOR, M. (1983), *Under Japanese Management – The Experience of British Workers*, London, Heinemann.

WIETERS, C. D. (1976), 'Vendor performance rating systems', *Journal of Purchasing and Materials Management*, 11, 31–6.

WILDAWSKY, A. (1983), 'Information as an organizational problem', *Journal of Management Studies*, 20, 30–40.

WILENSKY, H. L. (1967), *Organizational Intelligence*, New York, Basic Books.

WILKINS, M. (1970), *The Emergence of Multinational Enterprise*, Cambridge, Massachusetts, Harvard University Press.

WILSON, D. T., and MATTHEWS, H. C. (1971), 'Impact of management information systems upon purchasing decision making', *Journal of Purchasing*, 7, 48.

WINDOLF, P. (1982), *Recruitment and Selection in Enterprises – A Comparative View on Britain and Germany*, Berlin, International Institute of Management, Discussion Paper 82–17.

WINDOLF, P. (1983), 'Recruitment strategies and social closure' (mimeo).

WOOD, S. (ed.) (1982), *The Degradation of Work?*, London, Hutchinson.

WOODWARD, J. (1965), *Industrial Organization: Theory and Practice*, London, Oxford University Press.

WOODWARD, J. (ed.) (1970), *Industrial Organization: Behaviour and Control*, London, Oxford University Press.

YALMAN, N. (1967), 'Observations on *Le cru et le cuit*', in Leach, E. (ed.), *The Structure of Myth and Totemism*, London, Tavistock.

YODER, D. (1970), *Personnel Management and Industrial Relations*, Englewood Cliffs, New Jersey, Prentice-Hall.

YOSHINO, M. Y. (1968), *Japan's Managerial System: Tradition and Innovation*, Cambridge, Massachusetts, MIT Press.

ZACHMAN, J. A. (1982), 'Business systems planning and business information control study: a comparison', *IBM Systems Journal*, 21, 31–5.

ZAJONC, R. B. (1963), 'The effect of varying group task difficulty on individual and group performance', *Human Relations*, 16, 359–68.

ZEITLIN, M. (1974), 'Corporate ownership and control: the large corporation and the capitalist class', *American Journal of Sociology*, 79, 5.

ZIBRISKIE, N., and BROWNING, J. (1980), 'Professionalism in purchasing: a status report', *Journal of Purchasing and Materials Management*, 16, 2–10.

ZIMMERMAN, D. H. (1973), 'The practicalities of rule use', in Salaman, G. and Thompson, K., *People and Organisations*, London, Longman.

Notes on Contributors

JOHN BLAKE is lecturer in financial accounting at Loughborough University. After reading history at Oxford he qualified as a chartered accountant and worked for some years in the accountancy profession before entering higher education. He is the author of: *Accounting Standards*, Longman, 1981; *Inflation Accounting* (with P. Clayton), Longman, 1984; and *The Interpretation of Accounts*, Van Nostrand, 1984.

KEITH BLOIS is currently reader in marketing at the University of Loughborough. After graduating in economics from the University of Bristol he worked in operations research in both the public and private sectors, and in market research in a major engineering company. He came to the Department of Management Studies at Loughborough University, where he has been successively lecturer, senior lecturer and reader, and been awarded a Ph.D. for his research in economics and marketing, and is particularly well known for his work on quasi-vertical integration.

MATS BODIN, from Gothenburg, Sweden, did his first degree at the Royal Institute of Technology in Stockholm, and since 1980 has been a research fellow there in the Department of Industrial Economics and Management. His research and publications have centred on computerization decisions and use.

ALAN BRYMAN took a BA and MA in sociology at the University of Kent. He has been research assistant at the University of Aston and research fellow at the University of Birmingham. He is currently lecturer in sociology at the University of Loughborough. He is joint author of *Clergy Ministers and Priests*, Routledge and Kegan Paul, 1977, and is currently working on a book on leadership.

JOANNA BUCKINGHAM, a politics and sociology graduate from the University of Southampton, is research associate at Loughborough University. Her research interests include higher technical education and small-business operation, as well as the work of managers.

JOHN BURGOYNE graduated in psychology at University College, London, followed by an M.Phil. at Birkbeck College and a Ph.D. at Manchester University. After various posts at the Manchester University Business School he became Research Director at the Lancaster University Centre for the Study of Management Learning. He is joint author of *A Manager's Guide to Self-Development*, McGraw-Hill, 1978, and *Management Development: Context and Strategies*, Gower Press, 1978, as well as of numerous articles.

JON CLARK read German at Birmingham University where he got a first, followed by a Ph.D. at the University of Bremen in West Germany. He has been a research officer at the London School of Economics and a visiting research fellow at the University of Paris VII (Jussieu), and is presently lecturer in industrial relations at the University of Southampton as well as joint director of the ESRC–SERC-funded New Technology in the Workplace project. His publications, in all three languages, range across interests in comparative trade unionism and labour law.

PAUL FINLAY is a lecturer in management-information systems at the University of Loughborough. After a first degree and doctorate in physics he worked for six years in operations research for the Ministry of Defence. This was followed by several years in operations research and later corporate planning with British and American Tobacco Ltd, ending as Project Manager responsible for all production-related management services. He is author of *Mathematical Modelling in Business Decisions*, Croom Helm, 1985.

DAVID FORD is senior lecturer in marketing at the University of Bath, School of Management. He has also taught at the University of Texas at Austin and the University of Uppsala in Sweden. His teaching and research has mainly taken place in the areas of industrial and international marketing and he has a number of publications on these topics. His original background is in engineering and he is particularly interested in management education in the industrial-manufacturing and services sectors.

MICHAEL FORES is a freelance writer and consultant. He studied engineering at Cambridge, and was formerly a Senior Economic Adviser at the Department of Industry. He has been visiting fellow at the International Institute of Management in West Berlin, and has written extensively on engineering, management and national economic performance. He is co-editor with Ian Glover of *Manufacturing and Management*, HMSO, 1978.

IAN GLOVER studied at London, Bath, and the City University, and has degrees from all of them. He has been a research associate at City University, a senior research officer at Heriot-Watt University, and a consultant to the Department of Industry. He is currently lecturer in sociology at Dundee College of Technology. With Michael Fores he is co-editor of the influential *Manufacturing and Management*, HMSO, 1978.

WYNNE HARRIES, who died in 1984, was lecturer in organizational behaviour at the University of Loughborough. He had several years' experience in line supervision and management in the engineering industry, and was a research fellow at the London School of Economics as well as senior research fellow at the former Centre for Utilisation of Social Science Research at Loughborough. Before his death, he was pursuing SERC-funded research on microelectronic applications in the construction industry.

TERRY HILL is senior lecturer in production/operations management at the University of Warwick. After a BA in commerce and an M.Sc. in industrial administration at the University of Manchester, he worked for several years in a variety of companies, having been in succession PA to the managing director, purchasing manager, assistant works manager, a consultant and then general works manager. He is author of *Production/ Operations Management*, Prentice-Hall, 1983.

IAN JAMIESON, after a short period in business, taught sociology for eight years in the School of Business at Ealing College of Higher Education. His doctorate was on the effect of culture on business enterprise. He has subsequently done research on Asian business in London. In 1978 he was appointed the evaluator of the Schools Council Industry Project – a major national curriculum-development enterprise aimed at bringing schools and industry closer together – and in 1981 became Director of Research for schools–industry work at the Schools Council. His publications include *Capitalism and Culture*, Gower Press, 1980, and, with Martin Lightfoot, *Schools and Industry*, Methuen, 1982.

GERRY JOHNSON, after graduating from University College, London, where he was also president of the Students Union, worked in marketing and consultancy in a variety of companies before entering higher education. He is currently lecturer in business policy at the University of Aston. With Kevin Scholes he is author of *Understanding Corporate Strategy*, Prentice-Hall, 1984.

TONY KEENAN is head of the Department of Business Organisation at Heriot-Watt University. After working in industry for some years he read psychology at the University of Strathclyde and went on to do a doctorate at the University of Birmingham before coming to Heriot-Watt University as a lecturer in organizational behaviour. His main research interests are in occupational recruitment, work experience and higher technical education, and he has numerous research-based publications.

BOB LEE worked as a personnel manager in a major telecommunications company after graduating with a first-class degree in management science. He has since been a lecturer in business organization at Trent Polytechnic and a research fellow at the University of Loughborough, before being appointed to his present post of lecturer in organizational behaviour at Loughborough. He is joint author with Peter Lawrence of *Insight into Management*, OUP, 1984, and *Organisational Behaviour: A New Approach*, Hutchinson, 1985.

PÄR LIND took bachelors and masters degrees at the University of Lund in Sweden, where he became assistant lecturer in mathematics, before working for some years with IBM, Olivetti and Logica. He has returned to higher education and is now research fellow in the Department of Industrial Economics and Management at the Royal Institute of Technology in Stockholm. He has a specialist interest in computer use in the Third World.

JULIAN LOWE is senior lecturer in industrial economics at the University of Bath. After a BA in economics at the University of Wales, and an MA in economics at the University of Manchester, he worked in corporate planning at a major multinational company, before entering higher education with a lectureship at the University of Nottingham. He is the author of five books and numerous articles.

ELEANOR J. MORGAN graduated in economics at London University, and at the University of Massachusetts. After a research post at the University of Reading she became a lecturer in industrial economics in the School of Management at Bath University. As well as being co-author of a book on leasing, she has written various articles concerned with the application of economics for business issues and industry/government relationships.

JOHN SCOTT obtained a first in sociology at Kingston Polytechnic and later a Ph.D. at the University of Strathclyde. He has held lectureships at Strathclyde and the University of Leicester, and is the author of *Corporations, Classes and Capitalism*, Hutchinson, 1979; *Anatomy of Scottish Capital* (with Michael Hughes), Croom Helm, 1980; and *The Upper Classes*, Macmillan, 1982.

MICK SILVER is currently lecturer in industrial economics and statistics at the University of Bath. Prior to this he was lecturer in applied statistics at the University of Aston. He was educated at the University of Leeds, taking degrees in economics (BA) and industrial statistics (Ph.D). Aside from his work on R & D he has published on a range of subjects including industrial development in Tanzania, manpower planning, psephology, productivity analysis, theoretical and applied issues in index numbers, concentration measures, and mathematical and statistical texts. He has undertaken consultancy at government level in Iran, and for a number of UK organizations.

ARNDT SORGE, from Düsseldorf, studied economics and sociology at the Universities of Freiburg and Cologne after completing military service. He has been a lecturer at the University of Münster, where he obtained his Ph.D., and is now research fellow at the International Institute of Management in West Berlin. He is the author of two books on industrial democracy in West Germany, and of *Microelectronics and Manpower in Manufacturing: Applications of Computer Numerical Control in Great Britain and West Germany*, Gower, 1982.

JOHN STEVENS is senior lecturer in materials management at Lanchester Polytechnic. After graduating in economics at the University of Durham, John Stevens did an administrative traineeship with the CEGB and subsequently worked as a purchasing manager for several companies before joining the Business Studies Department of Lanchester. He is the author of *The Purchasing/Marketing Interface*, Associated Business Programmes Ltd, 1975, and of *Measuring Purchasing Performance*, Business Books Ltd, 1978, as well as of numerous articles on purchasing and materials management.

MICHAEL WHITE is a senior research fellow at the Policy Studies Institute. After working in industry in the 1960s he joined the Oxford Centre for Management Studies as a researcher. He continued research into industrial relations and worker attitudes at Ashbridge Management College, where he became Research Programme Director. He is author, with Malcolm Trevor, of *Under Japanese Management*, Heinemann, 1983.

PAUL WINDOLF was born in Düsseldorf, and worked for a leading West German engineering firm for several years after attending a business college. He later studied sociology and economics at the Universities of Freiburg and Berlin, as well as at Poitiers and the Sorbonne. He has taught at a polytechnic college in Berlin, at the University of Münster, and been a research fellow at the London School of Economics. He is currently a senior fellow at the International Institute of Management in West Berlin. His publications centre on unemployment, socialization, social science methods, industrial recruitment and industrial relations.

INDEX

The subject index follows the index of names on p. 488.